WE, TOO, SING AMERICA

A Reader for Writers

WE, TOO, SING AMERICA

A Reader for Writers

Chitra B. Divakaruni

Boston, Massachusetts   Burr Ridge, Illinois
Dubuque, Iowa   Madison, Wisconsin   New York, New York
San Francisco, California   St. Louis, Missouri

McGraw-Hill

*A Division of The **McGraw·Hill** Companies*

WE, TOO, SING AMERICA
A Reader for Writers

Copyright © 1998 by The McGraw-Hill Companies, Inc. All rights reserved. Printed in the United States of America. Except as permitted under the United States Copyright Act of 1976, no part of this publication may be reproduced or distributed in any form or by any means, or stored in a data base or retrieval system, without the prior written permission of the publisher.

1 2 3 4 5 6 7 8 9 0 DOC DOC 9 0 9 8 7

ISBN 0-07-017084-3

Sponsoring Editor: *Tim Julet.*
Project Manager: *Gladys True.*
Production supervisor: *Lori Koetters*
Cover Designer and Design Manager: *Kiera Cunningham*
Compositor: *COM COM.*
Photo Editor: *Natalia Yamrom.*
Printer: *R. R. Donnelley & Sons Company.*

PHOTO CREDITS:

Unit 1:	Edward Lettau/Photo Researchers.
Unit 2:	Richard Hutchings/Photo Researchers.
Unit 3:	Erich Hartmann/Magnum.
Unit 4:	Henri Cartier-Bresson/Magnum.
Unit 5:	Paul Fusco/Magnum.
Unit 6:	Danny Lyon/Magnum.
Unit 7:	Focus on Sports.
Unit 8:	Leonard Freed/Magnum.
Unit 9:	Eugene Richards/Magnum.
Unit 10:	Paul Fusco/Magnum.

Library of Congress Cataloging-in-Publication Data

We, too, sing America : a reader for writers / [edited by]
    Chitra B. Divakaruni.
        p.   cm.
    Includes index.
    ISBN 0-07-017084-3
    1. Readers—Social sciences.   2. Pluralism (Social sciences)—Problems, exercises, etc.
3. Ethnic groups—United States—Problems, exercises, etc.   4. English language—
Rhetoric.   5. Readers—United States.   6. College readers.   I. Divakaruni,
Chitra Banerjee, 1956–   .
PE1127.S6W38   1998
    808'.0427—dc21   97-17611
http://www.mhhe.com

ABOUT THE EDITOR

Chitra Banerjee Divakaruni is the editor of *Multitude: Cross Cultural Essays for Writers,* and the author of three books of poetry, the latest being *Black Candle.* Her book of stories, *Arranged Marriage,* has won several prizes including the American Book Award, the Gerbode award, and a Pushcart prize. Her novel is titled *The Mistress of Spices.* Divakaruni lives in California with her husband and two children, and teaches at Foothill College. She is also president of MAITRI, a helpline for South Asian women.

Photo by Dru Ariel Banerjee

For Gurumayi, teacher of teachers.

Table of Contents

Alternate Table of Contents
by Rhetorical Mode

Note: Selections using more than one rhetorical mode are listed under each pertinent category.

COMPARISON AND CONTRAST

CAUSE AND EFFECT

Preface

Designed for use by developing readers in college composition classes, *We, Too, Sing America* is an anthology of cross-cultural readings that examines many facets of living in America today. These readings have been carefully selected to expose students to the lifestyles, values, concerns, and problems of people and communities that might be very different from their own. The selections also allow students from different cultural backgrounds to relate more easily to classroom material and make meaningful contributions to discussions. Overall, dialogues begun in the classroom and continued through writing assignments will give students an opportunity to consider the complexities of the diverse mosaic that is American society.

We, Too, Sing America also has been designed to sharpen the reading and writing skills of students. To that end, selections have been chosen for their consistently high literary and stylistic quality, their varied rhetorical strategies, and their timely and accessible content.

DISTINCTIVE FEATURES OF THE TEXT

We, Too, Sing America offers its users the following special features:

- An overall focus on diversity, not just related to culture but also to gender, class, and community.
- Readings that are timely, easily accessible, and provide good starting-off points for student writing.
- Readings that are of varying length and difficulty to allow instructors to choose what is most suitable for their students.
- Readings that cover various genres and rhetorical modes.

xxi

- An extensive, easy-to-use **apparatus** focusing on the connection between reading, writing, and critical thinking, including an **introduction** discussing techniques related to effective reading and writing.
- Group activities focused on **collaborative learning.**
- **Student essays,** ranging from personal essays to research papers, with a different set of apparatus designed to focus on the writing process itself.

ORGANIZATION OF THE TEXT

The text is organized into 10 thematic units that approach the idea of diversity from different angles. The topics deal with aspects of the American experience that students are most likely to have come across and be interested in, and they move from the simple to the complex. Within each unit, instructors will find pieces of varying lengths and sophistication. Selections in each unit also are balanced in terms of the cultures or communities covered, the writers' gender and class, the genres presented (from essays to articles to poetry), and the styles (from the personal to the critical or analytic). Many times, selections present opposing views and create an interesting dialectic within units. Readings have been chosen to cover all the major rhetorical modes or patterns of organization taught in writing classes. For instructors who are interested in structuring their class in this manner, a supplementary **rhetorical table of contents** is provided. Each unit ends with a **student essay,** chosen to generate class discussion about the writing process and to serve as a possible model for further student writing.

TEACHING APPARATUS

We, Too, Sing America has been designed with the needs of the developing reader/writer in mind:

- The **Introduction** talks about how to read and annotate effectively, points to some of the common problems faced by writers (e.g., writer's block), and offers strategies to help with generating, developing, organizing, and revising ideas.
- Each selection is preceded by a **Pre-reading Activity** to draw students into the topic, give it some individual thought, and connect it with their own experience and understanding of society.
- **Journal Writing** activities with each prose selection give students an opportunity to explore the topic, take stock of their capabilities as readers, and respond to the writer's ideas.

- A section titled **As You Read** alerts students to stylistic or rhetorical strategies used by the writer and allows them to interact with the text by annotating it.
- A **headnote** gives the date of writing for each selection and background information about the writer to enable students to contextualize the piece.
- A **vocabulary building** activity picks out words that might not be familiar to students and has them try these words in their own writing.
- The questions under **Analyzing Content** deal with the subject matter of the readings, focus students on the main points, and are a good gauge of their understanding of the text.
- The questions under **Analyzing Writing Techniques** deal with matters of style and technique and focus students on how the writer has achieved a particular effect in the piece.
- A **Group Activity** brings students together to discuss, research, and write in groups, using each other as resources and critics.
- The suggestions under **Your Writing** allow students to formulate and develop their own ideas on the issue. A variety of suggestions enable students to find a subject or approach they are comfortable with.
- A separate set of **Structure and Strategy** questions follows the student essays and leads students to look more closely at the process of putting an essay together.
- The **Synthesis** questions at the end of each unit draw the different readings together and offer students more challenging and comprehensive writing ideas.
- A **glossary** provides the meanings of literary and writing terms discussed in the text.

In addition there are an alternate **rhetorical table of contents** for the instructor, an **index** for easy reference, and an accompanying **Instructor's Manual** with teaching suggestions.

Chitra B. Divakaruni

WE, TOO, SING AMERICA

A Reader for Writers

Introduction

TO THE READER: SOME NOTES
ON EFFECTIVE READING AND WRITING

Welcome to *We, Too, Sing America,* a book that is about growing up in America today, about being part of a rich and complex mix of people of different backgrounds, cultures, interests, and abilities—in short, about *you.* It is my hope that the readings in this book will enable you to explore issues that are meaningful to your life and, in the process, sharpen your reading and writing skills.

Through my years of teaching, I have seen that the connection between effective reading, writing, and thinking is crucial. I have, therefore, designed this book so that the questions and activities that go with each selection engage these different skills at the same time. This interaction will help you to become a more active, interested learner and make the process of reading and writing more enjoyable.

Before you begin on these selections, I would like to share with you some techniques related to reading, writing, and thinking that have worked for my students and myself. I hope they will work for you as well.

EFFECTIVE READING

The first important element of reading effectively is to allow yourself enough **time**. Many students understand a writer's ideas only superficially or partially, because they have rushed through the piece.

Look at a selection, and determine how long it will take you, at your normal speed, to read it. Now give yourself **three** times as much time. This will enable you to:

- Read it once for the overall idea and story content.
- Read it once more at a slower pace, this time using **critical thinking skills**, marking and highlighting and taking notes.

Marking

For some of you, **marking** will be an unfamiliar, uncomfortable activity. In the public school system, you may have been told not to write in your books, because others would be using them after you. In college, however, your books are your own, and I recommend marking them and writing comments in them as activities that will make you into a more active, thinking reader. In addition, it is good to have a notebook or journal in which you can jot down longer responses.

What Are Some Things You Will Be Looking For?   It is important to find and mark the **main idea** or **thesis** of a selection as soon as possible. This can be an actual sentence or a group of sentences in the piece, or (this is trickier) it can be an implied statement that you must deduce by examining the entire selection. Explicit thesis statements are often found in the introductions or conclusions of essays.

Once you find the **thesis**, you need to look for ways in which the writer has **supported** it. (Often, this is through the use of examples, facts, statistics, or reasons.) There are various ways of marking these:

- You can number the supporting points and the subsections under them.
- You can point out examples and underline important statistics that strengthen the main idea.
- You can highlight transition words that indicate the relationship between the supporting ideas (as in cause-and-effect essays or pro-and-con papers, in which the paper focuses on different aspects of the thesis as it moves along).

Another important element of writing is the author's **purpose**. Ultimately, all writers want you to agree with their thesis, but one who is attempting to make you laugh will (or should) write differently from one who wants to create sympathy in you, wants you to buy a product, or wants to anger you into action.

Keep the following questions in mind as you read:

- How does the writer want me to respond to this piece?
- Am I responding in the desired way? Why, or why not?

After you finish reading, write down your answers. The answer to the first question will give you a better understanding about the thrust of the entire piece. The answer to the second will allow you to critically evaluate the writer's tools and measure of success. What you learn as you do so will be directly helpful in your own writing as you attempt to move *your* readers in a particular manner.

Closely connected to the **purpose** of a piece is the notion of **audience**, which can have an enormous effect on a writer's style. You know this already—you would not write a letter to a close friend in the same way you would a report for your biology teacher.

Three questions to ask in this respect are:

- Who is the author writing this piece for?
- How do I know this?
- Has the author chosen the best possible methods for reaching this particular audience?

As you read, you should also be noting **questions**. Some will seek information related to the text: *When? What? How?* Some will express frustration with concepts: *What does this mean? Why is the writer saying this? What's the relevance of this example?* Some will be larger, exploring notions of *why,* leading you to research the topic in more depth and, perhaps, to come up with writing ideas of your own. Each kind of question is important, because it will lead you to think about the selection in meaningful ways.

Don't forget the questions that are already provided for you at the ends of selections, even if they are not assigned by your professor. These questions have been carefully formulated to address key issues in each selection, and they will help you to focus on what is most important about each essay.

Summary and Response

The last step in effective reading is to write a summary and a response to the text.

A **summary** encapsulates, as briefly as possible without losing the argument or confusing the reader, the main points made by the writer. Use your own words whenever you can, and delete all supporting evidence except the most important. Remain objective; do not confuse your own opinions with what the writer is saying. Writing a summary is a good way of checking how well you understand the writer's ideas.

A **response** is more personal and less structured. It can cover many things, from your emotional reaction to a piece to a description of a similar experience that happened to you to an evaluation of characters described or reasons why you disagree with the writer. The response is a good place to bring in your evaluation of the writer and your understanding of the issues involved, and it may be a starting point for a longer, more formal piece of writing on the subject.

EFFECTIVE WRITING

The readings in this book have been selected to stimulate you into writing effective essays of your own that are related to what you have read yet also express independent thought. I define an effective essay as one that is clear, is coherent, is focused on a main idea that demonstrates careful thinking and that the essay supports adequately, and is written in a style that is interesting to readers. Depending on your writing experience and background, such essays will come easier to some of you and may be more challenging for others. Described below are some techniques that should make the movement from reading to writing smoother for most of you.

Writer's Block

Most of you have experienced **writer's block**, that dreaded moment when you stare at a blank piece of paper or computer screen—*and nothing comes.* Before you panic, however, remember that you are not alone in this. Almost every writer, including those with several successful books to their credit, has suffered at some time from this syndrome. Also, there are several thinking and writing techniques you can practice to reduce the possibility of writer's block and, perhaps, to prevent it altogether.

Making Connections   Often, writer's block occurs because we feel we have nothing to say about a subject, either because we know very little about it or because we have not considered the issue and, therefore, have no opinion about it. What you need to do in this case is to read with a different focus, **looking for connections between what you are reading and your own experience**. This will be easiest when the writer is describing something familiar. When you are faced with something that seems totally alien to your lifestyle, however, remember that one reason we value reading is because it opens up worlds we would never otherwise have had access to. In either situation, you can ask yourself questions such as:

- How are my experience and background different from the writer's or those of the characters?
- Can I relate to the characters on a human level, because we share certain aspirations and passions?
- Has the writer provided enough information to convince me of his or her argument?

- What questions has he or she raised that I want to examine further?
- How might this issue impact my life, my community, or the larger society in which I live?
- Philosophically, do I agree with the writer? Why, or why not?

If you give yourself enough time to explore these questions, I am certain you will come up with several writing ideas.

Writer's block also may occur *after* we have selected—or been handed—a topic. This sometimes results from our belief that we should be able to create, all at once, a perfect piece of writing. If you experience this problem, one or more of the following pre-writing strategies for opening up the creative process may help: **brainstorming, focused freewriting**, and **clustering**. All of these activities allow us to see that writing is a manageable process with several steps leading, slowly, to a finished product.

Brainstorming

Write down in list form everything you can think of that is even remotely related to your topic. Do not worry about logic, consistency, structure, or orignality. Just let word associations lead you from one idea to the next. You will be surprised by what you come up with. Sometimes, you will begin seeing connections between different items. At others, you will come up with a subtopic that is sharply focused and will lead you to a **thesis**.

Here is an example of a **brainstorming** exercise done to develop ideas for Writing Idea #2 for the selection "Children of Divorce" (Unit 1, Selection 2):

Brainstorming

Topic: Attitude of a particular cultural group toward divorce

(Indians living in America)
— divorce not common
— looked down upon
— woman thought to be at fault
— this attitude is changing, but very slowly
— example of Mrs Raman
— quite different from "mainstream" America
— causes related to children (importance of)
— also many women don't work

— religious reasons
— many families will disown divorced daughters
— Neeta's case
— is this an advantage? Why?
— some negative aspects to not allowing divorce
— life for women after divorce
— what happens to divorced men?

Focused Freewriting

Write down, rapidly and without stopping, anything that comes to your mind as you think about your chosen topic. Once again, do not worry about logic, organization, grammar, diction, or the quality of the ideas. The purpose of this exercise is to loosen you up and allow you to access the subconscious areas of your mind. You will not be able to use everything you write, but once again, you might be surprised by unexpectedly perceptive ideas that you can then develop into an essay.

Here is an example of **focused freewriting** exercise done in response to Writing Idea #1 for "America's Scapegoats" (Unit 10, Selection 4):

Focused Freewriting

Question: Are immigrants causing America's problems? Choose a social problem you consider major & explore how immigrants have/have not affected it.

It's easy to blame immigrants for all of America's troubles. Many people are against immigrants because they think they take away jobs from "real" Americans. But once you enter this country legally, aren't you a "real" American, too? Also people think immigrants cause other problems like burdening the welfare system. But if statistics are checked, people would see most welfare recipients are people who were born in this country. Also, immigrants are mostly law abiding—maybe because they are afraid of the "system" and don't want to get into trouble. They also have relatively strong family structures with less divorce and broken families. Many immigrants have contributed to business, science, re-

search, etc. Going back to jobs, many successful immigrants even end up providing jobs for America!

Clustering or Mapping

This is similar to brainstorming but allows us to visualize relationships and to pursue a particular idea in depth. It is more logical than the other activities, but it shares with them the notion of freedom, of being allowed to follow an idea in any direction you wish. You may use this method when analyzing a reading as well as when generating ideas for your own writing. For a reading, you place the writer's main idea in a bubble in the center of the page, then branch out to the supporting points. Details and examples that support a point can be clustered around that point. For your own writing, you begin with your central topic in a bubble in the center of the page, then branch out in different directions with related ideas, examples, and details. The clustering process also allows you to formulate (and identify) sublevels of support that will be helpful when you begin to write your first draft.

Here is an example of **clustering** in response to Writing Idea #1 for the selection "American Men Don't Cry" (Unit 3, Selection 1):

Clustering

Question: Do we still bring little boys up differently from little girls?

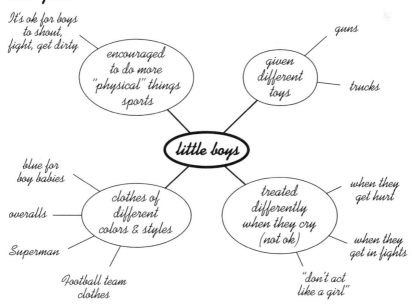

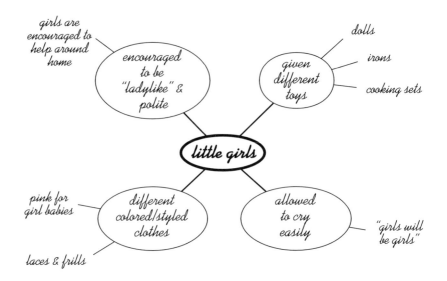

When you have completed one or more of the activities described, go over what you have generated and highlight the best, most interesting ideas. Throw the rest away. (This in itself is liberating—the realization that you are not bound to what you have written at any point in the process.) You will begin to see patterns and ideas emerge, and you are now ready for the actual writing of your paper.

Creating a Thesis

At this point, most writers know what they want to write about, but not necessarily what they want to say about it. This is a good point for you to look back at the prewriting you have done and try to formulate your ideas into a sentence that will encapsulate what you believe, feel, or understand about your subject.

For example, you might look back at the brainstorming exercise and realize that you know a great deal about the attitudes toward divorce in your community. Then, looking at the subsidiary points you have come up with, you may formulate a **thesis statement** such as: "Although divorce is a common phenomenon in America and generally accepted as such, in the Indian-American community it is still frowned on for several reasons, such as the traditional role of women, the emphasis on the family, and religious values."

This will be your **working thesis** as you begin to organize supporting evidence. Here are a few questions you can ask to check on the effectiveness of your thesis:

- Is it interesting? Can I say something unusual or unique as I develop it?

- Do I have enough information to develop it sufficiently?
- Is it clearly focused and narrow enough to allow me to examine an issue in depth?
- Is it an argument or opinion that needs to be supported rather than merely a factual statement?

Remember, the thesis is the heart of the paper. If you have a strong thesis, you are on your way to writing a good paper.

GATHERING AND ORGANIZING SUPPORTING MATERIAL

The Outline

It is now time to organize your supporting points. Look back over your prewriting activities and your thesis and make a new list consisting of your strongest supporting ideas. This time you are checking for logic and consistency and making sure that everything is related to your thesis. (Be prepared to modify the thesis if you come up with better ideas!) Begin ordering your supporting points—sometimes the thesis itself, as in the example above, will indicate what these are—starting with a strong one and saving, perhaps, your best point for a powerful ending).

Below is a sample outline. As you see, outlines need not be very elaborate. You can often use a word or a phrase as a cue for the actual writing of the essay.

The Attitude of Indian-Americans toward Divorce

Intro: Discuss how although they live in the United States, many Indian-Americans still hold on to their old values from India, especially those related to divorce. Negative attitude toward divorce is based on three reasons:

I. Emphasis on family stability, especially well-being of children
   a. Social activities center around children (give example of Indian parties)
   b. Parents very involved in children's schoolwork (give Nitin's parents' example)
   c. Each parent plays a different but important role in child's life, which would be much harder to achieve with divorce

> **d.** Because of the above, divorced parents would rarely con-
> sider remarriage
> **II.** Religious values
>   **a.** The Hindu religion, to which most Indians belong, rec-
>   ommends one marriage, especially for women
>   **b.** Therefore, a stigma is attached to divorced women, and
>   it would be very hard for them to get married or even par-
>   ticipate in festive occasions such as holy days, weddings,
>   etc. (example of Mrs. Raman)
>   (Look up more, maybe talk to temple priest)
> **III.** The traditional role played by women, followed in many
> families even here
>   **a.** the woman is expected to adjust to unpleasant situations
>   **b.** the woman is generally blamed for failure of marriage
>   **c.** many Indian women, even in the United States, have
>   chosen the traditional role of homemaker and would have
>   a hard time surviving financially after divorce
>
> **Conclusion:**   Maybe something about the different attitudes in
> mainstream and immigrant societies? Maybe something about
> how some of these attitudes are positive but some are negative
> and how they can harm people?
>
> Note: Come up with more specific examples under each category

The outline provides you with a good overview of the entire paper. It can alert you to weak sections or areas where you need more material. (This might require more thinking, and perhaps a trip to the library.) It also can allow you to move your points around relatively painlessly.

This is a good point at which to share your work with others and get some feedback. In my classes, I often assign group activities in which students examine and comment on the ideas in each other's outlines. Even if your class is not structured in this way, you can always try a similar activity yourself with a group of students with whom you feel comfortable.

Supporting Your Ideas and Developing Your Paragraphs

There are many different ways of developing ideas. Depending on the assignment and the appropriate rhetorical mode, there are particular structures that will be most effective for you. Your instructor will provide you with the details of these, but here are some basic items that can improve the structure and content of almost any paragraph:

- A clear topic sentence that indicates the focus of your paragraph.
- Facts and statistics to back up your assertions.
- Examples (specific ones are particularly good).
- Quotations.
- Descriptive detail where appropriate.
- Background or context information where needed.
- Clear step by step reasoning where needed.
- Transition words or phrases to show the logical connections between paragraphs.

Remember, it is not enough merely to bring in these elements. You must arrange them carefully to create the best effect on the reader.

Editing

Once you have a complete first draft, it is helpful to set it aside for a few days, because this will allow you both distance and perspective. It is good to have a classmate or someone with a writing background look at your draft. Here are some questions you might consider when going over it:

- Does the essay fit the assignment?
- Is the thesis clear and clearly related to the assignment?
- Has the paper stayed focused on the thesis?
- Has each part of the thesis (if there are more than one) been addressed?
- Is there sufficient evidence to convince the reader?
- Are the paragraphs focused, structured, and adequately developed?
- Is there an interesting introduction? A strong conclusion?
- Is the diction appropriate? Are words well chosen?
- Are the mechanics of the paper (e.g., grammar, spelling, punctuation) correct?
- Is the format (e.g., typing, spacing, cover page, footnotes) accurate?

Don't think of editing as merely changing words or sentences or correcting grammatical errors. Sometimes, editing might require an act of boldness—throwing out major sections because they do not belong in the paper, changing the thesis, or correcting a faulty premise on which the entire paper is based. If done carefully and intelligently, however, editing will repay your efforts amply; often, you will be amazed at the difference in quality between your first draft and the finished product.

I hope these suggestions for effective reading and writing, along with the more detailed techniques your instructor will provide, will help you in your own work. What I have recommended is certainly not proscriptive; there are many different ways of reading and writing well. Whichever you choose, I hope you will enjoy what is, in my belief, one of the most challenging, thought-provoking, and satisfying human activities.

Youth and Age

Youth and age, our first and last years, bracket our existence and are meaningful to our lives in particularly powerful and poignant ways. The experiences of our childhoods are perhaps felt most deeply, and those of our old age are perhaps understood most clearly. Together, they balance emotion and wisdom, and when they connect across generations, the relationships formed are complex and valuable.

Such relationships are the focus of many selections in this unit. In the poem "Grandmother," Lawson Fusao Inada writes of the valuable lessons, mythic and otherwise, that his grandmother was able to convey to him in the simplest of ways in the midst of adversity. In " 'See Spot Run': Teaching My Grandmother to Read," Ellen Tashie Frisina shows us a more unusual situation where she, the grandchild, is the teacher and the grandparent the learner, although it is clear that she too gains much from the interchange. And in "Old Before Her Time" by Katherine Barrett, Patty Moore picks up many valuable pointers about life from the old people she seeks out for conversation.

Childhood is a time of simplicity, of living life to its fullness, and of seeing the world in a way we never will again, and several selections illustrate this. "Circle of Children" by Brenda Anne Le Blanc reminds us of numerous valuable attributes of childhood, and it argues that we need to be around children to a greater extent than is our social custom. "The Kitchen" by Alfred Kazin shows us with amazing clarity his first home, a Brownsville tenement, and the mother who filled it with her presence and left her mark on him. The pain of the early years, however, can leave indelible impressions as well, as "Children of Divorce" by Anthony Brandt points out through a careful examination of case studies.

Attitudes toward old age in America also are the subject of a number of selections. In them, we see that these attitudes may be greatly influenced by a person's cultural or ethnic background and by the messages incessantly conveyed to us by the media. While "Never Too Old: The Art of Getting Better" by Louise Bernikow celebrates the joys of age, "Old Before Her Time" critically examines the fears and disadvantages that old people often live with. This last piece also points out the way in which America ostracizes the elderly, but fortunately, this is not always the case. As "Grandmother" and " 'See Spot Run' " point out, old age and its wisdom—and perhaps even its frailty—can be valued and loved, leading us to link the past with the present and enabling us to create a richer, more informed future.

Pre-reading Activity   Think of a place that is associated with your most vivid childhood memories. Using the technique of **clustering**, write down several descriptive details that bring the place to life.

As You Read   Observe the writer's use of **topic sentences** at the beginnings of paragraphs to create a unifying pattern throughout this excerpt.

THE KITCHEN
Alfred Kazin

Born in 1915, **Alfred Kazin** *is a Jewish-American writer and teacher who has held several distinguished fellowships. He is a member of the American Academy of Arts and Sciences and the author of several books, including* On Native Ground, The Inmost Leaf, Starting Out in the Thirties, New York Jew, An American Procession, *and* A Walker in the City *(1957), from which this selection is taken.*

In Brownsville tenements the kitchen is always the largest room and the 1 center of the household. As a child I felt we lived in a kitchen to which four other rooms were annexed. My mother, a "home" dressmaker, had her workshop in the kitchen. She told me once that she had begun dressmaking in Poland at thirteen; as far back as I can remember, she was always making dresses for the local women. She had an innate sense of design, a quick eye for all the subtleties in the latest fashions, even when she despised them, and great boldness. For three or four dollars she would study the fashion magazines with a customer, go with the customer to the remnants store on Belmont Avenue to pick out the material, argue the owner down—all remnants stores, for some reason, were supposed to be shady, as if the owners dealt in stolen goods—and then for days would patiently fit and baste and sew and fit again. Our apartment was always full of women in their housedresses sitting around the kitchen table waiting for a fitting. My little bedroom next to the kitchen was the fitting room. The sewing machine, an old nut-brown Singer with golden scrolls painted along the black arm and engraved along the two tiers of little drawers massed with needles and thread on each side of the treadle, stood next to the window and the great coal-black stove which up to my last year in college was our main source of heat. By December the two outer bedrooms were closed off, and used to chill bottles of milk and cream, cold borscht and jellied calves' feet.

2   The kitchen held our lives together. My mother worked in it all day long, we ate in it almost all meals except the Passover *seder,* I did my homework and first writing at the kitchen table, and in winter I often had a bed made up for me on three kitchen chairs near the stove. On the wall just over the table hung a long horizontal mirror that sloped to a ship's prow at each end and was lined in cherry wood. It took up the whole wall, and drew every object in the kitchen to itself. The walls were a fiercely stippled whitewash, so often rewhitened by my father in slack seasons that the paint looked as if it had been squeezed and cracked into the walls. A large electric bulb hung down the center of the kitchen at the end of a chain that had been hooked into the ceiling; the old gas ring and key still jutted out of the wall like antlers. In the corner next to the toilet was the sink at which we washed, and the square tub in which my mother did our clothes. Above it, tacked to the shelf on which were pleasantly ranged square, blue bordered white sugar and spice jars, hung calendars from the Public National Bank on Pitkin Avenue and the Minsker Progressive Branch of the Workman's Circle; receipts for the payment of insurance premiums, and household bills on a spindle; two little boxes engraved with Hebrew letters. One of these was for the poor, the other to buy back the Land of Israel. Each spring a bearded little man would suddenly appear in our kitchen, salute us with a hurried Hebrew blessing, empty the boxes (sometimes with a sidelong look of disdain if they were not full), hurriedly bless us again for remembering our less fortunate Jewish brothers and sisters, and so take his departure until the next spring, after vainly trying to persuade my mother to take still another box. We did occasionally remember to drop coins in the boxes, but this was usually only on the dreaded morning of "mid-terms" and final examinations, because my mother thought it would bring me luck. She was extremely superstitious, but embarrassed about it, and always laughed at herself whenever, on the morning of an examination, she counseled me to leave the house on my right foot. "I know it's silly," her smile seemed to say, "but what harm can it do? It may calm God down."

3   The kitchen gave a special character to our lives, my mother's character. All my memories of that kitchen are dominated by the nearness of my mother sitting all day long at her sewing machine, by the clacking of the treadle against the linoleum floor, by the patient twist of her right shoulder as she automatically pushed at the wheel with one hand or lifted the foot to free the needle where it had got stuck in a thick piece of material. The kitchen was her life. Year by year, as I began to take in her fantastic capacity for labor and her anxious zeal, I realized it was ourselves she kept stitched together. I can never remember a time when she was not working. She worked because the law of her life was work, work and anxiety; she worked because she would have found life meaningless without work. She read almost no English; she could read the Yiddish paper, but

never felt she had time to. We were always talking of a time when I would teach her how to read, but somehow there was never time. When I awoke in the morning she was already at her machine, or in the great morning crowd of housewives at the grocery getting fresh rolls for breakfast. When I returned from school she was at her machine, or conferring over *McCall's* with some neighborhood woman who had come in pointing hopefully to an illustration—"Mrs. Kazin! Mrs. Kazin! Make me a dress like it shows here in the picture!" When my father came home from work she had some-how mysteriously interrupted herself to make supper for us, and the dishes cleared and washed, was back at her machine. When I went to bed at night, often she was still there, pounding away at the treadle, hunched over the wheel, her hands steering a piece of gauze under the needle with a fi-nesse that always contrasted sharply with her swollen hands and broken nails. Her left hand had been pierced through when as a girl she had worked in the infamous Triangle Shirtwaist Factory on the East Side. A nee-dle had gone straight through the palm, severing a large vein. They had sewn it up for her so clumsily that a tuft of flesh always lay folded over the palm.

The kitchen was the great machine that set our lives running; it whirred   4 down a little only on Saturdays and holy days. From my mother's kitchen I gained my first picture of life as a white, overheated, starkly lit workshop redolent with Jewish cooking, crowded with women in housedresses, strewn with fashion magazines, patterns, dress material, spools of thread—and at whose center, so lashed to her machine that bolts of energy seemed to dance out of her hands and feet as she worked, my mother stamped the treadle hard against the floor, hard, hard, and silently, grimly at war, beat out the first rhythm of the world for me.

Building Vocabulary

Define the words below, using *context clues* wherever possible and checking in a dictionary when necessary. Use them in sentences of your own.

tenement (paragraph 1)	conferring (3)	disdain (2)
innate (1)	annexed (1)	Yiddish (3)
stippled (2)	borscht (1)	redolent (4)
zeal (3)		

Journal Writing

Choose one or more of the three activities listed below, and make an entry in your journal. Focus on writing spontaneously rather than on structure and mechanics.

1. **Exploring:** Recall what you remember from other sources—your reading, your life experiences, movies and television, stories told to you by others—about the topic discussed by the writer. Choose one or two of these to write about. Which aspects of the topic did they bring up? What additional information did they provide? What emotions did they create in you?
2. **Taking Stock:** Which parts of the selection were most difficult for you to grasp? Which parts needed more explanation? Which parts required outside information to be understood? What kind of information was required (e.g., historical, culture-specific, technical, etc.)? Where might such information be found? Were there aspects of the writer's style you found particularly effective? Particularly difficult? Why?
3. **Responding:** Identify one or two of the writer's main concerns. What personal knowledge, if any, do you have of these issues? What is your opinion on these issues? Examine your response carefully to see what it teaches you about yourself.

Analyzing Content

1. Why does Kazin call the kitchen "the center of the household" (1)?
2. Examine the details in paragraph 2. What do they tell us about Kazin's family?
3. Analyze the character of the mother.
4. How does Kazin feel toward his mother? What do you think he has learned from her?
5. State, in your own words, the **thesis** of this excerpt.

Analyzing Writing Techniques

1. The first three paragraphs in this excerpt are rather long. How, in each of them, has the writer developed the **controlling idea** of the paragraph? Give examples.
2. In paragraph 4, Kazin uses a **metaphor** to explain the role of the kitchen in his family's life. Pick out the metaphor, and explain its significance.

Group Activity

In this selection, Kazin's mother is an important influence in his life. As a group, use the technique of **brainstorming** to come up with a list of people who have been important in your lives. **Classify** these people into categories (e.g., parents, employers, teachers, strangers, etc.). Which category has the most people in it?

Your Writing

1. Using the ideas generated in the group activity, write an essay about a person who has been a significant influence, positive or negative, in your early life. **Describe** the person, and **explain** the nature of the influence.

2. **Compare/contrast** Kazin's mother's lifestyle with that of a contemporary mother. (This can be your own mother or any woman whose life you have observed in detail).

Pre-reading Activity What are some of the feelings, images, and thoughts you associate with the word *divorce?* **Freewrite** for 5 to 10 minutes, jotting down all related ideas that occur to you. Phrases and single words are OK.

As You Read Note the writer's use of statistics and scientific studies as evidence.

CHILDREN OF DIVORCE
Anthony Brandt

Anthony Brandt *is a freelance journalist who sometimes writes for* Parenting, *in which this article appeared in 1991. Judith Wallerstein, whom he profiles, is the coauthor of* Second Chances: Men, Women, and Children a Decade after Divorce.

1   I asked Sharon,[1] who is 45, to describe her most vivid memory of her parents' divorce. A specific image came immediately to her mind. "I remember my father framed in the doorway, leaving." She was five years old at the time. Right after that, her mother's new boyfriend and second-husband-to-be moved in.

2   Soon after this new arrangement was in place, Sharon had a nightmare that would recur for years. "I dreamt that I was alone in the apartment and 'it' was coming after me," she says. "I never saw 'it,' though when I woke up in the dream, the beds were made but no one was there. The dream was so awful that at dusk I would start to get knots in my stomach, I was so afraid of going to sleep. I was terrified of being abandoned."

3   Sometimes Sharon would hide in closets to escape her fears. "But my mother ignored the signs of distress," she says. "The fact is, her emotional energy was not focused on helping me and my brother adjust to the divorce. She was more interested in making her new relationship work." Sharon's mother and father each remarried within several years of their divorce, so there were stepparents in both of her homes. "I had the feeling that I didn't belong anywhere—that I never came first."

4   It has taken Sharon years of therapy to come to terms with all of this. She has been through a divorce of her own, and has had a great deal of

----

[1]These names have been changed.

trouble getting started in any sort of career. "My parents' divorce drove me crazy half of my life," she says. "My mother and father made me feel responsible for them. The only way I could be OK was to make them feel OK." There is anger in her voice. "If it weren't for therapy, I wouldn't be doing anything at all with my life right now."

Sharon's emotional difficulties may seem extreme, but the situation in which she found herself certainly is not. We all know the figures: If recent trends continue, fully 50 percent of marriages in this country will end in divorce. Compare that to a divorce rate of 30 percent in 1950, and you begin to see how dramatically the American family has been transformed over the past 40 years. In my own extended family, for instance, there was only one divorce in my parents' generation, and it so shocked my family that it was literally unspeakable. No one would talk about it; no one would even mention it. Today, at least four members of my generation have been divorced, including me, my brother, and two cousins, and no one is blinking an eye.   5

In the midst of this social revolution, we've also been fairly cavalier about the effect that divorce is having on our children. Perhaps it's wishful thinking, or a kind of willed ignorance, but people tend to assume that while children certainly will be disturbed by the breakup of their parents, they'll adjust in time, and whatever emotional scars they've acquired will eventually disappear. Indeed this optimistic attitude was justified by what, until recently, was considered the major scientific study of divorce in this country. Conducted in the late seventies by E. Mavis Hetherington at the University of Virginia, the study found that while divorce did have a destabilizing effect on preschool children—both at home and in school—they generally recovered within a two-year period.   6

Considering the lifelong devastation that other family traumas, such as child abuse or drug addiction, can cause, two years seemed like a manageable amount of time. Then along came Judith Wallerstein, executive director of the Center for the Family in Transition, in Corte Madera, California. In 1971 she began the longest running study in the country of the effects of divorce on children. She is the Columbus of her field, and the news she is bringing back from the world of divorce is sobering. Among her most shattering findings: Without adequate guidance and love, the psychological damage of divorce on children of all ages can be severe and longlasting. Furthermore, Wallerstein observed what she calls a "sleeper effect" of divorce; that is, even when children may seem to have adjusted quite well, it suddenly becomes clear, ten years later, that they have not. They hit some crisis point, often when romantic relationships become central in their lives, and all the fear and anger come back. Girls, especially, seem to suffer from this kind of delayed reaction.   7

The point that Wallerstein would like everyone to hear is not that parents should feel guilty about their marital trouble, or even that they should stay together for the sake of the children. In fact, she feels strongly that an unhappy marriage can be just as harmful to a child as a divorce. But what   8 parents often forget, she says, is that divorce is not a one-time event in the lives of their children: It lasts forever. Parents must realize that long after Mom and Dad have emotionally recovered, and perhaps even remarried, their children may still bear the scars of the divorce, and that tending to those scars—for as long as it takes—is something the adults must take responsibility for. Through the work she does at her family counseling center, and which she describes in her book (coauthored with Sandra Blakeslee), *Second Chances: Men, Women, and Children a Decade After Divorce,* Judith Wallerstein has set out to help parents do just that.

9   ## The Long-Term Effects

10 Human psychology is complicated, and the effects of divorce that Wallerstein describes are diverse. But one thread runs through them all, she writes. "These children all say that their lives have been overshadowed by their parents' divorces and that they feel deprived of a range of economic and psychological supports. . . . They feel less protected, less cared for, less comforted." Many of them said that their parents' divorce marked the end of their childhood.

11   Children of high-conflict divorces suffer the most, but according to Wallerstein, no one is totally immune. Teresa Peck, a clinical psychologist at Wallerstein's center, is conducting a research program in some of the local schools to investigate the relationship between divorce and adolescent underachievement. "What I've found is that 78 percent of the underachievers—kids with grade averages in the A–B range in the lower schools, who had fallen into the D–F range in high school—came from families of divorce, compared to only 30 percent of the achieving kids— those who maintained an A–B average consistently over the years," Peck explains. "And when you break the figures down by gender, boys did much worse. None of the male achievers came from families of divorce."

12   Underachievement is a way for kids to reach out to their parents for help, says Peck. But it's also a way of showing anger: " 'You've messed up my life, so I'm just going to mess it up more to show you.' And these weren't delinquents. These were basically decent kids whose life had taken a turn they couldn't adjust to," she says. Nearly half of the boys in Peck's study continued to fare poorly after leaving school.

13   Wallerstein also found, in her long-term study, that boys didn't seem to recover very well over time. Ten years after their parents' divorce, many of them were "unhappy and lonely, and had had few, if any, lasting relationships with women," she adds. A significant number of the girls, on the other hand, the same ones who seemed to have adjusted quite well to the divorce, were now suffering from the sleeper effect. Wallerstein explains that this typically occurs when "the man/woman relationship moves into center stage in their lives. All the ghosts rise from the basement at that point." Many of the women Wallerstein observed destroyed their own relationships with men before they got too close, or simply did not want to

get involved at all. Some became sexually promiscuous without forming attachments to anyone in particular.

Veronica, 25, is someone who's experiencing the sleeper effect with a vengeance. Her parents were divorced when she was six years old, and a year ago she would have said the divorce had no effect on her at all. "There were always conflicts between my parents, but I didn't think I had any scars." Recently, though, her boyfriend raised the issue of marriage, and all of a sudden she "started to panic." She even had an anxiety attack at a friend's wedding.   14

"I was totally unprepared for how difficult it was for me to trust him," Veronica explains. Eventually she went into therapy, which brought it all back: her parents' divorce, her father's leaving the country for four years, her own insecurity at the time, her mother's emotional withdrawal. "I developed this fear back then that my parents weren't going to be there." Sometimes when her mother would go out for the evening, Veronica would call 911 in a panic, trying to find out if she had been in an accident. Today, Veronica says, she keeps putting off her boyfriend—apparently out of a similar fear of abandonment. "He tells me that he loves me and wants to marry me, but I just can't believe him. I have no trust at all. Marriage feels like an enormous, scary thing to me."   15

Separating with Sensitivity   16

Beleaguered parents who already feel bad about the breakup of their marriage won't be eager, of course, to hear all this discouraging news. Indeed, critics often charge that Wallerstein simply makes people feel more guilty. But she insists that that's not her intention. In fact, she agrees with the conclusions of the seminal British study released to the press last June. For the first time ever, more than 17,000 children were observed over a period of several years, both before and after some of their parents had divorced. Researchers found that in the divorced families, the children were already suffering from behavioral and psychological problems long before their parents actually broke up.   17

These findings might seem to call into question the premise of Wallerstein's study—that divorce itself is to blame for the problems children suffer when families split apart. Wallerstein, though, sees no contradiction whatsoever. "This just confirms what we've known all along, that trouble in the family doesn't begin the day the papers are filed. Divorce is simply the climactic event in the life of the unhappy family." But—and it is an extremely important but—even though she doesn't believe that parents who can't get along should stay together for the sake of the children, Wallerstein thinks that they "have to divorce better than they're doing. That's the whole issue."   18

In 1980, Wallerstein founded the Center for the Family in Transition to do what no other agency in the country was doing: provide services specifically designed for divorcing families and their children. For the last   19

11 years, every couple with children who's filed for a divorce in Marin County, California, has received a letter from Judith Wallerstein inviting them to come in and discuss their problems. "The center provides an educational and a counseling service combined," she explains. "It's based on the simple principle that if you're going to have a society where divorce is so accessible, you have an equal responsibility to provide services to help both the children and the parents."

20   Couples who seek help at the center are first counseled on how to get through the actual divorce. Wallerstein believes that the manner in which a family separates can help determine the way everyone involved will adjust for years to come, so this is a pivotal part of the therapy. As she explains in *Second Chances,* the hardest, and perhaps the most important, task for parents who are breaking up is to give their children permission to love both of them equally. "Children need to feel that they have a right to their own feelings, and that they are not being asked to ally with one parent against the other." William Voltaire, a father of two in Sausalito, California, who used the center to help him through his divorce, found this to be a crucial first step. "It took plenty of time and reinforcement, but when my kids realized that they could have feelings that were independent of mine—if they were missing their mom, for instance, or wanted to spend an extra night at her house—and I would not feel betrayed, they began to relax."

21   Wallerstein also stresses how important it is for parents to present the divorce as a rational solution to an unhappy situation—something meant to restore peace and order, not just break the family apart. Then, once the divorce is final, parents are advised on how to be as direct and detailed as possible about all the changes that will result from the split. And, Wallerstein adds, they must take an active role in the process. If a four-year-old is going to visit her father, for instance, Wallerstein suggests that the mother prepare her enthusiastically. If possible, call the father and find out where he plans to take the child, and talk about it with her ahead of time. Give her permission, in other words, to have fun. When the child returns, the mother should observe her to determine what would most help her to settle back in.

22   Voltaire calls it "mood reading." Many kids like to be greeted at the door, for instance, while others need to be left alone for a while before reconnecting. Some of the children in Wallerstein's study would walk all around the house, touching the furniture just to make sure it was still there.

23   The point that Wallerstein cannot emphasize enough is that this vigilance toward their children is something divorced parents will need to maintain indefinitely. Whether there's a new school in the offing, a move, new caretaking arrangements, or, perhaps the most traumatic of all, a new parental relationship, it is the parents' job—not the child's—to initiate discussion and try to smooth the way.

But what about parents who don't have access to Judith Wallerstein's   24
center? Wallerstein admits that she is "very, very worried about families in
America, since there just doesn't seem to be any commitment on the part
of society to taking care of the children of divorce." Hers is the only program of its kind in the country, and even some of her funding for low-
income families has been cut. Wallerstein suggests that, whenever possible, a divorcing couple seek some kind of counseling or consult books on
divorce for ideas about how to do it themselves. The first and most important step, though, is simply to acknowledge that their children are hurting, and accept responsibility for it.

At this point Wallerstein draws her encouragement from the children   25
themselves; most of them show marked improvement with the loving attention they receive at the center. What heartens her the most, though, is
that they haven't given up on the idea of the family: If anything, they just
want to do it better than their parents did. "These children want a family
of their own," Wallerstein says. "And they don't want their children to go
through what they went through, so above all, they don't want a divorce."

If our children are ready to learn from our mistakes, maybe we can,   26
too.

Building Vocabulary

Define the words below, using *context clues* wherever possible and
checking in a dictionary when necessary. Use them in sentences of
your own.

trends (5)	transition (17)	seminal (15)
destabilizing (6)	cavalier (6)	vigilance (21)
immune (9)	coauthor (8)	

Journal Writing

Choose one or more of the three activities listed below, and make an
entry in your journal. Focus on writing spontaneously rather than on
structure and mechanics.

1. **Exploring:** Recall what you remember from other sources—your
   reading, your life experiences, movies and television, stories told
   to you by others—about the topic discussed by the writer. Choose
   one or two of these to write about. Which aspects of the topic did
   they bring up? What additional information did they provide?
   What emotions did they create in you?
2. **Taking Stock:** Which parts of the selection were most difficult for
   you to grasp? Which parts needed more explanation? Which parts
   required outside information to be understood? What kind of in-

formation was required (e.g., historical, culture-specific, technical, etc.)? Where might such information be found? Were there aspects of the writer's style you found particularly effective? Particularly difficult? Why?

3. **Responding:** Identify one or two of the writer's main concerns. What personal knowledge, if any, do you have of these issues? What is your opinion on these issues? Examine your response carefully to see what it teaches you about yourself.

Analyzing Content

1. What is a common assumption about the effects of divorce on children?
2. Explain why Brandt believes this assumption from question 1 to be incorrect. What proof has he provided to support his opinion?
3. Explain the term *sleeper effect,* and find an example of it in the essay.
4. Analyze the correlation between underachievement at school and being a child of divorce.
5. According to Wallerstein, what are some steps that divorcing parents can take to minimize the effects of divorce on their children?

Analyzing Writing Techniques

1. Throughout the essay, Brandt uses **quotations.** Who are some of the people he quotes? Why is the use of quotation an effective technique in an essay like this?
2. Analyze the first four paragraphs of the essay. Why does the writer choose to begin in this way? How does he use **transition** to move from the beginning to one of his major ideas?

Group Activity

People often have very strong opinions on divorce. **Discuss** the opinions of the members of your group on this issue. Each member of the group needs to explain why he or she holds this opinion. After discussion, write a **collaborative summary** of the different opinions.

Your Writing

1. **Interview** one or more people who are knowledgeable about the subject of divorce (either from having experienced it themselves

or because of their professions). Using the material gathered, write an essay that discusses the **pros and cons** of divorce.

2. In paragraph 5, Brandt tells us that divorce in America is a common, and a commonly accepted, phenomenon. Is this true for all cultural groups living in America or for cultural groups elsewhere? Write an essay in which you discuss the attitude of a particular cultural group (your own or one you know closely) toward divorce. Support your **thesis** with specific **examples** and, if possible, **quotations**.

Pre-reading Activity   Write about an important interaction you have had with an older adult. Who was the adult? What was unique about this interaction? What mark did it leave on you?

As You Read   Observe the writer's handling of time, moving from the events of the story back to the grandmother's childhood and then forward to her death. What transitions, if any, has Frisina used to indicate the movements in time?

"SEE SPOT RUN": TEACHING MY GRANDMOTHER TO READ
Ellen Tashie Frisina

Ellen Tashie Frisina is a second-generation Greek-American. This is one of her first published pieces.

1   When I was 14 years old, and very impressed with my teenage status (looking forward to all the rewards it would bring), I set for myself a very special goal—a goal that so differentiated me from my friends that I don't believe I told a single one. As a teenager, I was expected to have deep, dark secrets, but I was not supposed to keep them from my friends.

2   My secret was a project that I undertook every day after school for several months. It began when I stealthily made my way into the local elementary school—horror of horrors should I be seen; I was now in junior high. I identified myself as a *graduate* of the elementary school, and being taken under wing by a favorite fifth-grade teacher, I was given a small bundle from a locked storeroom—a bundle that I quickly dropped into a bag, lest anyone see me walking home with something from the "little kids" school.

3   I brought the bundle home—proudly now, for within the confines of my home, I was proud of my project. I walked into the living room, and one by one, emptied the bag of basic reading books. They were thin books with colorful covers and large print. The words were monosyllabic and repetitive. I sat down to the secret task at hand.

4   "All right," I said authoritatively to my 70-year-old grandmother, "today we begin our first reading lesson."

5   For weeks afterward, my grandmother and I sat patiently side by side— roles reversed as she, with a bit of difficulty, sounded out every word, then read them again, piece by piece, until she understood the short sentences. When she slowly repeated the full sentence, we both would smile and clap our hands—I felt so proud, so grown up.

My grandmother was born in Kalamata, Greece, in a rocky little farm- 6
ing village where nothing much grew. She never had the time to go to
school. As the oldest child, she was expected to take care of her brother
and sister, as well as the house and meals, while her mother tended to the
gardens, and her father scratched out what little he could from the soil.

So, for my grandmother, schooling was out. But she had big plans for 7
herself. She had heard about America. About how rich you could be. How
people on the streets would offer you a dollar just to smell the flower you
were carrying. About how everyone lived in nice houses—not stone huts
on the sides of mountains—and had nice clothes and time for school.

So my grandmother made a decision at 14—just a child, I realize 8
now—to take a long and sickening 30-day sea voyage alone to the United
States. After lying about her age to the passport officials, who would shake
their heads vehemently at anyone under 16 leaving her family, and after
giving her favorite gold earrings to her cousin, saying "In America, I will
have all the gold I want," my young grandmother put herself on a ship.
She landed in New York in 1916.

No need to repeat the story of how it went for years. The streets were 9
not made of gold. People weren't interested in smelling flowers held by
strangers. My grandmother was a foreigner. Alone. A young girl who
worked hard doing piecework to earn enough money for meals. No leisure
time, no new gold earrings—and no school.

She learned only enough English to help her in her daily business as 10
she traveled about Brooklyn. Socially, the "foreigners" stayed in neighborhoods where they didn't feel like foreigners. English came slowly.

My grandmother had never learned to read. She could make out a 11
menu, but not a newspaper. She could read a street sign, but not a shop
directory. She could read only what she needed to read as, through the
years, she married, had five daughters, and helped my grandfather with
his restaurant.

So when I was 14—the same age that my grandmother was when she 12
left her family, her country, and everything she knew—I took it upon myself to teach my grandmother something, something I already knew how
to do. Something with which I could give back to her some of the things
she had taught me.

And it was slight repayment for all she taught me. How to cover the 13
fig tree in tar paper so it could survive the winter. How to cultivate rose
bushes and magnolia trees that thrived on her little piece of property. How
to make baklava, and other Greek delights, working from her memory.
("Now we add some milk." "How much?" "Until we have enough.") Best
of all, she had taught me my ethnic heritage.

First, we phonetically sounded out the alphabet. Then, we talked 14
about vowels—English is such a difficult language to learn. I hadn't even
begun to explain the different sounds "gh" could make. We were still at
the basics.

15   Every afternoon, we would sit in the living room, my grandmother with an afghan covering her knees, giving up her crocheting for her reading lesson. I, with the patience that can come only from love, slowly coached her from the basic reader to the second-grade reader, giving up my telephone gossiping.

16   Years later, my grandmother still hadn't learned quite enough to sit comfortably with a newspaper or magazine, but it felt awfully good to see her try. How we used to laugh at her pronunciation mistakes. She laughed more heartily than I. I never knew whether I should laugh. Here was this old woman slowly and carefully sounding out each word, moving her lips, not saying anything aloud until she was absolutely sure, and then, loudly, proudly, happily saying, "Look at Spot. See Spot run."

17   When my grandmother died and we faced the sad task of emptying her home, I was going through her night-table drawer and came upon the basic readers. I turned the pages slowly, remembering. I put them in a paper bag, and the next day returned them to the "little kids" school. Maybe someday, some teenager will request them again, for the same task. It will make for a lifetime of memories.

Building Vocabulary

Define the words below, using *context clues* wherever possible and checking in a dictionary when necessary. Use them in sentences of your own.

stealthily (2)	afghan (15)	baklava (13)
authoritatively (4)	monosyllabic (3)	crocheting (15)
directory (11)	vehemently (8)	

Journal Writing

Choose one or more of the three activities listed below, and make an entry in your journal. Focus on writing spontaneously rather than on structure and mechanics.

1. **Exploring:** Recall what you remember from other sources—your reading, your life experiences, movies and television, stories told to you by others—about the topic discussed by the writer. Choose one or two of these to write about. Which aspects of the topic did they bring up? What additional information did they provide? What emotions did they create in you?

2. **Taking Stock:** Which parts of the selection were most difficult for you to grasp? Which parts needed more explanation? Which parts required outside information to be understood? What kind of information was required (e.g., historical, culture-specific, technical, etc.)? Where might such information be found? Were there aspects

of the writer's style you found particularly effective? Particularly difficult? Why?

3. **Responding:** Identify one or two of the writer's main concerns. What personal knowledge, if any, do you have of these issues? What is your opinion on these issues? Examine your response carefully to see what it teaches you about yourself.

Analyzing Content

1. What is the secret project that the 14-year-old Frisina undertakes? How does she feel about it at school? At home? What accounts for the difference in her attitude?
2. Why does Frisina undertake this project?
3. How does the project change the relationship between Frisina and her grandmother? Explain with details gathered from different parts of the essay.
4. Compare the myth of America with the reality encountered by the grandmother when she arrives here. What conclusion can you draw from this experience?
5. How does the grandmother feel about learning to read? Which details in the essay indicate her attitude?

Analyzing Writing Techniques

1. Pick out the **thesis** of the essay. Where does it occur? Why has the writer placed it here?
2. What kind of **diction** has the writer used in this essay: informal or formal, simple or complex? What are the reasons for her choice?

Group Activity

Discuss with your group experiences in which you were a "teacher" to someone else. Explain the situation. Now, **compiling** the group's ideas, **list** the qualities that a good teacher needs to possess.

Your Writing

1. Is Frisina's relationship with her grandmother typical of the relationship that teenagers in America have with their grandparents? From your experience and observation, write an essay explaining what this relationship is. What social factors influence this relationship?
2. Illiteracy is a problem for many adults in America today. **Research** this issue, and write an essay on the **causes** of this problem.

Pre-reading Activity **Freewrite** for 5 to 10 minutes about stories and legends that you were told as you were growing up.

As You Read Note the writer's use of **direct speech**. What does it add to the poem?

GRANDMOTHER
Lawson Fusao Inada

Lawson Fusao Inada *is the author of two books,* Before the War *and* Legends from Camp. *He is an editor of two landmark Asian-American anthologies,* Aiiieeee! *and* The Big Aiiieeee! *He has won several writing awards, including two fellowships from the National Endowment for the Arts, and teaches English at Southwest Oregon State College.*

1   For Grandmother: Mijiu Inada, Yoshiko Saito

2   Except for the fact that Grandmother taught me
chopsticks and Japanese before forks and English,
my relationship with Her wasn't all that much.

3   As a matter of fact, Grandmother, with Her old-
fashioned ways, was actually somewhat of an extravagant source of confusion and distraction.

4   For example, just to waste time on a rainy day
in a boring barrack-room in our ordinary
concentration camp in Arkansas, She'd say:

5   "The Great God, Thunder, is very powerful.
Listen to Him. When He storms, be careful.
Or He will send Lightning to take your navel!"

6   Or, on just another quiet night in Colorado,
on the way to the shower-house, She may pause
in the warm desert sand to simply say:

7   "Ah, the Full Moon! Look closely, Grandson.
It's the same Moon, and the same Story.
'Two Rabbits with Mallets Pounding Rice.' "

Time passes. Grandmother passes. I've learned   8
the facts since. Still, in some storms, I feel
a twitch, and, in the still of certain nights,

with the right chopsticks, I can eat with   9
the Rabbits, who have scattered all the Rice.

Building Vocabulary

Define the words below, using *context clues* wherever possible and
checking in a dictionary when necessary. Use them in sentences of
your own.

extravagant (6–7)   distraction (7)
barrack-room (9)   concentration camp (10)

Analyzing Content

1. What, according to the first stanza, did the poet learn from his
   grandmother? Is this the whole truth about their relationship?
2. How does the narrator react as a boy to the grandmother's stories?
3. How does he react to them as a grown-up, after her death?
4. Analyze the meaning of the last five lines of the poem.

Analyzing Writing Techniques

1. The poet uses two brief **allusions** (lines 8–9, lines 13–14) to indicate an important historical event. Explain the event and how it
   affected the lives of Japanese-Americans. Why does he not describe it in more detail? What do the allusions add to the poem?
2. What is the **tone** of this poem? Point to details that help to establish this tone.

Group Activity

Discuss some myths you have heard or read about. Where are they set?
How do they compare with the ones the grandmother taught the poet?

Your Writing

1. One of the themes of this poem is the conservation of one's heritage. Write an essay in which you examine the different ways that
   people do this. Be sure to give specific examples.
2. **Compare/contrast** the way the poet feels toward his grandmother
   with how you feel about an older adult who has been important
   in your life. If your feelings toward this individual have changed
   over time, indicate this clearly with examples.

Pre-reading Activity   Picture yourself 20 or 30 years from now. How do you imagine you will look? In what kinds of activities do you see yourself participating? How do you feel about this older self?

As You Read   Note the way in which Bernikow intermingles long and short sentences, including fragments and one-word sentences, into her writing. What does this add to her style?

NEVER TOO OLD: THE ART
OF GETTING BETTER
Louise Bernikow

Born in 1940 in New York, **Louise Bernikow** *holds degrees from Barnard and Columbia and has taught at Queens College, Barnard, and Hunter College, where she founded the Women's Studies program. Her books include* Among Women, Let's Have Lunch: Games of Sex and Power, *and* Alone in America: The Search for Companionship. *Her work has appeared in* Life, Ms., New York Times Book Review, *and* Mademoiselle, *in which this piece was first published in 1983.*

1   When I was twenty, I was afraid of a lot of things. I worried, for example, about finding myself in bed with Mr. Wonderful at last and looking down, only to discover I had forgotten to shave my legs. Mr. Wonderful would retch and leave. Or I was sure I would translate Dante entirely wrong in Italian class, say something obscene without knowing it, causing snickers from the fluent girls in the back row. I might, I feared, buy the wrong shade of pink cashmere sweater, eliciting similar snickers, now coupled with laughter, from the very same girls, whose perfect color coordination matched their perfect Italian, their perfect dorm rooms and their perfect hold on the universe. These were minor fears. Whatever pits I might fall into, I could always climb out because I was, after all, just twenty, with my whole life ahead of me. But what if I woke up one day to find that I was say, forty?

2   Aging meant sagging—in the face, the body, the spirits. At forty, I thought, a woman was gone, like a skier on a chair lift disappearing over the crest of the mountain. Men might become more powerful, worldly and attractive, but women withered. They inhabited the universe, like the old living room sofa, but nobody paid attention to them. They weren't beau-

tiful, sexy, compelling or exciting. They had no impact. They didn't jump gaily into fountains wearing sequins in the middle of the night or take up calculus or join expeditions to climb the highest mountain in Nepal.

I had, in this fear, an insidious cultural disease. Everything around me glorified youthfulness. The popular female stars were perpetual teenagers like Debbie Reynolds, Sandra Dee and Doris Day. Grown-up women existed in some other country, a dull country. There were "mature" women in ads for tranquilizers. There were "matronly" clothes for the over-forty woman, all grays and browns. There was Eleanor Roosevelt as the model of an older women, striding confidently through the world on half-inch heels. Me, I wanted to play tennis for hours, wear sexy clothes, write at the top of my form. I wanted to keep my zing for years, for decades, forever.

Fear of aging is still with us. The disease infects America more than any other country. In Europe, after all, such actresses as Jeanne Moreau, Simone Signoret and Melina Mercouri have remained appealing, exciting women well into what are delicately called their "riper" years. Some of America's current sex symbols, on the other hand, are under twenty-one; some are under seventeen. The market is flooded with products promising a fountain of youth: soaps to make you "fresh-faced," which means young; vitamins to turn your body into a teenager's, no matter how lumpy and sagging it is when you begin wolfing them down. If there is a twenty-year-old today who has masterfully overcome her fear of leg stubble, mistakes in Italian or uncoordinated clothes, but who still catches her breath at the thought of going "over the hill"—passing thirty or even forty—I can't say she's a lunatic. She simply has a bad case of the disease.

I'm cured. I got cured by waking up one morning and finding myself over thirty, over forty, not dead, feeling nothing like a sofa. My zing was still in place. I hardly felt that anything had ended. It all seemed to have just started.

This has something to do with my own idiosyncratic development and something to do with the cultural conditions under which I managed my arrival at what they used to call middle age. When women of my mother's generation reached forty, most of them had already raised families and were facing "empty nests." The older they got, the less they had to do. Women their age did not return to school or go to work. And because their lives became more constricted as the years passed, they looked and felt older than they actually were. To these women, the idea that life might begin at forty would have seemed crazy. And rightly so.

But it's not at all crazy now. Former First Lady Rosalynn Carter gave birth to Amy two months after her fortieth birthday. The number of women having their first child after thirty has more than doubled in the last decade. So has the number of women returning to college. (They do better at their studies, these doddering older women, than the kids do.) If having babies or hitting the books doesn't seem like the thrill of a lifetime, consider Janet Guthrie, the first and only woman to drive in the Indianapolis 500. (Do sofas drive racing cars?) She was a year shy of forty at the time. Do people over the hill perform with as much vigor or invent with as much audacity and originality as modern dance pioneer Martha Graham did, well past forty? Or paint like Georgia O'Keeffe, sculpt like Louise Nevelson?

8   I look around at my aging friends. The first thing that strikes me is how beautiful they are. I mean physically, although there is a great deal of the spiritual in this beauty. I could trot out a parade of public figures to prove the point—Sophia Loren, Jacqueline Kennedy Onassis, Lauren Bacall, Liv Ullmann, Jane Fonda, Raquel Welch—but I'll stick to the ordinary citizens of my world and to my humble self as a reasonable yardstick.

9   Kitty is sitting there with her legs crossed, red stockings gleaming, something simultaneously impish, excited, authoritative and full of wonder crossing her face as she talks about a project that interests her. Her clothes are wild and original. Her hair is full, flying, electric. Priscilla is standing at the naming ceremony for her newborn daughter, her second child since she turned forty. Her dress is lavender; her eyes brilliant, filled with deep happiness and satisfaction, the kind that comes out of experience rather than innocence.

10   There is experience, too, in Honor's confidence as she dresses to take me out to dinner on my birthday. In a soft black jersey pantsuit, she radiates swagger, elegance, authority; she has the aura of a woman who knows who she is. The younger Honor worried about being fat, bedeviled herself about food, hid, apologized, felt bad. "I feel I'm getting more attractive all the time," she says, brushing her hair. "Standards of beauty are changing. We're beautiful because of our wholeness. I'm so much more autonomous, self-generating. I have a greater sense of the uniqueness of the life I've built and confidence in its ability to sustain me." Clearly, how Honor feels and how she looks are inseparable.

11   This sends me to my personal archive, my photo album. Here, I find the history of my own face as I lay the pictures in a row, like a deck of tarot cards.

12   **1957.** The high school yearbook. The face of innocence and youth. I look awful. I'm wearing the required black sweater with white lace collar and there is a cheerleader megaphone on a gold chain around my neck. I haven't become anyone yet. I'm quite frantic, and it shows. I'm unhappy and that shows, too.

13   **1960.** The Columbia College Senior Prom. This one makes me cringe. A strand of pearls. Pageboy haircut. Deep-red lipstick. Trying to become what I saw in magazines, imitating grown-ups. I look as matronly as my mother.

14   **1961.** The college yearbook. The face of someone trying to be someone else. The mode here is obviously debutante. I remember arranging my face to achieve a hollow-cheeked look and worrying about unruly hair—

wanting, in every possible way, to be smooth and sophisticated. The following year, I had a nervous breakdown.

1970. The jacket photograph on my first book. My hair is nearly falling   15
across my face, but still, a face is beginning to emerge. I have some lines
around my eyes and some puffiness under them. I had been in love and
lived with the man. I had fallen apart and put myself back together. I had
a history.

1976. The face of a woman with confidence. This picture appeared   16
in a book called *Emergence,* by Cynthia MacAdams, which celebrates
what the feminist writer Kate Millett, in the introduction, calls "a new kind
of woman." Some of the strength that I like here comes out of a historical
context—this is the height of my connection with the Women's Movement—and some comes from being well into my thirties.

1981. The photograph on the cover of my most recent book, *Among*   17
Women. I am wearing a dress and eye makeup. I am just on the other side
of forty and somehow, at last, feel comfortable with all the women I am.

I use myself as an example because these personal documents tell what   18
is clearly not a unique story, although it surely goes counter to the cultural
mythology that has women growing frumpier and fainter as we age. I feel
a great spiritual kinship with Annie Edson Taylor, who celebrated her forty-
third birthday by going over Niagara Falls in a barrel. She was the first person and only woman to do so. The year was 1901. I think she'd like being
alive today.

Building Vocabulary

Define the words below, using *context clues* wherever possible and
checking in a dictionary when necessary. Use them in sentences of
your own.

retch (1)	autonomous (10)	idiosyncratic (6)
insidious (3)	eliciting (1)	audacity (7)
fountain of youth (4)	zing (3)	archive (10)
doddering (7)		

Journal Writing

Choose one or more of the three activities listed below, and make an
entry in your journal. Focus on writing spontaneously rather than on
structure and mechanics.

1. **Exploring:** Recall what you remember from other sources—your
   reading, your life experiences, movies and television, stories told
   to you by others—about the topic discussed by the writer. Choose
   one or two of these to write about. Which aspects of the topic did

they bring up? What additional information did they provide? What emotions did they create in you?

2. **Taking Stock:** Which parts of the selection were most difficult for you to grasp? Which parts needed more explanation? Which parts required outside information to be understood? What kind of information was required (e.g., historical, culture-specific, technical, etc.)? Where might such information be found? Were there aspects of the writer's style you found particularly effective? Particularly difficult? Why?

3. **Responding:** Identify one or two of the writer's main concerns. What personal knowledge, if any, do you have of these issues? What is your opinion on these issues? Examine your response carefully to see what it teaches you about yourself.

Analyzing Content

1. In paragraph 1, Bernikow lists a number of fears she had as a 20-year-old. What was her worst fear? Why?

2. Why does Bernikow, in paragraph 3, term this fear an "insidious cultural disease"? What supporting evidence does she provide?

3. In paragraph 5, Bernikow claims she has finally overcome this fear. How has she done it? Are you convinced by her argument? Explain why or why not.

4. Analyze the ways in which, according to Bernikow, the lives of women have changed between her mother's generation and her own?

Analyzing Writing Techniques

1. Bernikow ends the first paragraph with a question. Where does she answer it? What is the effect of this question–answer technique on the reader?

2. In this essay, Bernikow uses **illustration** as a major method of supporting her ideas. Pick out a few examples of this that you find particularly effective, and explain why they work for you.

3. The examples used by Bernikow can be divided into three main categories. What are they? Which do you find most effective as support?

Group Activity

In paragraph 4, Bernikow implies that America's current sex symbols are mostly very young. What is your group's opinion on this issue? Make a list of the people your group considers to be sex symbols. What role does youth play in their attractiveness?

Your Writing

1. Bernikow declares (paragraph 4) that the market is flooded with products that promise youth. Do you agree? Visit a mall or browse through magazines to collect supporting evidence. (Be prepared to change your mind if necessary!) Now, write an essay in which you incorporate the material you have **researched** to prove your point.
2. Make a list of the advantages of age, according to Bernikow. Now, **interview** an elderly person, and find out how far he or she agrees with the author. Write an essay in which you discuss your findings.

Pre-reading Activity   **List** some situations in which you have observed old people (e.g., on the bus, at a party, at the grocery store).
What were your attitudes toward them in each of these situations?

As You Read   Note the way in which the writer deduces a lesson
from each of the settings she describes. What kind of **transition** pattern has she used to introduce each lesson?

OLD BEFORE HER TIME
Katherine Barrett

Katherine Barrett is a contributing editor at Financial World *and* The
Ladies' Home Journal *as well as a monthly columnist for* Glamour. *Her articles and columns have appeared in numerous magazines, including*
Newsweek, Harper's, Better Homes and Gardens, Redbook, *and* Working
Woman. *In 1991, along with her husband Richard Green, Barrett coauthored* The Man Behind the Magic, *a biography of Walt Disney. The following essay originally appeared in 1983 in* The Ladies' Home Journal.

1   This is the story of an extraordinary voyage in time, and of a young woman
who devoted three years to a singular experiment. In 1979, Patty Moore—
then aged twenty-six—transformed herself for the first of many times into
an eighty-five-year-old woman. Her object was to discover firsthand the
problems, joys and frustrations of the elderly. She wanted to know for herself what it's like to live in a culture of youth and beauty when your hair
is gray, your skin is wrinkled and no men turn their heads as you pass.

2   Her time machine was a makeup kit. Barbara Kelly, a friend and professional makeup artist, helped Patty pick out a wardrobe and showed her
how to use latex to create wrinkles, and wrap Ace bandages to give the
impression of stiff joints. "It was peculiar," Patty recalls, as she relaxes in
her New York City apartment. "Even the first few times I went out I realized that I wouldn't have to *act* that much. The more I was perceived as
elderly by others, the more 'elderly' I actually became . . . I imagine that's
just what happens to people who really are old."

3   What motivated Patty to make her strange journey? Partly her career—as an industrial designer, Patty often focuses on the needs of the elderly. But the roots of her interest are also deeply personal. Extremely close
to her own grandparents—particularly her maternal grandfather, now
ninety—and raised in a part of Buffalo, New York, where there was a large
elderly population, Patty always drew comfort and support from the older

people around her. When her own marriage ended in 1979 and her life seemed to be falling apart, she dove into her "project" with all her soul. In all, she donned her costume more than two hundred times in fourteen different states. Here is the remarkable story of what she found.

Columbus, Ohio, May 1979. Leaning heavily on her cane, Pat Moore   4
stood alone in the middle of a crowd of young professionals. They were all attending a gerontology conference, and the room was filled with animated chatter. But no one was talking to Pat. In a throng of men and women who devoted their working lives to the elderly, she began to feel like a total nonentity. "I'll get us all some coffee," a young man told a group of women next to her. "What about me?" thought Pat. "If I were young, they would be offering me coffee, too." It was a bitter thought at the end of a disappointing day—a day that marked Patty's first appearance as "the old woman." She had planned to attend the gerontology conference anyway, and almost as a lark decided to see how professionals would react to an old person in their midst.

Now, she was angry. All day she had been ignored . . . counted out in   5
a way she had never experienced before. She didn't understand. Why didn't people help her when they saw her struggling to open a heavy door? Why didn't they include her in conversations? Why did the other participants seem almost embarrassed by her presence at the conference—as if it were somehow inappropriate that an old person should be professionally active?

And so, eighty-five-year-old Pat Moore learned her first lesson: The old   6
are often ignored. "I discovered that people really do judge a book by its cover," Patty says today. "Just because I looked different, people either condescended or they totally dismissed me. Later, in stores, I'd get the same reaction. A clerk would turn to someone younger and wait on her first. It was as if he assumed that I—the older woman—could wait because I didn't have anything better to do."

New York City, October 1979. Bent over her cane, Pat walked slowly   7
toward the edge of the park. She had spent the day sitting on a bench with friends, but now dusk was falling and her friends had all gone home. She looked around nervously at the deserted area and tried to move faster, but her joints were stiff. It was then that she heard the barely audible sound of sneakered feet approaching and the kids' voices. "Grab her, man." "Get her purse." Suddenly an arm was around her throat and she was dragged back, knocked off her feet.

She saw only a blur of sneakers and blue jeans, heard the sounds of   8
mocking laughter, felt fists pummeling her—on her back, her legs, her breasts, her stomach. "Oh, God," she thought, using her arms to protect her head and curling herself into a ball. "They're going to kill me. I'm going to die. . . ."

Then, as suddenly as the boys attacked, they were gone. And Patty was   9
left alone, struggling to rise. The boys' punches had broken the latex

makeup on her face, the fall had disarranged her wig, and her whole body ached. (Later she would learn that she had fractured her left wrist, an injury that took two years to heal completely.) Sobbing, she left the park and hailed a cab to return home. Again the thought struck her: What if I really lived in the gray ghetto . . . what if I couldn't escape to my nice safe home . . . ?

10   Lesson number two: The fear of crime is paralyzing. "I really understand now why the elderly become homebound," the young woman says as she recalls her ordeal today. "When something like this happens, the fear just doesn't go away. I guess it wasn't so bad for me. I could distance myself from what happened . . . and I was strong enough to get up and walk away. But what about someone who is really too weak to run or fight back or protect herself in any way? And the elderly often can't afford to move if the area in which they live deteriorates, becomes unsafe. I met people like this and they were imprisoned by their fear. That's when the bolts go on the door. That's when people starve themselves because they're afraid to go to the grocery store."

11   **New York City, February 1980.** It was a slushy, gray day and Pat had laboriously descended four flights of stairs from her apartment to go shopping. Once outside, she struggled to hold her threadbare coat closed with one hand and manipulate her cane with the other. Splotches of snow made the street difficult for anyone to navigate, but for someone hunched over, as she was, it was almost impossible. The curb was another obstacle. The slush looked ankle-deep—and what was she to do? Jump over it? Slowly, she worked her way around to a drier spot, but the crowds were impatient to move. A woman with packages jostled her as she rushed past, causing Pat to nearly lose her balance. If I really were old, I would have fallen, she thought. Maybe broken something. On another day, a woman had practically knocked her over by letting go of a heavy door as Pat tried to enter a coffee shop. Then there were the revolving doors. How could you push them without strength? And how could you get up and down stairs, on and off a bus, without risking a terrible fall?

12   Lesson number three: If small, thoughtless deficiencies in design were corrected, life would be so much easier for older people. It was no surprise to Patty that the "built" environment is often inflexible. But even she didn't realize the extent of the problems, she admits. "It was a terrible feeling. I never realized how difficult it is to get off a curb if your knees don't bend easily. Or the helpless feeling you get if your upper arms aren't strong enough to open a door. You know, I just felt so vulnerable—as if I was at the mercy of every barrier or rude person I encountered."

13   **Ft. Lauderdale, Florida, May 1980.** Pat met a new friend while shopping and they decided to continue their conversation over a sundae at a nearby coffee shop. The woman was in her late seventies, "younger" than Pat, but she was obviously reaching out for help. Slowly, her story unfolded. "My husband moved out of our bedroom," the woman said softly,

fiddling with her coffee cup and fighting back tears. "He won't touch me anymore. And when he gets angry at me for being stupid, he'll even sometimes. . . ." The woman looked down, embarrassed to go on. Pat took her hand. "He hits me . . . he gets so mean." "Can't you tell anyone?" Pat asked. "Can't you tell your son?" "Oh, no!" the woman almost gasped. "I would never tell the children; they absolutely adore him."

Lesson number four: Even a fifty-year-old marriage isn't necessarily a   14
good one. While Pat met many loving and devoted elderly couples, she was stunned to find others who had stayed together unhappily—because divorce was still an anathema in their middle years. "I met women who secretly wished their husbands dead, because after so many years they just ended up full of hatred. One woman in Chicago even admitted that she deliberately angered her husband because she knew it would make his blood pressure rise. Of course, that was pretty extreme. . . ."

Patty pauses thoughtfully and continues. "I guess what really made an   15
impression on me, the real eye-opener, was that so many of these older women had the same problems as women twenty, thirty or forty. Problems with men . . . problems with the different roles that are expected of them. As a 'young woman' I, too, had just been through a relationship where I spent a lot of time protecting someone by covering up his problems from family and friends. Then I heard this woman in Florida saying that she wouldn't tell her children their father beat her because she didn't want to disillusion them. These issues aren't age-related. They affect everyone."

Clearwater, Florida, January 1981. She heard the children laughing,   16
but she didn't realize at first that they were laughing at her. On this day, as on several others, Pat had shed the clothes of a middle-income woman for the rags of a bag lady. She wanted to see the extremes of the human condition, what it was like to be old and poor, and outside traditional society as well. Now, tottering down the sidewalk, she was most concerned with the cold, since her layers of ragged clothing did little to ease the chill. She had spent the afternoon rummaging through garbage cans, loading her shopping bags with bits of debris, and she was stiff and tired. Suddenly, she saw that four little boys, five or six years old, were moving up on her. And then she felt the sting of the pebbles they were throwing. She quickened her pace to escape, but another handful of gravel hit her and the laughter continued. They're using me as a target, she thought, horror-stricken. They don't even think of me as a person.

Lesson number five: Social class affects every aspect of an older per-   17
son's existence. "I found out that class is a very important factor when you're old," says Patty. "It was interesting. That same day, I went back to my hotel and got dressed as a wealthy woman, another role that I occasionally took. Outside the hotel, a little boy of about seven asked if I would go shelling with him. We walked along the beach, and he reached out to hold my hand. I knew he must have a grandmother who walked with a cane, because he was so concerned about me and my footing. 'Don't put

your cane there, the sand's wet,' he'd say. He really took responsibility for my welfare. The contrast between him and those children was really incredible. The little ones who were throwing the pebbles at me because they didn't see me as human. And then the seven-year-old taking care of me. I think he would have responded to me the same way even if I had been dressed as the middle-income woman. There's no question that money does make life easier for older people, not only because it gives them a more comfortable life-style, but because it makes others treat them with greater respect."

18   **New York City, May 1981.** Pat always enjoyed the time she spent sitting on the benches in Central Park. She'd let the whole day pass by, watching young children play, feeding the pigeons and chatting. One spring day she found herself sitting with three women, all widows, and the conversation turned to the few available men around. "It's been a long time since anyone hugged me," one woman complained. Another agreed. "Isn't that the truth. I need a hug, too." It was a favorite topic, Pat found—the lack of touching left in these women's lives, the lack of hugging, the lack of men.

19   In the last two years, she had found out herself how it felt to walk down Fifth Avenue and know that no men were turning to look after her. Or how, it felt to look at models in magazines or store mannequins and *know* that those gorgeous clothes were just not made for her. She hadn't realized before just how much casual attention was paid to her because she was young and pretty. She hadn't realized it until it stopped.

20   Lesson number six: You never grow old emotionally. You always need to feel loved. "It's not surprising that everyone needs love and touching and holding," says Patty. "But I think some people feel that you reach a point in your life when you accept that those intimate feelings are in the past. That's wrong. These women were still interested in sex. But more than that, they—like everyone—needed to be hugged and touched. I'd watch two women greeting each other on the street and just holding onto each other's hands, neither wanting to let go. Yet, I also saw that there are people who are afraid to touch an old person . . . they were afraid to touch me. It's as if they think old age is a disease and it's catching. They think that something might rub off on them."

21   **New York City, September 1981.** He was a thin man, rather nattily dressed, with a hat that he graciously tipped at Pat as he approached the bench where she sat. "Might I join you?" he asked jauntily. Pat told him he would be welcome and he offered her one of the dietetic hard candies that he carried in a crumpled paper bag. As the afternoon passed, they got to talking . . . about the beautiful buds on the trees and the world around them and the past. "Life's for the living, my wife used to tell me," he said. "When she took sick she made me promise her that I wouldn't waste a moment. But the first year after she died, I just sat in the apartment. I didn't want to see anyone, talk to anyone, or go anywhere. I missed her so much." He took a handkerchief from his pocket and wiped his eyes, and they sat in silence. Then he slapped his leg to break the mood and change

the subject. He asked Pat about herself, and described his life alone. He belonged to a "senior center" now, and went on trips and had lots of friends. Life did go on. They arranged to meet again the following week on the same park bench. He brought lunch—chicken salad sandwiches and decaffeinated peppermint tea in a thermos—and wore a carnation in his lapel. It was the first date Patty had had since her marriage ended.

Lesson number seven: Life does go on . . . as long as you're flexible   22 and open to change. "That man really meant a lot to me, even though I never saw him again," says Patty, her eyes wandering toward the gray wig that now sits on a wig-stand on the top shelf of her bookcase. "He was a real old-fashioned gentleman, yet not afraid to show his feelings—as so many men my age are. It's funny, but at that point I had been through months of self-imposed seclusion. Even though I was in a different role, that encounter kind of broke the ice for getting my life together as a single woman."

In fact, while Patty was living her life as the old woman, some of her   23 young friends had been worried about her. After several years, it seemed as if the lines of identity had begun to blur. Even when she wasn't in makeup, she was wearing unusually conservative clothing, she spent most of her time with older people and she seemed almost to revel in her role— sometimes finding it easier to be in costume than to be a single New Yorker.

But as Patty continued her experiment, she was also learning a great   24 deal from the older people she observed. Yes, society often did treat the elderly abysmally . . . they were sometimes ignored, sometimes victimized, sometimes poor and frightened, but so many of them were survivors. They had lived through two world wars, the Depression and into the computer age. "If there was one lesson to learn, one lesson that I'll take with me into *my* old age, it's that you've got to be flexible," Patty says. "I saw my friend in the park, managing after the loss of his wife, and I met countless other people who picked themselves up after something bad—or even something catastrophic—happened. I'm not worried about them. I'm worried about the others who shut themselves away. It's funny, but seeing these two extremes helped me recover from the trauma in my own life, to pull *my* life together."

Today, Patty is back to living the life of a single thirty-year-old, and   25 she rarely dons her costumes anymore. "I must admit, though, I do still think a lot about aging," she says. "I look in the mirror and I begin to see wrinkles, and then I realize that I won't be able to wash *those* wrinkles off." Is she afraid of growing older? "No. In a way, I'm kind of looking forward to it," she smiles. "I *know* it will be different from my experiment. I *know* I'll probably even look different. When they aged Orson Welles in *Citizen Kane* he didn't resemble at all the Orson Welles of today."

But Patty also knows that in one way she really did manage to cap-   26 ture the feeling of being old. With her bandages and her stooped posture, she turned her body into a kind of prison. Yet, inside she didn't change at all. "It's funny, but that's exactly how older people always say they feel," says Patty. "Their bodies age, but inside they are really no different than when they were young."

Building Vocabulary

Define the words below, using *context clues* wherever possible and checking in a dictionary when necessary. Use them in sentences of your own.

singular (1)	vulnerable (12)	disarrange (9)
gerontology (4)	jauntily (21)	threadbare (11)
pummel (8)	time machine (2)	anathema (14)
ordeal (10)	condescend (6)	catastrophic (24)

Journal Writing

Choose one or more of the three activities listed below, and make an entry in your journal. Focus on writing spontaneously rather than on structure and mechanics.

1. **Exploring:** Recall what you remember from other sources—your reading, your life experiences, movies and television, stories told to you by others—about the topic discussed by the writer. Choose one or two of these to write about. Which aspects of the topic did they bring up? What additional information did they provide? What emotions did they create in you?
2. **Taking Stock:** Which parts of the selection were most difficult for you to grasp? Which parts needed more explanation? Which parts required outside information to be understood? What kind of information was required (e.g., historical, culture-specific, technical, etc.)? Where might such information be found? Were there aspects of the writer's style you found particularly effective? Particularly difficult? Why?
3. **Responding:** Identify one or two of the writer's main concerns. What personal knowledge, if any, do you have of these issues? What is your opinion on these issues? Examine your response carefully to see what it teaches you about yourself.

Analyzing Content

1. What experiment does Patty Moore conduct? Why does she decide to do it? (Look for more than one reason.)
2. In how many states does Moore conduct her experiment? Why?
3. Analyze the lessons Moore learns through the experiment. Which lessons are positive and which negative?

4. How do Moore's interactions with the elderly help her to deal with the trauma in her own life?

Analyzing Writing Techniques

1. The essay is divided into several sections. Examine each section, and explain how it fits into the overall structure of the essay.
2. Find five **transition terms** used by Barrett. What relationship between ideas is indicated by each (e.g., similarity, contrast, consequence, etc.)?
3. In many parts of the essay, Barrett uses quotations or bits of dialogue. Pick out a few examples, and discuss how they strengthen the essay.

Group Activity

Discuss with other members of your group old people you have known—either personally or through reading or TV or film. What have you learned from these people? Write a **collaborative** paragraph in which you **summarize** your findings.

Your Writing

1. Do you agree or disagree with the lessons Moore learns about the state of being old? Write an essay in which you present your opinion about one of the lessons, and support it with examples from your observance of, or experience with, the elderly.
2. Barrett calls American culture one that focuses on "youth and beauty." Do you agree? In a **comparison/contrast** essay, analyze our society's attitude toward those who are no longer young. Use specific examples and different situations to support your thesis.

Pre-reading Activity   Write about an activity you used to enjoy as a child. Do you still do it? Why, or why not?

As You Read   Note the writer's juxtaposition of long and short sentences to add variety to her writing style.

CIRCLE OF CHILDREN
Brenda Anne Le Blanc

Of Sicilian, Portuguese, French, and German descent, Brenda Anne Le Blanc was born and raised in the San Francisco Bay Area. Her interests are drama and dance, and she is considering a dual major in English and Spanish. Brenda is a student at Foothill College.

1   Have you forgotten the importance of ice cream? When was the last time you made a snow angel? How long has it been since you jumped into a big, fluffy pile of leaves? How long? Shame on you. Remember the story of Peter Pan? Well, if you don't, read it again, or better yet, read it to a child. Maybe you can be saved, but chances are, you've already grown up. Chances are, you probably take things in your life—how shall I put this—too darn seriously! If this is the case, don't be alarmed. There's still hope. And that hope is children.

2   If you don't have children in your own family, surround yourself with them. Make them a part of your "extended" family and your life. Why? Because children play a very important role in our lives. They connect us to adventure, innocence, truth, and magic. "Feel the dignity of a child," said Robert Henri. "Do not feel superior to him, for you are not." All too often, however, we see children only as lacking the knowledge we possess. We forget that there is so much we can learn from them.

3   Children know how to have fun. Recently, I was at my boyfriend's house, just sitting around talking, when his sister Christina, who is nine, asked me to dance. I could have said no, letting my more dignified, "mature" side keep control. Instead, I said "yes," and we danced like two world-famous ballerinas across the living room "stage." We made up step after step until finally we had a complete routine, polished enough to perform. She was a princess that night, dancing across the floor in her pink nightgown, and I was her queen.

4   That night brought me back to the days of my own childhood, when I would make up dances. I would put on some music and create elaborate routines to each song, practicing them over and over again. I took my dances professionally and seriously, enjoying every moment. How old was

I when I stopped dancing like that, so freely? That is why we need children in our family or circle of special people—to remind us to dance.

Children believe in magic. I can remember seeing photographs of fairies in a book my father had when I was a little girl. The photographs showed them flying around flowers and trees. Thoughts of trick photography never occurred to me. I only hoped to meet one of these small, beautiful creatures one day. Even then, I was aware that my belief was much stronger than that of any adult. I can remember promising myself I would never stop believing, but as the years went by, my belief grew fainter and fainter. Trick photography, I say to myself now. If there is any hope at all for me to believe again, I must look at the pictures with a child. Through her mind and heart, perhaps it can all be real again, with no "common sense" to disrupt the dream. With children surrounding us, we can stay connected to the magical, unexplainable things we once believed.

Children are open. They speak from their hearts, without editing what they say or do. They simply "go for it." When I was in kindergarten, I drew a picture titled "My Mother Cooking Dinner." The drawing was of a woman in the kitchen, holding a small pan with gobs of black smoke rising up from it and filling the entire room. Here is a fine example of how "uncensored" a child truly is. My mother, being an artist herself, was rather proud of her young daughter expressing herself so freely. It is this kind of honesty that children bring to the home.

Children's senses are alive. "You have to ask children and birds how cherries and strawberries taste," said Goethe, and he was right. Did you know food tastes better eaten off the tips of your fingers? Children know. Children know that pizza should never be cut with a knife and fork, that ice cream should always be eaten on a cone and not in a cup with a spoon. Children even know you can eat peas with your hands, one at a time, like tiny gumballs. Children know this, because they are naturally sensuous. Thank God for children to liven the smells, sights, and tastes around us.

Children show emotion. As we get older, we lock our emotional instruments away, rarely taking them out and playing them, but a child's instrument is free to play whatever music he or she wishes. It can go from the happiest flute tune to a deep, sad cello in a matter of seconds. Children are free to let these songs play each time they become inspired by an emotion. Unfortunately, sometimes we tell them, "Don't cry," "Don't yell," or "Shhh." Injunctions like these make the instrument go out of tune. Instead of telling them to stop the emotion from coming out, we should learn from them that having a range of emotions is natural. Often, it is not just the sadness we hold back but the happiness, too. Children express their joy. They don't hold back their affection. If they want to show their love with a hug, they don't say to themselves, "Maybe I shouldn't." They just run up and wrap their arms around you, squeezing you until love fills you up. Pain, fear, anger, wonder, love, hope, joy—as we watch a child express these feelings, perhaps we can learn again to express them ourselves.

9   Children have a great sense of adventure. They are natural scientists, musicians, archeologists, doctors, and even ship captains. All they need is a little imagination added to their day-to-day lives. It is sad that as adults we often lose this sense of adventure. Remember how long the summers were as a child? How each new day we set off to explore the world? Part of the reason it can be so much fun to look at bugs in the backyard for hours has to do with time, and children have more of it. When we stop rushing around trying to get from one appointment to the next, maybe we can take the time again to look under rocks, to see what happens when we mix baking soda with vinegar or soak a tooth in Coca-Cola for a week. When we create time for children in our lives, we create time for adventure, time for scientific experiments, time to explore.

10   In today's society, where children are so often excluded from the adult world and adult events, it is important to remember that they need to be made a valuable part of one's intimate circle—for our sakes as much as theirs. Yes, children need us to teach them how to survive, but we need them to teach us how to live.

Structure and Strategy

1. Locate the **thesis** of this essay. Is it effectively placed?
2. What technique has the writer used in the first paragraph to engage the reader?
3. What are the major points that support her thesis?
4. Pick out some instances in which the writer has used descriptive detail effectively to support her major points.
5. Pick out some instances in which she has used specific examples.
6. Is the conclusion effective? Why, or why not? Which sentence in it reinforces the thesis?

Your Writing

1. Do you agree with Le Blanc's idea that children can teach us many important things? Write an essay in which you support your opinion with points that are different from hers.
2. Le Blanc focuses on the positive aspects of childhood. Write an essay in which you analyze some of the negative characteristics that children sometimes possess. Be sure to use examples.

SYNTHESIS: QUESTIONS FOR CRITICAL THINKING AND WRITING

1. "Never Too Old" and "Old Before Her Time" approach the phenomenon of aging from very different standpoints. **Compare/contrast** the major points presented by each writer, then write an essay explaining which viewpoint you agree with more closely.

2. " 'See Spot Run' " and "Grandmother" illustrate that children often have a special relationship with their grandparents. Write an essay in which you explore this relationship, taking into account the writers' ideas as well as adding your own and showing how it is different from a relationship with parents.

3. "Children of Divorce" points to a major problem that American children face today; a broken family. What, in your opinion, is another major problem faced by children? **Research** this problem, and write an essay about it.

4. In this unit, we are given portraits of children from many different ethnic backgrounds: Greek-American, Japanese-American, Jewish-American, etc. Analyze their experiences, looking for elements that you relate to in spite of the difference in ethnicity. Then, write an essay in which you analyze three important common elements of "growing up."

Family

What is a family? So much has changed in America in the last few decades that most find it difficult to answer this question. But even as the structure of the family undergoes immense transformations, the concept of family and its importance in our lives remains constant. This is illustrated by the diverse pieces in this unit.

Parental roles are the subjects of "The Train Cake" by Michael Dorris, "The Good Mother: Searching for an Ideal" by Susan Chira, and "Hold the Mayonnaise" by Julia Alvarez. In the first, a single father tries hard to prove himself—with some unexpected results. In the second, working mothers examine and redefine what it means to be a "good mother" today and come to terms with various kinds of guilt as they do. In the third, a Latina stepmother struggles with her role in an Anglo household.

These three pieces illustrate some ways in which the American family is moving away from the "traditional" ideal of the 1940s and 1950s. This issue is explored further in "Marriage as a Restricted Club" by Lindsy Van Gelder, in which the writer demands the same legal rights for gay couples as for heterosexual ones. A new twist is added in "Vietnamese Families: The Gap and the Bridge" by Trang Vo; here, the "American" children wish to move away from the traditional family values of their immigrant parents.

Finally, several selections alert us that the American family, whatever its structure may be, is struggling with some serious problems. In "Father and Child" and "The Orphanage: Is It Time to Bring It Back?" writers Shelley Moore and Tom Morganthau analyze what happens when parents do fail in their responsibilities to their offspring. In "Vietnamese Families" and "Hold the Mayonnaise," we see how the clash of two very different cultures can worsen the already frail bond in households. Happily, though, the writers do not leave us with a sense of hopelessness. The selections in this unit offer the reader a number of models and solutions to consider and evaluate.

Pre-reading Activity **Freewrite** for 5 to 10 minutes about the foods of your childhood. Which ones did you particularly like? Which did you dislike? Were there some foods that seem to you typical of your cultural background?

As You Read Observe the writer's use of Spanish words. Are they easy to understand? What kinds of **context clues** has she provided? What do they add or take away from the essay?

HOLD THE MAYONNAISE
Julia Alvarez

Julia Alvarez was born in 1950 in the Dominican Republic and moved to the United States when she was 10 years old. She holds a degree from Syracuse University and teaches at Middlebury, Vermont. Her books include Homecoming, *a poetry collection;* How the Garcia Girls Lost Their Accents, *a collection of stories; and* In the Time of Butterflies, *a novel.*

"If I die first and Papi ever gets remarried," Mami used to tease when we were kids, "don't you accept a new woman in my house. Make her life impossible, you hear?" My sisters and I nodded obediently and a filial shudder would go through us. We were Catholics, so of course, the only kind of remarriage we could imagine had to involve our mother's death.

We were also Dominicans, recently arrived in Jamaica, Queens, in the early 60's, before waves of other Latin Americans began arriving. So, when we imagined who exactly my father might possibly ever think of remarrying, only American women came to mind. It would be bad enough having a *madrastra,* but a "stepmother." . . .

All I could think of was that she would make me eat mayonnaise, a food I identified with the United States and which I detested. Mami understood, of course, that I wasn't used to that kind of food. Even a madrastra, accustomed to our rice and beans and tostones and pollo frito, would understand. But an American stepmother would think it was normal to put mayonnaise on food, and if she were at all strict and a little mean, which all stepmothers, of course, were, she would make me eat potato salad and such. I had plenty of my own reasons to make a potential stepmother's life impossible. When I nodded obediently with my sisters, I was imagining not just something foreign in our house, but in our refrigerator.

So it's strange now, almost 35 years later, to find myself a Latina stepmother of my husband's two tall, strapping, blond, mayonnaise-eating

1

2

3

4

daughters. To be honest, neither of them is a real aficionado of the condiment, but it's a fair thing to add to a bowl of tuna fish or diced potatoes. Their American food, I think of it, and when they head to their mother's or off to school, I push the jar back in the refrigerator behind their chocolate pudding and several open cans of Diet Coke.

5   What I can't push as successfully out of sight are my own immigrant childhood fears of having a *gringa* stepmother with foreign tastes in our house. Except now, I am the foreign stepmother in a gringa household. I've wondered what my husband's two daughters think of this stranger in their family. It must be doubly strange for them that I am from another culture.

6   Of course, there are mitigating circumstances—my husband's two daughters were teen-agers when we married, older, more mature, able to understand differences. They had also traveled when they were children with their father, an eye doctor, who worked on short-term international projects with various eye foundations. But still, it's one thing to visit a foreign country, another altogether to find it brought home—a real bear plopped down in a Goldilocks house.

7   Sometimes, a whole extended family of bears. My warm, loud Latino family came up for the wedding: my *tía* from Santo Domingo; three dramatic, enthusiastic sisters and their families; my papi, with a thick accent I could tell the girls found it hard to understand; and my mami, who had her eye trained on my soon-to-be stepdaughters for any sign that they were about to make my life impossible. "How are they behaving themselves?" she asked me, as if they were 7 and 3, not 19 and 16. "They're wonderful girls," I replied, already feeling protective of them.

8   I looked around for the girls in the meadow in front of the house we were building, where we were holding the outdoor wedding ceremony and party. The oldest hung out with a group of her own friends. The younger one whizzed in briefly for the ceremony, then left again before the congratulations started up. There was not much mixing with me and mine. What was there for them to celebrate on a day so full of confusion and effort?

9   On my side, being the newcomer in someone else's territory is a role I'm used to. I can tap into that struggling English speaker, that skinny, dark-haired, olive-skinned girl in a sixth grade of mostly blond and blue-eyed giants. Those tall, freckled boys would push me around in the playground. "Go back to where you came from!" *"No comprendo!"* I'd reply, though of course there was no misunderstanding the fierce looks on their faces.

10   Even now, my first response to a scowl is that old pulling away. (My husband calls it "checking out.") I remember times early on in the marriage when the girls would be with us, and I'd get out of school and drive around doing errands, killing time, until my husband, their father, would be leaving work. I am not proud of my fears, but I understand—as the lingo goes—where they come from.

And I understand, more than I'd like to sometimes, my stepdaughters' 11
pain. But with me, they need never fear that I'll usurp a mother's place.
No one has ever come up and held their faces and then addressed me,
"They look just like you." If anything, strangers to the remarriage are probably playing Mr. Potato Head in their minds, trying to figure out how my
foreign features and my husband's fair Nebraskan features got put together
into these two tall, blond girls. "My husband's daughters," I kept introducing them.

Once, when one of them visited my class and I introduced her as such, 12
two students asked me why. "I'd be so hurt if my stepmom introduced me
that way," the young man said. That night I told my stepdaughter what my
students had said. She scowled at me and agreed. "It's so weird how you
call me Papa's daughter. Like you don't want to be related to me or something."

"I didn't want to presume," I explained. "So it's O.K. if I call you my 13
stepdaughter?"

"That's what I am," she said. Relieved, I took it for a teensy inch of ac- 14
ceptance. The takings are small in this stepworld, I've discovered. Sort of
like being a minority. It feels as if all the goodies have gone somewhere
else.

Day to day, I guess I follow my papi's advice. When we first came, 15
he would talk to his children about how to make it in our new country.
"Just do your work and put in your heart, and they will accept you!" In
this age of remaining true to your roots, of keeping your Spanish, of fighting from inside your culture, that assimilationist approach is highly suspect. My Latino students—who don't want to be called Hispanics anymore—would ditch me as faculty adviser if I came up with that play-nice
message.

But in a stepfamily where everyone is starting a new life together, it 16
isn't bad advice. Like a potluck supper, an American concept my mami
never took to. ("Why invite people to your house and then ask them to
bring the food?") You put what you've got together with what everyone
else brought and see what comes out of the pot. The luck part is if everyone brings something you like. No potato salad, no deviled eggs, no little
party sandwiches with you know what in them.

Building Vocabulary

Define the words below, using *context clues* wherever possible and
checking in a dictionary when necessary. Use them in sentences of
your own.

filial (1)	stepworld (14)	whizzed (8)
potential (3)	detested (3)	usurp (11)
mitigating (6)	strapping (4)	assimilationist (15)
tap (9)		

Journal Writing

Choose one or more of the three activities listed below, and make an entry in your journal. Focus on writing spontaneously rather than on structure and mechanics.

1. **Exploring:** Recall what you remember from other sources—your reading, your life experiences, movies and television, stories told to you by others—about the topic discussed by the writer. Choose one or two of these to write about. Which aspects of the topic did they bring up? What additional information did they provide? What emotions did they create in you?
2. **Taking Stock:** Which parts of the selection were most difficult for you to grasp? Which parts needed more explanation? Which parts required outside information to be understood? What kind of information was required (e.g., historical, culture-specific, technical, etc.)? Where might such information be found? Were there aspects of the writer's style you found particularly effective? Particularly difficult? Why?
3. **Responding:** Identify one or two of the writer's main concerns. What personal knowledge, if any, do you have of these issues? What is your opinion on these issues? Examine your response carefully to see what it teaches you about yourself.

Analyzing Content

1. What does Alvarez's mother tell her never to do in the beginning of the essay? What is the **tone** of her request?
2. Describe the horrifying thoughts that Alvarez has when she thinks of a "stepmother." Why is this **ironic** later?
3. Analyze Alvarez's relationship with her stepdaughters. Why is it a difficult one?
4. What does Alvarez mean by the statement, "The takings are small in this stepworld"?

Analyzing Writing Techniques

1. In this piece, mayonnaise, an ordinary food item, has become a symbol. How has Alvarez managed to do this? What does mayonnaise **symbolize** for her?
2. Pick out some **transition words** Alvarez uses in this essay. What kind of link does each one establish between paragraphs or sections?

Group Activity

Discuss how living with a stepparent would be different from living with a parent. Draw on the group's actual experiences as well as imagined fears and expectations. **Summarize** the group's ideas in a **collaboratively written** paragraph.

Your Writing:

1. In paragraph 15, Alvarez's father gives her some advice. How far do you agree or disagree with the effectiveness of this advice? In an essay, clarify your viewpoint, and give reasons for it.
2. Write an essay in which you discuss the role of stepparents in shaping the American family today. What are some situations, problems, challenges, and gains that children face because of stepparents? Incorporate some **research** along with personal or observed examples.

Pre-reading Activity   Using the technique of **clustering**, write down 10 images or ideas you associate with a "good mother." Compare your **list** with a classmate's, and discuss where these images came from: Your own experience? The media? Some other source?

As You Read: Observe the writer's use of quotations from women who have different viewpoints on the same subject. Why is this a good technique?

THE GOOD MOTHER:
SEARCHING FOR AN IDEAL
Susan Chira

Susan Chira is a journalist who writes for the New York Times, *in which this article first appeared in 1992.*

1   The American mother—that self-sacrificing, self-effacing, cookie-baking icon—has been shoved into the center of a political morality play, one where stick-figure mothers battle in a debate that does not begin to suggest the complexity, diversity and confusion of being a mother in 1992.

2   Instead of Marilyn Quayle and Hillary Clinton, those emblems of stay-at-home and working mothers, talk to Toni Rumsey, who cried when her first child was born and [she] realized she would have to keep her factory job at Gerber Baby Foods here in Fremont or face living in a trailer.

3   Or Stacy Murdock, who watches every penny on her farm in Murray, Ky., because her family's income dropped by more than half when she quit teaching, unable to bear leaving her children.

4   Or Nancy Cassidy, a garment worker in Easton, Pa., who loves to work and believes her children are the better for it.

5   These mothers are haunted by the ghost of the mythical 1950's television mother—one that most women today cannot be, even if they want to. Caught between a fictional ideal, changing expectations of women's roles and the reality that many mothers now work because they must, women around the country are groping for a new definition of the good mother.

6   **Reshaping Motherhood**

7   The old images linger, but they fit fewer people's lives. Motherhood in America has undergone a breathtaking transformation in little more than

30 years, propelled by shrinking wages of husbands and changing social attitudes.

In 1960, 20 percent of mothers with children under 6 years old were in the labor force; by last year the figure had swelled to 58 percent, with most of them working full time. Twenty-nine percent of all American families are now headed by one parent. 8

Some more affluent women choose to work for self-fulfillment, and some who started out that way found that they could not afford to leave their jobs as the economy soured. Whether or not a conservative backlash movement is trying to shame women into staying at home, more and more mothers see work as a financial and personal necessity. 9

Small wonder, then, that Republican strategists quickly folded their family values banner when they found the reality of motherhood in this election year at odds with campaign slogans. With politicians in both parties now courting middle America, many of these same working-class women have been forced to take jobs outside the home, often monotonous and regimented ones at low wages that may not allow them to buy help with child care and housecleaning. 10

As interviews with more than 30 mothers around the country show, politicians have waded into one of the most wrenching issues of American life. 11

"I never feel like I'm a full mom," said Mrs. Rumsey, a 34-year-old mother of two who checks Gerber's baby food for shards of glass and signs of spoilage from 7 A.M. to 3 P.M. "I make the cookies, the homemade costumes for Halloween. I volunteer for everything to make up to them for not being here. When I do all that, I make myself so tired that they lose a happy cheerful mom, and then I'm cheating them again. It's hard when you were raised with Donna Reed and the Beav's mom." 12

In another factory in Easton, Pa., Mrs. Cassidy inspects sportswear, and her life as a working mother, for flaws. "I think you can work and be a good mother," said the 42-year-old mother of two. "We're doing it. When people compliment you that they're nice children, then I think you've been a terrific mother." 13

The Old Ideal: Mythic Verities and Apple Pie   14

Some women have found that they could not be good mothers in the old sense because working has become so important to their identities. These women say they know in their hearts that being at home all day does not automatically make a good mother. 15

"You can be there without being there," said Cheryl Moorefield, a labor nurse in Winston-Salem, N.C., who has two children. 16

Yet ask most women their image of a good mother, and the old verities come tumbling forth. "A mother doesn't have a right to be tired or sick," said Deborah Gray, a 38-year-old mother of six whose shift can run 12 17 hours a day during the busy summer season at Heinz's pickling plant in Holland, Mich. "A mother must be available no matter what. A mother is a person that can perform miracles."

18   In Murray, Ky., which boasts the National Scouting Museum, tobacco and soybean farms, a state university branch and what seems like a church on every corner, Stacy Murdock comes close to this cherished ideal. Mrs. Murdock, who gave up her teaching job, is up at 6 A.M., starts breakfast and then wakes her three children a half-hour later. The whole family eats breakfast at 7 A.M., and then her husband drives the two older children to school. Her husband, one of a vanishing breed of small farmers who can work close to home, tends his 600 acres of corn, beans, wheat and cattle while his wife plays with her 14-month-old daughter, cleans, cooks and pays bills. At noon he returns for a hot meal with his family.

19   By 2:30 P.M., Mrs. Murdock is on her way to school to pick up her older daughters. Some afternoons she takes them to dancing school, which she pays for by keeping the school's books. On Wednesdays the children's grandmother drops by to baby-sit so that Mrs. Murdock can volunteer at the older children's school.

20   "The most important thing you're going to get in your life is your children," Mrs. Murdock said, explaining why the family has given up eating out, planning for a bigger house and having many other extras. "I just can't imagine giving that responsibility to someone else."

21   It is precisely because convictions about what kind of mother is best run so strong and deep that family values became such an explosive issue. Despite all the talk about fathers' becoming more involved with children, it is mothers who remain at the center of this debate, and mothers who shoulder the praise or blame. Most women interviewed said they were worried about the future of the family, but many said the debate, at least as conducted by politicians, seemed irrelevant or insulting.

22   "Family values is a cheap way out," Mrs. Rumsey said. "We all believe in family morals and values. I'm not going to put down what you're doing and don't put me down for what I'm trying to do."

23   For some, the debate intensified their own guilt. "My heart pounds a little bit," said Kris Northrop, the mother of a 4-month-old girl, who has just returned to her job running a candy-wrapping machine at the Life Savers plant in Holland, Mich. "I think, Is this right? Should I try to not be a working mother, even though my image is of an independent mother?"

24   And for others the verdict is clear: working and mothering small children cannot mix. "I had these children and I wanted to raise them," said Celisa Cunningham, a Baptist minister's wife who returned to work designing and supervising asphalt mixes once her children started school. "I've given 10 years to my children and I'm going to give 30 to my career, and I'm going to see more from those 10 years in the long run than from the 30. I think many mothers cop out and make a life-style choice."

The New Reality: Harried Jugglers on a Tightrope   25

But for many working-class women, Mrs. Murdock's life, and the com-   26
fortable certainties invoked by the champions of family values, are as re-
mote as the television characters that helped shape their idea of the good
mother.

Instead of family breakfasts and school volunteer work, Jan Flint works   27
nights and her husband works days in a Welch's juice and jam plant in
Lawton, Mich., so that one of them can always be home with the children.

"That's what God meant for me—to stay at home, cook and sew, and   28
I can't do that," said Mrs. Flint, who had to return to work seven years ago
when money got tight. "I used to have a clean house all the time. I always
enjoyed being involved in my older two's education. Last night was open
house and my children wanted me to go. I bribed them—'I'll let you bring
friends over if I don't go.' That's what's happening to the American family.
Nobody's there, and children don't have full-time guidance."

Measuring themselves against such an exacting, idealized standard,   29
where good mothering equals how much time is spent with the children
rather than how secure or happy the children are, many working women
feel they fall short. For the most part, these women struggle without help
from society or their employers, who seldom give them long maternity
leaves or flexible hours.

And because motherhood itself has been transformed in less than a   30
generation, these mothers have no guides. "What is happening now is that
parents are relying on child care who themselves were often raised by their
mothers," said Deborah Phillips, a psychologist and expert in child development at the University of Virginia. "So there is incredible anxiety and
uncertainty, especially in a society that holds firmly to the belief that
mother care is superior."

Sheila Lencki, a mother of four who works as a school secretary in   31
Murray, Ky., says she fears she is failing to meet the standard her own
mother set.

"My own mother stayed at home, and that's what I wanted to do," she   32
said. "I respect my mother so much. I think that everything she does is
right."

Even more troubling, many women fear they have somehow relin-   33
quished their children. "When I put them in day care, I did feel a pull; I'm
not the one raising my children," said Mrs. Moorefield, who raised her two
children alone for seven years until her remarriage several years ago.
"Who's teaching them values?"

That anxiety deepens if mothers suspect their child care is not very   34
good, a suspicion that experts in the field say is often correct. Working-
class women usually cannot afford to buy one-on-one attention for their
children; most of the women interviewed either left their children with rel-

atives or took them to the home of another mother who was looking after several children for pay.

35   The quality of such care, in both the physical settings and the attention the children receive, varies considerably. The best care is also often the most expensive, and many women said government could help them most by giving them some financial help with child care.

36   Many women said they felt lucky to have found help from their families or loving baby sitters. But some said they were making compromises that disturbed them, either leaving children as young as 9 at home alone until they returned from work or having to switch baby sitters frequently.

37   Although she loves her work, Mrs. Moorefield is torn because she believes her recent change to a 12-hour shift may be hurting her children, who are not doing well in school. She is considering sharing a job, but she must first wait to see whether her husband, who works in an airline stockroom, goes on strike.

38   Generally, though, most women say, with an air of surprise, that they believe their children are actually turning out all right, even if working interferes with their ideal of a good mother.

39   "For me, looking at my kids tells me I'm doing O.K.," Mrs. Rumsey said. "My kids are excellent students. They are outgoing. They have minds of their own. No matter how much I've never wanted to work, there's never been any drastic indication from my kids that I shouldn't."

40   ## Blazing a New Path: Leaving the Land of Make-Believe

41   With little chance of living out their ideal of the good mother, many mothers are searching for a new way to think about motherhood.

42   Elesha Lindsay works days checking references at Forsyth Memorial Hospital in Winston-Salem, N.C., and two nights a week studying for a higher-paying job as a medical stenographer while her husband juggles four jobs as a cook. She leaves her 16-month-old daughter at the hospital's day-care center, where she believes her daughter is happy and well-cared for. Yet she cried all week when she first had to return to work, when her daughter was 9 weeks old. She and a friend filled in for each other so she could add three weeks onto the hospital's normal six-week maternity leave.

43   Although she would rather work part time when her daughter is small, Mrs. Lindsay sees herself as a good mother, and work as a welcome part of her life.

44   "Being a good mother depends on what type of person you are and what you instill," she said. "My mother wasn't there the majority of the time, but I was watching her, knowing the type of person she was. We knew what our mother expected from us. That child is spending more time with that day-care giver than you, but I still feel like I'm a better person for her, out working, financially helping the family."

Mrs. Cassidy, the garment worker, also believes that too many moth-   45
ers become obsessed with motherhood's gestures rather than its substance.
"It doesn't matter if you bake cookies for them, and don't take them to Cub
Scouts every time," she said. "You're not going to be there for their first
step. But I never heard mine say, 'You were never there when I needed
you.'"

Still, many mothers worry that they may be deluding themselves. "It   46
looks fine to me," Mrs. Lencki said, "but maybe I'm not looking."

While there is debate about the effects of extensive nonmaternal care   47
early in life, experts agree that with conscientious, loving parents and
high-quality care the vast majority of children do just fine, by any mea-
surement of intellectual and emotional development. Some studies suggest that mothers' attitudes are crucial; if they are happy, whether staying
at home or working, that will have an enormous impact on their relationship with their children.

Employer flexibility clearly makes a difference, said Arlie Hochschild,   48
a sociologist and author of *The Second Shift: Working Parents and the Revolution at Home* (Viking, 1989), who is now studying the workplace and
its effects on family life. "We have to acknowledge that the majority of
American women will work for the majority of their lives through their
childbearing years and we have to adapt the workplace," she said. "Don't
pretend they're men who have wives at home to do this."

One reason Mrs. Cassidy feels little guilt is that she was able to take   49
off work to watch her children in school plays, or tend them when they
were sick. But other companies, particularly factories where workers' ab-
sences may slow assembly lines, are not so lenient. Several women said
their employers required 24-hour notice for sick days—an impossibility
with children—or docked their pay if they wanted to go to an event at their
children's schools.

But even if they did not choose to work, some mothers have found   50
that working has brought unexpected benefits: a new sense of identity, a
role in a broader community, pride in their independence, a temporary escape from children that may allow them to be better mothers in the time
they share.

And while women may yearn for the safe world of mythic families,   51
they have seen enough of the sobering reality of divorce and widowhood
to cherish the financial independence that working confers. "My mother
stayed home, and when my father divorced her she had nothing to fall back
on," said Donna King, a hospital laboratory supervisor who is a mother of
four.

In fact, most of the women interviewed said they would prefer work-   52
ing to staying at home—but most wanted to work part time.

These days, some more affluent and educated women say they would   53
feel embarrassed to tell their friends that they did not work. Yet many
working-class mothers who have found that they are happy working treat

it like a guilty secret. Mrs. Lencki dropped her voice almost to a whisper when she talked about enjoying her job, despite her guilt that her youngest son had not had her full-time presence.

54   Pride, embarrassment and defiance competed as Mrs. Moorefield talked about work. "For me, the ideal mother is one who is able to choose," Mrs. Moorefield said. "Even if we could financially afford that I could not work, I still think I would need at least some other contact, part time. You want to be there for your children, and on the other hand you want to be able to provide for them well. This sounds like I'm anti-family values. . . ."

Building Vocabulary

Define the words below, using *context clues* wherever possible and checking in a dictionary when necessary. Use them in sentences of your own.

self-effacing (1)	relinquish (30)	exacting (26)
slogans (9)	fictional ideal (5)	sobering (47)
irrelevant (19)	verities (15)	

Journal Writing

Choose one or more of the three activities listed below, and make an entry in your journal. Focus on writing spontaneously rather than on structure and mechanics.

1. **Exploring:** Recall what you remember from other sources—your reading, your life experiences, movies and television, stories told to you by others—about the topic discussed by the writer. Choose one or two of these to write about. Which aspects of the topic did they bring up? What additional information did they provide? What emotions did they create in you?
2. **Taking Stock:** Which parts of the selection were most difficult for you to grasp? Which parts needed more explanation? Which parts required outside information to be understood? What kind of information was required (e.g., historical, culture-specific, technical, etc.)? Where might such information be found? Were there aspects of the writer's style you found particularly effective? Particularly difficult? Why?
3. **Responding:** Identify one or two of the writer's main concerns. What personal knowledge, if any, do you have of these issues? What is your opinion on these issues? Examine your response carefully to see what it teaches you about yourself.

Analyzing Content

1. Why do some mothers today feel guilty about working outside the home?
2. What are some of the disadvantages of being a working mother?
3. What are some benefits of being a working mother?
4. Why, according to paragraph 27, do most working mothers today feel anxious?
5. What has been the traditional attitude toward nonmaternal care? How far is this accurate? Summarize the arguments on this issue as presented in paragraphs 40 to 43.

Analyzing Writing Techniques

1. Note the writer's use of short paragraphs (e.g., paragraphs 28–36). Why do you think she chose to do this?
2. Does this piece have an **implied thesis** or an **explicit thesis**? What is the advantage of each kind of thesis?

Group Activity

Define, by putting together ideas and examples from the lives of each member of the group, a "good mother." How close is your definition to the ones presented by Chira?

Your Writing

1. Chira claims that "motherhood in America has undergone a breathtaking transformation in little more than 30 years." Do you agree or disagree? **Interview** two women, one of your mother's generation and one of your own, and write an essay based on your findings.
2. Do you think the concept of the "good mother" differs from culture to culture? Write an essay in which you examine this concept from two different cultural perspectives you are familiar with or have researched.

Pre-reading Activity   Write about an early birthday that made a deep impression on you. Explain why.

As You Read   Note the writer's use of descriptive detail to bring this excerpt alive. Where do we find the most detail? Why?

THE TRAIN CAKE
Michael Dorris

*A Native-American writer and single father, **Michael Dorris** taught at Dartmouth College. His writings include* Native Americans: Five Hundred Years After, A Yellow Raft in Blue Water, *and* The Crown of Columbus, *which he coauthored with his former wife, Louise Erdrich. The selection below is taken from* The Broken Cord, *an autobiographical work about his son Adam, who suffered from the effects of fetal alcohol syndrome.*

1   . . . Adam was enrolled in what I assumed to be an enlightened day-care center, and I had thrown myself into the role of professional single parent. Still in my twenties, I was young enough to believe that all it took to juggle family and career was organization and good intent. I was aggressively confident, well versed in the literature and jargon of child rearing, and prepared to quote statistics to prove that nurturing was a *human,* and not exclusively female, potential.

2   I was ready for the doubtful look or the arched eyebrow, I was ready to exchange recipes and remedies while folding clothes in laundromats or waiting in line at Sears to have family portraits taken. I was not, however, expecting to vie with a population of high-achieving working parents—single or married—every bit as defensive as I about being employed outside the home.

3   The competition, I soon realized, would not be easy. The other moms and dads had read and taken notes on every how-to-be-perfect manual on the market. Their progeny arrived in the morning dressed in color-coordinated outfits with matching watches and down-filled winter gear. Each boy and girl sported hairstyles that had to have taken an hour of dextrous adult early-morning labor to create. These kids all had famous idiosyncratic habits—aversions to synthetic cloth or allergies to dust—that required special instructions.

4   Birthdays were the one occasion for each child to be center stage. And so lavish had the festivities apparently become the year before we arrived that the day-care center had made a rule limiting the gala spread to foods

explicitly made *by* the actual parents *in* their actual homes. This seemed reasonable enough, but as fall turned into winter and I witnessed, at the end of occasional days, the excessive remains of one extravaganza after another, I began to suspect that some people were cheating. How else to explain the ice-cream cupcakes, the individual hot-dog-and-baked-bean quiches, the fluted papaya cups filled with *crème fraîche?*

Adam and I still lived in the small wooden house by Mascoma Lake— the price was right for an instructor's salary. It was there that I retreated to think and plan as Adam's January birthday neared. Under no circumstances was I about to send him off with a concoction sneakily purchased at the bakery. I had something to prove.   5

I considered briefly the phyla of cream puffs and éclairs but rejected them as too risky. I was not an experienced cook, and my oven, while dutifully heating, was not up to wild extremes or precise temperature calibrations. I contemplated the possibilities of puddings but rejected them as too unorthodox, too bizarre. From every unconventional excursion, I came back to cake.   6

"What would be the best cake you could imagine?" I asked Adam one night as he played on the carpet with our Husky, Skahota. His reply was immediate and unsurprising, the declaration of his enduring passion.   7

"A choo choo train!" he announced, and went back to his game.   8

It was his birthday, so I didn't argue, didn't try to widen his horizon. This once I took his fierce attachment seriously and called Nina, who knew more about baking than I. Culling through her recipe collection, she uncovered directions for specialized pans made from cardboard wrapped in aluminum foil. Boxcars and caboose were a cinch, the coal car was a problem, and the locomotive was a challenge. But it was possible, it was Adam's enduring, maddening fantasy, and done right, it could be the most spectacular dessert ever to grace the two-foot-high day-care table. I gave the project a week of my life.   9

Mounted on a piece of plywood, each of the six cars was at base an eight-by-four-inch-long rectangle of trimmed sponge cake, to which I attached paper wheels and connected toggles made of taffy. No food colors at the local grocery seemed bright or impressive enough, so I traveled one Sunday afternoon to a specialty outlet where, for two dollars each, I purchased small vials of blues and reds and yellows and greens so vivid, so ceramic in their luster, that a mere drop was sufficient to tint a bowl of white icing. But I was looking for more than a tint; I was after *bold,* so for good measure I mixed more and more edible dye into my palette until the hues that confronted me were dazzling. No caboose was ever so barnred, no passenger car so grass-green, no plucky little locomotive, decorated with gumdrops, a hand mirror and a cheerful expression, so sky-blue. This was a little engine that *could,* and knew it. Black, for the coal car, was trickier, but I solved that dilemma with melted licorice that, when spread warm and allowed to harden, cemented the fragile sides into indestructible steel.   10

I got behind in my lecture preparations, but finished the train at midnight the day before Adam's party. All around it I had constructed toy houses, cutout happy families (more than one shepherded by a lone adult male), grazing cartoon animals. Before going to bed, exhausted but smug, I asked Bea to come over and take photographs of Adam, Nina, and me standing before my creation. My son would have nothing to apologize for.

11 And it all came to pass just as I had imagined. When I carefully carried the plywood base from the car, and negotiated the door of the center, the train cake was greeted with exclamations of delight and disbelief by the staff and children alike. Other parents, disrobing their sons and daughters from layers of mittens and boots and snowsuits, looked from the cake to me with expressions of betrayal and chagrin.

12 I had become the act to beat, the standard against which to measure. With a spin of the mixer I had achieved the status of Ideal Parent, the adult for whom no task was too great, no child's dream too onerous to grant. Yes, I was employed full-time, but did I let that get in the way of my fatherly duties? The train cake told the story in capital letters.

13 The party, to which I returned to preside over later in the day, was memorable. In the flickering light of six candles (one to grow on), the children's eyes were sugar-glazed. The volume of their voices was loud with greed, and once the clapping ceased, they made fast work of all my labors. Within twenty minutes my ordered platter had become a surrealistic swatch of colors, with only the indestructible coal car, chipped at but undismantled, remaining as solitary witness.

14 Adam, who had eaten almost none of the cake in his excitement, was everyone's best friend, the hero of the day, and when we got into our blue VW station wagon to go home, he leaned across the seat with a smile so wide and happy it startled me.

15 "Thank you, Daddy," he said.

16 I looked at him, this little boy who really was, after all, what this was for and about. In his dark eyes there was one message only, one idea: his wish had come true. And I looked back in turn with a single realization of my own: in him, my wish had come true, too.

17 "Happy Birthday," I said.

18 The story should have ended there, with the cake eaten and Adam content and me reacquainted with the real meaning of things, but there was one final chapter. About ten o'clock that night, I was at the kitchen table trying hard to organize the next day's class notes when the phone rang. It was the director of the day-care center, and her voice was frantic.

19 "What did you put in that thing?" she demanded.

20 "Why, nothing," I answered, worried that I had somehow violated some interdiction about natural ingredients. "Just flour and sugar and a few pieces of candy. What's wrong?"

21 "The parents have been calling me all night," she said. "They're hysterical. They're ready to take their children to the emergency room at the hospital."

"Why?" Now I was scared.   22

"It's when they put the kids to bed," she said. "When they took them   23
to the potty. They noticed before they flushed! The water in the toilet bowl
was green! Or bright blue! Electric yellow! *Orange!*"

I closed my eyes and saw again the jaunty cars, lined up and ready to   24
roll. The train cake had made more of an impression than I had planned.

Days later, when every expensive hue had passed safely but remark-   25
ably through the digestive system of each child, the day-care center's gov-
erning council inaugurated an amendment to the party rule: henceforth,
all birthday fixings must be normal. The like of the train cake would never
be seen again.

Building Vocabulary

Define the words below, using *context clues* wherever possible and
checking in a dictionary when necessary. Use them in sentences of
your own.

nurturing (1)	indestructible (13)	contemplate (6)
dextrous (3)	progeny (3)	chagrin (11)
extravaganza (4)	aversions (3)	reacquainted (18)
taffy (10)		

Journal Writing

Choose one or more of the three activities listed below, and make an
entry in your journal. Focus on writing spontaneously rather than on
structure and mechanics.

1. **Exploring:** Recall what you remember from other sources—your
   reading, your life experiences, movies and television, stories told
   to you by others—about the topic discussed by the writer. Choose
   one or two of these to write about. Which aspects of the topic did
   they bring up? What additional information did they provide?
   What emotions did they create in you?
2. **Taking Stock:** Which parts of the selection were most difficult for
   you to grasp? Which parts needed more explanation? Which parts
   required outside information to be understood? What kind of information was required (e.g., historical, culture-specific, technical,
   etc.)? Where might such information be found? Were there aspects
   of the writer's style you found particularly effective? Particularly
   difficult? Why?
3. **Responding:** Identify one or two of the writer's main concerns.
   What personal knowledge, if any, do you have of these issues?
   What is your opinion on these issues? Examine your response
   carefully to see what it teaches you about yourself.

Analyzing Content

1. What is Dorris trying to prove to the other parents and staff at the day-care center? Who else might he be trying to convince?
2. What do we learn of Dorris' character from the details provided in the essay?
3. Why, in paragraph 11, does Dorris write that the other parents looked at him with "expressions of betrayal and chagrin"?
4. What does he discover toward the end of the excerpt? How?

Analyzing Writing Techniques

1. Although the excerpt is about a serious topic, the writer establishes a humorous **tone** early in the piece. Pick out examples of his humor. What does it add to the piece?
2. What does the train cake **symbolize** for Dorris?

Group Activity

Discuss, in a group, gifts you have each received that made an impression on you. Examine the motives of the gift-givers. Using this information, make a **list** of reasons why people choose to give gifts. Do these reasons differ from culture to culture?

Your Writing

1. In this piece, Dorris is battling some of the views that society holds about single fathers. Write an essay in which you examine these views, and explain whether or not you agree with them, using Dorris and other single fathers as supporting evidence.
2. One theme of this essay is the desire to keep up with one's peers. Is this, according to your understanding of society, a common problem that encompasses different age groups, or is it more intense at certain periods in one's life? Write an essay in which you **classify** different groups of people (e.g., teenagers, single adults, parents, senior citizens, etc.), and examine how they attempt to "keep up."

Pre-reading Activity What do you consider a suitable age to start having children? Write a paragraph explaining why you chose this age.

As You Read Underline the facts about teenage fathers that you find most striking in this essay.

FATHER AND CHILD
Shelley Moore

Shelley Moore is an African-American journalist. This piece originally appeared in The Crisis, *a journal published by the NAACP.*

James was in a bind. He was behind in his child support payments, and the Department of Social Services was on his back.   1

James was 19 years old, making eighty dollars a week. Sheila, the   2
mother of his baby, was under 18, so Social Services had been sending benefits to her father instead of to her. James did not trust that arrangement. That is why he started giving his money directly to Sheila instead of to Social Services. And that is why Social Services was on his back. James did not know what to do about it.

Fortunately, James found out about the Fatherhood Project, a coun-   3
seling and training program at the local Albany (NY) area Urban League for young men who are parents. Today, James no longer has any hassle with Social Services. He is employed in a full-time job *and* a part-time job, and he and his young family have an apartment. Sheila has gone back to high school. After she graduates this year, James will return to school, too. But for now, he is working hard enough, taking care of business and baby, too.

The Fatherhood Project is part of a growing movement of community-   4
based initiatives around the country addressing teen parenthood from the male side of the issue, for a change. And a lot of young fathers care more about their young families than they are given credit for.

"We get a lot of bad press," says one young father named Robert.   5

Traditionally, responsibilities for parenthood and parenthood preven-   6
tion have fallen most heavily on those most likely to get pregnant—women and girls. And for a teenage girl without an income or a high school diploma, parenthood usually forecasts a bleak future for both mother and child.

7   Yet, it happens all the time. In 1982, more than one-half million girls under the age of 20 in the United States became mothers. Over 145,000 of those young mothers were black, and 87 percent of black teen mothers were unmarried at the time their babies were born. According to a research study by Child Trends, 22 percent of black girls, married and unmarried, become mothers by age 18. By the time they turn 20, the motherhood rate zooms to 41 percent.

8   One might assume that teenage pregnancies are fathered by teenage boys. That is not always the case. Many of the fathers are young men in their early twenties. Some are older than that. The data is sketchy, however, since fatherhood patterns are difficult to research, and research results are not extremely reliable.

9   But it appears that being a teenager, being black and being male is a likely recipe for becoming a father in this country. Consider some of the findings of a 1986 Planned Parenthood poll of teenagers about sex and contraception: Sexual activity starts younger among teenagers of the lowest socio-economic backgrounds. Among black teens who had sex before age 18, 71 percent were sexually active by the time they turned 14. Forty percent of sexually active black teenagers never use any form of contraception. Thirty-five percent of black teenagers feel contraceptives are too expensive.

10   Black teenagers are less knowledgeable about conception and contraception than white teenagers are, and boys are less knowledgeable than girls. Black teenagers are less likely than white teenagers, and boys are less likely than girls to have taken sex education courses in school. Fifty-two percent of black teenagers have had no sex education courses at all. And boys are less likely than girls to talk about sex, conception and contraception with their parents.

11   Teenage parenting is not just a "black" problem, but it is now considered one of the major stumbling blocks to economic progress in the black community. Babies come along before their parents have an opportunity to finish school, start careers, or stash any money away.

12   In a recent study of young men just beyond their teens, researchers for the Children's Defense Fund found that the average inflation-adjusted earnings of men aged 20 to 24 fell by nearly 30 percent between 1973 and 1984. For black men in that age group, earnings fell a staggering 50 percent. This decline resulted largely from the nation's employment shift from high-paying manufacturing jobs to low-paying service jobs during that decade. The percentage of young men earning enough to lift a family of three out of poverty fell from 60 percent to 42 percent, and the percentage of such men who were married fell from 40 percent to 20 percent.

13   The study concluded that as the earnings of young men declined, so did their marriage prospects. As a result, the rate of babies born out of wedlock has skyrocketed.

If times are hard for black fathers in their early twenties, the plight of   14
black fathers in their early teens can be only worse.

That is why organizations like Alpha Phi Alpha Fraternity, the Coun-   15
cil of Black Churchmen and the National Urban League are addressing teen
fatherhood issues more aggressively than they have in the past.

Three years ago, the National Urban League launched an award-   16
winning public service advertising campaign to reach young black men
with the messages: "Don't Make a Baby If You Can't Be a Father" and
"Think Before You Do." Produced by Mingo-Jones Advertising on the
Urban League's behalf, the campaign consists of radio commercials,
posters and a television spot.

"We want to encourage boys to do their part in preventing pregnancy,"   17
said Ed Pitt of the National Urban League. "And if they do become parents, we want to help them become more responsible parents." As a result of the national advertising, at least 21 local Urban Leagues across the
country have launched programs to serve teen fathers.

Other grassroots projects are cropping up, too—like the Teen Fathers   18
program at the Youth and Family Center in Lawndale, California, just outside of Los Angeles; the Black Fathers Collective in Brooklyn, New York;
the March of Dimes' Male Involvement Project in Washington, DC, and
the Teen Fathers Program at the Medical College of Pennsylvania Hospital. Typically, the programs help fathers find jobs, train for careers, get back
in school or negotiate social service systems. Counseling and support
groups are also important components of the programs. Teen fathers bear
a lot of pressures in the face of sudden adult responsibility.

In a recent interview in *People* magazine, Ron Johnson, director of the   19
program in Lawndale, stated: "Most teenage fathers want to be with their
children, but they can't support the child, and it's hard to feel good about
yourself as a man if you earn only $4 to $5 an hour."

"My sister has money she can lend me," says Raymond, a father of   20
two young boys, "but she won't let me have it. She wants me to learn a
lesson."

"It's not easy," says Robert, who recently married his baby daughter's   21
mother. "Sometimes I have to borrow money from my folks." He adds
proudly: "I always pay it back."

Most young fathers feel public funds should not have to support their   22
children. They also feel there is no other alternative. Some community-
based programs teach fathers the basics of caretaking, like diapering, feeding and rocking babies to sleep. In the process, fathers not only learn practical skills; they also form close, personal bonds with their children and
strengthen their sense of commitment.

"They look so much like me," says Raymond of his boys. "I love it   23
when they call me Daddy. I still have a good relationship with my girlfriend, too. We may get married, but I want to go slow. I want to find a
steady job first."

24   "I don't feel like I'm stuck," says Robert. "I got the girl I wanted, and I don't feel a need to see other girls. I also stay away from old friends who I know would be a bad influence on me, although I'd like them to see how well I'm doing."

25   Robert is grateful for the moral support he and his wife have received from both sets of parents. Families can make or break successful teen fathering. It is not unusual for the baby's maternal grandparents to shut the father out. He is seen as the problem, not the solution. Goodbye and good riddance.

26   "I want to get it together before too many people start coming between us," says Raymond. "I don't want a lot of family and friends telling us what to do."

27   "Her mother takes control and tries to do everything for her daughter. She just excludes me completely," complains another young father named Kevin. "Why should she be angry with me? Having children is natural."

28   For Michael, his emotional bonds to his children cause him a lot of pain. He is one of thousands of teen parents who have given up their rights to their children. Today, his two-year-old son lives in a foster home in another state. "I haven't seen him in 10 months," he says, biting his lip. "I try not to think about him, because it hurts so bad—especially around Christmas and his birthday."

29   Local teen fatherhood programs, most of which are less than three years old, have been highly successful. "Seventy-five percent of the young men that have come to us have been successful in getting their lives back on track," reports Harold Robinson of Albany's Fatherhood Project. "We surprised everybody with those results. We even surprised ourselves."

30   In Baltimore this past January, the Urban League paid tribute to a number of local fathers at a celebration in honor of Martin Luther King, Jr.'s birthday. Men and boys alike were recognized for their exemplary commitments to parenting.

31   Good fathering is not an issue for teenage boys who avoid making babies in the first place. That is why many pregnancy prevention efforts are now targeting boys as well as girls. Planned Parenthood and other family planning clinics that were once considered "female" facilities are now reaching out more strongly to males. The most common advice given to boys is, in a word, condoms—the most effective preventative measure they can use, next to abstinence. Communities have also put pressure on school systems to balance their sex education curricula, which tend to focus on the female side of the issues. Boys are therefore less likely to sign up for the courses. But knowing the details about making babies is not enough. Boys as well as girls need to clearly understand that becoming parents too soon is not in their best interest.

32   The Planned Parenthood study observed that: "Contraceptives are more likely to be used by those teenagers who objectively have a lot at stake and who stand to lose a lot by being involved in an unintended pregnancy."

Teenagers with strong, realistic plans for college and careers are least likely to become parents. Too many low-income teenagers—and black teenage boys in particular—do not have such bright hopes for their futures.

　　Believing in one's self is perhaps the best contraceptive of all.   33

Building Vocabulary

Define the words below, using *context clues* wherever possible and checking in a dictionary when necessary. Use them in sentences of your own.

in a bind (1)	abstinence (31)	caretaking (22)
initiatives (4)	on his back (1)	preventative (31)
negotiate (18)	grassroots (18)	curricula (31)
exemplary (30)		

Journal Writing

Choose one or more of the three activities listed below, and make an entry in your journal. Focus on writing spontaneously rather than on structure and mechanics.

1. **Exploring:** Recall what you remember from other sources—your reading, your life experiences, movies and television, stories told to you by others—about the topic discussed by the writer. Choose one or two of these to write about. Which aspects of the topic did they bring up? What additional information did they provide? What emotions did they create in you?
2. **Taking Stock:** Which parts of the selection were most difficult for you to grasp? Which parts needed more explanation? Which parts required outside information to be understood? What kind of information was required (e.g., historical, culture-specific, technical, etc.)? Where might such information be found? Were there aspects of the writer's style you found particularly effective? Particularly difficult? Why?
3. **Responding:** Identify one or two of the writer's main concerns. What personal knowledge, if any, do you have of these issues? What is your opinion on these issues? Examine your response carefully to see what it teaches you about yourself.

Analyzing Content

1. Explain the reasons for James' problem. What disadvantages is he facing as a father? How does he overcome them?

2. What are some diferences between male and female black teenagers in terms of sex education?
3. Why is teenage parenting considered a major stumbling block to economic progress in the black community?
4. What are some ways of solving this problem? Which do you consider the most effective?

Analyzing Writing Techniques

1. Note the writer's use of single-sentence paragraphs. What is the effect of such paragraphs on readers?
2. **List** the solutions to the problem of teenage parents in the order that they are presented in the essay. **Analyze** the writer's organizational logic in ordering them this way.

Group Activity

Using the technique of **brainstorming**, come up with a list of disadvantages to having children while one is a teenager. **Organize** the items in order of importance, starting with the most important.

Your Writing

1. The group activity focuses on the (often obvious) disadvantages of becoming a teenage parent, but can it be a positive learning experience as well? Write an essay in which you examine the important lessons a teenager may learn after becoming a parent.
2. Consider some other important problems that affect American families today. Choose one, and **research** the problem, establishing some basic statistics. What is being done to reduce the negative effects of this problem?

Pre-reading Activity   What **connotations** does the word *orphanage* hold for you? Where did these associations come from?

As You Read   Enumerate the quotations used by the writer. What kinds of sources has he used?

THE ORPHANAGE: IS IT TIME TO BRING IT BACK?
Tom Morganthau

Tom Morganthau writes regularly for Newsweek, *in which this piece first appeared in 1994.*

Jimmy is real, though his real name isn't Jimmy. He is 17 and lives in a   1
group home for troubled teens not far from New York City. The home is OK and Jimmy is OK: he's doing well in school and intends to go to college. Jimmy is a survivor against overwhelming odds—and his life story, as told by Jimmy himself, proves it.

"It all started when my father and mother met in a bar," Jimmy said in   2
an autobiography written for his English class. "Most relationships that start like this usually don't turn out okay." This one didn't. Jimmy's father smoked crack and drank; his mother smoked pot. They had kids—three boys and a girl—but, as Jimmy says, his parents "were so disorganized and dependent upon drugs that they would leave a pot of food on the ground and make us eat from it. While we were eating, they would both leave and go their separate ways."

The state intervened and put the kids in foster homes. Foster care can   3
work. But Jimmy was beaten by his foster parents and moved many times to different homes. (This period of his life is mostly a blur.) At 9, he was placed in a Roman Catholic home for boys. Four years later he moved in with his grandmother. Jimmy loves her, but she was very poor and the neighborhood was terrifying. After two rocky years, Jimmy wound up at the group home where he now lives. He is still at risk, and he knows it. "The drugs, the drink—it's in my family history," he says. "I want to get away from it."

There are nearly 500,000 kids like Jimmy in America today, and the   4
chaotic pattern of his young life, in a child-welfare system that is appallingly overburdened and routinely destructive, is an example of a national dilemma that is rapidly getting worse. That is partly (but only partly)

because the family is breaking down. Divorce and illegitimacy are up. Child abuse and child neglect are up. Proper nurture—by stable, responsible, loving parents—is increasingly hard to find. Most Americans already know this. What is new and different, and what clearly portends a fundamental shift change in America's approach to the problem of unwanted and uncared-for kids, is our national frustration with welfare.

5   Welfare reform is a hot subject in Washington these days, and even liberals are playing the game. Now, however, the Republican majorities in both houses of Congress are escalating the debate to new and tougher levels. Essentially, the conservatives want to end welfare because they believe it fosters dependency and creates a financial incentive for young women to have babies they cannot care for. The theory is clearly debatable: whatever is going through the mind of a 14-year-old girl at the moment of conception, a monthly check totaling, say, $322 cannot be decisive. But the Republicans are targeting welfare anyway, and that means drastic restrictions on AFDC (Aid to Families with Dependent Children) and potentially vast disruption in the child-welfare system that AFDC supports. Ultimately, it may very well mean resurrecting the old and long-discredited idea of The Orphanage.

6   The word sticks in the craw. It evokes the moral hypocrisies of the Victorian Age—its heartless distinction between the deserving and the undeserving poor, its belief in harsh discipline for the young and its pious acceptance of institutional warehouses packed with pathetic waifs. Those connotations are the reason orphanages have suddenly become a red-hot partisan issue inside the Beltway—why Democrats demoralized by the 1994 election results are using the word to caricature the conservative approach to welfare reform and why Republicans are furiously backpedaling. It is a fact that Rep. Newt Gingrich's newly announced welfare-reform bill would allow (but not direct) state governments to use federal funds to establish orphanages if they chose. And it is a fact that some Democrats—George Stephanopoulos, for example—are jeering. "We'll mail all the Republican members [of Congress] a copy of 'Oliver Twist'," Stephanopolous said recently. The orphanage idea, Hillary Rodham Clinton declared in a speech last week, is "unbelievable and absurd."

7   But the other impulse behind the orphanage revival is the concern, now verging on panic, for the catastrophic decline of proper child-rearing practices among the poor. The alarm over single-parent families, a fixture of the welfare debate for the past 20 years, seems almost nostalgic at a time when many thousands of welfare mothers are addicted to crack. "Just as heroin in the 1960s contributed to the rise of single-parent families, so will crack soon give us the no-parent child as a social problem," New York Sen. Daniel Patrick Moynihan wrote in 1989. "We are likely to respond to this development by reestablishing orphanages."

8   In essence, Moynihan and many others argue that America must intervene to save the children of the drug-dependent poor to avert an even

larger social crisis in the next generation. This belief is buttressed by evidence that the child-welfare system is close to breaking down. Foster care is the most important case in point. The number of children in some kind of "out-of-home care" has jumped from 300,000 to at least 460,000 since 1987, and Eileen McCaffery, executive director of the Orphan Foundation of America, says "The numbers will soon overwhelm the system." Foster-parenting is tough, emotionally exhausting work, and the pay is lousy: between 1985 and 1990, according to the National Foster Parent Association of America, the number of families participating dropped by 27 percent.

Meanwhile, the churches and private charities that operate group   9
homes—today's orphanages—uniformly report a huge increase in applicants and a chronic shortage of funds. Boys Town, the legendary home for troubled teens near Omaha, Neb., says it turns down eight to nine applicants for every child it admits—and that the cost of housing and educating each kid now ranges from $40,000 to $48,000 a year. Father James Close, superintendent of the Mercy Home for Boys and Girls in Chicago, says the mushrooming costs of institutional care probably dooms the movement to bring back the orphanage. "Let's say we had an unlimited budget and 5,000 Mercy Homes. So what? They're going to keep coming in droves—they're just multiplying out there." Worse yet, he says, the behavior problems exhibited by kids 15 years from now "are going to be far more severe."

Only very large orphanages could handle the flood. But those are the   10
very institutions that progressives shuttered decades ago—and with good reason. Ronald Feldman, dean of the Columbia University School of Social Work, helped redesign Boys Town into a series of group homes in the 1970s. "By and large, orphanages weren't fiscally responsible and large numbers of kids came out of them with serious problems," he explains. "How are you going to put 500, 800, 1,000 kids in a large institution that is at once caring and confining?" says social and medical historian David Rothman. "When custody meets care, custody always wins."

Though the barracks-style buildings may be gone, the notion of the   11
orphanage as a shelter of last resort is thriving. Now they're called group homes—usually clusters of eight to 10 kids living in small houses that are more supportive, and expensive, than the spartan warehouses Gingrich's plan evokes. Small group homes struggle to avoid the traps of their oversize predecessors. From the outside, the Worcester Group Home looks like any of the other sprawling Victorian houses lining a well-traveled street in Worcester, Mass. Inside, the atmosphere strives for the homey, though the institutional sometimes wins out. The living-room sofas are comfy, though a bit too upright; the video library—"Sister Act," "E.T."—is more cute than hip; individual "hygiene boxes" for items like toothbrushes guarantee privacy. But in the hallway, a bulletin board listing laundry days and the weekly chores is a reminder that this is a community. It's more sorority

house than Mom's house, but what distinguishes Worcester from either is the oversize desk in the second-floor hallway, where staffers sit 24 hours a day, watching over the kids. For most, it's the first time anyone has cared to. "I came in here and didn't consider anybody my friend. I just considered them my associates," says Jean, 17, slipping into pink flowered slippers and trying to sound philosophical that her closest friend, Carrie, is moving back home.

12   By the time children land in a group home, they've usually been in the child-welfare system for years, bouncing from mother to aunts to foster homes so often that most couldn't fit into a traditional family even if one would have them. These are kids whose lives have roller-coastered through the social upheavals of the '60s. Their mothers are often drug addicts, for whom Spock, at best, is a character on TV; their fathers don't exist, not even in faded photographs. Few of the kids know what it's like to live in a house where no one yells or takes advantage of them: 80 percent of the girls who arrive at Boys Town have been sexually abused; 90 percent of the kids at the Mount St. Joseph–St. Elizabeth Home in San Francisco have alcohol and drug problems. Just as frightening, "Half the kids are active cutters," says Mount St. Joseph director Mary Barry. "Cutters" refers to kids who cut their veins in suicide attempts, not cutting classes in school.

13   There are no quick fixes for broken children, only structure, consistency and love—the sort of things families on the verge of collapse don't have a store of. To compensate, most group homes strive for a balance. One part is family—each home usually has two parent figures who live with them round the clock. The other is an almost-military devotion to cleanliness (try to find a messy bathroom anywhere), orderliness (at Worcester, 13 pairs of shoes sit in a row inside the back door) and rules (at Boys Town, the dress code is simple: one girl who arrived with orange-and-green hair was told to shower and come back looking "like a 16-year-old, not a streetwalker"). The point, says Father Val J. Peter, director of Boys Town, is to teach kids how to live with others—and themselves.

14   Someday soon, the politicized babble in Washington will collide with the gritty and complicated realities of caring for unwanted children—and when it does, the politicians and policy wonks now pushing orphanages will be confronted with some very tough issues. One of them, of course, is cost. There are now nearly 9.7 million children on AFDC nationwide. If Gingrich's welfare-reform plan were in full effect today, more than 5 million of those children would lose their financial support. Who will care for them? Gingrich's bill doesn't say, although conservatives clearly hope the vast majority would be housed and fed by relatives. But even if that's true, experts foresee a massive increase in the number of kids who will need someplace to go. Assume, optimistically, that four out of five welfare kids are taken in by uncles and aunts and grandmas and grandpas. That still leaves 1 million children who will need some form of institutionalized care—a tripling of the kiddie caseload and a massive social cost. At

----
What It Costs

Institutional care for children is not
cheap. Here is how the 78-bed Mercy
Home in Chicago spends its money:

ANNUAL COST PER CHILD

Staff	**$35,000**
Room, heat, light, gas	**8,000**
Clothes, camp, transport	**5,000**
Food	**4,000**
Tuition	**3,500**
Counseling	**2,500**
Medical, dental	**1,500**
Total	**59,500**

Only 7 percent of total is government-
funded

$100 per child per day, about average for group homes, caring for those
kids would cost at least $36.5 billion.

Who will pay the bill? In a recent interview, Gingrich talked in broadly   15
optimistic terms about the need to "expand private charities" to care for
those who lose their benefits under welfare reform. But David Liederman,
executive director of the Child Welfare League of America, says that private philanthropy is already carrying its share of the load. "About 30 percent of the cost of residential care in the United States is subsidized by char-
itable dollars," Liederman says. "The homes are run by nonprofits, many
of which have large endowments. There isn't a state in America that pays
the actual cost of care."

Or take the custody question. Parents—even welfare mothers—have   16
rights. Current federal law, embodied in the Adoption Assistance and Child
Welfare Act of 1980, is a mind-boggling attempt to balance the rights of
parents with the state's responsibility to protect children. It made "family
reunification" a primary goal of the child-welfare system, which means that
it limits the government's power to take children away from their parents
except in well-documented cases of neglect or abuse. Now the politicians
want welfare mothers to give up their kids—but no one wants to give that
kind of power to a "welfare bureaucrat." Mothers—even unmarried,
teenage mothers—resent those who say they should abandon their children. Patricia James is an 18-year-old mother who lives in a group home
in New York City with her 2-year-old daughter Del-Shá. Would she send
her daughter to an orphanage? "Del-Shá is my shadow," Patricia says.
"She's all I've got—I don't have nobody." The answer is no.

17   And what about the kids? Child-welfare advocates think the conservatives have lost sight of true family values, and they may have a point. Welfare reform, they say, is really about *adults*—it's an attempt to cure adult welfare dependency that may have the side effect of forcing many thousands of children into institutional care. "Get them off the dole, two years and out? What does that mean if you're *a 2-year-old?*" asks Carol Statuto Bevan of the National Council for Adoption. Still, almost everyone agrees that millions of kids are in jeopardy. And so the real question is: if orphanages aren't the answer, what is?

Building Vocabulary

Define the words below, using *context clues* wherever possible and checking in a dictionary when necessary. Use them in sentences of your own.

intervened (3)	sprawling (11)	connotation (6)
chaotic (4)	philanthropy (15)	mushrooming (9)
escalating (5)	wound up (3)	consistency (12)
nostalgic (7)	appalling (4)	advocate (17)

Journal Writing

Choose one or more of the three activities listed below, and make an entry in your journal. Focus on writing spontaneously rather than on structure and mechanics.

1. **Exploring:** Recall what you remember from other sources—your reading, your life experiences, movies and television, stories told to you by others—about the topic discussed by the writer. Choose one or two of these to write about. Which aspects of the topic did they bring up? What additional information did they provide? What emotions did they create in you?
2. **Taking Stock:** Which parts of the selection were most difficult for you to grasp? Which parts needed more explanation? Which parts required outside information to be understood? What kind of information was required (e.g., historical, culture-specific, technical, etc.)? Where might such information be found? Were there aspects of the writer's style you found particularly effective? Particularly difficult? Why?
3. **Responding:** Identify one or two of the writer's main concerns. What personal knowledge, if any, do you have of these issues? What is your opinion on these issues? Examine your response carefully to see what it teaches you about yourself.

Analyzing Content

1. Why does the writer think the orphanage might have to be resurrected? How does he feel about it?
2. The writer expresses concern about "the catastrophic decline of proper child rearing practices among the poor." Pick out evidence that supports this statement.
3. Describe a group home. How does it provide security for a child coming from a broken home? How is it different from a traditional orphanage?
4. What is a primary goal of the current child-welfare system?

Analyzing Writing Techniques

1. This essay has an **implied thesis**. What is it? Point to facts and statements that lead you to this thesis.
2. **Analyze** the structure of paragraph 12. What is the topic sentence of the paragraph? How has the writer supported it? Pick out one detail that you find particularly effective, and explain why.

Group Activity

In paragraph 4, the writer claims that the family is breaking down. As a group, discuss how far you agree with this statement. **Compile** the responses of the group to this issue, using specific examples to back up your opinions.

Your Writing

1. Examine the concept of welfare as it exists in America today. Does it need to be reformed? Abandoned? Continued as is? Write an essay in which you discuss your opinion on the future of this institution, supported by relevant facts and examples.
2. **Compare/contrast** what happens to children in America with those in other cultures when their parents are not available to take care of them. Analyze the pros and cons of each situation. This paper might require some **research**.

Pre-reading Activity   What ideas come to your mind when you read the title? What do you think this essay is about?

As You Read   Observe the writer's use of personal examples to support her views. What are the strengths and weaknesses of such examples?

MARRIAGE AS A RESTRICTED CLUB
Lindsy Van Gelder

Born in 1944 in Plainfield, NJ, **Lindsy Van Gelder** *holds degrees from Northwestern University and Sarah Lawrence College. She has contributed articles to* Redbook, Esquire, *and* Rolling Stone *and has worked as a commentator for WNEW-TV news and a reporter for the* New York Post. *She also writes regularly for* Ms., *in which this piece originally appeared in 1984.*

1   Several years ago, I stopped going to weddings. In fact, I no longer celebrate the wedding anniversaries or engagements of friends, relatives, or anyone else, although I might wish them lifelong joy in their relationships. My explanation is that the next wedding I attend will be my own—to the woman I've loved and lived with for nearly six years.

2   Although I've been legally married to a man myself (and come close to marrying two others), I've come, in these last six years with Pamela, to see heterosexual marriage as very much a restricted club. (Nor is this likely to change in the near future, if one can judge by the recent clobbering of what was actually a rather tame proposal to recognize "domestic partnerships" in San Francisco.) Regardless of the *reason* people marry—whether to save on real estate taxes or qualify for married students housing or simply to express love—lesbians and gay men can't obtain the same results should they desire to do so. It seems apparent to me that few friends of Pamela's and mine would even join a club that excluded blacks, Jews, or women, much less assume that they could expect their black, Jewish, or female friends to toast their new status with champagne. But probably no other stand of principle we've ever made in our lives has been so misunderstood, or caused so much bad feeling on both sides.

3   Several people have reacted with surprise to our views, it never having occurred to them that gay people *can't* legally marry. (Why on earth did they think that none of us had bothered?) The most common reaction, however, is acute embarrassment, followed by a denial of our main point—that the about-to-be-wed person is embarking on a privileged status. (One friend of Pamela's insisted that lesbians are "lucky" not to have to agonize

over whether or not to get married.) So wrapped in gauze is the institution of marriage, so ingrained the expectation that brides and grooms can enjoy the world's delighted approval, that it's hard for me not to feel put on the defensive for being so mean-spirited, eccentric, and/or politically rigid as to boycott such a happy event.

Another question we've fielded more than once (usually from our most radical friends, both gay and straight) is why we'd want to get married in the first place. In fact, I have mixed feelings about registering my personal life with the state, but—and this seems to me to be the essence of radical politics—I'd prefer to be the one making the choice. And while feminists in recent years have rightly focused on puncturing the Schlaflyite[1] myth of the legally protected homemaker, it's also true that marriage does confer some very real dollars-and-cents benefits. One example of inequity is our inability to file joint tax returns, although many couples, both gay and straight, go through periods when one partner in the relationship is unemployed or makes considerably less money than the other. At one time in our relationship, Pamela—who is a musician—was between bands and earning next to nothing. I was making a little over $37,000 a year as a newspaper reporter, a salary that put me in the 42 percent tax bracket— about $300 a week taken out of my paycheck. If we had been married, we could have filed a joint tax return and each paid taxes on half my salary, in the 25 or 30 percent bracket. The difference would have been nearly $100 a week in our pockets.

Around the same time, Pamela suffered a months'-long illness which would have been covered by my health insurance if she were my spouse. We were luckier than many; we could afford it. But on top of the worry and expense involved (and despite the fact that intellectually we believe in the ideal of free medical care for everyone), we found it almost impossible to avoid internalizing a sense of personal failure—the knowledge that *because of who we are, we can't take care of each other.* I've heard of other gay people whose lovers were deported because they couldn't marry them and enable them to become citizens; still others who were barred from intensive-care units where their lovers lay stricken because they weren't "immediate family."

I would never begrudge a straight friend who got married to save a lover from deportation or staggering medical bills, but the truth is that I no longer sympathize with most of the less tangible justifications. This includes the oft-heard "for the sake of the children" argument, since (like many gay people, especially women) I *have* children, and I resent the implication that some families are more "legitimate" than others. (It's important to safeguard one's children's rights to their father's property, but a legal contract will do the same thing as marriage.)

----

[1]Phyllis Schlafly, a political activist, opposed the Equal Rights Amendment. [Ed.]

7   But the single most painful and infuriating rationale for marriage, as far as I'm concerned, is the one that goes, "We wanted to stand up and show the world that we've made a *genuine* commitment." When one is gay, such sentiments are labeled "flaunting." My lover and I almost never find ourselves in public settings outside the gay ghetto where we are (a) perceived to be a couple at all (people constantly ask us if we're sisters, although we look nothing like each other), and (b) valued as such. Usually we're forced to choose between being invisible and being despised. "Making a genuine commitment" in this milieu is like walking a high-wire without a net—with most of the audience not even watching and a fair segment rooting for you to fall. A disproportionate number of gay couples do.

8   I think it's difficult for even my closest, most feminist straight women friends to empathize with the intensity of my desire to be recognized as Pamela's partner. (In fact, it may be harder for feminists to understand than for others; I know that when I was straight, I often resented being viewed as one half of a couple. My struggle was for an independent identity, not the cojoined one I now crave.) But we are simply not considered *authentic,* and the reminders are constant. Recently at a party, a man I'd known for years spied me across the room and came over to me, arms outstretched, big happy-to-see-you grin on his face. Pamela had a gig that night and wasn't at the party, my friend's wife was there but in another room, and I hadn't seen her yet. "How's M————?" I asked the man. "Oh, she's fine," he replied, continuing to smile pleasantly. "Are you and Pam still together?"

9   Our sex life is against the law in many states, of course, and like all lesbians and gay men, we are without many other rights, both large and small. (In Virginia, for instance, it's technically against the law for us to buy liquor.) But as a gay couple, we are also most likely to be labeled and discriminated against in those very settings that, for most heterosexual Americans, constitute the most relaxed and personal parts of life. Virtually every tiny public act of togetherness—from holding hands on the street to renting a hotel room to dancing—requires us constantly to risk humiliation (I think, for example, of the two California women who were recently thrown out of a restaurant that had special romantic tables for couples), sexual harassment (it's astonishing how many men can't resist coming on to a lesbian couple), and even physical assault. A great deal of energy goes into just expecting possible trouble. It's a process which, after six years, has become second nature for me—but occasionally, when I'm in Provincetown or someplace else with a large lesbian population, I experience the *absence* of it as a feeling of virtual weightlessness.

10   What does all this have to do with my friends' weddings? Obviously, I can't expect my friends to live my life. But I do think that lines are being drawn in this "profamily" Reagan era, and I have no choice about what side I'm placed on. My straight friends do, and at the very least, I expect them to acknowledge that. I certainly expect them to understand why I

don't want to be among the rice-throwers and well-wishers at their weddings; beyond that, I would hope that they would commit themselves to fighting for my rights—preferably in personally visible ways, like marching in gay-pride parades. But I also wish they wouldn't get married, period. And if that sounds hard-nosed, I hope I'm only proving my point—that not being able to marry isn't a minor issue.

Not that my life would likely be changed as the result of any individual straight person's symbolic refusal to marry. (Nor, for that matter, do all gay couples want to be wed.) But it's a political reality that heterosexual live-together couples are among our best tactical allies. The movement to repeal the state sodomy laws has profited from the desire of straight people to keep the government out of *their* bedrooms. Similarly, it was a heterosexual New York woman who went to court several years ago to fight her landlord's demand that she either marry her live-in boyfriend or face eviction for violating a lease clause prohibiting "unrelated" tenants—and whose struggle led to the recent passage of a state rent law that had ramifications for thousands of gay couples, including Pamela and me. 11

The right wing has seized on "homosexual marriage" as its bottom-line scare phrase in much the same way that "Would you want your sister to marry one?" was brandished twenty-five years ago. *They* see marriage as their turf. And so when I see feminists crossing into that territory of respectability and "sinlessness," I feel my buffer zone slipping away. I feel as though my friends are taking off their armbands, leaving me exposed. 12

Building Vocabulary

Define the words below, using *context clues* wherever possible and checking in a dictionary when necessary. Use them in sentences of your own.

embarking (3)	hard-nosed (10)	disproportionate (7)
radical (4)	wrapped in gauze (3)	ramifications (11)
rationale (7)	internalizing (5)	

Journal Writing

Choose one or more of the three activities listed below, and make an entry in your journal. Focus on writing spontaneously rather than on structure and mechanics.

1. **Exploring:** Recall what you remember from other sources—your reading, your life experiences, movies and television, stories told to you by others—about the topic discussed by the writer. Choose one or two of these to write about. Which aspects of the topic did they bring up? What additional information did they provide? What emotions did they create in you?

2. **Taking Stock:** Which parts of the selection were most difficult for you to grasp? Which parts needed more explanation? Which parts required outside information to be understood? What kind of information was required (e.g., historical, culture-specific, technical, etc.)? Where might such information be found?

3. **Responding:** Identify one or two of the writer's main concerns. What personal knowledge, if any, do you have of these issues? What is your opinion on these issues? Examine your response carefully to see what it teaches you about yourself.

Analyzing Content

1. Why has Van Gelder stopped going to weddings? What might be the positive and negative effects of this act?

2. Van Gelder states that both heterosexual and homosexual couples wish to marry for similar reasons. What are these reasons? **List** them in order of importance.

3. Throughout the essay, Van Gelder refers to laws that are biased against gay couples. **Summarize** these laws in a paragraph; in a second paragraph, **evaluate** their fairness.

4. Why does Van Gelder say "heterosexual live-together couples are among our best tactical allies"? What does she want such couples to do? How far do you agree with her thinking?

Analyzing Writing Techniques

1. Examine the writer's use of **metaphor** in the title. What **connotations** is she able to create through the metaphor? What other metaphors does she use in the essay?

2. Where does the writer use the technique of **comparison/contrast** in the essay? What argument is she presenting through this technique?

Group Activity

Write a group letter to the writer expressing your collective attitude toward her wish that laws be changed to recognize gay and lesbian marriages. Give reasons for your opinion.

Your Writing

1. Write an essay in which you **analyze** four or five important reasons why couples today get married. **Evaluate** each reason, and support it with examples.

2. What is the attitude toward gay couples in your community, family, place of work, or culture? **Interview** members of the group you are writing about, and present their views in an essay.

Pre-reading Activity   Write about a communication problem you have faced in your family. What were its causes? How did it change relationships among family members?

As You Read   Note the writer's use of **division** and **classification** to organize the problem she is discussing.

VIETNAMESE FAMILIES:
THE GAP AND THE BRIDGE
Trang Vo

Originally from a small town in South Vietnam, **Trang Vo** *came to the United States in 1992 and enrolled in English as a Second Language classes. The eldest of four children, Trang plans to major in biological technology and to go into research. Her other languages are Vietnamese and French.*

From the small groups of refugee families that trickled into the United States after the end of the Vietnam War in 1975, the Vietnamese community has expanded steadily past the confines of San Francisco's Chinatown and Santa Ana's Little Saigon. They have overcome many of the challenges that face immigrant families: learning a new language, finding jobs, adapting to a new culture. As a result of adapting, however, they now face a new problem: the communication gap between parents and daughters as regards dating and marriage. This gap is so large that it often results in tragedy.

    Although Vietnamese families are each different, they can be divided into two main categories. The first consists of families in which the children came to the United States when they were in their teens or older. These families have to cope with the cultural conflicts between the traditional Vietnamese viewpoints of the parents and the children's Americanized attitude toward dating. To resolve this conflict, the children either tend to lie to their parents, or cut off connections from them completely. The second consists of families in which the children grew up in this country. These families have to deal with another kind of friction, because the children often feel very differently from their parents about the entire issue of marriage.

    In the first type of family, the parents are deeply influenced by traditional Vietnamese culture. Although they live in the freest nation in the world, their minds are still strictly conservative. They believe that they have

1

2

3

the right to choose mates for their children, especially their daughters. Their children must obey totally to be "good children." Meanwhile, the children have been observing other young people enjoying personal freedom in this society. They, too, hunger for their own freedom. They desire to pick out their own mates. They do not want anyone, not even their parents, to make these decisions for them. An invisible gap has grown between them and their parents.

4   The gap becomes visible when the children introduce their boyfriends or girlfriends to the family. Because the tastes of the elderly and the young are very different, the people who fit the children's dream generally fail the tests of their parents. Conflict arises. The parents insist that the children break off the romantic relationship. Depending on their personality, the children respond to this demand in different ways.

5   Hanh is a timid girl who came to the United States when she was 20 years old. After studying in an American college for a few years, she saw how unfettered Americans were in their lives and thoughts. This affected her. Slowly, she began to express her own opinions instead of silently obeying her mother all the time. She wanted something for herself: her own freedom.

6   At a recent Christmas party, Hanh met a handsome Vietnamese man with a warm smile. They fell in love not long after. With a heart full of happiness, she took her "prince" home to introduce to her family. That was when troubles began. The young man, who had lived on his own in America since he was a teenager, did not know much about traditional customs. He merely nodded and said "hello" to Hanh's mother instead of crossing his arms and bowing respectfully. Thus, he created a bad impression on the mother. In addition, she had heard rumors of his "no-good" love life. He had had several girlfriends before Hanh. To the mother, this was a playboy, the worst kind of mate for her daughter. She forbade Hanh to see this man "if she wanted to remain her daughter."

7   Afraid of her mother's anger, Hanh pretended that she broke up with her boyfriend, but she continues to see him in secret and loves him passionately. Torn in two between her mother and her love, she lives with daily stress. There is no longer any true communication between herself and her family. "I don't know what I'll do when my mom figures out the truth," she says.

8   Thuy, a talkative, outgoing girl who came to America at 16, dealt differently with her situation. At 18, she brought home her first love, a 19-year-old white boy with long blond hair and a silver earring. He was just like her, laughing and joking all the time. At first, her father did not say much, but as Thuy began to go out more often with him and to stay out later, he began to show more displeasure. He was particularly upset because the young man would not come upstairs to greet him when he came to pick up Thuy. She and her father fought about this issue almost every day.

One night, Thuy's father stayed up till midnight waiting for Thuy to   9
return. When she did not, he crammed her belongings into two suitcases
and left them at the front door. In the morning, the cases were gone. There
were no calls or letters from Thuy. From common friends, the family knew
she lived with her boyfriend in a one-room apartment in San Jose, but if
they talked about contacting her, the father would put on a terrible frown
and puff furiously on his cigarette.

Many Vietnamese parents and children find themselves in this sad sit-   10
uation, caught in their anger and pride, suffering. They miss one another
and try to find out in secret how the other is doing, but each side waits for
the other one to give in and call first. The cold war can sometimes last a
long time. In Thuy's case, it lasted over 2 years, and although now she is
finally talking to her father, they speak awkwardly and uneasily, without
the laughter, jokes, and openness of earlier times.

The second type of family faces a different problem. In these fami-   11
lies, the children were very young when they came here. Therefore, they
have assimilated almost completely into American culture. Their parents,
too, are more open-minded. They do not mind their children choosing
their own mates. The conflict arises when it comes to the issue of marriage.

Vietnamese parents, no matter how long they have been here, dream   12
about their children's weddings. The moment when their children will walk
down the aisle, beautiful and full of happiness in their noble black tuxe-
does or lovely white bridal gowns, is one they long for. Thus, parents would
like their children to get married early. If their daughters are not married
by 25 and their sons by 30, they tend to start questioning them, but the
children have other plans. They are busy thinking of where they would
like to go on their next vacation, Hawaii or Las Vegas, or of the new bur-
gundy Corvette they are planning to buy, or of what to wear to the party
on Saturday. Many of them already have a boyfriend or girlfriend they are
happy with. Some are even living with their partners and see no need for
a big wedding. They try to avoid their parents' chronic questions, and when
they cannot, the arguments escalate.

My friend Nga is 30-years-old and has lived in America for the past   13
20 years. She is a beautiful woman who runs a small and elegant beauty
salon. She has a boyfriend, but they are not planning on marriage. Last
week, she called me, extremely upset, and said that she was not going
to talk to her mother anymore. I was surprised. I knew that Nga's mother
has been trying to convince her to get married, but I had not realized the
situation was so bad. It seems Nga's mother had tried a new tactic this
time.

Nga's mother had sent her sisters, Nga's two aunts, to influence her to   14
get married. The sisters came to the salon saying they wanted to get their
hair styled, but while Nga was styling their hair, they began telling her the
story of an acquaintance, Auntie Huong. Auntie Huong had been a pretty

woman with several boyfriends, but she had waited too long to get married. And one day, it was too late. "Now she sits sadly in her old house and counts dawns and sunrises, her heart full of regret," said one aunt. "Time has wings," said the other, "and so has beauty." Then, they both asked her if she wanted to become an old maid like Auntie Huong. If not, they advised, she had better catch a man and have him marry her right away.

15   Nga was so upset she couldn't say a word. She was insulted by her aunts' insinuations, and hurt and angry that her mother had discussed her situation with relatives and asked them to help. She felt her mother was pressuring her unjustly, forcing her into a marriage she wasn't ready for. The only way left for her, she felt, was to cut off communication with her mother. The result: another broken family.

16   It seems to me that in each case the problem arises because the parents and children just cannot relate to each other. The parents have forgotten that once they, too, were as young as their children, careless and enthusiastic, impulsive and romantic. The children do not realize that in a few decades they will be as old as their parents, and as cautious. Thus, although they love each other, their love hurts each other because there is no understanding. They need a bridge, something beyond the blood connection, to join them.

17   That bridge, I feel, is discussion. Not one person talking at the other, but both sides sitting down and listening. Parents should try to explain *why* they think their decisions are better, not just yell and order the children as they did in the old country. Children should think about the logic and the caring behind their parents' advice, and offer reasons of their own for their lifestyle choices. They should not rebelliously reject the advice merely by claiming it is out of date and prejudiced. Instead of stubbornly wanting only their own way, both sides should consider compromises. In this way, they can successfully reach each other across the gap that living in America has caused in the Vietnamese family.

Structure and Strategy

1. Analyze the introductory paragraph. With what idea does the writer begin the paragraph? How is it related to the thesis?
2. What might be another way of starting the essay (without changing the thesis)?
3. In which paragraphs does Vo offer **explanation** and **analysis**? In which does she offer **illustration**?
4. In this selection, Vo uses **extended examples** that are developed in detail, sometimes taking up more than one paragraph. What is the effect of this on the reader? What are some pros and cons of extended examples versus shorter ones?

Your Writing

1. In this essay, Vo demonstrates that individuals may have very different attitudes toward marriage. What is your attitude? Write an essay in which you evaluate its importance in your life, giving reasons for your view.

2. As Vo indicates, dating and courtship practices can differ greatly from culture to culture. **Compare/contrast** American dating/courtship practices with those of another culture that you are familiar with. What social values are implied in each?

QUESTIONS FOR CRITICAL THINKING AND WRITING

1. "The Good Mother" and "The Train Cake" illustrate that many parents today are crucially concerned with the question, "Who is a good parent?" Write a **definition** essay in which you answer this question for yourself, bringing in examples of "good" parents from different kinds of cultural backgrounds.

2. Several selections in this unit point to the fact that the American family is rapidly changing. Write an essay in which you **evaluate** the changes in the American family today, comparing it with families of a generation ago and analyzing gains and losses.

3. "Father and Child" and "The Orphanage" discuss the issue of government intervention between parents and children. Do you believe such intervention should be allowed? Write an essay in which you present your standpoint on this issue, examining actual cases you have researched.

4. A number of selections in this unit focus on the non-traditional family (i.e., a family **not** consisting of two parents and their biological children). Analyze **one** of these alternate family structures, and show how relationships might be different in such a family.

Men and Women

1. Ashley Montagu, **"American Men Don't Cry"**

2. Shirley Chisholm, **"I'd Rather Be Black than Female"**

3. Joy Harjo, **"Three Generations of Native American Women's Birth Experience"**

4. Adair Lara, **"Cheap Men"**

5. Steve Tesich, **"Focusing on Friends"**

6. Charnjeet Bhogal, **"Boys and Girls, Indian Style"** (Student Essay)

Foremost among the features that distinguish one culture (or sub-culture) from another are gender roles. What men and women do and how they behave toward one another depend greatly on the societal forces and taboos that have shaped their consciousness. Within the United States, this takes on an added complexity, because so many peoples have come together here, each with their own tenets of what constitutes manhood and womanhood.

Several selections in this unit focus on the behavioral expectations that a particular society places on men and women. "American Men Don't Cry" by Ashley Montagu discusses the problems created when men are held up to be pillars of strength, while "Cheap Men" by Adair Lara ironically examines the female belief that men should pay when out on a date. "Focusing on Friends" by Steve Tesich approaches the issue from a different angle: the way that we behave with friends of the same sex, claims the writer, is totally different from our interactions with friends of the opposite sex.

A number of the pieces go further and examine the relative power held by men and women in society. Their findings, not surprisingly, indicate that women are still at a disadvantage. In "Boys and Girls, Indian Style," Charnjeet Bhogal decries the preferential treatment given to males in traditional Indian families. In "I'd Rather Be Black than Female," Shirley Chisholm points to the difficulties women face when venturing into traditionally "male" careers. In "Three Generations of Native American Women's Birth Experience," Joy Harjo shows us that the helplessness of being female is compounded by a minority background.

Together, the selections in this unit invite us to analyze gender roles, including our own, to ascertain how far they are shaped by the culture that surrounds us, to identify problem areas, and to think about how they may be changed for the better.

Pre-reading Activity   Think back to memories you have of crying during your childhood or early adult years. How did people respond? How much of the response was determined by your sex?

As You Read   Note the writer's use of terms within quotation marks. What is the effect of this device?

AMERICAN MEN DON'T CRY
Ashley Montagu

Born in London, **Ashley Montagu** *is a professor of anthropology who has taught at many universities, including Harvard and Princeton. His books include* On Being Human, The Natural Superiority of Women, Culture and the Evolution of Man, Man and the Computer, *and* The American Way of Life, *from which the following excerpt is taken.*

American men don't cry because it is considered unmasculine to do so.   1
Only sissies cry. Crying is a "weakness" characteristic of the female, and no American male wants to be identified with anything in the least weak or feminine. Crying, in our culture, is identified with childishness, with weakness and dependence. No one likes a crybaby, and we disapprove of crying even in children, discouraging it in them as early as possible. In a land so devoted to the pursuit of happiness as ours, crying really is rather un-American. Adults must learn not to cry in situations in which it is permissible for a child to cry. Women being the "weaker" and "dependent" sex, it is only natural that they should cry in certain emotional situations. In women, crying is excusable. But in men, crying is a mark of weakness. So goes the American credo with regard to crying.

"A little man," we impress on our male children, "never cries. Only   2
sissies and crybabies do." And so we condition males in America not to cry whenever they feel like doing so. It is not that American males are unable to cry because of some biological time clock within them which causes them to run down in that capacity as they grow older, but that they are trained not to cry. No "little man" wants to be like that "inferior creature," the female. And the worst thing you can call him is a sissy or a crybaby. And so the "little man" represses his desire to cry and goes on doing so until he is unable to cry even when he wants to. Thus do we produce a trained incapacity in the American male to cry. And this is bad. Why is it bad? Because crying is a natural function of the human organism which is designed to restore the emotionally disequilibrated person to a state of

equilibrium. The return of the disequilibrated organ systems of the body to steady states or dynamic stability is known as homeostasis. Crying serves a homeostatic function for the organism as a whole. Any interference with homeostatic mechanisms is likely to be damaging to the organism. And there is good reason to believe that the American male's trained incapacity to cry is seriously damaging to him.

3   It is unnecessary to cry whenever one wants to cry, but one should be able to cry when one ought to cry—when one needs to cry. For to cry under certain emotionally disequilibrating conditions is necessary for the maintenance of health.

4   To be human is to weep. The human species is the only one in the whole of animated nature that sheds tears. The trained inability of any human being to weep is a lessening of his capacity to be human—a defect which usually goes deeper than the mere inability to cry. And this, among other things, is what American parents—with the best intentions in the world—have achieved for the American male. It is very sad. If we feel like it, let us all have a good cry—and clear our minds of those cobwebs of confusion which have for so long prevented us from understanding the ineluctable necessity of crying.

Building Vocabulary

Define the words below, using *context clues* wherever possible and checking in a dictionary when necessary. Use them in sentences of your own.

unmasculine (1)	devoted (1)
credo (1)	trained incapacity (2)
equilibrium (2)	homeostasis (2)
animated (4)	ineluctable (4)

Journal Writing

Choose one or more of the three activities listed below, and make an entry in your journal. Focus on writing spontaneously rather than on structure and mechanics.

1. **Exploring:** Recall what you remember from other sources—your reading, your life experiences, movies and television, stories told to you by others—about the topic discussed by the writer. Choose one or two of these to write about. Which aspects of the topic did they bring up? What additional information did they provide? What emotions did they create in you?
2. **Taking Stock:** Which parts of the selection were most difficult for you to grasp? Which parts needed more explanation? Which parts required outside information to be understood? What kind of information was required (e.g., historical, culture-specific, technical,

etc.)? Where might such information be found? Were there aspects of the writer's style you found particularly effective? Particularly difficult? Why?

3. **Responding:** Identify one or two of the writer's main concerns. What personal knowledge, if any, do you have of these issues? What is your opinion on these issues? Examine your response carefully to see what it teaches you about yourself.

Analyzing Content

1. Why can American men not cry while it is acceptable for women to do so?
2. What negative effect may not crying have on a human being?
3. Explain the writer's statement, "To be human is to weep." What is he **implying** about the American male?
4. What are the "cobwebs of confusion" the writer is referring to in the last paragraph? Analyze the **metaphor** used and what it says about the problem.

Analyzing Writing Techniques

1. What is the tone of the writer's statement, "In a land so devoted to the pursuit of happiness as ours, crying is really rather un-American"?
2. In this excerpt, there are several important ideas, but they do not have specific examples supporting them. Where could examples be added effectively?

Group Activity

Montagu's excerpt brings up the question of what is masculinity. **Brainstorm**, as a group, to create a list of 10 people that group members consider "masculine." Analyzing this material, write a **collaborative** paragraph in which you define masculinity.

Your Writing

1. Montagu's piece, which was written in 1952, states that we bring little boys up differently from girls. How far is this still true today? Write an essay in which you examine this question, supporting it with examples and with quotations from experts in the fields.
2. What men may or may not do varies from culture to culture. Choose a culture you are familiar with (excluding mainstream American), and examine the concept of masculinity in that culture. **Interview** men from that culture to gain a deeper insight into the views and beliefs of that culture.

Pre-reading Activity   What are some professions that you are interested in pursuing? Are any of them considered traditionally "male"
or "female" fields? Explain.

As You Read   Note the writer's use of **rhetorical questions** as a **stylistic device** in this essay. What effect does it have on the reader?

I'D RATHER BE BLACK THAN FEMALE
Shirley Chisholm

*Active in education and politics, **Shirley Chisholm** has taught in nursery
school, been an educational consultant, served as a New York State Assembly member and a congresswoman, and lectured widely on education,
race, and women's issues.*

1   Being the first black woman elected to Congress has made me some kind
of phenomenon. There are nine other blacks in Congress; there are ten
other women. I was the first to overcome both handicaps at once. Of the
two handicaps, being black is much less of a drawback than being female.

2   If I said that being black is a greater handicap than being a woman,
probably no one would question me. Why? Because "we all know" there
is prejudice against black people in America. That there is prejudice against
women is an idea that still strikes nearly all men—and, I'm afraid, most
women—as bizarre.

3   Prejudice against blacks was invisible to most white Americans for
many years. When blacks finally started to "mention" it, with sit-ins, boycotts, and freedom rides, Americans were incredulous. "Who, us?" they
asked in injured tones. "We're prejudiced?" It was the start of a long,
painful reeducation for white America. It will take years for whites—including those who think of themselves as liberals—to discover and eliminate the racist attitudes they all actually have.

4   How much harder will it be to eliminate the prejudice against women?
I am sure it will be a longer struggle. Part of the problem is that women in
America are much more brainwashed and content with their roles as
second-class citizens than blacks ever were.

5   Let me explain. I have been active in politics for more than twenty
years. For all but the last six, I have done the work—all the tedious details
that make the difference between victory and defeat on election day—
while men reaped the rewards, which is almost invariably the lot of women
in politics.

It is still women—about 3 million volunteers—who do most of this 6 work in the American political world. The best any of them can hope for is the honor of being district or county vice-chairman, a kind of separate-but-equal position with which a woman is rewarded for years of faithful envelope stuffing and card-party organizing. In such a job, she gets a number of free trips to state and sometimes national meetings and conventions, where her role is supposed to be to vote the way her male chairman votes.

When I tried to break out of that role in 1963 and run for the New 7 York State Assembly seat from Brooklyn's Bedford-Stuyvesant, the resistance was bitter. From the start of that campaign, I faced undisguised hostility because of my sex.

But it was four years later, when I ran for Congress, that the question 8 of my sex became a major issue. Among members of my own party, closed meetings were held to discuss ways of stopping me.

My opponent, the famous civil rights leader James Farmer, tried to project a black, masculine image; he toured the neighborhood with sound trucks filled with young men wearing Afro haircuts, dashikis, and beards. While the television crews ignored me, they were not aware of a very important statistic, which both I and my campaign manager, Wesley MacD. Holder, knew. In my district there are two and a half women for every man registered to vote. And those women are organized—in PTA's, church societies, card clubs, and other social and service groups. I went to them and asked their help. Mr. Farmer still doesn't quite know what hit him.

When a bright young woman graduate starts looking for a job, why is 10 the first question always: "Can you type?" A history of prejudice lies behind that question. Why are women thought of as secretaries, not administrators? Librarians and teachers, but not doctors and lawyers? Because they are thought of as different and inferior. The happy homemaker and the contented darky are both stereotypes produced by prejudice.

Women have not even reached the level of tokenism that blacks are 11 reaching. No women sit on the Supreme Court. Only two have held Cabinet rank, and none do at present. Only two women hold ambassadorial rank. But women predominate in the lower-paying, menial, unrewarding, dead-end jobs, and when they do reach better positions, they are invariably paid less than a man gets for the same job.

If that is not prejudice, what would you call it? 12

A few years ago, I was talking with a political leader about a promising young woman as a candidate. "Why invest time and effort to build the girl up?" he asked me. "You know she'll only drop out of the game to have a couple of kids just about the time we're ready to run her for mayor."

Plenty of people have said similar things about me. Plenty of others 14 have advised me, every time I tried to take another upward step, that I should go back to teaching, a woman's vocation, and leave politics to the men. I love teaching, and I am ready to go back to it as soon as I am convinced that this country no longer needs a woman's contribution.

15   When there are no children going to bed hungry in this rich nation, I may be ready to go back to teaching. When there is a good school for every child, I may be ready. When we do not spend our wealth on hardware to murder people, when we no longer tolerate prejudice against minorities, and when the laws against unfair housing and unfair employment practices are enforced instead of evaded, then there may be nothing more for me to do in politics.

16   But until that happens—and we all know it will not be this year or next—what we need is more women in politics, because we have a very special contribution to make. I hope that the example of my success will convince other women to get into politics—and not just to stuff envelopes, but to run for office.

17   It is women who can bring empathy, tolerance, insight, patience, and persistence to government—the qualities we naturally have or have had to develop because of our suppression by men. The women of a nation mold its morals, its religion, and its politics by the lives they live. At present, our country needs women's idealism and determination, perhaps more in politics than anywhere else.

Building Vocabulary

Define the words below, using *context clues* wherever possible and checking in a dictionary when necessary. Use them in sentences of your own.

phenomenon (1)	bizarre (2)
brainwashed (4)	tedious (5)
tokenism (11)	menial (11)
evade (15)	empathy (17)

Journal Writing

Choose one or more of the three activities listed below, and make an entry in your journal. Focus on writing spontaneously rather than on structure and mechanics.

1. **Exploring:** Recall what you remember from other sources—your reading, your life experiences, movies and television, stories told to you by others—about the topic discussed by the writer. Choose one or two of these to write about. Which aspects of the topic did they bring up? What additional information did they provide? What emotions did they create in you?
2. **Taking Stock:** Which parts of the selection were most difficult for you to grasp? Which parts needed more explanation? Which parts required outside information to be understood? What kind of information was required (e.g., historical, culture-specific, technical, etc.)? Where might such information be found? Were there aspects

of the writer's style you found particularly effective? Particularly difficult? Why?

3. **Responding:** Identify one or two of the writer's main concerns. What personal knowledge, if any, do you have of these issues? What is your opinion on these issues? Examine your response carefully to see what it teaches you about yourself.

Analyzing Content

1. Why, according to the writer, is it harder to be female than to be black? Why would most people disagree with her?
2. What, according to her, are some of the disadvantages faced by women in politics? What might be a hidden advantage?
3. Why is the writer unwilling to return to teaching as yet?
4. In what way, according to her, can a woman make a special contribution to politics? Do you agree or disagree?

Analyzing Writing Techniques

1. Where in the essay has the writer used the **rhetorical device** of **repetition** to strengthen her point? What is the effect of this device?
2. Who is the intended audience of this essay? What clues indicate this?

Group Activity

Discuss Chisholm's claim that "women predominate in the lower-paying, menial, unrewarding, dead-end jobs." How far is this true today? Have any of the facts that she mentioned changed since this essay was written? Collect examples from each member of the group, and prepare a brief **presentation** to share with the entire class.

Your Writing

1. Do you agree or disagree with Chisholm's premise that men and women have intrinsically different qualities? Write an essay in which you examine males and females who work in the same field (e.g., men and women doctors, teachers, construction workers, etc.) Do they behave differently? Do they deal with people and problems in different ways? Are they more similar than Chisholm states?
2. Examine Chisholm's statement that the happy homemaker is a stereotype produced by prejudice. What does she mean by it? How far do you agree with her? **Interview** several women to determine how they feel about the role of the homemaker, and write an essay, clearly focused around a main idea or **thesis** of your own, in which you **report** your findings.

Pre-reading Activity   Write a short description of what you know about your own birth experience. (You might wish to consult with parents or older relatives on this.) If you don't know much, explain why.

As You Read   Note the writer's use of allusion to Native-American customs and myths.

THREE GENERATIONS OF NATIVE AMERICAN WOMEN'S BIRTH EXPERIENCE
Joy Harjo

Joy Harjo is a Native-American of Creek, Cherokee, and white ancestry. An artist, essayist, and poet, she has taught at colleges throughout the Southwest and served as a consultant for the National Indian Youth Council, the Native American Broadcasting Consortium, and the National Endowment for the Arts. Her poetry collections include Secrets from the Center of the World *and* In Mad Love and War.

1   It was still dark when I awakened in the stuffed back room of my mother-in-law's small rented house with what felt like hard cramps. At 17 years of age I had read everything I could from the Tahlequah Public Library about pregnancy and giving birth. But nothing prepared me for what was coming. I awakened my child's father and then ironed him a shirt before we walked the four blocks to the Indian hospital because we had no car and no money for a taxi. He had been working with another Cherokee artist silk-screening signs for specials at the supermarket and making $5 a day, and had to leave me alone at the hospital because he had to go to work. We didn't awaken his mother. She had to get up soon enough to fix breakfast for her daughter and granddaughter before leaving for her job at the nursing home. I knew my life was balanced at the edge of great, precarious change and I felt alone and cheated. Where was the circle of women to acknowledge and honor this birth?

2   It was still dark as we walked through the cold morning, under oaks that symbolized the stubbornness and endurance of the Cherokee people who had made Tahlequah their capital in the new lands. I looked for handholds in the misty gray sky, for a voice announcing this impending miracle. I wanted to change everything; I wanted to go back to a place before childhood, before our tribe's removal to Oklahoma. What kind of life was I bringing this child into? I was a poor, mixed-blood woman heavy with a child who would suffer the struggle of poverty, the legacy of loss.

For the second time in my life I felt the sharp tug of my own birth cord, still connected to my mother. I believe it never pulls away, until death, and even then it becomes a streak in the sky symbolizing that most important warrior road. In my teens I had fought my mother's weaknesses with all my might, and here I was at 17, becoming as my mother, who was in Tulsa, cooking breakfasts and preparing for the lunch shift at a factory cafeteria as I walked to the hospital to give birth. I should be with her; instead, I was far from her house, in the house of a mother-in-law who later would try to use witchcraft to destroy me.

After my son's father left me I was prepped for birth. This meant my pubic area was shaved completely and then I endured the humiliation of an enema, all at the hands of strangers. I was left alone in a room painted government green. An overwhelming antiseptic smell emphasized the sterility of the hospital, a hospital built because of the U.S. government's treaty and responsibility to provide health care to Indian people. 3

I intellectually understood the stages of labor, the place of transition, of birth—but it was difficult to bear the actuality of it, and to bear it alone. Yet in some ways I wasn't alone, for history surrounded me. It is with the birth of children that history is given form and voice. Birth is one of the most sacred acts we take part in and witness in our lives. But sacredness seemed to be far from my lonely labor room in the Indian hospital. I heard a woman screaming in the next room with her pain, and I wanted to comfort her. The nurse used her as a bad example to the rest of us who were struggling to keep our suffering silent. 4

The doctor was a military man who had signed on this watch not for the love of healing or out of awe at the miracle of birth, but to fulfill a contract for medical school payments. I was another statistic to him; he touched me as if he were moving equipment from one place to another. During my last visit I was given the option of being sterilized. He explained to me that the moment of birth was the best time to do it. I was handed the form but chose not to sign it, and am amazed now that I didn't think too much of it at the time. Later I would learn that many Indian women who weren't fluent in English signed, thinking it was a form giving consent for the doctor to deliver their babies. Others were sterilized without even the formality of signing. My light skin had probably saved me from such a fate. It wouldn't be the first time in my life. 5

When my son was finally born I had been deadened with a needle in my spine. He was shown to me—the incredible miracle nothing prepared me for—then taken from me in the name of medical progress. I fell asleep with the weight of chemicals and awoke yearning for the child I had suffered for, had anticipated in the months proceeding from this unexpected genesis when I was still 16 and a student at Indian school. I was not allowed to sit up or walk because of the possibility of paralysis (one of the drug's side effects), and when I finally got to hold him, the nurse stood guard as if I would hurt him. I felt enmeshed in a system in which the wis- 6 dom that had carried my people from generation to generation was ignored. In that place I felt ashamed I was an Indian woman. But I was also proud of what my body had accomplished despite the rape by the bureaucracy's machinery, and I got us out of there as soon as possible. My son would flourish on beans and fry bread, and on the dreams and stories we fed him.

7   My daughter was born four years later, while I was an art student at the University of New Mexico. Since my son's birth I had waitressed, cleaned hospital rooms, filled cars with gas (while wearing a miniskirt), worked as a nursing assistant, and led dance classes at a health spa. I knew I didn't want to cook and waitress all my life, as my mother had done. I had watched the varicose veins grow branches on her legs, and as they grew, her zest for dancing and sports dissolved into utter tiredness. She had been born with a caul over her face, the sign of a gifted visionary.

8   My earliest memories are of my mother writing songs on an ancient Underwood typewriter after she had washed and waxed the kitchen floor on her hands and knees. She too had wanted something different for her life. She had left an impoverished existence at age 17, bound for the big city of Tulsa. She was shamed in a time in which to be even part Indian was to be an outcast in the great U.S. system. Half her relatives were Cherokee full-bloods from near Jay, Oklahoma, who for the most part had nothing to do with white people. The other half were musically inclined "white trash" addicted to country-western music and Holy Roller fervor. She thought she could disappear in the city; no one would know her family, where she came from. She had dreams of singing and had once been offered a job singing on the radio but turned it down because she was shy. Later one of her songs would be stolen before she could copyright it and would make someone else rich. She would quit writing songs. She and my father would divorce and she would be forced to work for money to feed and clothe four children, all born within two years of each other.

9   As a child growing up in Oklahoma, I liked to be told the story of my birth. I would beg for it while my mother cleaned and ironed. "You almost killed me," she would say. "We almost died." That I could kill my mother filled me with remorse and shame. And I imagined the push-pull of my life, which is a legacy I deal with even now when I am twice as old as my mother was at my birth. I loved to hear the story of my warrior fight for my breath. The way it was told, it had been my decision to live. When I got older, I realized we were both nearly casualties of the system, the same system flourishing in the Indian hospital where later my son Phil would be born.

10   My parents felt lucky to have insurance, to be able to have their children in the hospital. My father came from a fairly prominent Muscogee Creek family. *His* mother was a full-blood who in the early 1920s got her degree in art. She was a painter. She gave birth to him in a private hospital in Oklahoma City; at least that's what I think he told me before he died at age 53. It was something of which they were proud.

This experience was much different from my mother's own birth. She and five of her six brothers were born at home, with no medical assistance. The only time a doctor was called was when someone was dying. When she was born her mother named her Wynema, a Cherokee name my mother says means beautiful woman, and Jewell, for a can of shortening stored in the room where she was born. 11

I wanted something different for my life, for my son, and for my daughter, who later was born in a university hospital in Albuquerque. It was a bright summer morning when she was ready to begin her journey. I still had no car, but I had enough money saved for a taxi for a ride to the hospital. She was born "naturally," without drugs. I could look out of the hospital window while I was in labor at the bluest sky in the world. Her father was present in the delivery room—though after her birth he disappeared on a drinking binge. I understood his despair, but did not agree with the painful means to describe it. A few days later Rainy Dawn was presented to the sun at her father's pueblo and given a name so that she will always be recognized as a part of the people, as a child of the sun. 12

That's not to say that my experience in the hospital reached perfection. The clang of metal against metal in the delivery room had the effect of a tuning fork reverberating fear in my pelvis. After giving birth I held my daughter, but they took her from me for "processing." I refused to lie down to be wheeled to my room after giving birth: I wanted to walk out of there to find my daughter. We reached a compromise and I rode in a wheelchair. When we reached the room I stood up and walked to the nursery and demanded my daughter. I knew she needed me. That began my war with the nursery staff, who deemed me unknowledgeable because I was Indian and poor. Once again I felt the brushfire of shame, but I'd learned to put it out much more quickly, and I demanded early release so I could take care of my baby without the judgment of strangers. 13

I wanted something different for Rainy, and as she grew up I worked hard to prove that I could make "something" of my life. I obtained two degrees as a single mother. I wrote poetry, screenplays, became a professor, and tried to live a life that would be a positive influence for both of my children. My work in this life has to do with reclaiming the memory stolen from our peoples when we were dispossessed from our lands east of the Mississippi; it has to do with restoring us. I am proud of our history, a history so powerful that it both destroyed my father and guarded him. It's a history that claims my mother as she lives not far from the place her mother was born, names her as she cooks in the cafeteria of a small college in Oklahoma. 14

When my daughter told me she was pregnant, I wasn't surprised. I had known it before she did, or at least before she would admit it to me. I felt despair, as if nothing had changed or ever would. She had run away from Indian school with her boyfriend and they had been living in the streets of Gallup, a border town notorious for the suicides and deaths of Indian 15 peoples. I brought her and her boyfriend with me because it was the only way I could bring her home. At age 16, she was fighting me just as I had so fiercely fought my mother. She was making the same mistakes. I felt as if everything I had accomplished had been in vain. Yet I felt strangely empowered, too, at this repetition of history, this continuance, by a new possibility of life and love, and I steadfastly stood by my daughter.

16   I had a university job, so I had insurance that covered my daughter. She saw an obstetrician in town who was reputed to be one of the best. She had the choice of a birthing room. She had the finest care. Despite this, I once again battled with a system in which physicians are taught the art of healing by dissecting cadavers. My daughter went into labor a month early. We both knew intuitively the baby was ready, but how to explain that to a system in which numbers and statistics provide the base of understanding? My daughter would have her labor interrupted: her blood pressure would rise because of the drug given to her to stop the labor. She would be given an unneeded amniocentesis and would have her labor induced—after having it artificially stopped! I was warned that if I took her out of the hospital so her labor could occur naturally my insurance would cover nothing.

17   My daughter's induced labor was unnatural and difficult, monitored by machines, not by touch. I was shocked. I felt as if I'd come full circle, as if I were watching my mother's labor and the struggle of my own birth. But I was there in the hospital room with her, as neither my mother had been for me, nor her mother for her. My daughter and I went through the labor and birth together.

18   And when Krista Rae was born she was born to her family. Her father was there for her, as were both her grandmothers and my friend who had flown in to be with us. Her paternal great-grandparents and aunts and uncles had also arrived from the Navajo Reservation to honor her. Something *had* changed.

19   Four days later, I took my granddaughter to the Saguaro forest before dawn and gave her the name I had dreamed for her just before her birth. Her name looks like clouds of mist settling around a sacred mountain as it begins to speak. A female ancestor approaches on a horse. We are all together.

Building Vocabulary

Define the words below, using *context clues* wherever possible and checking in a dictionary when necessary. Use them in sentences of your own.

precarious (1)	cadavers (16)	notorious (15)
impoverished (8)	caul (7)	amniocentesis (16)
reclaiming (14)	prominent (10)	

Journal Writing

Choose one or more of the three activities listed below, and make an entry in your journal. Focus on writing spontaneously rather than on structure and mechanics.

1. **Exploring:** Recall what you remember from other sources—your reading, your life experiences, movies and television, stories told to you by others—about the topic discussed by the writer. Choose one or two of these to write about. Which aspects of the topic did they bring up? What additional information did they provide? What emotions did they create in you?
2. **Taking Stock:** Which parts of the selection were most difficult for you to grasp? Which parts needed more explanation? Which parts required outside information to be understood? What kind of information was required (e.g., historical, culture-specific, technical, etc.)? Where might such information be found? Were there aspects of the writer's style you found particularly effective? Particularly difficult? Why?
3. **Responding:** Identify one or two of the writer's main concerns. What personal knowledge, if any, do you have of these issues? What is your opinion on these issues? Examine your response carefully to see what it teaches you about yourself.

Analyzing Content

1. What is the writer's overall impression of her first birth experience? What **metaphor** does she use in paragraph 6 to sum up her ideas?
2. List the similarities and differences between the writer's birth experiences and her mother's. What do the details **imply** about the changes in their lives?
3. What are some things the writer is proud of having provided for her daughter? Which of these is the most important? Why?
4. Explain the writer's attitude toward her culture, picking out one or two quotations that embody this attitude most strongly.

Analyzing Writing Techniques

1. What is the (implied) main point of the piece?
2. What is the **tone** of this essay? Which details indicate this tone?

Group Activity

Do some **collaborative research** on the medical procedures related to delivering babies in this country and how they have or have not changed in the last 20 years. (Each member of the group can choose a sub-area that Harjo has discussed for research, such as prepping, use of pain medications, physician's intervention, presence of family in the delivery room, etc.) In a brief, group report, put together your findings. Do you see a movement in a particular direction?

Your Writing

1. Harjo implies, through references, that the traditional Native-American birth experience was very different from what she and her mother underwent. Write a research paper describing such an experience, and analyze the cultural values it implies.
2. The birth experience is unique to women, changing their lives in amazing ways. Write about an experience that is typically male and has immense effects on men's lives. Describe this experience (which can come out of any culture you are familiar with), and explain its effects.

Pre-reading Activity   What are your views on who should pay for dates? Why do you feel this way?

As You Read   Note the writer's use of humorous examples to support her point.

CHEAP MEN
Adair Lara

Adair Lara *lives in San Francisco, teaches writing, and is a columnist for the* San Francisco Chronicle *and the author of several collections of essays, the latest being* At Adair's House.

It was our second date, and we had driven one hundred miles up the coast   1
in my car to go abalone-diving. When I stopped to fill the tank at the only gas station in sight, Craig scowled and said, "You shouldn't get gas here. It's a rip-off."

But he didn't offer to help pay. And that night, after dinner in a restau-   2
rant, he leaned over and whispered intimately, "You get the next one." Though he was sensitive and smart, and looked unnervingly good, Craig was as cheap as a two-dollar watch.

This is not an ethical dilemma, you're all shouting. *Lose the guy,* and   3
fast.

Lose the guy? Is this fair? My friend Jill is always heading for the john   4
when the check comes, but I don't hear anybody telling me to lose *her.* And she's far from the only cheap woman I know. A lot of us make decent money these days, yet I haven't seen women knocking over tables in fights for the lunch tab. In fact, many women with 20/20 vision seem to have trouble distinguishing the check from the salt, pepper and other tabletop items. But if a guy forgets to chip in for gas or gloats too long over the deal he got on his Nikes, he's had it.

Why is this double standard so enduring? One reason is that, while   5
neither sex has a monopoly on imperfection, there *are* such things as flaws that are much more distasteful in one sex than in the other. Women seem especially unpleasant when they get drunk, swear or even insist on pursuing an argument they'll never win. And men seem beneath contempt when they're cheap.

These judgments are a holdover from the days when women stayed   6
home and men earned the money. Though that old order has passed, we

still associate men with paying for things. And besides, there's just something appealing about generosity. Buying something for someone is, in a sense, taking care of her. The gesture says, "I like you, I want to give you something." If it comes from a man to whom we are about to entrust our hearts, this is a comforting message. We miss it when it's not forthcoming.

7   Then why *not* dump on cheap men?

8   Some men are just skinflints and that's it. My friend Skye broke up with her boyfriend because when they went to the movies he doled out M&M's to her one at a time. Craig, my date back at the gas station, liked to talk about how he'd bought his car—which in California, where I live, is like buying shoes—as a special present to himself.

9   This kind of cheapness is ingrained; you'll never change it. That guy who parks two miles away to avoid the parking lot fee was once a little boy who saved his birthday money without being told to. Now he's a man who studies the menu and sputters, "Ten dollars for *pasta?*" His stinginess will always grate on you, since he is likely to dole out his feelings as parsimoniously as his dollars.

10   On the other hand, I know a wonderful man, crippled with debts from a former marriage, who had to break up with a woman because she never paid her share, and he was simply running out of money. Though she earned a lot more than he did, she couldn't expand her definition of masculinity to include "sometimes needs to go Dutch treat."

11   To men, such women seem grasping. One friend of mine, who spends a lot of money on concerts and theater and sailing but not on restaurants he considers overpriced, has evolved a strategy for women who are annoyed at the bohemian places he favors. If his date complains, he offers to donate to the charity of her choice the cost of an evening at her favorite spot. "Some women have bad values," he says. "And if the idea of spending money on a good cause, but not on her, makes her livid, I know she's one of them."

12   I had a bracing encounter with my own values when I told my friend Danny the humorous (I thought) story of a recent date who asked if I wanted a drink after a concert, then led me to the nearest water fountain.

13   Danny gave me one of his wry looks. "Let's get this straight," he said, laughing. "As a woman, you are so genetically precious that you deserve attention just because you grace the planet. So, of course, he should buy you drinks. He should also drive the car, open the door, ask you to dance, coax you to bed. And then when you feel properly pampered, you can let out that little whine about how he doesn't treat you as an equal."

14   On second thought, I guess I'd rather buy my own drink.

15   So here's the deal. Before dumping a guy for ordering the sundowner dinner or the house white, better first make sure that you aren't burdening the relationship with outdated ideas of how the sexes should behave. Speaking for myself, I know that if a man looks up from the check and says,

"Your share is eleven dollars," part of me remembers that, according to my mother, *my* share was to look charming in my flowered blouse.

Wanting the man to pay dies hard. What many of us do now is *offer* 16 to split the check, then let our purses continue to dangle from the chair as we give him time to realize that the only proper response is to whip out his own wallet.

Is this a game worth playing? It's up to you, but consider that offering 17 to help pay implies that the check is his responsibility. And this attitude can work both ways. My sister gets angry when her husband offers to help clean the house. "Like it's *my* house!" she snorts.

Like it's *his* check.   18

Building Vocabulary

Define the words below, using *context clues* wherever possible and checking in a dictionary when necessary. Use them in sentences of your own.

unnervingly good (2)	wry (14)	skinflint (8)
20/20 vision (4)	ethical dilemma (3)	evolved (12)
holdover (6)	distinguishing (4)	pampered (14)
dole (8)		

Journal Writing

Choose one or more of the three activities listed below, and make an entry in your journal. Focus on writing spontaneously rather than on structure and mechanics.

1. **Exploring:** Recall what you remember from other sources—your reading, your life experiences, movies and television, stories told to you by others—about the topic discussed by the writer. Choose one or two of these to write about. Which aspects of the topic did they bring up? What additional information did they provide? What emotions did they create in you?
2. **Taking Stock:** Which parts of the selection were most difficult for you to grasp? Which parts needed more explanation? Which parts required outside information to be understood? What kind of information was required (e.g., historical, culture-specific, technical, etc.)? Where might such information be found? Were there aspects of the writer's style you found particularly effective? Particularly difficult? Why?
3. **Responding:** Identify one or two of the writer's main concerns. What personal knowledge, if any, do you have of these issues?

What is your opinion on these issues? Examine your response carefully to see what it teaches you about yourself.

Analyzing Content

1. What double standard does the writer point out in the essay? What is your opinion on this issue?
2. Why, according to the writer, does this double standard still continue?
3. What might be a valid reason for "dumping on" cheap men?
4. What might be some reasons for not "dumping on" cheap men?
5. What is the main point the writer is making? Do you agree? Why, or why not?

Analyzing Writing Techniques

1. Why does the writer use questions in the essay?
2. Why does she use one-sentence paragraphs?
3. Who is the intended audience of the essay? **Quote** a brief passage to support your answer.

Group Activity

Debate the pros and cons of having men and women observe traditional roles. Write a **collabortative sentence** about the conclusion reached by the group. What examples did the members use to support their opinions?

Your Writing

1. Dating customs and roles often differ from culture to culture as well as from generation to generation. **Interview** an individual of the same sex as you but from a different culture *or* a different generation, and write a paper **comparing/contrasting** your dating experiences.
2. Write a **process** paper on how to behave on a date. At the end of the paper, **analyze** the cultural values implied by your ideas.

Pre-reading Activity   Write about your best friend. Is he or she of the same sex as you? What do you talk about with each other?

As You Read   Note the writer's use of **comparison/contrast** techniques. Where in the essay do they occur?

FOCUSING ON FRIENDS
Steve Tesich

Born in Yugoslavia, **Steve Tesich** *came to the United States when he was 14. He has two degrees in Russian literature and is the author of several plays and a novel. He received an Academy Award for his screenplay of the movie* Breaking Away. *This selection was originally published in* The New York Times Magazine *in 1983.*

When I think of people who were my good friends, I see them all, as I do   1
everything else from my life, in cinematic terms. The camera work is entirely different for men and women.

I remember all the women in almost extreme close-ups. The settings   2
are different—apartments, restaurants—but they're all interiors, as if I had never spent a single minute with a single woman outside. They're looking right at me, these women in these extreme close-ups; the lighting is exquisite, worthy of a Fellini or Fosse film,[1] and their lips are moving. They're telling me something important or reacting to something even more important that I've told them. It's the kind of movie where you tell people to keep quiet when they chew their popcorn too loudly.

The boys and men who were my friends are in an entirely different   3
movie. No close-ups here. No exquisite lighting. The camera work is rather shaky but the background is moving. We're going somewhere, on foot, on bicycles, in cars. The ritual of motion, or action, makes up for the inconsequential nature of the dialogue. It's a much sloppier film, this film that is not really a film but a memory of real friends: Slobo, Louie, Sam. Male friends. I've loved all three of them. I assumed they knew this, but I never told them.

----

[1]**Fellini, Fosse:** Federico Fellini and Bob Fosse, movie directors whose films are noted for visual extravagance

4   Quite the contrary is true in my female films. In close-up after close-up, I am telling every woman who I ever loved that I love her, and then lingering on yet another close-up of her face for a reaction. There is a perfectly appropriate musical score playing while I wait. And if I wait long enough, I get an answer. I am loved. I am not loved. Language clears up the suspense. The emotion is nailed down.

5   Therein lies the difference, I think, between my friendships with men and with women. I can tell women I love them. Not only can I tell them, I am compulsive about it. I can hardly wait to tell them. But I can't tell the men. I just can't. And they can't tell me. Emotions are never nailed down. They run wild, and I and my male friends chase after them, on foot, on bicycles, in cars, keeping the quarry in sight but never catching up.

6   My first friend was Slobo. I was still living in Yugoslavia at the time, and not far from my house there was an old German truck left abandoned after the war. It had no wheels. No windshield. No doors. But the steering wheel was intact. Slobo and I flew to America in that truck. It was our airplane. Even now, I remember the background moving as we took off down the street, across Europe, across the Atlantic. We were inseparable: The best of friends. Naturally, not one word concerning the nature of our feelings for one another was ever exchanged. It was all done in actions.

7   The inevitable would happen at least once a day. As we were flying over the Atlantic, there came, out of nowhere, that wonderful moment: engine failure! "We'll have to bail out," I shouted. "A-a-a-a-a!" Slobo made the sound of a failing engine. Then he would turn and look me in the eye: "I can't swim," he'd say. "Fear not." I put my hand on his shoulder. "I'll drag you to shore." And, with that, both of us would tumble out of the truck onto the dusty street. I swam through the dust. Slobo drowned in the dust, coughing, gagging. "Sharks!" he cried. But I always saved him. The next day the ritual would be repeated, only then it would be my turn to say "I can't swim," and Slobo would save me. We saved each other from certain death over a hundred times, until finally a day came when I really left for America with my mother and sister. Slobo and I stood at the train station. We were there to say goodbye, but, since we weren't that good at saying things and since he couldn't save me, he just cried until the train started to move.

8   The best friend I had in high school was Louie. It now seems to me that I was totally monogamous when it came to male friends. I would have several girl friends but only one real male friend. Louis was it at that time. We were both athletes, and one day we decided to "run till we drop." We just wanted to know what it was like. Skinny Louie set the pace as we ran around our high-school track. Lap after lap. Four laps to a mile. Mile after mile we ran. I had the reputation as being a big-time jock. Louie didn't. But this was Louie's day. There was a bounce in his step and, when he turned back to look at me, his eyes were gleaming with the thrill of it all.

I finally dropped. Louie still looked fresh; he seemed capable, on that day, of running forever. But we were the best of friends, and so he stopped. "That's it," he lied. "I couldn't go another step farther." It was an act of love. Naturally, I said nothing.

Louie got killed in Vietnam. Several weeks after his funeral, I went to   9
his mother's house, and, because she was a woman, I tried to tell her how much I had loved her son. It was not a good scene. Although I was telling the truth, my words sounded like lies. It was all very painful and embarrassing. I kept thinking how sorry I was that I had never told Louie himself.

Sam is my best friend now, and has been for many years. A few years   10
ago, we were swimming at a beach in East Hampton. The Atlantic! The very Atlantic I had flown over in my German truck with Slobo. We had swum out pretty far from the shore when both of us simultaneously thought we spotted a shark. Water is not only a good conductor of electricity but of panic as well. We began splashing like madmen toward shore. Suddenly, at the height of my panic, I realized how much I loved my friend, what an irreplaceable friend he was, and, although I was the faster swimmer, I fell back to protect him. Naturally, the shark in the end proved to be imaginary. But not my feelings for my friend. For several days after that I wanted to share my discovery with him, to tell him how much I loved him. Fortunately, I didn't.

I say fortunately because on reflection, there seems to be sufficient ev-   11
idence to indicate that, if anybody was cheated and shortchanged by me, it was the women, the girls, the very recipients of my uncensored emotions. Yes, I could hardly wait to tell them I loved them. I did love them. But once I told them, something stopped. The emotion was nailed down, but, with it, the enthusiasm and the energy to prove it was nailed down, too. I can remember my voice saying to almost all of them, at one time or another: "I told you I love you. What else do you want?" I can now recoil at the impatient hostility of that voice but I can't deny it was mine.

The tyranny of self-censorship forced me, in my relations with male   12
friends, to seek alternatives to language. And just because I could never be sure they understood exactly how I felt about them, I was forced to look for ways to prove it. That is, I now think, how it should be. It is time to make adjustments. It is time to pull back the camera, free the women I know, and myself, from those merciless close-ups and have the background move.

Building Vocabulary

Define the words below, using *context clues* wherever possible and checking in a dictionary when necessary. Use them in sentences of your own.

cinematic (1)   shortchanged (11)   inevitable (7)
exquisite (3)   self-censorship (12)   simultaneously (10)
quarry (5)   close-ups (2)   recoil (11)
monogamous (8)   inconsequential (3)

Journal Writing

Choose one or more of the three activities listed below, and make an entry in your journal. Focus on writing spontaneously rather than on structure and mechanics.

1. **Exploring:** Recall what you remember from other sources—your reading, your life experiences, movies and television, stories told to you by others—about the topic discussed by the writer. Choose one or two of these to write about. Which aspects of the topic did they bring up? What additional information did they provide? What emotions did they create in you?
2. **Taking Stock:** Which parts of the selection were most difficult for you to grasp? Which parts needed more explanation? Which parts required outside information to be understood? What kind of information was required (e.g., historical, culture-specific, technical, etc.)? Where might such information be found? Were there aspects of the writer's style you found particularly effective? Particularly difficult? Why?
3. **Responding:** Identify one or two of the writer's main concerns. What personal knowledge, if any, do you have of these issues? What is your opinion on these issues? Examine your response carefully to see what it teaches you about yourself.

Analyzing Content

1. **Summarize**, in one or two sentences, the main difference between the ways the writer communicates with his women friends and with his men friends.
2. With which sex does the writer have deeper friendships? How do we **infer** this from the essay?
3. At the end of paragraph 9, what appears to be the thesis of the essay?
4. What is the actual thesis of this essay? Where in the essay has the writer placed it? Why?

Analyzing Writing Techniques

1. Analyze the cinematic **metaphor** that the writer uses at the beginning and end of the essay. What point does he make through this metaphor?

2. Analyze the writer's use of **extended examples**. Where in the essay do these occur? What do they allow the writer to do?

Group Activity

Have members of the group discuss whether they prefer friendships with people of the same sex or the opposite sex, and also the reasons for their preference.

Your Writing

1. Do you agree with Tesich's idea that one's relationship with male friends is very different from that one has with female friends? Write an essay examining this topic, supporting your points with personal and nonpersonal examples.
2. In American society, as Tesich illustrates, it is acceptable for individuals to have friendships with people of the opposite sex. This is not always the case in other societies, or even in other cultures within the United States (see, for example, "Cultural Barriers and the Press to Americanize" in Unit 9). Write about one such culture, analyzing the prevalent attitude to friendships of the opposite sex and using **research** or **interviews** where necessary.

Pre-reading Activity   List five ways in which you are expected to behave (because of your gender) in your family. How might these expectations be different if you were of the opposite sex?

As You Read   Note the tone of the essay. How would you describe this tone? What words or expressions have helped to create this tone?

BOYS AND GIRLS, INDIAN STYLE
Charnjeet Bhogal

*Of Indian descent, **Charnjeet Bhogal** was born in 1976 in Chicago and has lived in Texas and California. She is the fourth of five daughters. A student at Foothill College, she is considering a major in Sociology. Charnjeet loves to read and write, and she has done freelance work for several Indian-American newspapers.*

1   Born and raised in the United States, I was exposed to the "American Dream" at an early age. I, too, wanted to sit at Marsha Brady's vanity and brush my hair out 100 times each morning. But I didn't have silky blond hair, and I didn't have a vanity table, either. The teachers at school and the sitcoms on TV were always saying that everyone was entitled to his or her shot at the American Dream. Everyone had unique gifts, everyone was equal, and everyone had rights. But were they talking about me?

2   My father didn't think so. He had come to the United States in search of a better life for himself and his family, but what he found was religion. Perhaps it was because of what he considered his bad luck. Four tries at a son, and he was left with four daughters and another on the way. Growing up, we found ourselves attending the temple more and more often and practicing the orthodox laws of the Sikh religion increasingly strictly. And although in theory our religion preached equality of the sexes (this is why all Sikh names are sexless), in practice it seemed that we girls were at the bottom of the stairs, watching the men sit triumphantly at the top of a long climb we might not ever be allowed to make.

3   My father allowed the theories and ideals of his religion to consume his mind, thought, and better judgment. Everything he did, everything he decided, was dictated by his religion, or by those around him. His daughters were to be perfect, God-fearing women (as perfect as women could possibly get). No one should be able to say of them, "Look at those shameless girls! How did their parents raise them?" So, we were no longer allowed to cut our hair or remove it from our bodies, for true Sikhs consider

hair sacred. We were not allowed to go to parties, for true Sikhs would never waste time so frivolously when they could be learning the holy scriptures. And we weren't allowed to associate with boys, which was considered the worst sin of all.

At one point, we sisters were placed in Punjabi classes so we could learn to read and write the language and thus study the scriptures. It was our parents' idea, and they were all for it—until they found out there were boys in our class. We were immediately removed from this "dangerous" situation. When we tried to find out why, we met with shakes of the head and the cryptic remark that "boys will be boys." We weren't quite sure what that meant, because hadn't our parents always pointed to boys as superior beings, law-abiding and parent-fearing, unlike us girls? Perhaps they really meant that we weren't worthy to be in their presence. 4

Regular American school presented us with other challenges. Here, we had no other choice but to sit with boys, and slowly, we learned that they weren't evil beings out to taint our minds (and, worse, our bodies). It was a hard process, beset with guilt, but eventually, we even made friends with some of them. Of course, when we came home and spoke to our parents about school, we carefully omitted all mention of boys. We never gave our male classmates our phone numbers, and we emphasized that they were never to say hello if they ever saw us with our parents. 5

The educational aspect of school presented us with another problem. We were expected to study hard and excel at school, but we were discouraged from displaying any intelligence or superior knowledge, especially at home or in the presence of other Punjabis. In effect, we were forced to run the race but never allowed the joy of the victory. 6

On the one hand, we weren't allowed to express our thoughts; desire and curiosity were met with punishment. On the other hand, because of our grasp of what my parents considered the "foreign tongue," they sometimes had to ask us to explain American matters to them. My elder sisters especially (I was still in elementary school) helped with the reading of such documents as insurance policies and leases, and they even gave our parents advice about them. 7

We were living in Texas at this time, and my uncle (my father's brother), who lived close by, made himself a large presence in our lives. One day, he came by as my older sister Barbie was discussing some bills with my parents. He watched in displeased surprise for a while, then tore the bills out of her hand. He said that he just couldn't believe his brother would ask an ignorant girl for advice on such things. Barbie, who is a surprisingly strong character, gathered her courage and protested. This just further proved to my uncle what terrible children we were, because in our culture, talking back to parents is considered very disrespectful and talking back to other adults even worse. "Useless, stupid ***girl,***" he shouted at my sister. When my older sisters protested at the insult, to my astonishment my parents, afraid of losing face, joined in with my uncle. They yelled at 8 my sisters and cursed them for being girls and ruining their parents' lives. They bemoaned the bad luck that had brought them daughters instead of sons.

9   Shocked and too afraid to speak, I watched the entire scene in silence. I would never forget it. What had changed? Why were my sisters, who had only been trying to help, all of a sudden the "bad guys"? It wasn't just a matter of my sisters speaking out against my parents. Their main fault was that they were girls and had minds they put to use.

10   Perhaps it was at this time we began rebelling. Growing up in the shadow of brothers who weren't there had bred an understandable resentment in us. When male cousins came over to spend time in our house, we were expected to dress conservatively, serve them food, and take care of their every need. Now, however, we began to insist that they do household chores like all of us sisters. Countless times, we were pulled aside by my mother and warned to keep our mouths shut, but we no longer listened.

11   Rakare, a special day in August, is a festival when all girls and women tie ribbons around their brothers' wrists to wish them long and prosperous lives; in return, the sisters receive money and the promise of protection. When I was 9-years-old, one of my cousins came to stay with us. This was the first time we had met him, and when Rakare came along, we were handed the ribbons and made to undergo the ceremony. The whole family took part in the celebration, with my father at the center. I couldn't help but notice the contrast, for every year when our birthdays rolled around, my father would be off at one religious event or another and nowhere to be found.

12   Recently, we sisters have refused to celebrate Rakare with our male cousins. Why should we celebrate the existence of men when their being alive only suppressed our lives more? When people wonder why we have stopped celebrating this festival, my mom laughs it off, explaining, "It's only because they haven't any brothers of their own around to celebrate, or else they would do it." I think deep down, however, she knows the real reason.

13   For a long time when I was growing up, I hated this aspect of my culture, the unequal treatment of boys and girls. Ashamed and angry, I pretended to myself that I wasn't Indian. At school, I acted different, talked different, and carefully avoided other Indian children, especially the girls, who I imagined as accepting all the traditions I rejected. Sometimes, I would watch them interacting with each other, talking, playing. I both feared and envied the closeness they seemed to possess. It was something I couldn't risk. If I accepted the common bond I shared with these girls, I would also have to accept our common bondage to a culture that suppressed us.

14   This inner battle charged my every move through high school, depriving me of a much needed understanding and camaraderie. It is only now, years later, having finally opened myself up to a few Indian friends,

that I realize many of them were also going through the same process of rebellion and rejection.

Culture forms a new shape as it rolls off my tongue today, a shape I fi-   15
nally openly admit to being a part of. I now realize that I will always be Indian, that I have no choice but to be Indian. It is there every time I greet an elder respectfully, every time I agree to do something he or she asks even though I don't want to. But I also realize that being Indian doesn't mean I have to agree with everything in my culture. I can be who I am and still continue my fight to be treated with respect, to be considered equal to the "boys."

Structure and Strategy

1. Analyze the introduction to Bhogal's essay. What elements make it striking? How else might she have structured it?
2. This essay has an implied thesis. What is it? Which sections or statements in the essay most clearly indicate/support this thesis?
3. The essay can be divided into three sections that point to three different movements of thought. What are these? What transitions has the writer used to indicate them?

Your Writing

1. Write an essay in which you compare the way you (or someone you know well or have interviewed) were brought up with the way siblings of the opposite sex were treated in the family. Were there similarities? Were there differences? What philosophical attitudes do you think accounted for these?
2. Bhogal's essay touches on the fact that in many cultures, the education given to men and women are quite different, and the purposes for which men and women are educated are different as well. What is your view on this aspect of education in the United States? Your paper can focus on the educational situation as it is today or use **research** and **interviews** to examine an earlier time.

SYNTHESIS: QUESTIONS FOR CRITICAL THINKING AND WRITING

1. "American Men Don't Cry" and "Focusing on Friends" claim that men deal with emotions and emotional situations in a very different way than women do. In "American Men," the writer believes this is negative; in "Friends," the writer believes this is positive. Which writer do you agree with most? Write an essay defending your chosen writer's position, bringing in supporting evidence of your own.
2. "Three Generations of Native American Women's Birth Experience" illustrates that women of "minority" cultures can be at a disadvantage when dealing with American society or institutions. **Analyze**, in an essay, the different reasons why these women experience difficulties.
3. "Cheap Men" and "I'd Rather Be Black than Female" challenge some traditional assumptions about the roles of men and women in social and career contexts. Choose some other traditional assumptions you have noticed about gender roles in a social *or* a career context, and write an **argumentative** essay giving reasons why such assumptions should be nurtured or abolished.
4. "Three Generations of Native American Women's Birth Experience" and "I'd Rather Be Black than Female" depict ways in which communities of women support each other during challenging situations. In your opinion, how common are such communities, male or female, in America today? Are you part of such a community? Do you feel that such a community plays an important role? Are such communities more prevalent in "minority" cultures? Write an essay exploring these or other related ideas, focused in a clear **thesis** of your own.

Lifestyles

Rituals, habits, beliefs, ways of thinking—all of these constitute our many lifestyles, and in America today, they are indeed many, as the readings in this unit illustrate. Lifestyle is affected by numerous, diverse factors: our ethnicity; our past; the way our parents raised us; the dictates of a changing, increasingly technological society; and our disillusion with trends that we consider harmful. The writers in this unit analyze all of these, and they come to some surprising discoveries.

"Modern Courtesy" by Lore Segal and "My Horse" by Barry Lopez look at contemporary lifestyles from the vantage point of a very different past, weighing what has changed and what has been gained or lost. They find ways in which compromises may be reached between the old and the new ways of doing things and how valuable traditions may be kept alive, even if in a different guise.

Several readings examine the difference between how things are done in mainstream American culture versus a particular ethnic tradition. In "Kwanzaa: Holiday of 'Principles to Live By,' " Eugene Morris discusses how African-Americans have reached into their heritage for values to replace the increasing commercialization of Christmas. In "They Shut My Grandmother's Room Door," Andrew Lam contrasts the attitudes toward both death and the dying in Vietnam and America. And in "Womanwork," Paula Gunn Allen describes the age-old tasks carried out by Native-American women, even today, and the healing power they hold.

Two pieces that approach this issue from a different angle are "Mi Pueblo" by student Leticia Reyes and "Shaved Heads and Pop-Tarts" by Jeannine Stein. Reyes shows us how a particular place—in this case, a Mexican grocery—can help to preserve values and traditions from the old land. Stein gives us a glimpse into the counterculture and an unusual aspect of the lives of rockers, which reveals them as more human and vulnerable than perhaps we have thought them to be.

Finally, the readings in this unit show us the humanness in diversity, that no matter where people come from and how they do things, they are, ultimately, people. And through the characters and voices that come alive here, they are largely successful.

Pre-reading Activity Think back on a subject about which you and your parents (or some other authority figure) did not agree. What was the subject? Why did you disagree?

As You Read Observe the writer's use of conversation to develop her **thesis**.

MODERN COURTESY
Lore Segal

Born in Vienna and settled in New York, **Lore Segal** *is an author of both adult and children's books, including* Other People's Houses, Tell Me a Mitzi, Tell Me a Trudy, *and* Her First American. *She contributes stories regularly to* The New Yorker, Saturday Evening Post, Epoch, The New Republic, *and other periodicals. This piece first appeared in the* New York Times *in 1987.*

My son and I were having one of our rare quarrels. Jacob is a formidable 1
person and our difference was on a matter of substance—modern manners versus the old courtesies. Signor Giuseppe, an elderly neighbor from the Old World, had complained that Jacob didn't say good morning when he got on the elevator and that he answered Signor Giuseppe's questions reluctantly.

My son said Signor Giuseppe's questions were phonies. Signor 2
Giuseppe did not give a hoot about how many inches my son had grown and couldn't care less what subjects he was taking in school. My son said these were questions that didn't deserve answers.

I argued that it is the business of courtesy to cover up the terrible truth 3
that we don't give a hoot about the other person in the elevator.

"Why is that terrible and why cover it up?" my son asked sensibly. 4

Jacob belongs to the generation that says "Me and Joe are going out," 5
and whichever walks through the door first trusts the other to take care its back swing doesn't catch him in the head. My generation says "Signor Giuseppe and I are going out," and Signor Giuseppe opens the door and holds it for me.

Jacob said: "Why? You can open it for yourself." 6

This is true. It is also true that "me and Joe" is the formulation that cor- 7
responds to my experience. It's my own passage through the door that occupies my mind. It's because Signor Giuseppe might, in the press of the things on *his* mind, forget that I'm coming behind, that courtesy tells him

to let me go ahead. Courtesy makes me pass him the cookies, keeping me artificially aware of his hunger, which I don't experience. My own appetite can be trusted to take care of *my* cookies.

8   Signor Giuseppe and I reach the corner. His anachronistic hand under my forearm presumes that a lady cannot step off the curb without a supporting gentleman—a presumption for which modern men have been hit across the head with umbrellas. That is why my graduate student, who chats amusingly as we walk down the corridor, does *not* open the door for me.

9   "Why should he?" Jacob asked.

10   "Because I'm carrying two packages in my right hand, my books in my left, and my handbag and umbrella under my armpit," I said.

11   If my son or my graduate student were boors, we would not be addressing this matter. A boor is a boor and was always a boor. But I can tell that the muscles of my graduate student's back are readying to bend and pick up the book and umbrella I have dropped. He struggles between his natural courtesy and the learned inhibition that *I* have taught him: My being a woman is no reason for him to pick my things up for me. I crawl on the floor retrieving my property. He remains standing.

12   My son is not only formidable, he is a person of good will. He said: "That's stupid! If you see someone is in trouble you go and help them out. What's it got to do with courtesy?"

13   This is what it has to do with it: Having thrown out the old, dead, hypocritical rules about napkins, knives, and how to address the ladies, it is Jacob's and it is my graduate student's business to recover the essential baby that went down the drain as well. They must invent their own rules for eating so they don't look and sound nasty, and my student must count my packages to see if I need his help. When Jacob enters the elevator, he is required to perform a complex act of the imagination: Is Signor Giuseppe a plain pain in the neck or does he have trouble?

14   "His trouble is he's a pain in the neck," Jacob said.

15   "And your business is to keep him from finding it out."

16   "Why?" Jacob shouted.

17   "Because once Signor Giuseppe understands that he's too great a pain to chat with for the time the elevator takes to descend from the 12th to the ground floor, he will understand that he will die alone."

18   My son guffawed. He is not required to join me in this leap: The old courtesy was in the essential business of the cover-up. It was the contract by which I agreed to pretend to find your concerns of paramount interest, in return for which you took care not to let on that you did not care a hoot about mine.

19   Jacob said he still thought one should say what one meant and talk to the people one liked. But he said next time he got in the elevator with Signor Giuseppe, he was going to tell him good morning.

Building Vocabulary

Define the words below, using *context clues* wherever possible and checking in a dictionary when necessary. Use them in sentences of your own.

formidable (1)	guffaw (18)	boor (11)
formulation (7)	phonies (2)	hypocritical (13)
presumption (8)	anachronistic (8)	paramount (18)
inhibition (11)		

Journal Writing

Choose one or more of the three activities listed below, and make an entry in your journal. Focus on writing spontaneously rather than on structure and mechanics.

1. **Exploring:** Recall what you remember from other sources—your reading, your life experiences, movies and television, stories told to you by others—about the topic discussed by the writer. Choose one or two of these to write about. Which aspects of the topic did they bring up? What additional information did they provide? What emotions did they create in you?
2. **Taking Stock:** Which parts of the selection were most difficult for you to grasp? Which parts needed more explanation? Which parts required outside information to be understood? What kind of information was required (e.g., historical, culture-specific, technical, etc.)? Where might such information be found? Were there aspects of the writer's style you found particularly effective? Particularly difficult? Why?
3. **Responding:** Identify one or two of the writer's main concerns. What personal knowledge, if any, do you have of these issues? What is your opinion on these issues? Examine your response carefully to see what it teaches you about yourself.

Analyzing Content

1. What is the **thesis** of the essay? Where is it placed? Where do we first get a hint of it?
2. Describe the traditional view of courtesy, especially as it relates to women. What is the modern attitude toward this? Give an example of this attitude from the text.
3. What is the inherent philosophical difference between the two quotations Segal presents in paragraph 5 as indicative of the "old" and the "modern" generation?

4. Explain the dilemma Segal introduces in paragraph 11. What solution does she propose for it?

Analyzing Writing Techniques

1. What is the **tone** of this essay? In which paragraph does the writer begin to establish this tone?
2. Pick out other examples that help to develop the tone. What has the tone added to the argument?

Group Activity

Compare/contrast Segal's attitude toward courtesy with her son's, listing the pros and cons of each. Discuss the courtesy practices of each member of your group as they relate to the essay. With which of the two viewpoints in the essay does the group agree more closely? Why?

Your Writing

1. An underlying idea in Segal's essay is that the relationship between individuals has changed greatly within the span of a generation in American society—and not necessarily for the better. What is your viewpoint? Write an essay in which you analyze how a young person today relates to other individuals. In addition to personal or observed examples, use at least one outside source.
2. Write a **letter** to Signor Giuseppe, explaining to him the concept of "modern courtesy" as you understand it and either defending it or pointing out its flaws.

Pre-reading Activity   Describe a scene of death that you saw on TV or in a movie. How realistic do you think it was? What thoughts did it bring up in you?

As You Read   Note the writer's **comparison/contrast** of America and Vietnam and of the present and the past.

THEY SHUT MY GRANDMOTHER'S ROOM DOOR
Andrew Lam

Originally from Vietnam, **Andrew Lam** *lives in San Francisco, where he is the Associate Editor for the Pacific News Service. His articles have appeared in* Nation, Mother Jones, *and the* Washington Post. *He has been awarded a Rockefeller Fellowship and an Asian-American Journalism Award.*

When someone dies in the convalescent home where my grandmother 1
lives, the nurses rush to close all the patients' doors. Though as a policy death is not to be seen at the home, she can always tell when it visits. The series of doors being slammed shut remind her of the firecrackers during Tet.

The nurses' efforts to shield death are more comical to my grandmother 2
than reassuring. "Those old ladies die so often," she quips in Vietnamese, "everyday's like New Year."

Still, it is lonely to die in such a place. I imagine some wasted old body 3
under a white sheet being carted silently through the empty corridor on its way to the morgue. While in America a person may be born surrounded by loved ones, in old age one is often left to take the last leg of life's journey alone.

Perhaps that is why my grandmother talks now mainly of her home- 4
town, Bac-Lieu, its river and green rich rice fields. Having lost everything during the war, she can now offer me only her distant memories: Life was not disjointed back home; one lived in a gentle rhythm with the land; people died in their homes surrounded by neighbors and relatives. And no one shut your door.

So it goes. The once gentle, connected world of the past is but the lan- 5
guage of dreams. In this fast-paced society of disjointed lives, we are swept along and have little time left for spiritual comfort. Instead of relying on

neighbors and relatives, on the river and land, we deal with the language of materialism: overtime, escrow, stress, down payment, credit cards, tax shelter. Instead of going to the temple to pray for good health we pay life and health insurance religiously.

6   My grandmother's children and grandchildren share a certain pang of guilt. After a stroke which paralyzed her, we could no longer keep her at home. And although we visit her regularly, we are not living up to the filial piety standard expected of us in the old country. My father silently grieves and my mother suffers from headaches. (Does she see herself in such a home in a decade or two?)

7   Once, a long time ago, living in Vietnam we used to stare death in the face. The war in many ways had heightened our sensibilities toward living and dying. I can still hear the wails of widows and grieving mothers. Though the fear of death and dying is a universal one, the Vietnamese did not hide from it. Instead we dwelt in its tragedy. Death pervaded our poems, novels, fairy tales and songs.

8   But if agony and pain are part of Vietnamese culture, pleasure is at the center of America's culture. While Vietnamese holidays are based on death anniversaries, birthdays are celebrated here. American popular culture translates death with something like nauseating humor. People laugh and scream at blood and guts movies. The wealthy freeze their dead relatives in liquid nitrogen. Cemeteries are places of big business, complete with colorful brochures. I hear there are even drive-by funerals where you don't have to get out of your own car to pay your respects to the deceased.

9   That America relies upon the pleasure principle and happy endings in its entertainments does not, however, assist us in evading suffering. The reality of the suffering of old age is apparent in the convalescent home. There is an old man, once an accomplished concert pianist, now rendered helpless by arthritis. Every morning he sits staring at the piano. One feeble woman who outlived her children keeps repeating, "My son will take me home." Then there are those mindless, bedridden bodies kept alive through a series of tubes and pulsating machines.

10   But despair is not newsworthy. Death itself must be embellished or satirized or deep-frozen in order to catch the public's attention.

11   Last week on her 82[d] birthday I went to see my grandmother. She smiled her sweet sad smile.

12   "Where will you end up in your old age?" she asked me, her mind as sharp as ever.

13   The memories of monsoon rain and tropical sun and relatives and friends came to mind. Not here, not here, I wanted to tell her. But the soft moaning of a patient next door and the smell of alcohol wafting from the sterile corridor brought me back to reality.

14   "Anywhere is fine," I told her instead, trying to keep up with her courageous spirit. "All I am asking for is that they don't shut my door."

Building Vocabulary

Define the words below, using *context clues* wherever possible and checking in a dictionary when necessary. Use them in sentences of your own.

convalescent home (1)	nauseating (8)	pervaded (7)
wasted (3)	quip (2)	embellished (10)
filial piety (6)	disjointed (4)	

Journal Writing

Choose one or more of the three activities listed below, and make an entry in your journal. Focus on writing spontaneously rather than on structure and mechanics.

1. **Exploring:** Recall what you remember from other sources—your reading, your life experiences, movies and television, stories told to you by others—about the topic discussed by the writer. Choose one or two of these to write about. Which aspects of the topic did they bring up? What additional information did they provide? What emotions did they create in you?
2. **Taking Stock:** Which parts of the selection were most difficult for you to grasp? Which parts needed more explanation? Which parts required outside information to be understood? What kind of information was required (e.g., historical, culture-specific, technical, etc.)? Where might such information be found? Were there aspects of the writer's style you found particularly effective? Particularly difficult? Why?
3. **Responding:** Identify one or two of the writer's main concerns. What personal knowledge, if any, do you have of these issues? What is your opinion on these issues? Examine your response carefully to see what it teaches you about yourself.

Analyzing Content

1. Why is it a policy for death not to be seen at the convalescent home? What does this **imply** about the American attitude toward death?
2. In which paragraph(s) does the writer elaborate on this idea? **Summarize** the points he makes about death in America.
3. In this essay, the writer makes a related point about the treatment of old people in America and in Vietnam. **Compare/contrast** the treatment of the elderly in the two cultures. What reasons are indicated for the differences?

Analyzing Writing Techniques

1. The closed door becomes a **symbol** in this essay. Analyze its significance.
2. Throughout the essay, the writer has used **generalizations** to give a sense of American life. Pick out some of these. What are some pros and cons of using generalizations?

Group Activity

Discuss the writer's overall attitude toward how death is handled in America. How correct is he? Is his opinion **objective** or **subjective**? How far do you agree with his thinking? Write a **group letter** to the writer describing your response to this essay.

Your Writing

1. How far do you agree with the writer's claim that "pleasure is at the center of American culture"? Write an **argumentative** essay in which you examine the daily activities of Americans to **support** or **refute** this statement. Be sure to use specific examples and quotations.
2. **Visit** a convalescent home, and record your impressions in an essay. **Compare/contrast** your feelings about the place with the writer's descriptions.

Pre-reading Activity Describe, from your childhood, a holiday ritual that was important to your family. How much of the meaning of the ritual was explained to you?

As You Read Outline the basic steps that make up the Kwanzaa celebration.

KWANZAA: HOLIDAY OF "PRINCIPLES TO LIVE BY"
Eugene Morris

Eugene Morris *writes for* The Atlanta Journal and Constitution, *in which this piece first appeared in 1987.*

Alice Lovelace said her five children don't complain each holiday season 1
when they get handmade African toys and books written by African-American authors instead of computerized laser games and combat-fighter planes. They also understand why their home is decorated with candies, fruit, and place mats instead of a Christmas tree and stockings. Like millions of other black Americans, the Lovelace family celebrates *Kwanzaa* (also spelled *Kwanza*), a holiday when African-Americans give thanks for their heritage. Beginning [December 26], Kwanzaa is celebrated the seven days after Christmas.

Derived from an East African Swahili phrase, *matunda ya kwanza* or 2
"first fruits," Kwanzaa is neither an African holiday nor a black Christmas. It is an African-American cultural celebration that draws on African harvest festival traditions, like giving thanks for the first crops of the year. It also stresses principles for better living and offers guides to achieve inner peace.

"We started celebrating Kwanzaa as an alternative to the commer- 3
cialization of Christmas and because Kwanzaa is grounded in moral and cultural values," said Ms. Lovelace, executive director of an art gallery. "Kwanzaa teaches principles to live by," she said, "and we thought that was more valuable than celebrating Christmas, which has become so commercial."

Kwanzaa was founded in 1966 by Dr. Maulana Karenga, a black stud- 4
ies professor at California State University campuses in Los Angeles and Long Beach. Karenga initiated the holiday because he felt blacks needed a holiday that had historical relevance for blacks and Africans. Longtime Kwanzaa observers said small celebrations also began about the same time in Atlanta in the homes of some blacks. Other programs and celebrations

were held at community centers, black college campuses, and other sites. . . . National Kwanzaa officials said more than 13 million African-Americans celebrate Kwanzaa. In Atlanta, Kwanzaa . . . celebrations . . . include displays and demonstrations throughout the city. . . .

5   Kwanzaa was founded under seven principles, referred to as the *Nguzo Saba.* They are unity, self-determination, collective work and re-sponsibility, cooperative economics, purpose, creativity, and faith. During Kwanzaa, traditional holiday decorations are replaced by red, black, and green African colors of liberation. Kwanzaa symbols are placed upon a *mkeka* or place mat, which represents the African foundation of the holi-day. A *kinara* (seven-piece candleholder) and the *mishumaa saba* (seven candles) are also displayed. One candle is lighted each day. Other displays include *vibunzi* (corn), which symbolizes children, *mazao* (fruits, nuts, and vegetables), which represent the holiday's origins, African harvest, the re-wards of collective efforts, and the *zawadi* (gifts) primarily given to the chil-dren. However the gifts should be creative, cultural, and educational and not merely for entertainment. Each night some families sip a libation (or *tambiko*) from a unity cup (or *kikombe*) to honor black ancestors. Songs and dances are also performed.

6   Although Ikenna Ubaka and her daughter celebrate Kwanzaa and Christmas, Ms. Ubaka stresses the religious impact of Christmas and down-plays its commercialization. "We try to send the message during Kwanzaa that it is more important to give of yourselves than to spend money on pre-sents," she said. "Kwanzaa deals with our heritage and our culture."

7   Dr. Omowale Amuleru-Marshall, a member of the Atlanta Chapter of the Association of Black Psychologists and the faculty of the Morehouse School of Medicine, said his family celebrates Kwanzaa because of a dis-illusionment with Christmas. "My rejection of Christmas is not a rejection of Christ," he said, "just the way the holiday creates a psychological de-nial of one's own self and one's own culture."

Building Vocabulary

Define the words below, using *context clues* wherever possible and checking in a dictionary when necessary. Use them in sentences of your own.

stresses (2)	collective (5)	self-determination (5)
initiated (4)	grounded (3)	libation (5)

Journal Writing

Choose one or more of the three activities listed below, and make an entry in your journal. Focus on writing spontaneously rather than on structure and mechanics.

1. **Exploring:** Recall what you remember from other sources—your reading, your life experiences, movies and television, stories told to you by others—about the topic discussed by the writer. Choose one or two of these to write about. Which aspects of the topic did they bring up? What additional information did they provide? What emotions did they create in you?
2. **Taking Stock:** Which parts of the selection were most difficult for you to grasp? Which parts needed more explanation? Which parts required outside information to be understood? What kind of information was required (e.g., historical, culture-specific, technical, etc.)? Where might such information be found? Were there aspects of the writer's style you found particularly effective? Particularly difficult? Why?
3. **Responding:** Identify one or two of the writer's main concerns. What personal knowledge, if any, do you have of these issues? What is your opinion on these issues? Examine your response carefully to see what it teaches you about yourself.

Analyzing Content

1. When was Kwanzaa founded? Why?
2. What additional reasons for the founding are given by some African-Americans who celebrate this festival? **Paraphrase** their quotations.
3. **List** the seven principles of Kwanzaa, and explain what you understand to be the importance of each.
4. How does Kwanzaa contrast with Christmas? Do you see any similarities between it and other holiday celebrations you know?

Analyzing Writing Techniques

1. In paragraph 1, the writer uses two objects that seem to symbolize a certain aspect of Christmas. What are these objects? What do they say about Christmas?
2. At the end of the first paragraph, the writer has placed a sentence that indicates the topic of the article. What would you add to that sentence to make it into a comprehensive **thesis**?

Group Activity

Discuss Alice Lovelace's complaint that Christmas has become too commercialized. Do you agree? **Compile** a **group list** of examples based on personal **anecdotes**, observed experiences, and media advertisements that indicate how accurate she is.

Your Writing

1. As this article indicates, we often lose sight of the original meanings of holiday celebrations. *Excluding* Christmas, choose a holiday that is considered important in your culture, and **research** its beginnings. How closely are people able to keep to its original meaning? **Illustrate** with examples.
2. Examine Amuleru-Marshall's claim that Christmas "creates a psychological denial of one's own self and one's own culture." Write an essay in which you discuss why African-Americans might feel this way.

Pre-reading Activity What is your concept of "rockers"? Using the technique of **clustering**, come up with 10 words that you associate with them.

As You Read Underline interesting descriptive details that tell you something significant about the lifestyles of rockers.

SHAVED HEADS AND POP-TARTS
Jeannine Stein

Jeannine Stein *writes for* The Los Angeles Times, *in which this piece first appeared in 1992.*

Almost every night at 10, you'll find heavy-metal rock 'n' rollers with long   1
hair, pierced noses, tattoos, biker boots and leather jackets cruising the
aisles of the Hollywood Ralphs on Sunset.

It's not how you'd envision a rocker's natural habitat, but even head-   2
bangers have to eat. Sure, any 7-Eleven will do when you have a craving
for beef jerky and Junior Mints, but metal-heads do not live by preserved
meat and candy alone.

So in Hollywood, the grocery store of choice has been dubbed Rock   3
'N' Roll Ralphs. It's a hulking structure on the east end of the strip, near
Poinsettia, a few minutes' drive to rock clubs like Gazzari's, the Roxy and
Coconut Teaszer.

At the clubs, the long hair, tattoos and motorcycles belong. Seeing   4
those same people at Ralphs is a case of when worlds collide, a surrealistic blend of shaved heads, Pop-Tarts and Muzak, where baskets contain
generic corn flakes and Metal Edge magazine and punkers share space with
more mainstream types.

On a Thursday night in the liquor aisle, a woman hoists a large bot-   5
tle of whiskey and hands it to her male companion. She is barely in her
20s. She wears Kabuki-ish makeup, her face whited out and accented with
bright pink lipstick and eye shadow; she has a small hoop in her pierced
eyebrow. She wears a black and white polka-dot floppy hat, an old T-shirt,
pink and black horizontal striped tights and pink bouclé bike shorts. The
man with her is yin to her yang—middle aged, dressed in brown trousers
and a plaid shirt. They disappear down the aisle.

Two young guys stand in front of the deli counter. One keeps comb-   6
ing his hand through his dark Pre-Raphaelite hair. They stare and stare at

the selection of luncheon meats for several minutes before Mr. Hair says, "Uhhhhh . . . so d'you like pickle loaf?"

7   Two more rockers, one with long bleached blond hair, the other with long blue-black hair, lope on gangly legs to the bread aisle, where they pick up a few loaves, squeeze and then abandon the bread. They take two cookies from the bakery pantry and eat them.

8   A tall, skinny guy with a skull and crossbones T-shirt and black base-ball cap with "Suicidal Tendencies" stitched on it rushes over to the frozen food section clutching a coupon. He looks furtively up and down the case until he finds a box of Nestle's Crunch ice cream bars, grabs it, then picks up four six-packs of Coke and heads for the express line.

9   In the household aisle, a young woman with hair dyed to match her purple mini-skirt methodically eats California rolls and contemplates ex-tension cords.

10   Meanwhile, a touching scene is unfolding by the cat food. A man with chunky silver rings and biker boots crouches down and takes about 10 min-utes to decide between the 9-Lives chicken and cheese and the tuna for his pampered pet.

11   It's fair to say that most rockers who shop here aren't stocking up for the long haul. They come for the essentials, what it's going to take to get them through the night. The most frequently purchased items appear to be:

12   • Beer (usually 12-can packs in the cardboard carrying case)
   • Water (gallon jugs)
   • Luncheon meats
   • Chips (tortilla, potato)
   • Canned chili and soup
   • Dried pasta
   • Hamburger and hot dog buns
   • Steak
   • Pet food

13   Female rockers tend to make healthier choices, going for yogurt, fresh fruit, tuna and low-cholesterol margarine.

14   Even the wildest clubbies appear somehow tamed in this benign world of the grocery store. While they may spend every night in clubs, banging heads to Metallica, Megadeth and L7, here they're entranced by the Zen-like calm.

15   Maybe it's the flatness of the fluorescent lights, or the Muzak. It's hard to get jumpy when a syrupy rendition of the already syrupy "Garden Party" plays over the loudspeakers, or when the Video Recipe of the Week offers tips on how to cook a pork tenderloin. ("Sprinkle with parsley and serve!")

16   It's an atmosphere that's conducive to spending quantity time vacil-lating between hamburger dill chips and zesty bread-and-butter pickles. Faces go slack and eyes glaze over as the staggering number of choices

renders people passive. Conversations rarely consist of anything more substantial than "Should we get the low-salt chips?"

Building Vocabulary

Define the words below, using *context clues* wherever possible and checking in a dictionary when necessary. Indicate if words have a particular connotation or more than one meaning, and use them in sentences of your own.

heavy-metal (1)	furtively (8)	Muzak (4)
natural habitat (2)	Zen-like (14)	lope (7)
surrealistic (4)	cruising (1)	benign (14)
Pre-Raphaelite (6)	headbangers (2)	vacillating (16)

Journal Writing

Choose one or more of the three activities listed below, and make an entry in your journal. Focus on writing spontaneously rather than on structure and mechanics.

1. **Exploring:** Recall what you remember from other sources—your reading, your life experiences, movies and television, stories told to you by others—about the topic discussed by the writer. Choose one or two of these to write about. Which aspects of the topic did they bring up? What additional information did they provide? What emotions did they create in you?
2. **Taking Stock:** Which parts of the selection were most difficult for you to grasp? Which parts needed more explanation? Which parts required outside information to be understood? What kind of information was required (e.g., historical, culture-specific, technical, etc.)? Where might such information be found? Were there aspects of the writer's style you found particularly effective? Particularly difficult? Why?
3. **Responding:** Identify one or two of the writer's main concerns. What personal knowledge, if any, do you have of these issues? What is your opinion on these issues? Examine your response carefully to see what it teaches you about yourself.

Analyzing Content

1. What is the **implied thesis** of this piece?
2. Which surprising aspects of rockers does this selection reveal?
3. What are some differences in food habits between male and female rockers? What might this **imply**?

4. Explain why even the wildest rockers seem "tamed" in the grocery store.

Analyzing Writing Techniques

1. Analyze the writer's use of lists as a structural device. (She uses two different kinds in the piece.)
2. This writer likes to use very short paragraphs. Why? Which paragraphs develop the same topic and might be combined?

Group Activity

Discuss the title. What point is the writer trying to make through it? Come up with some alternate titles for the essay.

Your Writing

1. The writer of this piece breaks through some of our sterotypes about rockers. Many other groups in society are also stereotyped or marginalized for various reasons. Choose one such group, and write about the stereotyped image that society holds of them and how far it is based on truth.
2. "You are what you eat," goes an old saying. How far is it true that culture, lifestyle, and values affect your eating habits? Or, conversely, that your food habits affect your lifestyle? Write an essay in which you explore this issue by contrasting the eating habits of two distinct groups of people.

Pre-reading Activity   Thinking back on your childhood, describe the tasks that you remember women in your family or community performing.

As You Read   Underline all of the **visual images** you find in this poem.

WOMANWORK
Paula Gunn Allen

*Born in New Mexico, **Paula Gunn Allen** is part Laguna Pueblo, part Sioux, and part Chicana. Out of this rich and complex heritage comes her novel* The Woman Who Owned the Shadows *and poetry collections such as* Coyote's Daylight Trip. *Allen is also known for her poems and essays. She has taught at various universities, including the University of California at Berkeley and Los Angeles.*

some make potteries
some weave and spin
remember
the Woman/celebrate
webs and making
out of own flesh
earth
bowl and urn
to hold water
and ground corn   10
balanced on heads
and springs lifted
and rivers in our eyes
brown hands shaping
earth into earth
food for bodies
water for fields
they use old pots
broken
fragments   20
castaway

bits
to make new
mixed with clay
it makes strong
bowls, jars
new
She
brought
30 light
we remember this
as we make
the water bowl
broken
marks the grandmother's grave
so she will shape water
for bowls
for food growing
for bodies
40 eating
at drink
thank Her

Analyzing Content and Technique

1. **Classify** the different activities that women in this poem are engaged in. From these categories, what do you think is the role of women in this society?
2. Explain the references to "the Woman," doing some **research** if needed.
3. What is done with the old, broken pots? In what way might this be symbolic?
4. Analyze the structure of the poem, commenting on line lengths, stanza formation, and lack of punctuation.

Group Activity

Discuss the title as it relates to mainstream American society. Do we have "womanwork"? Is there a difference between men's work and women's? Do you feel there should be? Write a **collaborative** paragraph into which you incorporate the group's opinions.

Your Writing

1. Write an essay titled "Manwork." In it, analyze the activities that men are commonly expected/encouraged to undertake by the com-

munity or society in which you grew up or now live. What generalizations about men's roles can you draw from this?

2. Allen portrays a particular lifestyle for the women in her poem. How accurate is this depiction in terms of contemporary Native-American life? Write an essay in which you research the lifestyle of contemporary Native-American men or women, including their ties to their culture.

Pre-reading Activity   If you own a car, write about how you feel toward it. If you don't own a car, how do you feel about not having one?

As You Read   Think about the role of automobiles in our lives today.

MY HORSE
Barry Lopez

Born in 1945 in Port Chester, N.Y., **Barry Lopez** *holds degrees from the University of Notre Dame and the University of Oregon. His books include* Desert Notes *and* Coyote: A Collection of American Indian Trickster Tales. *His essays and photographs have appeared in* Harper's, Audubon, *and* North American Review, *in which this piece first appeared in 1975.*

1   It is curious that Indian warriors on the northern plains in the nineteenth century, who were almost entirely dependent on the horse for mobility and status, never gave their horses names. If you borrowed a man's horse and went off raiding for other horses, however, or if you lost your mount in battle and then jumped on mine and counted coup on an enemy—well, those horses would have to be shared with the man whose horse you borrowed, and that coup would be mine, not yours. Because even if I gave him no name, he was my horse.

2   If you were a Crow warrior and I a young Teton Sioux out after a warrior's identity and we came over a small hill somewhere in the Montana prairie and surprised each other, I could tell a lot about you by looking at your horse.

3   Your horse might have feathers tied in his mane, or in his tail, or a medicine bag tied around his neck. If I knew enough about the Crow, and had looked at you closely, I might make some sense of the decoration, even guess who you were if you were well-known. If you had painted your horse I could tell even more, because we both decorated our horses with signs that meant the same things. Your white handprints high on his flanks would tell me you had killed an enemy in a hand-to-hand fight. Small horizontal lines stacked on your horse's foreleg, or across his nose, would tell me how many times you had counted coup. Horse hoof marks on your horse's rump, or three-sided boxes, would tell me how many times you had stolen horses. If there was a bright red square on your horse's neck I would know you were leading a war party and that there were probably others out there in the coulees behind you.

You might be painted all over as blue as the sky and covered with white   4
dots, with your horse painted the same way. Maybe hailstorms were your
power—or if I chased you a hailstorm might come down and hide you.
There might be lightning bolts on the horse's legs and flanks, and I would
wonder if you had lightning power, or a slow horse. There might be white
circles around your horse's eyes to help him see better.

Or you might be like Crazy Horse, with no decoration, no marks on   5
your horse to tell me anything, only a small lightning bolt on your cheek,
a piece of turquoise tied behind your ear.

You might have scalps dangling from your rein.   6

I could tell something about you by your horse. All this would come   7
to me in a few seconds. I might decide this was my moment and shout my
war cry—*Hoka hey!* Or I might decide you were like the grizzly bear: I
would raise my weapon to you in salute and go my way, to see you again
when I was older.

I do not own a horse. I am attached to a truck, however, and I have   8
come to think of it in a similar way. It has no name; it never occurred to
me to give it a name. It has little decoration; neither of us is partial to decoration. I have a piece of turquoise in the truck because I had heard once
that some of the southwestern tribes tied a small piece of turquoise in a
horse's hock to keep him from stumbling. I like the idea. I also hang sage
in the truck when I go on a long trip. But inside, the truck doesn't look
much different from others that look just like it on the outside. I like it that
way. Because I like my privacy.

For two years in Wyoming I worked on a ranch wrangling horses. The   9
horse I rode when I had to have a good horse was a quarter horse and his
name was Coke High. The name came with him. At first I thought he'd
been named for the soft drink. I'd known stranger names given to horses
by whites. Years later I wondered if some deviate Wyoming cowboy wise
to cocaine had not named him. Now I think he was probably named after
a rancher, an historical figure of the region. I never asked the people who
owned him for fear of spoiling the spirit of my inquiry.

We were running over a hundred horses on this ranch. They all had   10
names. After a few weeks I knew all the horses and the names too. You
had to. No one knew how to talk about the animals or put them in order
or tell the wranglers what to do unless they were using the names—
Princess, Big Red, Shoshone, Clay.

My truck is named Dodge. The name came with it. I don't know if it   11
was named after the town or the verb or the man who invented it. I like it
for a name. Perfectly anonymous, like Rex for a dog, or Old Paint. You can't
tell anything with a name like that.

The truck is a van. I call it a truck because it's not a car and because   12
"van" is a suburban sort of consumer word, like "oxford loafer," and I don't
like the sound of it. On the outside it looks like any other Dodge Sports-

man 300. It's a dirty tan color. There are a few body dents, but it's never been in a wreck. I tore the antenna off against a tree on a pinched mountain road. A boy in Midland, Texas, rocked one of my rear view mirrors off. A logging truck in Oregon squeeze-fired a piece of debris off the road and shattered my windshield. The oil pan and gas tank are pug-faced from high-centering on bad roads. (I remember a horse I rode for a while named Targhee whose hocks were scarred from tangles in barbed wire when he was a colt and who spooked a lot in high grass, but these were not like "dents." They were more like bad tires.)

13   I like to travel. I go mostly in the winter and mostly on two-lane roads. I've driven the truck from Key West to Vancouver, British Columbia, and from Yuma to Long Island over the past four years. I used to ride Coke High only about five miles every morning when we were rounding up horses. Hard miles of twisting and turning. About six hundred miles a year. Then I'd turn him out and ride another horse for the rest of the day. That's what was nice about having a remuda. You could do all you had to do and not take it all out on your best horse. Three car family.

14   My truck came with a lot of seats in it and I've never really known what to do with them. Sometimes I put the seats in and go somewhere with a lot of people, but most of the time I leave them out. I like riding around with that empty cavern of space behind my head. I know it's something with a history to it, that there's truth in it, because I always rode a horse the same way—with empty saddle bags. In case I found something. The possibility of finding something is half the reason for being on the road.

15   The value of anything comes to me in its use. If I am not using something it is of no value to me and I give it away. I wasn't always that way. I used to keep everything I owned—just in case. I feel good about the truck because it gets used. A lot. To haul hay and firewood and lumber and rocks and garbage and animals. Other people have used it to haul furniture and freezers and dirt and recycled newspapers. And to move from one house to another. When I lend it for things like that I don't look to get anything back but some gas (if we're going to be friends). But if you go way out in the country to a dump and pick up the things you can still find out there (once a load of cedar shingles we sold for $175 to an architect) I expect you to leave some of those things around my place when you come back— if I need them.

16   When I think back, maybe the nicest thing I ever put in that truck was timber wolves. It was a long night's drive from Oregon up into British Columbia. We were all very quiet about it; it was like moving clouds across the desert.

17   Sometimes something won't fit in the truck and I think about improving it—building a different door system, for example. I am forever going to add better gauges on the dash and a pair of driving lamps and a sun-

roof, but I never get around to doing any of it. I remember I wanted to improve Coke High once too, especially the way he bolted like a greyhound through patches of cottonwood on a river flat. But all I could do with him was to try to rein him out of it. Or hug his back.

Sometimes, road-stoned in a blur of country like southwestern 18 Wyoming or North Dakota, I talk to the truck. It's like wandering on the high plains under a summer sun, on plains where, George Catlin wrote, you were "out of sight of land." I say what I am thinking out loud, or point at things along the road. It's a crazy, sun-stroked sort of activity, a sure sign it's time to pull over, to go for a walk, to make a fire and have some tea, to lie in the shade of the truck.

I've always wanted to pat the truck. It's basic to the relationship. But 19 it never works.

I remember when I was on the ranch, just at sunrise, after I'd saddled 20 Coke High, I'd be huddled down in my jacket smoking a cigarette and looking down into the valley, along the river where the other horses had spent the night. I'd turn to Coke and run my hand down his neck and slap-pat him on the shoulder to say I was coming up. It [would] make a bond, an agreement we started the day with.

I've thought about that a lot with the truck, because we've gone out 21 together at sunrise on so many mornings. I've even fumbled around trying to do it. But metal won't give.

The truck's personality is mostly an expression of two ideas: "with-you" 22 and "alone." When Coke High was "with-you" he and I were the same animal. We could have cut a rooster out of a flock of chickens, we were so in tune. It's the same with the truck: rolling through Kentucky on a hilly two-lane road, three in the morning under a full moon and no traffic. Picture it. You roll like water.

There are other times when you are with each other but there's no con- 23 nection at all. Coke got that way when he was bored and we'd fight each other about which way to go around a tree. When the truck gets like that—"alone"—it's because it feels its Detroit fat-ass design dragging at its heart and making a fool out of it.

I can think back over more than a hundred nights I've slept in the truck, 24 sat in it with a lamp burning, bundled up in a parka, reading a book. It was always comfortable. A good place to wait out a storm. Like sleeping inside a buffalo.

The truck will go past 100,000 miles soon. I'll rebuild the engine and 25 put a different transmission in it. I can tell from magazine advertisements that I'll never get another one like it. Because every year they take more of the heart out of them. One thing that makes a farmer or a rancher go sour is a truck that isn't worth a shit. The reason you see so many old pickups in ranch country is because these are the only ones with any heart. You can count on them. The weekend rancher runs around in a new pickup with too much engine and not enough transmission and with the wrong sort of tires because he can afford anything, even the worst. A lot of them have names for their pickups too.

26   My truck has broken down, in out of the way places at the worst of times. I've walked away and screamed the foulness out of my system and gotten the tools out. I had to fix a water pump in a blizzard in the Panamint Mountains in California once. It took all day with the Coleman stove burning under the engine block to keep my hands from freezing. We drifted into Beatty, Nevada, that night with it jury-rigged together with—I swear—baling wire, and we were melting snow as we went and pouring it in to compensate for the leaks.

27   There is a dent next to the door on the driver's side I put there one sweltering night in Miami. I had gone to the airport to meet my wife, whom I hadn't seen in a month. My hands were so swollen with poison ivy blisters I had to drive with my wrists. I had shut the door and was locking it when the window fell off its runners and [slid] down inside the door. I couldn't leave the truck unlocked because I had too much inside I didn't want to lose. So I just kicked the truck a blow in the side and went to work on the window. I hate to admit kicking the truck. It's like kicking a dog, which I've never done.

28   Coke High and I had an accident once. We hit a badger hole at a full gallop. I landed on my back and blacked out. When I came to, Coke High was about a hundred yards away. He stayed a hundred yards away for six miles, all the way back to the ranch.

29   I want to tell you about carrying those wolves, because it was a fine thing. There were ten of them. We had four in the truck with us in crates and six in a trailer. It was a five hundred mile trip. We went at night for the cool air and because there wouldn't be as much traffic. I could feel from the way the truck rolled along that its heart was in the trip. I liked the wolves inside it, the sweet odor that came from the crates. I could feel that same tireless wolf-lope developing in its wheels; it was like you might never have to stop for gas, ever again.

30   The truck gets very self-focused when it works like this; its heart is strong and it's good to be around it. It's good to be *with* it. You get the same feeling when you pull someone out of a ditch. Coke High and I pulled a Volkswagen out of the mud once, but Coke didn't like doing it very much. Speed, not strength, was his center. When the guy who owned the car thanked us and tried to pat Coke, the horse snorted and swung away, trying to preserve his distance, which is something a horse spends a lot of time on.

31   So does the truck.

32   Being distant lets the truck get its heart up. The truck has been cold and alone in Montana at 38 below zero. It's climbed horrible, eroded roads in Idaho. It's been burdened beyond overloading, and made it anyway. I've asked it to do these things because they build heart, and without heart all

you have is a machine. You have nothing. I don't think people in Detroit know anything at all about heart. That's why everything they build dies so young.

One time in Arizona the truck and I came through one of the worst 33 storms I've ever been in, an outrageous, angry blizzard. But we went down the road, right through it. You couldn't explain our getting through by the sort of tires I had on the truck, or the fact that I had chains on, or was a good driver, or had a lot of weight over my drive wheels or a good engine, because it was more than this. It was a contest between the truck and the blizzard—and the truck wouldn't quit. I could have gone to sleep and the truck would have just torn a road down Interstate 40 on its own. It scared the hell out of me; but it gave me heart, too.

We came off the Mogollon Rim that night and out of the storm and 34 headed south for Phoenix. I pulled off the road to sleep for a few hours, but before I did I got out of the truck. It was raining. Warm rain. I tied a short piece of red avalanche cord into the grill. I left it there for a long time, like an eagle feather on a horse's tail. It flapped and spun in the wind. I could hear it ticking against the grill when I drove.

When I have to leave that truck I will just raise up my left arm—*Hoka* 35 *hey!*—and walk away.

Building Vocabulary

Define the words below, using *context clues* wherever possible and checking in a dictionary when necessary. Use them in sentences of your own.

coulees (3)	sweltering (27)	bolted (17)
deviate (9)	hock (8)	build heart (32)
spooked (12)	pug-faced (12)	

Journal Writing

Choose one or more of the three activities listed below, and make an entry in your journal. Focus on writing spontaneously rather than on structure and mechanics.

1. **Exploring:** Recall what you remember from other sources—your reading, your life experiences, movies and television, stories told to you by others—about the topic discussed by the writer. Choose one or two of these to write about. Which aspects of the topic did they bring up? What additional information did they provide? What emotions did they create in you?
2. **Taking Stock:** Which parts of the selection were most difficult for you to grasp? Which parts needed more explanation? Which parts required outside information to be understood? What kind of in-

formation was required (e.g., historical, culture-specific, technical, etc.)? Where might such information be found? Were there aspects of the writer's style you found particularly effective? Particularly difficult? Why?

3. **Responding:** Identify one or two of the writer's main concerns. What personal knowledge, if any, do you have of these issues? What is your opinion on these issues? Examine your response carefully to see what it teaches you about yourself.

Analyzing Content

1. Analyze the significance of the title. What is it referring to?
2. How might examining a horse give someone information about its rider?
3. Why does the writer call his vehicle a truck rather than a van (paragraph 12)? What does this indicate about his lifestyle?
4. Pick out some other details that tell us about the writer's lifestyle and values.

Analyzing Writing Techniques

1. Point out some of the **analogies** the writer makes between the truck and the horse he used to ride. What surprising similarities do we discover between the truck and the horse?
2. In several places, the writer uses the **metaphor** of "heart." Look at these passages. What does the metaphor mean?

Group Activity

Examine the writer's statement, "I could tell something about you by your horse." How far does this apply to cars? Discuss whether group members have seen or had cars that reflected the owner's personality, lifestyle, values, or culture. Make a **collaborative list** of examples.

Your Writing

1. An automobile is not the only thing that can reflect the owner's or user's personality. What other items, in your culture, may be similarly reflective? Choose one, and write an essay in which you use the techniques of **description** and **explanation**.
2. The movement from the horse to the car, as illustrated by Lopez, says something interesting about the changes that have occurred in American culture. Write an essay in which you analyze the role of the automobile in current American life and draw a general **conclusion** about today's lifestyle from it.

Pre-reading Activity   Write about a place that gives you a sense of belonging and comfort. How is it able to do this?

As You Read   Note the writer's use of **sense images** to strengthen the reasons she is presenting.

MI PUEBLO
Leticia Reyes

*Born in 1974 in Mountain View, Calif., **Leticia Reyes** was raised by a single mother who has been a strong, positive influence on her life. She is the oldest of three children and plans to major in psychology. Her interests include reading, watching people, and spending time by herself. Leticia is a student at Foothill College.*

Most ethnic groups living in America have a place that they feel embraces   1
and preserves their culture. For some, it may be a religious gathering place, such as a church or a temple. For others, it may be a place of entertainment, such as a movie theater, or it may be a restaurant where they can taste the traditional dishes they grew up with. For the Spanish-speaking community in the San Francisco Bay Area, one example of such a place is the local Mexican market, Mi Pueblo. Mi Pueblo is special because of its authentic Mexican atmosphere and the sense of community that is created as one shops with people of the same race.

As I walk into the market, I experience the warmth and comfort that   2
comes from entering a place associated with many pleasant memories. My attention is immediately drawn to the donkey-shaped piñata made of cardboard and colorful papier-mâché. The piñata, which can be made in many different shapes and sizes, ranging from a fruit to a Batman figure, is a popular object of entertainment at children's birthday parties. As I look at this one, I am reminded of my mother purchasing a watermelon piñata here many years ago and filling it with candy and small toys. On my birthday, it was hung from the tallest tree in our yard by a rope that could move it up and down, and children were blindfolded, spun around, and handed a long, wooden stick. The object was to swing the stick as hard as possible and try to break the piñata open. I still remember the piñata finally crashing down, dispersing its contents over the yard, and all the excited children rushing in to try and get the most candy.

Nothing compares to the fragrance that lingers throughout Mi Pueblo.   3
This fragrance comes from the glass cases containing the freshly made pan

dulce, or sweet bread. I can go to the Safeway store and buy similar bread there, but how can there be any comparison between the still warm, fresh-baked pan and bread that has been sitting pre-packaged on the shelf? I pick up a tray and help myself to the different varieties of pan dulce offered: animal-shaped, shell-shaped, cream-filled, etc. Later, I will pick up a chunk of chocolate Ibarra as well, for I love to eat my pan dulce with freshly made chocolate caliente, or hot chocolate. This is a habit from my childhood. I remember my mother preparing these items every weekend, breaking the slab of chocolate into small pieces and dissolving it in simmering milk, watching carefully to see that it didn't boil, then adding sugar to taste. I remember our kitchen filling with the smell of bread. Chocolate caliente and pan dulce, the Mexican equivalent to hamburger and fries. Now, living on my own, I reenact the ritual, thankful there is a Mi Pueblo where I can find the foods that reinforce my cultural inheritance.

4   Throughout the store, I'm sure to find many items common enough in Mexico but difficult to locate in the United States. Fanta, a bottled soft drink popular in Mexico, is one example. Here, under one roof, are also all the ingredients you need for the preparation of special dishes such as tamales, steamed ground corn stuffed in corn husks, or menudo, tripe soup. And if you want authentic products like queso fresca, the soft Mexican cheese, or chorizo, the spicy Mexican sausage, don't go to the American grocery chains. Even if the items are there, the quality is just not the same.

5   The music playing in the store further strengthens the atmosphere. The songs are all in Spanish, the rhythms are typically Latin, and the singers and musicians can range from Julio Iglesias to Gloria Estefan. Listening to these Latin-American artists is sure proof that I'm in Spanish-speaking territory. For a brief moment, I don't feel like a "minority" anymore but am the "majority."

6   Language, too, helps with this impression. In the store, Spanish is the dominant form of communication. The language that in many places is still not accepted is spoken here with pride. For many of the shoppers, English is a barrier, so for them, shopping here instead of at Safeway is far more comfortable. Here, it is OK for them to speak their native language. They do not have to struggle to pronounce the few English words they know, only to end up feeling foolish. They do not need to deal with scornful checkout clerks or impatient customers waiting in line behind them. And for someone like me, who speaks English fluently, it is a wonderful opportunity to use the language that my parents gave me.

7   Perhaps the most important advantage of shopping at Mi Pueblo is the feeling of community one gets through interacting with people of a similar background. Everyone seems to know everyone, and even if they don't, they are willing to talk to you, to help you with ideas or suggestions, even to give you recipes and share cooking tips. A dozen personal conversations are going on at the same time in the store. People don't mind putting off their shopping to gossip or just catch up on news. The counterperson

talks to all the customers on a personal level. Every time I go to Mi Pueblo, I am amazed at how I am constantly bumping into people I know.

For many people who pass by the store, Mi Pueblo is just another gro-   8
cery, but for me and many like me, it is part of who we are. A store like Mi Pueblo is one of the few remaining places that captures the essence of the land where we originated. It brings back a little of Mexico to people in America. For me, this is particularly significant. I was not born in Mexico, but it is still an important part of who I am. A place like Mi Pueblo allows me to connect to my culture through the food, language, and people I find here.

I believe I am not alone in feeling in this way, because all across Amer-   9
ica, Spanish-speaking communities have their own version of Mi Pueblo, which is essential to their lifestyle. Through these markets, our culture is passed down from one generation to the next. I watch mothers bringing their children to Mi Pueblo for shopping and remember when my mother used to do the same. I'm sure she never realized how important these trips were in creating an awareness and appreciation of my heritage.

Structure and Strategy

1. What is the **thesis** of the essay? Where has the writer located it? Is it reinforced in some other part of the essay?
2. **Outline** the major points of the essay. Where is the most important point placed? Is this an effective placement? Why, or why not?
3. **Underline** Reyes' **topic sentences**. Where in the paragraph do they occur? Take one of the paragraphs and rewrite it, placing the **topic sentence** elsewhere.

Your Writing

1. Write an essay about a place that is culturally significant for you. Describe the place, and explain why.
2. Write an essay in which you contrast the shopping experience at Mi Pueblo with that in a large grocery chain. What are the advantages and disadvantages of shopping at each place?

SYNTHESIS: QUESTIONS FOR CRITICAL THINKING AND WRITING

1. "My Horse" takes an old Native-American tradition and gives it modern relevance; "Kwanzaa" invents a new tradition to fit the lives of present-day African-Americans. Write an essay about a new or reinvented tradition that is significant in your life or the life of your community, and analyze the **effects** of such a tradition.
2. "They Shut My Grandmother's Room Door" and "Modern Courtesy" point out that America often differs from other cultures in how it views the world. Make a list of your own about other philosophical differences in worldview between American culture and another you know well or can research. Choose one of these topics, and develop it into an essay.
3. "They Shut My Grandmother's Room Door" deals with an important taboo in mainstream American society: the topic of death. What is another taboo topic, either in this society or in your own cultural community? Discuss the topic, and analyze the **causes** for its forbiddenness.
4. "Modern Courtesy" and "My Horse" point out that there is often a cultural conflict between the old ways and new ways, between an earlier generation and a later one. Write about another cultural conflict you have noticed, either in the mainstream culture or in a particular ethnic one. Present a **solution** to improve the situation.

Education

We learn in many ways, both inside as well as outside the classroom, and depending on who we are, we may feel very differently about the whole notion of education itself. Often, our ethnicity, race, class, or ability influences our educational experience. Sometimes, it becomes an advantage, but more often, it places us in a disadvantageous position that only a special person—an inspiring teacher, perhaps—can help us break out of.

The writers in this section explore these ideas in several unique ways. In "On Being Seventeen, Bright, and Unable to Read," David Raymond shares the challenging and often frustrating experience of being dyslexic in a system not quite equipped to deal with this difference. In "The Struggle to Be an All-American Girl," Elizabeth Wong faces a different problem of "otherness" as her parents force her to attend Chinese school, which stands for all she would rather forget about her identity.

In "My Prison Studies," Malcolm X shows how the unlikeliest places can become havens of learning, and for the unlikeliest of reasons—for him, it is the desire to write perfect letters to a man he has never met. More often, however, inspiration is direct and simple, although no less powerful. Carl T. Rowan's "Unforgettable Miss Bessie," a tribute to a high school teacher, proves this.

Some pieces in this section raise interesting, and perhaps unsettling, questions. Is this the worst of times regarding race relations on campus? asks Tom Morganthau and his coauthors as they list incident after incident of hate crimes in "Race on Campus: Failing the Test?" Student Billy McClelland points to the different approaches to problem solving in Japanese and American pre-schools and their long-reaching effects, and he makes us wonder whether our individualistic stance is always for the best. Finally, in his essay "America Needs Its Nerds," Leonid Fridman forces us to look at the low value this society sets on education and the thinking life.

Pre-reading Activity   Write about a situation in which a parent or authority figure forced you to take a class or to learn something you didn't like.

As You Read   Note the different kinds of sentence structures used by Wong—simple, compound, complex, etc.

THE STRUGGLE TO BE AN ALL-AMERICAN GIRL
Elizabeth Wong

Born in 1958, **Elizabeth Wong** *is a first-generation Chinese-American. She is a playwright and a reporter for the* Hartford Courant *and the* San Diego Tribune.

1   It's still there, the Chinese school on Yale Street where my brother and I used to go. Despite the new coat of paint and the high wire fence, the school I knew 10 years ago remains remarkably, stoically the same.

2   Every day at 5 P.M., instead of playing with our fourth- and fifth-grade friends or sneaking out to the empty lot to hunt ghosts and animal bones, my brother and I had to go to Chinese school. No amount of kicking, screaming, or pleading could dissuade my mother, who was solidly determined to have us learn the language of our heritage.

3   Forcibly, she walked us the seven long, hilly blocks from our home to school, depositing our defiant tearful faces before the stern principal. My only memory of him is that he swayed on his heels like a palm tree, and he always clasped his impatient twitching hands behind his back. I recognized him as a repressed maniacal child killer, and knew that if we ever saw his hands we'd be in big trouble.

4   We all sat in little chairs in an empty auditorium. The room smelled like Chinese medicine, an imported faraway mustiness. Like ancient mothballs or dirty closets. I hated that smell. I favored crisp new scents. Like the soft French perfume that my American teacher wore in public school.

5   There was a stage far to the right, flanked by an American flag and the flag of the Nationalist Republic of China, which was also red, white and blue but not as pretty.

6   Although the emphasis at the school was mainly language—speaking, reading, writing—the lessons always began with an exercise in politeness. With the entrance of the teacher, the best student would tap a bell and

everyone would get up, kowtow, and chant, "Sing san ho," the phonetic for "How are you, teacher?"

7   Being ten years old, I had better things to learn than ideographs copied painstakingly in lines that ran right to left from the tip of a *moc but,* a real ink pen that had to be held in an awkward way if blotches were to be avoided. After all, I could do the multiplication tables, name the satellites of Mars, and write reports on "Little Women" and "Black Beauty." Nancy Drew, my favorite book heroine, never spoke Chinese.

8   The language was a source of embarrassment. More times than not, I had tried to disassociate myself from the nagging loud voice that followed me wherever I wandered in the nearby American supermarket outside Chinatown. The voice belonged to my grandmother, a fragile woman in her seventies who could outshout the best of the street vendors. Her humor was raunchy, her Chinese rhythmless, patternless. It was quick, it was loud, it was unbeautiful. It was not like the quiet, lilting romance of French or the gentle refinement of the American South. Chinese sounded pedestrian. Public.

9   In Chinatown, the comings and goings of hundreds of Chinese on their daily tasks sounded chaotic and frenzied. I did not want to be thought of as mad, as talking gibberish. When I spoke English, people nodded at me, smiled sweetly, said encouraging words. Even the people in my culture would cluck and say that I'd do well in life. "My, doesn't she move her lips fast," they would say, meaning that I'd be able to keep up with the world outside Chinatown.

10   My brother was even more fanatical than I about speaking English. He was especially hard on my mother, criticizing her, often cruelly, for her pidgin speech—smatterings of Chinese scattered like chop suey in her conversation. "It's not 'What it is,' Mom," he'd say in exasperation. "It's 'What *is* it, what *is* it, what *is* it!' " Sometimes Mom might leave out an occasional "the" or "a," or perhaps a verb of being. He would stop her in mid-sentence: "Say it again, Mom. Say it right." When he tripped over his own tongue, he'd blame it on her: "See, Mom, it's all your fault. You set a bad example."

11   What infuriated my mother most was when my brother cornered her on her consonants, especially "r." My father had played a cruel joke on Mom by assigning her an American name that her tongue wouldn't allow her to say. No matter how hard she tried, "Ruth" always ended up "Luth" or "Roof."

12   After two years of writing with a *moc but* and reciting words with multiples of meanings, I finally was granted a cultural divorce. I was permitted to stop Chinese school.

13   I thought of myself as multicultural. I preferred tacos to egg rolls; I enjoyed Cinco de Mayo more than Chinese New Year.

14   At last, I was one of you; I wasn't one of them.

15   Sadly, I still am.

Building Vocabulary

Define the words below, using *context clues* wherever possible and checking in a dictionary when necessary. Use them in sentences of your own.

stoically (1)   raunchy (8)   ideograph (7)
defiant (3)   dissuade (2)   smatterings (10)
kowtow (6)   maniacal (3)

Journal Writing

Choose one or more of the three activities listed below, and make an entry in your journal. Focus on writing spontaneously rather than on structure and mechanics.

1. **Exploring:** Recall what you remember from other sources—your reading, your life experiences, movies and television, stories told to you by others—about the topic discussed by the writer. Choose one or two of these to write about. Which aspects of the topic did they bring up? What additional information did they provide? What emotions did they create in you?
2. **Taking Stock:** Which parts of the selection were most difficult for you to grasp? Which parts needed more explanation? Which parts required outside information to be understood? What kind of information was required (e.g., historical, culture-specific, technical, etc.)? Where might such information be found? Were there aspects of the writer's style you found particularly effective? Particularly difficult? Why?
3. **Responding:** Identify one or two of the writer's main concerns. What personal knowledge, if any, do you have of these issues? What is your opinion on these issues? Examine your response carefully to see what it teaches you about yourself.

Analyzing Content

1. **List** the reasons why the writer does not wish to go to Chinese school.
2. From the details she gives of her likes and dislikes, what can you **infer** about the writer's attitude to her culture?
3. **Compare** her descriptions of the Chinese language to her descriptions of European languages. What characteristics does each language seem to possess?
4. Are we to interpret the term *multicultural* in paragraph 13 in a positive or a negative way? Why?

Analyzing Writing Techniques

1. Cite some examples, from the text, of **similes** and **metaphors**. What **tone** do they help to create?
2. Who is the audience of the essay? Which sentence gives us the clearest sense of this?
3. Where is the **thesis** of this essay placed? Where is it **foreshadowed**?

Group Activity

Discuss the term *All-American*. What does it mean to the members of your group? How far do group members consider themselves "All-American"? Generate a **group list** of physical and mental qualities associated with an "All-American" person. Is there an irony in the epithet?

Your Writing

1. Think back to a situation in which you, or someone you know, felt uncomfortable about or ashamed of an aspect of your culture. Describe the situation, and **analyze** how the negative emotions were created. (You may choose, alternately, to examine another reading from the book that deals with this idea.)
2. This essay indicates that a change has occurred in Wong's attitude toward the "cultural divorce" she fought to obtain when she was younger. What is her new, "re-educated" attitude? Write an essay exploring the reasons such a change may occur.

Pre-reading Activity   Write about a teacher who left a strong impression on you. Discuss what you learned from this person.

As You Read   Underline all of the **allusions** to other writers in this piece. How many are you familiar with? Look up the rest.

UNFORGETTABLE MISS BESSIE
Carl T. Rowan

Born in 1925, **Carl T. Rowan** *grew up in Tennessee and was educated at Oberlin College and the University of Minnesota. He has been a colum-nist for the* Minneapolis Tribune, *the* Chicago Sun-Times, *and* Reader's Di-gest. *He is a former ambassador to Finland and was director of the United States Information Agency.*

She was only about five feet tall and probably never weighed more than   1
110 pounds, but Miss Bessie was a towering presence in the classroom.
She was the only woman tough enough to make me read *Beowulf* and
think for a few foolish days that I liked it. From 1938 to 1942, when I attended Bernard High School in McMinnville, Tenn., she taught me English, history, civics—and a lot more than I realized.

   I shall never forget the day she scolded me into reading *Beowulf*.   2
   "But Miss Bessie," I complained, "I ain't much interested in it."   3
   Her large brown eyes became daggerish slits. "Boy," she said, "how   4
dare you say 'ain't' to me! I've taught you better than that."
   "Miss Bessie," I pleaded, "I'm trying to make first-string end on the foot-   5
ball team, and if I go around saying 'it isn't' and 'they aren't,' the guys are
gonna laugh me off the squad."
   "Boy," she responded, "you'll play football because you have guts. But   6
do you know what *really* takes guts? Refusing to lower your standards to
those of the crowd. It takes guts to say you've got to live and be somebody
fifty years after all the football games are over."
   I started saying "it isn't" and "they aren't," and I still made first-string   7
end—and class valedictorian—without losing my buddies' respect.
   During her remarkable 44-year career, Mrs. Bessie Taylor Gwynn   8
taught hundreds of economically deprived black youngsters—including
my mother, my brother, my sisters and me. I remember her now with grat-
itude and affection—especially in this era when Americans are so wrought-
up about a "rising tide of mediocrity" in public education and the prob-

lems of finding competent, caring teachers. Miss Bessie was an example of an informed, dedicated teacher, a blessing to children and an asset to the nation.

9   Born in 1895, in poverty, she grew up in Athens, Ala., where there was no public school for blacks. She attended Trinity School, a private institution for blacks run by the American Missionary Association, and in 1911 graduated from the Normal School (a "super" high school) at Fisk University in Nashville. Mrs. Gwynn, the essence of pride and privacy, never talked about her years in Athens; only in the months before her death did she reveal that she had never attended Fisk University itself because she could not afford the four-year course.

10   At Normal School she learned a lot about Shakespeare, but most of all about the profound importance of education—especially, for a people trying to move up from slavery. "What you put in your head, boy," she once said, "can never be pulled out by the Ku Klux Klan, the Congress or anybody."

11   Miss Bessie's bearing of dignity told anyone who met her that she was "educated" in the best sense of the word. There was never a discipline problem in her classes. We didn't dare mess with a woman who knew about the Battle of Hastings, the Magna Carta and the Bill of Rights—and who could also play the piano.

12   This frail-looking woman could make sense of Shakespeare, Milton, Voltaire, and bring to life Booker T. Washington and W. E. B. DuBois. Believing that it was important to know who the officials were that spent taxpayers' money and made public policy, she made us memorize the names of everyone on the Supreme Court and in the President's Cabinet. It could be embarrassing to be unprepared when Miss Bessie said, "Get up and tell the class who Frances Perkins is and what you think about her."

13   Miss Bessie knew that my family, like so many others during the Depression, couldn't afford to subscribe to a newspaper. She knew we didn't even own a radio. Still, she prodded me to "look out for your future and find some way to keep up with what's going on in the world." So I became a delivery boy for the Chattanooga *Times.* I rarely made a dollar a week, but I got to read a newspaper every day.

14   Miss Bessie noticed things that had nothing to do with schoolwork, but were vital to a youngster's development. Once a few classmates made fun of my frayed, hand-me-down overcoat, calling me "Strings." As I was leaving school, Miss Bessie patted me on the back of that old overcoat and said, "Carl, never fret about what you *don't* have. Just make the most of what you *do* have—a brain."

15   Among the things that I did not have was electricity in the little frame house that my father had built for $400 with his World War I bonus. But because of her inspiration, I spent many hours squinting beside a kerosene lamp reading Shakespeare and Thoreau, Samuel Pepys and William Cullen Bryant.

No one in my family had ever graduated from high school, so there   16
was no tradition of commitment to learning for me to lean on. Like millions of youngsters in today's ghettos and barrios, I needed the push and
stimulation of a teacher who truly cared. Miss Bessie gave plenty of both,
as she immersed me in a wonderful world of similes, metaphors and even
onomatopoeia. She led me to believe that I could write sonnets as well as
Shakespeare, or iambic-pentameter verse to put Alexander Pope to shame.

In those days the McMinnville school system was rigidly "Jim Crow,"   17
and poor black children had to struggle to put anything in their heads. Our
high school was only slightly larger than the once-typical little red schoolhouse, and its library was outrageously inadequate—so small, I like to say,
that if two students were in it and one wanted to turn a page, the other one
had to step outside.

Negroes, as we were called then, were not allowed in the town library,   18
except to mop floors or dust tables. But through one of those secret Old
South arrangements between whites of conscience and blacks of stature,
Miss Bessie kept getting books smuggled out of the white library. That is
how she introduced me to the Brontës, Byron, Coleridge, Keats and Ten-
nyson. "If you don't read, you can't write, and if you can't write, you might
as well stop dreaming," Miss Bessie once told me.

So I read whatever Miss Bessie told me to, and tried to remember the   19
things she insisted that I store away. Forty-five years later, I can still recite
her "truths to live by," such as Henry Wadsworth Longfellow's lines from
"The Ladder of St. Augustine":

The heights by great men reached and kept   20
Were not attained by sudden flight.
But they, while their companions slept,
Were toiling upward in the night.

Years later, her inspiration, prodding, anger, cajoling and almost os-   21
motic infusion of learning finally led to that lovely day when Miss Bessie
dropped me a note saying, "I'm so proud to read your column in the
Nashville *Tennessean.*"

Miss Bessie was a spry 80 when I went back to McMinnville and vis-   22
ited her in a senior citizens' apartment building. Pointing out proudly that
her building was racially integrated, she reached for two glasses and a pint
of bourbon. I was momentarily shocked, because it would have been
scandalous in the 1930s and '40s for word to get out that a teacher drank,
and nobody had ever raised a rumor that Miss Bessie did.

I felt a new sense of equality as she lifted her glass to mine. Then she   23
revealed a softness and compassion that I had never known as a student.

"I've never forgotten that examination day," she said, "when Buster   24
Martin held up seven fingers, obviously asking you for help with question
number seven, 'Name a common carrier.' I can still picture you looking at

your exam paper and humming a few bars of 'Chattanooga Choo Choo.' I was so tickled, I couldn't punish either of you."

25   Miss Bessie was telling me, with bourbon-laced grace, that I never fooled her for a moment.

26   When Miss Bessie died in 1980, at age 85, hundreds of her former students mourned. They knew the measure of a great teacher: love and motivation. Her wisdom and influence had rippled out across generations.

27   Some of her students who might normally have been doomed to poverty went on to become doctors, dentists and college professors. Many, guided by Miss Bessie's example, became public-school teachers.

28   "The memory of Miss Bessie and how she conducted her classroom did more for me than anything I learned in college," recalls Gladys Wood of Knoxville, Tenn., a highly respected English teacher who spent 43 years in the state's school system. "So many times, when I faced a difficult classroom problem, I asked myself, *How would Miss Bessie deal with this?* And I'd remember that she would handle it with laughter and love."

29   No child can get all the necessary support at home, and millions of poor children get *no* support at all. This is what makes a wise, educated, warm-hearted teacher like Miss Bessie so vital to the minds, hearts and souls of this country's children.

Building Vocabulary

Define the words below, using *context clues* wherever possible and checking in a dictionary when necessary. Use them in sentences of your own.

towering (1)	osmotic (21)	stature (18)
profound (10)	mediocrity (8)	scandalous (22)
barrios (16)	prodded (13)	

Journal Writing

Choose one or more of the three activities listed below, and make an entry in your journal. Focus on writing spontaneously rather than on structure and mechanics.

1. **Exploring:** Recall what you remember from other sources—your reading, your life experiences, movies and television, stories told to you by others—about the topic discussed by the writer. Choose one or two of these to write about. Which aspects of the topic did they bring up? What additional information did they provide? What emotions did they create in you?

2. **Taking Stock:** Which parts of the selection were most difficult for you to grasp? Which parts needed more explanation? Which parts required outside information to be understood? What kind of information was required (e.g., historical, culture-specific, technical, etc.)? Where might such information be found? Were there aspects of the writer's style you found particularly effective? Particularly difficult? Why?

3. **Responding:** Identify one or two of the writer's main concerns. What personal knowledge, if any, do you have of these issues? What is your opinion on these issues? Examine your response carefully to see what it teaches you about yourself.

Analyzing Content

1. What is the first lesson that Miss Bessie teaches the writer? How is it typical of all the other things he learns from her?

2. How does Miss Bessie get around some of the difficulties of the racially segregated system in which her students grew up?

3. In what way does she inspire the writer to overcome his financial handicap? Give examples.

4. **Summarize** the statement made by Miss Bessie's former student in paragraph 27. What does it tell us about the teacher?

Analyzing Writing Techniques

1. The piece is made up of several **anecdotes. Define** an anecdote, and pick out two that you consider strongest in the piece. What does an anecdote add to an essay?

2. Find some **transition terms** used in this essay. What relationship between ideas does each one indicate?

Group Activity

Discuss the qualities of a good teacher. Have each member of the group supply a quality that he or she thinks is central to good teaching, and explain why. Combine all these qualities into a **collaborative paragraph**.

Your Writing

1. What did Miss Bessie mean when she said, "If you can't write, you might as well stop dreaming" (paragraph 18)? How far do you agree with this idea? Looking at the lives of successful and un-

successful people around you, write an essay in which you explore this concept about the importance of writing.

2. As this piece illustrates, there are many ways a teacher can inspire students, both in and out of the classroom. Write a **process essay** titled "How to Inspire Students" in which you analyze several of the ways presented by Rowan as well as some ideas of your own. Try to use **anecdotes** to support your points.

Pre-reading Activity Think back on a situation in which you, or someone you know, was set apart from the crowd because of a "problem," a difference, or a handicap. Describe the situation.

As You Read Note the conversational **tone** of this piece. How is it created?

ON BEING SEVENTEEN, BRIGHT, AND UNABLE TO READ
David Raymond

David Raymond has dealt with dyslexia all his life. He wrote this essay, which first appeared in the New York Times *in 1976, while still in high school.*

One day a substitute teacher picked me to read aloud from the textbook. 1
When I told her, "No, thank you," she came unhinged. She thought I was acting smart, and told me so. I kept calm, and that got her madder and madder. We must have spent ten minutes trying to solve the problem, and finally she got so red in the face I thought she'd blow up. She told me she'd see me after class.

Maybe someone like me was a new thing for that teacher. But she 2
wasn't new to me. I've been through scenes like that all my life. You see, even though I'm seventeen and a junior in high school, I can't read because I have dyslexia. I'm told I read "at a fourth-grade level," but from where I sit, that's not reading. You can't know what that means unless you've been there. It's not easy to tell how it feels when you can't read your homework assignments or the newspaper or a menu in a restaurant or even notes from your own friends.

My family began to suspect I was having problems almost from the 3
first day I started school. My father says my early years in school were the worst years of his life. They weren't so good for me, either. As I look back on it now, I can't find the words to express how bad it really was. I wanted to die. I'd come home from school screaming, "I'm dumb. I'm dumb—I wish I were dead!"

I guess I couldn't read anything at all then—not even my own name— 4
and they tell me I didn't talk as good as other kids. But what I remember about those days is that I couldn't throw a ball where it was supposed to go, I couldn't learn to swim, and I wouldn't learn to ride a bike, because no matter what anyone told me, I knew I'd fail.

5   Sometimes my teachers would try to be encouraging. When I couldn't read the words on the board they'd say, "Come on, David, you know that word." Only I didn't. And it was embarrassing. I just felt dumb. And dumb was how the kids treated me. They'd make fun of me every chance they got, asking me to spell "cat" or something like that. Even if I knew how to spell it, I wouldn't; they'd only give me another word. Anyway, it was awful, because more than anything I wanted friends. On my birthday when I blew out the candles I didn't wish I could learn to read; what I wished for was that the kids would like me.

6   With the bad reports coming from school, and with me moaning about wanting to die and how everybody hated me, my parents began looking for help. That's when the testing started. The school tested me, the child guidance center tested me, private psychiatrists tested me. Everybody knew something was wrong—especially me.

7   It didn't help much when they stuck a fancy name onto it. I couldn't pronounce it then—I was only in second grade—and I was ashamed to talk about it. Now it rolls off my tongue, because I've been living with it for a lot of years—dyslexia.

8   All through elementary school it wasn't easy. I was always having to do things that were "different," things the other kids didn't have to do. I had to go to a child psychiatrist, for instance.

9   One summer my family forced me to go to a camp for children with reading problems. I hated the idea, but the camp turned out pretty good, and I had a good time. I met a lot of kids who couldn't read and somehow that helped. The director of the camp said I had a higher IQ than 90 percent of the population. I didn't believe him.

10   About the worst thing I had to do in fifth and sixth grade was go to a special education class in another school in our town. A bus picked me up, and I didn't like that at all. The bus also picked up emotionally disturbed kids and retarded kids. It was like going to a school for the retarded. I always worried that someone I knew would see me on that bus. It was a relief to go to the regular junior high school.

11   Life began to change a little for me then, because I began to feel better about myself. I found the teachers cared; they had meetings about me and I worked harder for them for a while. I began to work on the potter's wheel, making vases and pots that the teachers said were pretty good. Also, I got a letter for being on the track team. I could always run pretty fast.

12   At high school the teachers are good and everyone is trying to help me. I've gotten honors some marking periods and I've won a letter on the cross-country team. Next quarter I think the school might hold a show of my pottery. I've got some friends. But there are still some embarrassing times. For instance, every time there is writing in the class, I get up and go to the special education room. Kids ask me where I go all the time. Sometimes I say, "To Mars."

13   Homework is a real problem. During free periods in school I go into the special ed room and staff members read assignments to me. When I get home

my mother reads to me. Sometimes she reads an assignment into a tape recorder and then I go into my room and listen to it. If we have a novel or something like that to read, she reads it out loud to me. Then I sit down with her and we do the assignment. She'll write, while I talk my answers to her. Lately, I've taken to dictating into a tape recorder, and then someone—my father, a private tutor or my mother—types up what I've dictated. Whatever homework I do takes someone else's time, too. That makes me feel bad.

We had a big meeting in school the other day—eight of us, four from   14 the guidance department, my private tutor, my parents and me. The subject was me. I said I wanted to go to college, and they told me about colleges that have facilities and staff to handle people like me. That's nice to hear.

As for what happens after college, I don't know and I'm worried about   15 that. How can I make a living if I can't read? Who will hire me? How will I fill out the application form?

The only thing that gives me any courage is the fact that I've learned   16 about well-known people who couldn't read or had other problems and still made it. Like Albert Einstein, who didn't talk until he was four and flunked math. Like Leonardo da Vinci, who everyone seems to think had dyslexia.

I've told this story because maybe some teacher will read it and go   17 easy on a kid in the classroom who has what I've got. Or maybe some parent will stop nagging his kid, and stop calling him lazy. Maybe he's not lazy or dumb. Maybe he just can't read and doesn't know what's wrong. Maybe he's scared, like I was.

Building Vocabulary

Define the words below, using *context clues* wherever possible and checking in a dictionary when necessary. Use them in sentences of your own.

unhinged (1)   psychiatrists (6)   dictated (13)
IQ (9)   retarded (10)   facilities (14)

Journal Writing

Choose one or more of the three activities listed below, and make an entry in your journal. Focus on writing spontaneously rather than on structure and mechanics.

1. **Exploring:** Recall what you remember from other sources—your reading, your life experiences, movies and television, stories told to you by others—about the topic discussed by the writer. Choose one or two of these to write about. Which aspects of the topic did they bring up? What additional information did they provide? What emotions did they create in you?

2. **Taking Stock:** Which parts of the selection were most difficult for you to grasp? Which parts needed more explanation? Which parts required outside information to be understood? What kind of information was required (e.g., historical, culture-specific, technical, etc.)? Where might such information be found? Were there aspects of the writer's style you found particularly effective? Particularly difficult? Why?

3. **Responding:** Identify one or two of the writer's main concerns. What personal knowledge, if any, do you have of these issues? What is your opinion on these issues? Examine your response carefully to see what it teaches you about yourself.

Analyzing Content

1. How did being dyslexic affect the writer's self-image?
2. **Classify** the different kinds of responses educators had to the writer's problem.
3. Once he was diagnosed as being dyslexic, what activities did he have to undertake? How did he feel about this?
4. What is one fact that gives the writer courage?

Analyzing Writing Techniques

1. In many places in this piece, the writer uses **slang. Define** *slang,* and pick out some examples. What does it add to, or take away from, the piece?
2. What is the underlying **purpose** of the essay? Where is this stated?

Group Activity

Have each member of the group take on a **role** that the writer discusses: teachers, parents, other students, and the dyslexic person. Each person should write a paragraph from the point of view of his or her chosen character, discussing emotions as well as practical difficulties, and read it to the group for further discussion.

Your Writing

1. Research a learning problem *other than* dyslexia, including a description of the problem, its effects, and what kinds of help is available for people suffering from it. Write a **report** based on your findings.
2. This essay demonstrates that a teacher's negative attitude can leave lasting impressions on a student's psyche. Write a **letter** to the teacher in paragraph 1 explaining this, choosing several examples from the text and adding others from your own observation and experience.

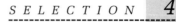

Pre-reading Activity　Consider the title. What do you think the writer means by it? How far do you agree with the statement?

As You Read　Note the **comparison/contrast** techniques used by the writer throughout the essay.

AMERICA NEEDS ITS NERDS
Leonid Fridman

Leonid Fridman *studied mathematics at Harvard University and was the founder of the Society of Nerds and Geeks.*

There is something very wrong with the system of values in a society that has only derogatory terms like nerd and geek for the intellectually curious and academically serious.　1

A geek, according to "Webster's New World Dictionary," is a street performer who shocks the public by biting off heads of live chickens. It is a telling fact about our language and our culture that someone dedicated to pursuit of knowledge is compared to a freak biting the head off a live chicken.　2

Even at a prestigious academic institution like Harvard, anti-intellectualism is rampant: Many students are ashamed to admit, even to their friends, how much they study. Although most students try to keep up their grades, there is but a minority of undergraduates for whom pursuing knowledge is the top priority during their years at Harvard. Nerds are ostracized while athletes are idolized.　3

The same thing happens in U.S. elementary and high schools. Children who prefer to read books rather than play football, prefer to build model airplanes rather than get wasted at parties with their classmates, become social outcasts. Ostracized for their intelligence and refusal to conform to society's anti-intellectual values, many are deprived of a chance to learn adequate social skills and acquire good communication tools.　4

Enough is enough.　5

Nerds and geeks must stop being ashamed of who they are. It is high time to face the persecutors who haunt the bright kid with thick glasses from kindergarten to the grave. For America's sake, the anti-intellectual values that pervade our society must be fought.　6

There are very few countries in the world where anti-intellectualism runs as high in popular culture as it does in the U.S. In most industrialized nations, not least of all our economic rivals in East Asia, a kid who studies hard is lauded and held up as an example to other students.　7

8   In many parts of the world, university professorships are the most prestigious and materially rewarding positions. But not in America, where average professional ballplayers are much more respected and better paid than faculty members of the best universities.

9   How can a country where typical parents are ashamed of their daughter studying mathematics instead of going dancing, or of their son reading Weber while his friends play baseball, be expected to compete in the technology race with Japan or remain a leading political and cultural force in Europe? How long can America remain a world-class power if we constantly emphasize social skills and physical prowess over academic achievement and intellectual ability?

10   Do we really expect to stay afloat largely by importing our scientists and intellectuals from abroad, as we have done for a major portion of this century, without making an effort to also cultivate a pro-intellectual culture at home? Even if we have the political will to spend substantially more money on education than we do now, do we think we can improve our schools if we deride our studious pupils and debase their impoverished teachers?

11   Our fault lies not so much with our economy or with our politics as within ourselves, our values and our image of a good life. America's culture has not adapted to the demands of our times, to the economic realities that demand a highly educated workforce and innovative intelligent leadership.

12   If we are to succeed as a society in the 21st century, we had better shed our anti-intellectualism and imbue in our children the vision that a good life is impossible without stretching one's mind and pursuing knowledge to the full extent of one's abilities.

13   And until the words "nerd" and "geek" become terms of approbation and not derision, we do not stand a chance.

Building Vocabulary

Define the words below, using *context clues* wherever possible and checking in a dictionary when necessary. Use them in sentences of your own.

derogatory (1)	prowess (9)	anti-intellectualism (3)
rampant (3)	approbation (13)	persecutors (6)
idolized (3)	dedicated (2)	deride (10)

Journal Writing

Choose one or more of the three activities listed below, and make an entry in your journal. Focus on writing spontaneously rather than on structure and mechanics.

1. **Exploring:** Recall what you remember from other sources—your reading, your life experiences, movies and television, stories told to you by others—about the topic discussed by the writer. Choose one or two of these to write about. Which aspects of the topic did they bring up? What additional information did they provide? What emotions did they create in you?
2. **Taking Stock:** Which parts of the selection were most difficult for you to grasp? Which parts needed more explanation? Which parts required outside information to be understood? What kind of information was required (e.g., historical, culture-specific, technical, etc.)? Where might such information be found? Were there aspects of the writer's style you found particularly effective? Particularly difficult? Why?
3. **Responding:** Identify one or two of the writer's main concerns. What personal knowledge, if any, do you have of these issues? What is your opinion on these issues? Examine your response carefully to see what it teaches you about yourself.

Analyzing Content

1. What does the writer believe to be a major problem in America's attitude toward intellectuals?
2. List the examples he provides to support his point.
3. Which other countries does he bring into his argument? How does this strengthen his position?
4. What are the "economic realities" he refers to in paragraph 11? Use your own ideas and observations to support his claims.

Analyzing Writing Techniques

1. Analyze the **diction** of the essay. What is the general level of the vocabulary used? Why are slang terms such as *nerd* and *geek* included?
2. What is the writer's **intention** in this essay? **Outline** the arguments he uses to achieve these intentions.

Group Activity

Make a group list of the highest-paid jobs in American society today, using **research** tools if necessary. Do your findings support Fridman's thesis? Why, or why not?

Your Writing

1. One of the related problems the writer points out is that educators in the United States are not adequately valued, either monetarily

or through prestige (paragraphs 8 and 10). Write an essay in which you explore this topic, using **statistics** to support your opinion.

2. In paragraphs 11 and 12, the writer brings up the idea of the "good life." **Define** what you understand by the "good life." What, in your opinion, is the relationship between the "good life," education, and an "intellectual" approach to things?

Pre-reading Activity   Describe an event in your life that inspired you to learn something.

As You Read   Note the writer's use of descriptive detail. What effect does it have on you?

MY PRISON STUDIES
Malcolm X

Malcolm X (1925–1965) was born in Nebraska as Malcolm Little, but he changed his name when he joined the Black Muslims, a militant group led by Elijah Muhammad. He advanced to a position of power within the group but later, disillusioned with certain aspects of it, established a separate organization of his own. Soon afterward, he was assasinated. Malcolm X was one of the strongest proponents of black power and black nationalism. The excerpt below is taken from The Autobiography of Malcolm X, *which was coauthored by Alex Haley.*

It was because of my letters that I happened to stumble upon starting to acquire some kind of a homemade education.   1

I became increasingly frustrated at not being able to express what I wanted to convey in letters that I wrote, especially those to Mr. Elijah Muhammad. In the street, I had been the most articulate hustler out there—I had commanded attention when I said something. But now, trying to write simple English, I not only wasn't articulate, I wasn't even functional. How would I sound writing in slang, the way I would *say* it, something such as, "Look, daddy, let me pull your coat about a cat, Elijah Muhammad—"   2

Many who today hear me somewhere in person, or on television, or those who read something I've said, will think I went to school far beyond the eighth grade. This impression is due entirely to my prison studies.   3

It had really begun back in the Charlestown Prison, when Bimbi first made me feel envy of his stock of knowledge. Bimbi had always taken charge of any conversation he was in, and I had tried to emulate him. But every book I picked up had few sentences which didn't contain anywhere from one to nearly all of the words that might as well have been in Chinese. When I just skipped those words, of course, I really ended up with little idea of what the book said. So I had come to the Norfolk Prison Colony still going through only book-reading motions. Pretty soon, I would have quit even these motions, unless I had received the motivation that I did.   4

5   I saw that the best thing I could do was get hold of a dictionary—to study, to learn some words. I was lucky enough to reason also that I should try to improve my penmanship. It was sad. I couldn't even write in a straight line. It was both ideas together that moved me to request a dictionary along with some tablets and pencils from the Norfolk Prison Colony school.

6   I spent two days just riffling uncertainly through the dictionary's pages. I'd never realized so many words existed! I didn't know *which* words I needed to learn. Finally, just to start some kind of action, I began copying.

7   In my slow, painstaking, ragged handwriting, I copied into my tablet everything printed on that first page, down to the punctuation marks.

8   I believe it took me a day. Then, aloud, I read back, to myself, everything I'd written on the tablet. Over and over, aloud, to myself, I read my own handwriting.

9   I woke up the next morning, thinking about those words—immensely proud to realize that not only had I written so much at one time, but I'd written words that I never knew were in the world. Moreover, with a little effort, I also could remember what many of these words meant. I reviewed the words whose meanings I didn't remember. Funny thing, from the dictionary first page right now, that "aardvark" springs to my mind. The dictionary had a picture of it, a long-tailed, long-eared, burrowing African mammal, which lives off termites caught by sticking out its tongue as an anteater does for ants.

10   I was so fascinated that I went on—I copied the dictionary's next page. And the same experience came when I studied that. With every succeeding page, I also learned of people and places and events from history. Actually the dictionary is like a miniature encyclopedia. Finally the dictionary's A section had filled a whole tablet—and I went on into the B's. That was the way I started copying what eventually became the entire dictionary. It went a lot faster after so much practice helped me to pick up handwriting speed. Between what I wrote in my tablet, and writing letters, during the rest of my time in prison I would guess I wrote a million words.

11   I suppose it was inevitable that as my word-base broadened, I could for the first time pick up a book and read and now begin to understand what the book was saying. Anyone who has read a great deal can imagine the new world that opened. Let me tell you something: from then until I left that prison, in every free moment I had, if I was not reading in the library, I was reading on my bunk. You couldn't have gotten me out of books with a wedge. Between Mr. Muhammad's teachings, my correspondence, my visitors—usually Ella and Reginald—and my reading of books, months passed without my even thinking about being imprisoned. In fact, up to then, I never had been so truly free in my life.

12   The Norfolk Prison Colony's library was in the school building. A variety of classes was taught there by instructors who came from such places as Harvard and Boston universities. The weekly debates between inmate

teams were also held in the school building. You would be astonished to know how worked up convict debaters and audiences would get over subjects like "Should Babies Be Fed Milk?"

Available on the prison library's shelves were books on just about every general subject. Much of the big private collection that Parkhurst had willed to the prison was still in crates and boxes in the back of the library—thousands of old books. Some of them looked ancient: covers faded, old-time parchment-looking binding. Parkhurst, I've mentioned, seemed to have been principally interested in history and religion. He had the money and the special interest to have a lot of books that you wouldn't have in general circulation. Any college library would have been lucky to get that collection.   13

As you can imagine, especially in a prison where there was heavy emphasis on rehabilitation, an inmate was smiled upon if he demonstrated an unusually intense interest in books. There was a sizable number of well-read inmates, especially the popular debaters. Some were said by many to be practically walking encyclopedias. They were almost celebrities. No university would ask any student to devour literature as I did when this new world opened to me, of being able to read and *understand.*   14

I read more in my room than in the library itself. An inmate who was known to read a lot could check out more than the permitted maximum number of books. I preferred reading in the total isolation of my own room.   15

When I had progressed to really serious reading, every night at about ten P.M. I would be outraged with the "lights out." It always seemed to catch me right in the middle of something engrossing.   16

Fortunately, right outside my door was a corridor light that cast a glow into my room. The glow was enough to read by, once my eyes adjusted to it. So when "lights out" came, I would sit on the floor where I could continue reading in that glow.   17

At one-hour intervals the night guards paced past every room. Each time I heard the approaching footsteps, I jumped into bed and feigned sleep. And as soon as the guard passed, I got back out of bed onto the floor area of that light-glow, where I would read for another fifty-eight minutes—until the guard approached again. That went on until three or four every morning. Three or four hours of sleep a night was enough for me. Often in the years in the streets I had slept less than that.   18

Every time I catch a plane, I have with me a book that I want to read—and that's a lot of books these days. If I weren't out here every day battling the white man, I could spend the rest of my life reading, just satisfying my curiosity—because you can hardly mention anything I'm not curious about. I don't think anybody ever got more out of going to prison than I did. In fact, prison enabled me to study far more intensively than I would have if my life had gone differently and I had attended some college. I   19 imagine that one of the biggest troubles with colleges is there are too many distractions, too much panty-raiding, fraternities, and boola-boola and all of that. Where else but in a prison could I have attacked my ignorance by being able to study intensely sometimes as much as fifteen hours a day?

Building Vocabulary

Define the words below, using *context clues* wherever possible and checking in a dictionary when necessary. Use them in sentences of your own.

penmanship (5)	afflicting (18)	dormant (18)
painstaking (7)	riffling (6)	alma mater (18)
feigned (18)	inevitable (11)	

Journal Writing

Choose one or more of the three activities listed below, and make an entry in your journal. Focus on writing spontaneously rather than on structure and mechanics.

1. **Exploring:** Recall what you remember from other sources—your reading, your life experiences, movies and television, stories told to you by others—about the topic discussed by the writer. Choose one or two of these to write about. Which aspects of the topic did they bring up? What additional information did they provide? What emotions did they create in you?
2. **Taking Stock:** Which parts of the selection were most difficult for you to grasp? Which parts needed more explanation? Which parts required outside information to be understood? What kind of information was required (e.g., historical, culture-specific, technical, etc.)? Where might such information be found? Were there aspects of the writer's style you found particularly effective? Particularly difficult? Why?
3. **Responding:** Identify one or two of the writer's main concerns. What personal knowledge, if any, do you have of these issues? What is your opinion on these issues? Examine your response carefully to see what it teaches you about yourself.

Analyzing Content

1. Why did Malcolm X decide to educate himself? What did he realize about the nature of language?
2. How did he begin his education? From the details given in this excerpt, what do we learn of his character?

3. Explain his statement in paragraph 10, "Up to then, I never had been so truly free in my life." Why is this **ironic**?
4. Why does the writer feel that he learned more in prison than he would have at a regular college?

Analyzing Writing Techniques

1. What effect does the early inclusion of slang in this excerpt have on the reader? How does it support the writer's argument?
2. What is the **thesis** of the piece? Where is it most explicitly stated? **Paraphrase** it in your own words.

Group Activity

Have each member in the group write a paragraph about a significant educational experience he or she had *outside of* a classroom setting. Read and discuss the pieces, then write a **collaborative** paragraph about the kind of learning experiences one can gain "out in the world."

Your Writing

1. Taking some of the ideas from the **group activity** assignment, write an essay **comparing/contrasting** the kind of education one gains in an educational institute with that one gains outside such an institute. What are the strengths of each kind of education? Be sure to support with specific detail.
2. Malcolm X's life demonstrates that the most unexpected events or people may turn our life around. **Research** the life of another public figure for whom this is true, and write a paper in which you demonstrate clearly how the change was **caused**.

Pre-reading Activity Describe the student population of your campus. How diverse is it in terms of race?

As You Read List the racial incidents mentioned in the piece, and observe how they are organized. In which paragraph do most of them occur? Why?

RACE ON CAMPUS: FAILING THE TEST?
Tom Morganthau with Marcus Mabry, Laura Genao, and Frank Washington

Tom Morganthau *writes regularly for* Newsweek, *in which this piece first appeared in 1991.*

1   The real truth about race relations on college campuses today is that they have never been better—and that they are, as Ohio State University student Sheron Smith puts it, "Terrible. Horrid. Stinky!" Got it? This is the best of times, the worst of times and, without doubt, the noisiest of times in America's long march toward equal opportunity in higher education. Almost everyone, it seems, is mad about something: racial slurs, affirmative action, separatism, multiculturalism or the tyranny of manners that is known as the PC ("politically correct") movement. The lofty notion of college campuses as havens of tolerance, free inquiry and reasoned discourse seems as archaic as panty raids. "I lament the loss of civility and accommodation," sighs Marjorie Garber, associate dean for affirmative action at Harvard. "It's not 'fascistic' or 'politically correct' to be aware of others' sensitivities. Think, with imagination, of others. Think of how what you're saying will be heard."

2   But good advice is rarely heeded, even at Harvard. . . . The nation's oldest university has been transfixed by one of the more perverse and complex controversies of a contentious academic year—a brouhaha over symbolic speech in the form of a Confederate flag. It began when Brigit Kerrigan, a senior from Great Falls, Va., displayed the Stars and Bars from the window of her dormitory room. Kerrigan, insisting that the flag was merely a statement of regional pride, steadfastly resisted pressure from fellow students and university officials to take it down. The university, recognizing the legal and political pitfalls of cracking down on a student's First Amendment rights, declined to compel her. And this impasse led Jacinda Townsend, 19, a junior from Bowling Green, Ky., to hang a bedsheet spray-painted with a swastika from *her* dormitory window. "I wanted peo-

ple to know what the Confederate flag really means," she said. "I don't see it so much as a part of free speech, but as a threat of violence."

The battle of the symbols continued until Townsend, succumbing to protests from Jewish students and criticism from the Harvard Black Students Association, finally removed the swastika bedsheet. Kerrigan's Confederate flag, on the other hand, remains defiantly in view, and it is worth considering her motives in touching off this *opéra-bouffe* dispute. Kerrigan is a conservative activist, and she seems to want to give Harvard's liberal sensibilities a vigorous neocon tweak. "If they talk about 'diversity,' they're gonna get it," she told The Boston Globe. "If they talk about tolerance, they'd better be ready to have it."

You could make the case that the race-relations debate now buffeting many U.S. colleges and universities is like the flag war at Harvard—a shadow play, for the most part harmless, of larger social conflicts. But the analogy is probably wrong. There are real stakes, real losses and real victims as schools all over the country struggle to negotiate the kind of social accommodations that most Americans avoid. The catchword for all this— Kerrigan is exactly right—is "diversity," and like all bureaucratic euphemisms, it covers a multitude of sins. . . . Diversity is achieved, in the bare statistical sense; by including minority students and teachers in the university community. But the *ethos* of diversity, which is tolerance and mutual respect, is much harder to come by—and there is ample evidence that the grand experiment in race relations may be failing. It is like a college mixer where no one mixes—and it is leading, in the view of Troy Duster, a Berkeley sociologist, to the "balkanization" of campus life.

Tension between the races is, of course, nothing new on campus. What *is* new, and surpassingly ugly, is the apparent rise in racial incidents of all sorts—name-calling, scapegoating, accusations and recriminations. There are no truly comprehensive statistics. But Adele Terrell, program director of the National Institute against Prejudice and Violence at the University of Maryland's Baltimore campus, says one in five black students reports some form of racial harassment and that racist episodes have been reported at more than 300 colleges and universities over the past five years. An incident at Ohio State . . . is a depressing example. A woman graduate student claimed she had been raped by a black student. She later recanted her story, but the case led to altercations between campus police and black students and a series of student confrontations along racial lines. "There is some very serious tension," an OSU official concedes. "It seems to be a national trend."

He may be right. The list of name schools that have been rocked by race-related controversies in recent years includes Yale, Brown, Penn State, Georgetown, the University of Texas, the University of Michigan and many others. At Yale, 10 black law students received anonymous "nigger" notes in their dormitory mailboxes after a reported rape last fall; not long afterward, eight black undergraduates got into a dispute at a local pizza parlor that further roiled the waters. A Georgetown University law student, Timothy Maguire, recently prompted an uproar over affirmative action with an article charging that the LSAT scores and grade-point averages of many black law-school students are significantly lower than whites'. (Maguire has apologized.) Racially offensive fraternity pranks have led to disciplinary action at the University of Texas and George Mason University in Virginia. An official at the University of Georgia, where fraternity rushes are still segregated by race, says flatly that the school is 20 years behind the times.

7   There's no disputing that big issues are in play here: affirmative action, free speech, the competition between liberty and justice. There is also no disputing, as many university administrators maintain, that the social and economic tensions of society at large will inevitably be played out on campus. Blacks (not to mention Hispanics and Asian-Americans) are becoming more assertive of their separate ethnic identities, of their right to protest even the most casual snub or slight, and of their need for firmer support from college authorities. Whites, wary of increasing competition for jobs and mindful of conservative attacks on liberal social policies, increasingly object to affirmative action and to the accusation that they are racists, too. Both sides—all sides—seem to harbor a sense of grievance and victimization. The great battles of the '60s and '70s are only history to the twentysomething generation, and blacks and other minorities are now questioning the very idea of integration. That does not mean the progress of the past two decades is actually in jeopardy. But the dream of racial amity—of blacks and whites learning and playing together—still seems sadly elusive.

Building Vocabulary

Define the words below, using *context clues* wherever possible and checking in a dictionary when necessary. Use them in sentences of your own.

haven (1)	ethos (4)	impasse (2)
transfixed (2)	discourse (1)	catchword (4)
brouhaha (2)	controversies (2)	scapegoating (5)
succumb (3)		

Journal Writing

Choose one or more of the three activities listed below, and make an entry in your journal. Focus on writing spontaneously rather than on structure and mechanics.

1. **Exploring:** Recall what you remember from other sources—your reading, your life experiences, movies and television, stories told to you by others—about the topic discussed by the writers. Choose one or two of these to write about. Which aspects of the topic did

they bring up? What additional information did they provide? What emotions did they create in you?

2. **Taking Stock:** Which parts of the selection were most difficult for you to grasp? Which parts needed more explanation? Which parts required outside information to be understood? What kind of information was required (e.g., historical, culture-specific, technical, etc.)? Where might such information be found? Were there aspects of the writers' style you found particularly effective? Particularly difficult? Why?

3. **Responding:** Identify one or two of the writers' main concerns. What personal knowledge, if any, do you have of these issues? What is your opinion on these issues? Examine your response carefully to see what it teaches you about yourself.

Analyzing Content

1. Why do the writers say that in terms of race relations, "this is the best of times, the worst of times"?
2. Which educational institutes have been affected by racial tension? What can you **deduce** from this fact?
3. What "big issues" are in play on campus? **Define** each term.
4. What, according to the writers, do minorities on campus want today? What do the whites want? How does this escalate tension?

Analyzing Writing Techniques

1. In this essay, the writers use many **allusions** to enrich the social, political, and literary context of the piece. Pick out some of these, and explain them.
2. In paragraphs 2 and 3, the writers discuss **symbols. Define** the term, and then explain in what way the items mentioned in the second paragraph are symbols.

Group Activity

Evaluate the writers' statement, "this is the best of times, the worst of times" in terms of race relations on campus. Do you agree? What has each member of the group noticed on your campus? Together, write a **collaborative** statement that reflects the state of race relations on your campus.

Your Writing

1. The writers claim in paragraph 7 that "the great battles of the '60s and the '70s are only history to the twentysomething generation." **Interview** two or three people in their late teens or early twenties

to check on whether this is true. How much do they know of this era? How much do *you* know? Write an essay, filling in the gaps with **research**, in which you evaluate the importance of that time.

2. What are some pros and cons of attempting to create diversity on campus? Write an essay in which you explore this topic, presenting a conclusion, supported by evidence, as to whether or not this is a worthwhile effort.

Pre-reading Activity   Write about your earliest school memories of interacting with other children. How did your teacher deal with conflict?

As You Read   Note the anecdote with which the essay begins. When is it reintroduced? How does it relate to the **thesis**?

AMERICAN AND JAPANESE PRESCHOOLS: WHAT'S THE DIFFERENCE?
Billy McClelland

*Born in 1976 in Paris, **Billy McClelland** moved to the United States at the age of two. He grew up in Georgia and wrote this essay while studying at Foothill College. He is currently continuing his studies at the Air Force Academy and plans to become a jet pilot. His other major interest is Tae Kwon Do, in which he has a black belt.*

The sun rises over the Pacific Ocean to start a new day in Japan. Young   1
Hiroki arrives at his preschool, Komatsudani Hoika, located in East Kyoto. Here, like children in many American preschools, he begins his day by playing with his classmates. The morning clean-up song sounds over the loudspeakers, followed by the exercise song, and after this, Hiroki runs to his classroom with his classmates. During the rest of the day, he is loud and boisterous. He calls out answers to many questions the teacher asks and yells answers to questions the teacher does not ask. He entertains the class with rude jokes and wrestles with some of the boys. He purposely steps on one boy's hands and interrupts a game by taking the flashcards and throwing them everywhere. While Hiroki is misbehaving, the teacher seemingly ignores his bad behavior (Tobin [et al.] 12–17).

A similar scene at an American preschool is handled very differently.   2
At St. Jonathan's in Hayward, California, when Phil and Ryan have a problem with sharing toy trucks and come close to fighting, the teacher intervenes right away, stopping the fight before it begins. She encourages the children to express how they feel and solve their problem with words instead of physical force. She talks to them about cooperation, and soon the boys are playing peacefully again.

Why do the preschool teachers in Japan allow their students to mis-   3
behave in such a manner? Compared with American preschools, this method is unorthodox, but the inaction is intentional. It results from the Japanese ideal of *groupism,* whereas the American teacher's reaction re-

flects the American educational philosophy of *individualism*. These different emphases reflect the larger cultural values of the two countries, which are clearly evident in their business practices.

4   Japanese preschools give their students a strong feeling of being part of a group. One way this feeling is created is with school uniforms. Each preschool has its own uniform, and they vary in design and color. In preschools where the parents cannot afford uniforms, name tags are issued; these have the child's family name, given name, preschool name, and name of the class written on them. The children are often collectively called by this class name when the teachers are speaking to them. All of this provides the children with a sense of belonging (Tobin [et al.] 40).

5   In Japanese preschools, teachers develop groupism with their deliberately passive attitude toward behavior problems. This allows the other classmates to deal with the problems themselves, as a group. In Hiroki's case, the other children couldn't stop Hiroki from fighting, but cleaning up the mess he made and taking care of the little boy who was stepped on generated a group effort. Even more interesting is how the children dealt with Hiroki and how he reacted to it. They refused to sit with him at lunch or play with him. As a result, 9 months later, Hiroki was behaving much better. When asked about the situation, the teacher said that the children came up with the idea themselves (Tobin et al., pp. 20–30). An analysis of the situation shows the way in which groupism works: the teachers and students have created a group atmosphere in which all students want to participate. If someone is excluded because of bad behavior, he will desire so strongly to be part of the group that he will change how he acts to be included again.

6   In America, individualism is the most important trait that children develop in preschool. Uniforms are uncommon, and children are encouraged to choose what they want to wear. An orientation packet from another preschool, St. Timothy's, tells parents:

7   We plan experiences and opportunities in all areas so that your children can develop a wide variety of skills. Since the children choose activities that interest them, they are meeting their own needs. Consequently, children develop feelings of confidence, responsibility and creativity. (Tobin [et al.] 140)

8   Individualism is developed through activities like show-and-tell, in which children are allowed to talk about an object from home or an experience they have had. They are also allowed to choose who they sit with during lunch and which playground equipment to play on. All of this helps to develop independence.

9   The way the teacher handled Phil and Ryan's problem demonstrates individualism, too. Each student is dealt with on an individual basis. The

rest of the class is not expected to be concerned with Phil and Ryan's fight. The two boys are responsible for resolving the conflict themselves (with a little encouragement from their teacher).

The behavior the children of each country are taught in preschool directly relates to how each country conducts business. Groupism plays a major role in Japanese business, in which decisions are made by committee. Members of the committee are all responsible for the results of the decision. The Japanese will generally work together and sacrifice their personal interests for the good of the team. For example, Japanese workers will not leave until their boss does. This is not to finish extra work but to be available if they are needed by their boss. Many workers are so dedicated to their group that they will miss vacations or come in to work even when they are sick just so they will not let down their group. Companies reward this loyalty with programs such as subsidized housing and bonuses (Hall [and Hall] 68–9).   10

The opposite is true in American businesses, in which individuals make decisions and are individually responsible for bad choices (Ouchi 42, 58). Most American workers are looking for personal gain, and they work for several companies in a short period of time. It is quite common for Americans to leave a company if a better job offer comes up. This high turnover rate causes workers not to rely on others, who might leave in the middle of an important project, but only to rely on themselves.   11

Interestingly, these business practices may have stemmed from old-time farming situations. In Japan, villages during feudal times were responsible for providing feudal lords with a steady supply of food, mostly rice. The villagers needed to work together to cultivate and harvest the rice, which required a large irrigation system that created a need for task-oriented teamwork within the community. It was important to work cooperatively, because failure meant punishment of the entire village (Hall [and Hall] 42). On the other hand, the American farmer had much more land to cultivate and machines with which to work. As a result, American farmers lived miles apart from each other and worked their own land. In areas with severe winters, they had no choice but to be independent, because help was often out of reach (Ouchi 66). Without the ability to help themselves, they would not have survived.   12

A study of preschools in different countries conducted by Joseph Tobin, David Wu, and Dana Davidson illustrated some interesting attitudes. When asked "Why should society have preschools?" 61% of the Japanese interviewed said, "To give children the experience of being a member of a group." Most Americans, however, said "to make young children more independent and self-reliant" (Tobin [et al.] 192). A study of the preschools in Japan and America, then, tells us not only about the countries' educational systems but also about deep-rooted and deeply different cultural values that ultimately influence their business practices.   13

Works Cited

Hall, Edward T. and Hall, Mildred Reed. *Hidden Differences: Doing Business with the Japanese.* Garden City, Anchor Press, 1987.

Ouchi, William. *Theory Z: How American Business Can Meet the Japanese Challenge.* Menlo Park, Calif., Addison Wesley, 1981.

Tobin, Joseph, David Wu, and Dana Davidson. *Preschool in Three Cultures: Japan, China and the United States.* Binghamton, Yale University Press, 1989.

Structure and Strategy

1. This is a **research** essay as opposed to a **personal** one. How is such an essay different in **tone** and **intention**? What are the strengths of a research essay? What are the strengths of a personal essay?
2. What is the major **rhetorical mode** of this essay (e.g., narration, description, etc.)? What is a minor rhetorical mode that also is used?
3. What kinds of **transitions** has the writer used? Are there any places where you might need to add a transition?
4. What is the function of the conclusion in this essay? What tools has the writer used to make it an effective conclusion?

Your Writing

1. Write an essay in which you analyze a particular teaching practice (perhaps something you've observed in the classroom) and the philosophy behind it. Is it effective? What is it teaching students in terms of behavior, social interactions, problem solving, etc.? What larger values are implied in it?
2. In this essay, McClelland connects what is learned in preschool to business practices the students will follow as adults. Do you see other connections between what students learn in school and what is happening in American society? Write an essay expressing your opinion on this topic.

SYNTHESIS: QUESTIONS FOR CRITICAL THINKING AND WRITING

1. "On Being Seventeen, Bright, and Unable to Read" and "The Struggle to Be an All-American Girl" illustrate how ethnicity or disability may contribute to a sense of isolation in the classroom. Choose *one other* factor that may contribute to such isolation, and write a paper exploring the problem and ways in which it may be solved.

2. "America Needs Its Nerds" and "Race on Campus: Failing the Test?" deal with issues of prejudice against groups. Who are some other groups on campus that find themselves stereotyped? Write a paper discussing the stereotypes faced by such a group, examining the reasons for these stereotypes and presenting at least one way of dealing with them.

3. "The Struggle to Be an All-American Girl" describes a Chinese school the writer had to attend. Many other cultures in America have these additional, cultural schools. Write about *one* such school (not necessarily an academic one), researching your topic if needed. What is taught at this school? What can a child learn from such a place?

4. When studying the selections in this unit, one notes that particular attitudes in the mind of the student can promote learning. What are these? Write a paper in which you analyze the mental "recipe" for success, giving examples from the readings.

At Work

For most American adults, work—be it in or outside of the home—takes up more of our time than any other single activity. Thus, our jobs, whether we feel positively or negatively toward them, are an extremely important part of our lives. The writers in this unit examine a wide variety of work situations and attitudes toward them. They also examine the roles of minorities, women, and the disabled in the work force, and point to problematic areas and suggested solutions.

In "Racism in Corporate America," Manning Marable looks at the positions open to minorities and pronounces the situation inequitable, while Eric Bigler, in "Give Us Jobs, Not Admiration," describes vividly the prejudices of a potential employer against a disabled candidate. "Equality, Yes—Militarism, No" by Annette Fuentes points to the ironies of women being given "equal" footing in the armed forces. And in "Earth Ambassador Aiding Indian Youth," Rick Heredia records one man's struggle to improve the conditions of his people.

"Year of the Blue-Collar Guy" by Steve Olson and "Who Burns for the Perfection of Paper" by Martin Espada establish an interesting dialogue. While the first piece celebrates manual labor and those who perform it, the second looks ruefully at their difficulties and disadvantages. Perhaps a balance between these two viewpoints is achieved by student Roz Batt, in "Fishy Business," as she observes Asian workers at a San Francisco fish market. She admires their dedication and pride even as she is aware of how hard they must toil to achieve a semblance of financial success.

Pre-reading Activity   What does the term *Earth Ambassador* mean to you? What values are implied in it?

As You Read   Pick out paragraphs that are unconventional in structure. What makes them different and effective?

EARTH AMBASSADOR AIDING
INDIAN YOUTH
Rick Heredia

Rick Heredia *writes for the* Bakersfield Californian, *in which this piece first appeared in 1991.*

Porterville—Larry De Soto's office door opens and you hear the Tule River   1
as it rushes past the tribal building on the Tule River Indian reservation.

The door shuts, muting the river.   2

Inside, the only sound is the clicking of a keyboard as De Soto [a   3
Yowlumni/Paiute], working through a stack of membership applications,
enters into an amber-screened computer the names of those wishing to be
added to the tribal rolls.

Helping the [Yokut] . . . tribe's membership committee is one of many   4
responsibilities De Soto, 21, has assumed. Others include holding down
a job in the tribe's Natural Resources Department, singing with a drum
group that promotes alcohol- and drug-free lifestyles, and starting a youth
council that De Soto hopes will be self-supporting through a recycling program. Recycling complements De Soto's latest effort: He has been chosen
as one of 48 American Indian youth from across the country to serve as
Earth Ambassadors.

Under the auspices of the United National Indian Tribal Youth, head-   5
quartered in Oklahoma City, the Earth Ambassador program prepares De
Soto and the others to take an active role in environmental issues at the
tribal and national levels. The 48 Indian youth will be formally recognized
during special American Indian Earth Day activities Monday in Washington, D.C. Included is a reception on Capitol Hill. In a gesture that's largely
symbolic, the Ambassadors will demonstrate their commitment to the environment by taking part in a staking ceremony. The youth were introduced
to it during a week-long training session held in December in a rural part
of Ramona, northeast of San Diego. The ceremony is rooted in the warrior tradition. On the battlefield, warriors sometimes tied themselves to

stakes driven into the ground, a sign that they would stay and fight until the enemy was defeated.

6   "Now, we're involved in a spiritual war," said Phil Lane Jr., coordinator of the Four Worlds Development Project in Lethbridge, Alberta, Canada, who conducts the ceremony. "We're fighting to heal the wounds inflicted on our people by drugs, alcohol and other hurts, and we're fighting to protect and heal our Mother Earth. By participating in the staking ceremony, our youth are committing themselves to the work of healing our human family and Mother Earth. We're not going to retreat—ever again."

7   Strong words.

8   But, said De Soto, a tall, slender man with penetrating dark eyes who is dressed in a colorful ribbon shirt and whose hair tapers into a single braid, "If you set your mind to something, the sky's the limit."

9   Tule River is a country away from the nation's capital, and De Soto knows that once he returns, the real work of accomplishing the Ambassador program's 12 goals—ranging from improving Indian communities' economies to promoting unity and self esteem—begins. "A lot of people hear 'reservation' and they hear 'negative,' 'negative,' 'negative,' " De Soto said, echoing a sentiment shared by other reservation residents. They complain that this is an unfair description of their community. So, one of De Soto's aims will be, through the youth council, to break down barriers and attitudes that separate people both on and off the reservation.

10   In addition to planning a recycling program, De Soto worries about pollution in the river and wonders about relocating the site where residents dump their trash.

11   On a larger scale, he and the other Ambassadors have discussed such issues as nuclear power and the depleting ozone layer.

12   Like De Soto, the rest of the Ambassadors—they are from 23 states and represent 20 Indian tribes—are encouraged to set up youth councils in their respective communities. If they succeed, it will be a testament to their skill and leadership and to that of their sponsors, UNITY.

13   Leadership is important to De Soto, the proud father of a son, Laryn, born in mid-March. De Soto dreams of studying law, someday working with the Native American Rights Fund in Boulder, Colorado, and taking a stronger role in helping shape the environmental and political destiny of American Indians.

14   Education, he believes, will help him accomplish that. But not at the expense of his cultural training—an ongoing process for De Soto. In addition to his drumming and singing, he makes frequent trips to the sweat lodge, a few miles up the two-lane road that winds through the heart of the reservation, past looming mountain peaks lush with growth. They are a reminder of what an elder once told De Soto.

15   "The Earth will be here forever. The people will kill themselves off. The Earth will remain."

Building Vocabulary

Define the words below, using *context clues* wherever possible and checking in a dictionary when necessary. Use them in sentences of your own.

muting (2)	testament (12)	tapers (8)
environmental issues (5)	auspices (5)	ozone (11)
penetrating (8)	rooted (5)	looming (14)
depleting (11)		

Journal Writing

Choose one or more of the three activities listed below, and make an entry in your journal. Focus on writing spontaneously rather than on structure and mechanics.

1. **Exploring:** Recall what you remember from other sources—your reading, your life experiences, movies and television, stories told to you by others—about the topic discussed by the writer. Choose one or two of these to write about. Which aspects of the topic did they bring up? What additional information did they provide? What emotions did they create in you?
2. **Taking Stock:** Which parts of the selection were most difficult for you to grasp? Which parts needed more explanation? Which parts required outside information to be understood? What kind of information was required (e.g., historical, culture-specific, technical, etc.)? Where might such information be found? Were there aspects of the writer's style you found particularly effective? Particularly difficult? Why?
3. **Responding:** Identify one or two of the writer's main concerns. What personal knowledge, if any, do you have of these issues? What is your opinion on these issues? Examine your response carefully to see what it teaches you about yourself.

Analyzing Content

1. Make a list of De Soto's responsibilities. From them, what can you **deduce** about his values?
2. Describe a staking ceremony, and explain why it was done in the past. How is it relevant today?
3. What barriers does De Soto hope to break down in paragraph 9? How?
4. What does De Soto hope to do eventually?

Analyzing Writing Techniques

1. In paragraph 7, the writer discusses the negative **connotations** of the word *reservation.* **Define** connotation, then make a list of words that have negative and positive connotations.
2. What does the first paragraph of this article do? What might be another effective way of beginning it?

Group Activity

What images do you associate with the term *Native-American?* Make a group list of the images, then analyze where they came from.

Your Writing

1. This article makes several references to reservation life, the stereotyping of reservation inhabitants, and the values learned by living on a reservation. Write a **report** about life on a reservation, exploring both its pros and cons.
2. In paragraph 14, the writer discusses the "cultural training" that De Soto continues to undergo. What is the importance of such training? Write an essay in which you describe the cultural training available to members of another ethnic group, and analyze its effects.

Pre-reading Activity   Think back to a time when you interacted
with a disabled person. Describe the situation and the interaction.
How did you feel? If you are disabled, bring that element into the description.

As You Read   Observe the examples used by the writer, and divide
them into two categories: personal, and researched.

GIVE US JOBS, NOT ADMIRATION
Eric Bigler

*Born in Ohio in 1958, **Eric Bigler** had a driving accident when he was in
high school that left his entire lower body paralyzed. He went on to earn
degrees in social work and in business and industrial counseling manage-
ment. He works part-time at a research laboratory in Wright State University in Dayton, Ohio, on adapting computer technology to help the disabled
work with computers. This piece first appeared in* Newsweek *in 1987.*

Tuesday I have another job interview. Like most I have had so far, it will   1
probably end with the all-too-familiar words, "We'll let you know of our
decision in a few days."

Many college-graduates searching for their first career job might sim-   2
ply accept that response as, "Sorry, we're not interested in you," and blame
the rejection on inexperience or bad chemistry. For myself and other disabled people, however, this response often seems to indicate something
more worrisome: a reluctance to hire the handicapped even when they're
qualified. I have been confined to a wheelchair since 1974, when a high-
school diving accident left me paralyzed from the chest down. But that
didn't prevent me from earning a bachelor's in social work in 1983, and
I am now finishing up a master's degree in business and industrial man-
agement, specializing in employee relations and human-resource development.

Our government spends a great deal of money to help the handi-   3
capped, but it does not necessarily spend it all wisely. For example, in 1985
Ohio's Bureau of Vocational Rehabilitation (BVR) spent more than $4 mil-
lion in tuition and other expenses so that disabled students could obtain
a college education. BVR's philosophy is that the amount of money spent
educating students will be repaid in disabled employees' taxes. The agency
assists graduates by offering workshops on résumé writing and interview-

ing techniques, skills many already learned in college. BVR also maintains files of résumés that are matched with help-wanted notices from local companies and employs placement specialists to work directly with graduates during their job search.

4   Even with all this assistance, however, graduates still have trouble getting hired. Such programs might do better if they concentrated on the perceptions of employers as well as the skills of applicants. More important, improving contacts with prospective employers might encourage them to actively recruit the disabled.

5   Often, projects that *do* show promise don't get the chance to thrive. I was both a client and an informal consultant to one program, Careers for the Disabled in Dayton, which asked local executives to make a commitment to hire disabled applicants whenever possible. I found this strategy to be on target, since support for a project is more likely when it is ordered from the top. The program also offered free training seminars to corporations on how they can work effectively with the disabled candidate. In April of 1986—less than a year after it was started and after only three disabled people were placed—the program was discontinued because, according to the director, they had "no luck at getting [enough] corporations to join the program."

6   Corporations need to take a more independent and active part in hiring qualified handicapped persons. Today's companies try to show a willingness to innovate, and hiring people like myself would enhance that image. Madison Avenue has finally recognized that the disabled are also consumers; more and more often, commercials include them. But advertisers could break down even more stereotypes. I would like to see one of those Hewlett-Packard commercials, for instance, show an employee racing down the sidewalk in his wheelchair, pulling alongside a pay phone and calling a colleague to ask "What if . . . ?"

7   Corporate recruiters also need to be better prepared for meeting with disabled applicants. They should be ready to answer queries about any barriers that their building's design may pose, and they should be forthright about asking their own questions. It's understandable that employers are afraid to mention matters that are highly personal and may prove embarassing—or, even worse, discriminatory. There's nothing wrong, however, with an employer reassuring him or herself about whether an applicant will be able to reach files, operate computers or even get into the bathroom. Until interviewers change their style, disabled applicants need to initiate discussion of disability-related issues.

8   **Cosmetic acts:** Government has tried to improve hiring for the disabled through Affirmative Action programs. The Rehabilitation Act of 1973 says institutions or programs receiving substantial amounts of federal money can't discriminate on the basis of handicap. Yet I was saddened and surprised to discover how many companies spend much time and money writ-

ing great affirmative-action and equal-opportunity guidelines but little time following them. Then there are the cosmetic acts, such as the annual National Employ the Handicapped Week every October. If President Reagan (or anyone else) wants to help the disabled with proclamations, more media exposure is necessary. I found out about the last occasion in 1985 from a brief article on the back of a campus newspaper—a week after it had happened.

9   As if other problems were not enough, the disabled who search unsuccessfully for employment often face a loss of self-esteem and worth. In college, many disabled people I have talked to worked hard toward a degree so they would be prepared for jobs after graduation. Now they look back on their four or more years as wasted time. For these individuals, the days of earning good grades and accomplishing tough tasks fade away, leaving only frustrating memories. Today's job market is competitive enough without prejudice adding more "handicaps."

10   About that interview . . . five minutes into it, I could feel the atmosphere chill. The interviewer gave me general information instead of trying to find out if I was right for the job. I've been there before. Then the session closed with a handshake, and those same old words: "We'll let you know." They said I should be so proud of myself for doing what I am doing. That's what they always say. I'm tired of hearing how courageous I am. So are other disabled people. We need jobs, and we want to work like anyone else.

11   But still, I remain an optimist. I know someday soon a company will be smart enough to realize how much I have to offer them in both my head and my heart.

12   Maybe then I'll hear the words so many of us really want to hear: "You're hired."

Building Vocabulary

Define the words below, using *context clues* wherever possible and checking in a dictionary when necessary. Use them in sentences of your own.

bad chemistry (2)	discriminatory (7)	pose (7)
strategy (5)	prospective (4)	initiate (7)
enhance (6)	innovate (6)	

Journal Writing

Choose one or more of the three activities listed below, and make an entry in your journal. Focus on writing spontaneously rather than on structure and mechanics.

1. **Exploring:** Recall what you remember from other sources—your reading, your life experiences, movies and television, stories told to you by others—about the topic discussed by the writer. Choose one or two of these to write about. Which aspects of the topic did they bring up? What additional information did they provide? What emotions did they create in you?
2. **Taking Stock:** Which parts of the selection were most difficult for you to grasp? Which parts needed more explanation? Which parts required outside information to be understood? What kind of information was required (e.g., historical, culture-specific, technical, etc.)? Where might such information be found? Were there aspects of the writer's style you found particularly effective? Particularly difficult? Why?
3. **Responding:** Identify one or two of the writer's main concerns. What personal knowledge, if any, do you have of these issues? What is your opinion on these issues? Examine your response carefully to see what it teaches you about yourself.

Analyzing Content

1. Why does the writer say that the government's strategy to help the handicapped is not wise?
2. What changes does he suggest in the strategy?
3. In paragraph 6, the writer mentions "stereotypes" faced by the handicapped. What do you think these are? How would the commercial he imagines break down some of these stereotypes?
4. How do handicapped people often feel about their educational achievements? Why?

Analyzing Writing Techniques

1. How does the writer connect the beginning and the end of this essay? Is this an effective strategy? Suggest an alternative method of ending this piece.
2. Who is the intended audience of this essay? How do we know this? What is the **tone** of the essay? Is this suited to the audience? Why, or why not?

Group Activity

Answer question 2 under "Analyzing Writing Techniques." Now, decide on a **different audience** for the essay. In what ways would you change the tone, and perhaps even the information, to fit this new audience? Write a **collaborative** beginning to this new essay.

Your Writing

1. Write a **letter** to a disabled person who is planning to embark on a job search. What advice and cautions would you give?
2. This selection was written in 1987. How has the situation for the handicapped changed since then? Do some of the problems mentioned by the writer remain? Write a **research** paper examining how easy or difficult it is for the handicapped to get a job today. Some questions to consider are: What programs are available to help them? How effective are these programs? What stereotypes still exist?

Pre-reading Activity   What is your response to the title? Do you believe that such racism exists?

As You Read   Note the writer's use of statistics. How do these
strengthen his thesis?

RACISM IN CORPORATE AMERICA
Manning Marable

Born in 1950 in Dayton, Ohio, **Manning Marable** *holds degrees from Earl-
ham College, the University of Wisconsin, and the University of Maryland. He has taught at many educational institutions, including Cornell
University, Fisk University, and Williams College. He currently teaches
at the Center for Race and Ethnic Studies at the University of Colorado.
He is an award-winning poet whose work focuses on the African-
American experience. His books include* How Capitalism Underdevel-
oped Black America *and* Race, Reform and Rebellion: The Second Re-
construction. *This selection is taken from his book* The Crisis of Color and
Democracy *(1991).*

1   For years, Reagan economist Milton Friedman asserted that the free enterprise system is virtually "free" of racism. More recently, black Reagan-
ites such as Thomas Sowell and Walter Williams have championed the corporations as being interested in the uplifting and development of African
Americans. But the actual record of the relationship between blacks and
corporate America, particularly in terms of black employment in managerial positions, has been similar to *apartheid* in South Africa.

2   Before 1965, the white corporate establishment didn't realize that
African Americans even existed. College-trained blacks and middle-class
businesspeople were attached to the separate economy of the ghetto.
African Americans who applied for jobs at white-owned companies found
that their resumes weren't accepted. Blacks who were hired were placed
in low-paying clerical or maintenance positions.

3   With the impact of the civil rights movement, the public demonstrates
and boycotts against corporations which Jim Crowed blacks, businesses
were forced to change their hiring policies. However, most blacks were
placed in minority neighborhoods, having little contact with whites in su-
pervisory roles. In the 1960s and 1970's, the careers of most black exec-

utives were "racialized." They were given responsibilities which focused exclusively on racial matters, rather than the broad issues which affected the profit and loss of the corporation as a whole. They were assigned to mediate black employees' grievances, or to direct affirmative action policies, rather than being placed in charge of a major division of the company. Their managerial experiences were limited, and therefore their prospects for upward mobility into senior executive positions were nonexistent.

In 1977, only 3.6 percent of all managers in the United States were 4 people of color. The *Fortune* magazine survey of the 1,000 largest U.S. companies that year indicated that, out of 1,708 senior executives, there were only three African Americans, two Asians, two hispanics, and eight women.

In the 1980s and 1990s, progress for African Americans inside cor- 5 porations slowed, and in some cases has been reversed. African Americans now represent about 13 percent of the total U.S. population, but less than 5 percent of all managers, and less than 1 percent of all mid-to-upper level executives. Why this pattern of corporate apartheid?

One reason is the racial segregation of U.S. business schools. African 6 Americans represent only 3 to 4 percent of all students in MBA programs. Blacks are less than 2 percent in graduate level programs in the sciences and computer programming. With the Bush administration's threat to eliminate minority scholarships at universities and a decline in federal enforcement of affirmative action, universities aren't as aggressive in recruiting students of color.

Many heads of major corporations have racial attitudes which are dis- 7 criminatory. But even more pervasive is what I would term the "passive racism" inside the corporate suites. White executives recognize that racism exists within their corporations, but they are unwilling to do anything about it. They refuse to compensate victims of past or current discrimination, or to take positive steps to subsidize development programs within minority communities, such as internships or scholarships.

Black and Hispanic executives usually lack the informal connections 8 most whites take for granted. They usually don't belong to the same social clubs, churches, fraternities or political parties. They aren't mentored for possible openings for career advancement by senior white executives. From their perspective, a "glass ceiling" exists which blocks their mobility.

Unless policies of greater corporate accountability and social re- 9 sponsibility are pursued, blacks, Latinos and women will continue to be marginalized inside corporations. Part of this strategy for reform must transcend the request for jobs within the corporate structure. The private sector must be forced to address the basic needs of the black community. This will not occur until the system of corporate capitalism is transformed, and economic decisions are based first upon human needs rather than private profits.

Building Vocabulary

Define the words below, using *context clues* wherever possible and checking in a dictionary when necessary. Use them in sentences of your own.

ghetto (2)   accountability (9)   compensate (7)
eliminate (6)   grievances (3)   transcend (9)

Journal Writing

Choose one or more of the three activities listed below, and make an entry in your journal. Focus on writing spontaneously rather than on structure and mechanics.

1. **Exploring:** Recall what you remember from other sources—your reading, your life experiences, movies and television, stories told to you by others—about the topic discussed by the writer. Choose one or two of these to write about. Which aspects of the topic did they bring up? What additional information did they provide? What emotions did they create in you?
2. **Taking Stock:** Which parts of the selection were most difficult for you to grasp? Which parts needed more explanation? Which parts required outside information to be understood? What kind of information was required (e.g., historical, culture-specific, technical, etc.)? Where might such information be found? Were there aspects of the writer's style you found particularly effective? Particularly difficult? Why?
3. **Responding:** Identify one or two of the writer's main concerns. What personal knowledge, if any, do you have of these issues? What is your opinion on these issues? Examine your response carefully to see what it teaches you about yourself.

Analyzing Content

1. **Compare/contrast** the pre-1965 and post-1965 situations in terms of employment opportunities for blacks in corporate America.
2. How has the situation improved? How has it worsened?
3. Explain the term *passive racism*.
4. According to the writer, what larger social change must occur before the employment problem can be solved?

Analyzing Writing Techniques

1. **Analyze** the opening paragraph, which uses a technique that is sometimes called *pivoting.* By observing the structure of this paragraph, explain the technique.
2. Of what is the writer trying to persuade the reader? Where in the essay is this indicated? What does the rest of the essay do?

Group Activity

Marable uses several specific terms with complex meanings to bring his ideas across. Some of these are *free enterprise, apartheid, Jim Crow, affirmative action, glass ceiling,* and *capitalism.* Each group should **research** *one* of these terms and do a brief presentation to the class on how it came into being, what its connotations are, and the history associated with it. You may add other words from the essay to this list.

Your Writing

1. Marable mentions Hispanics, women, and Asians but focuses on African-Americans. Write an essay in which you take *one* of the groups he has not discussed in detail, and analyze their problems in the workplace. You may use personal and observed examples as well as statistics.
2. What are your views on affirmative action? Write an essay in which you evaluate the arguments presented by groups who are for affirmative action as well as those who are against it. With whom do you agree more? Why?

Pre-reading Activity   What kind of language would you expect from a "blue-collar guy" who is writing an essay? Why?

As You Read   Underline descriptive words, phrases, and ideas that surprise you by their unusualness. What impression of the writer's abilities do they create in your mind?

YEAR OF THE BLUE-COLLAR GUY
Steve Olson

*Born in 1946 in Rice Lake, Wisconsin, **Steve Olson** lives in northern Wisconsin with his wife and two sons. He is a construction worker who claims he writes "mostly for himself." This piece first appeared in the "My Turn" column of* Newsweek *in 1989.*

1   While the learned are attaching appropriate labels to the 1980s and speculating on what the 1990s will bring, I would like to steal 1989 for my own much maligned group and declare it "the year of the blue-collar guy (BCG)." BCGs have been portrayed as beer-drinking, big-bellied, bigoted rednecks who dress badly. Wearing a suit to a cement-finishing job wouldn't be too bright. Watching my tie go around a motor shaft followed by my neck is not the last thing I want to see in this world. But, more to the point, our necks are too big and our arms and shoulders are too awesome to fit suits well without expensive tailoring. Suits are made for white-collar guys.

2   But we need big bellies as ballast to stay on the bar stool while we're drinking beer. And our necks are red from the sun and we are somewhat bigoted. But aren't we all? At least our bigotry is open and honest and worn out front like a tattoo. White-collar people are bigoted, too. But it's disguised as the pat on the back that holds you back: "You're not good enough so you need affirmative action." BCGs aren't smart enough to be that cynical. I never met a BCG who didn't respect an honest day's work and a job well done—no matter who did it.

3   True enough, BCGs aren't perfect. But, I believe this: we are America's last true romantic heroes. When some twenty-first-century Louis L'Amour writes about this era he won't eulogize the greedy Wall Street insider. He won't commend the narrow-shouldered, wide-hipped lawyers with six-digit unearned incomes doing the same work women can do. His wide-shouldered heroes will be plucked from the ranks of the blue-collar guy.

They are the last vestige of the manly world where strength, skill and hard work are still valued.

To some extent our negative ratings are our own fault. While we were building the world we live in, white-collar types were sitting on their ever-widening butts redefining the values we live by. One symbol of America's opulent wealth is the number of people who can sit and ponder and comment and write without producing a usable product or skill. Hey, get a real job—make something—then talk. These talkers are the guys we drove from the playgrounds into the libraries when we were young and now for 20 years or more we have endured the revenge of the nerds.

BCGs fidgeted our way out of the classroom and into jobs where, it seemed, the only limit to our income was the limit of our physical strength and energy. A co-worker described a BCG as "a guy who is always doing things that end in the letter 'n'—you know—huntin', fishin', workin'. . . ." My wise friend is talking energy! I have seen men on the job hand-nail 20 square of shingles (that's 6,480 nails) or more a day, day after day, for weeks. At the same time, they were remodeling their houses, raising children, and coaching Little League. I've seen crews frame entire houses in a day—day after day. I've seen guys finish concrete until 11 P.M., go out on a date, then get up at 6 A.M. and do it all over again the next day.

These are amazing feats of strength. There should be stadiums full of screaming fans for these guys. I saw a 40-year-old man neatly fold a 350-pound piece of rubber roofing, put it on his shoulder and, alone, carry it up a ladder and deposit it on a roof. Nobody acknowledged it because the event was too common. One day at noon this same fellow wrestled a 22-year-old college summer worker. In the prime of his life, the college kid was a 6-foot-3, 190-pound body-builder and he was out of his league. He was on his back to stay in 90 seconds flat.

Great Skilled Work Force

Mondays are tough on any job. But in our world this pain is eased by stories of weekend adventure. While white-collar types are debating the value of reading over watching TV, BCGs are doing stuff. I have honest to God heard these things on Monday mornings about BCG weekends: "I tore out a wall and added a room," "I built a garage," "I went walleye fishing Saturday and pheasant hunting Sunday," "I played touch football both days" (in January), "I went skydiving." "I went to the sports show and wrestled the bear." Pack a good novel into these weekends.

My purpose is not so much to put down white-collar people as to stress the importance of blue-collar people to this country. Lawyers, politicians, and bureaucrats are necessary parts of the process, but this great skilled work force is so taken for granted it is rarely seen as the luxury it truly is. Our plumbing works, our phones work, and repairs are made as quickly as humanly possible. I don't think this is true in all parts of the world. But this blue-collar resource is becoming endangered. Being a tradesman is viewed with such disdain these days that most young people I know treat the trades like a temporary summer job. I've seen young guys take minimum-wage jobs just so they can wear suits. It is as if any job without a dress code is a dead-end job. This is partly our own fault. We even tell our own sons, "Don't be like me, get a job people respect." Blue-collar guys ought to brag more, even swagger a little. We should drive our families past the latest job site and say, "That house was a piece of junk, and now it's the best one on the block. I did that." Nobody will respect us if we don't respect ourselves.

10   Our work is hard, hot, wet, cold, and always dirty. It is also often very satisfying. Entailing the use of both brain and body there is a product—a physical result of which to be proud. We have fallen from your roofs, died under heavy equipment, and been entombed in your dams. We have done honest, dangerous work. Our skills and energy and strength have transformed lines on paper into physical reality. We are this century's Renaissance men. America could do worse than to honor us. We still do things the old-fashioned way, and we have earned the honor.

Building Vocabulary

Define the words below, using *context clues* wherever possible and checking in a dictionary when necessary. Use them in sentences of your own.

speculating (1)	opulent (4)	cynical (2)
awesome (1)	swagger (9)	vestige (3)
bigoted (2)	maligned (1)	disdain (9)
eulogize (3)	ballast (2)	Renaissance men (10)

Journal Writing

Choose one or more of the three activities listed below, and make an entry in your journal. Focus on writing spontaneously rather than on structure and mechanics.

1. **Exploring:** Recall what you remember from other sources—your reading, your life experiences, movies and television, stories told to you by others—about the topic discussed by the writer. Choose one or two of these to write about. Which aspects of the topic did they bring up? What additional information did they provide? What emotions did they create in you?
2. **Taking Stock:** Which parts of the selection were most difficult for you to grasp? Which parts needed more explanation? Which parts required outside information to be understood? What kind of information was required (e.g., historical, culture-specific, technical, etc.)? Where might such information be found? Were there aspects

of the writer's style you found particularly effective? Particularly difficult? Why?

3. **Responding:** Identify one or two of the writer's main concerns. What personal knowledge, if any, do you have of these issues? What is your opinion on these issues? Examine your response carefully to see what it teaches you about yourself.

Analyzing Content

1. What reasons does the writer give for the way in which the BCG dresses?
2. Why does he say the BCGs are America's last true romantic heroes?
3. Twice in the essay, the writer states that the negative attitude of the world toward the BCG is "our own fault." Explain what he means by this.
4. What does the writer most appreciate about the BCG? What can you **deduce** from this about his values?

Analyzing Writing Techniques

1. How does the writer use humor as a tool? What does it add to the essay? Where is the humor particularly effective?
2. Under what **rhetorical modes** (e.g., narration, description, argument, etc.) would this essay fit? Point to areas employing these specific modes.

Group Activity

How does the media portray BCGs? As a group, research various areas in which images of BCGs appear. Discuss whether these support the writer's complaints about ways that BCGs have been stereotyped and undervalued.

Your Writing

1. Write a paper about *another* group of people in a particular field of work who, according to you, have been stereotyped. These could be people from a particular ethnic group (e.g., Chicano farm laborers) or a particular profession (e.g., athletes, blues singers, etc.). Explain some of the stereotypes, and **contrast** them with the reality of this group's life.
2. In paragraph 9, the writer states, "Our plumbing works, our phones work, and repairs are made as quickly as humanly possible. I don't think this is true in all parts of the world." Is the writer accurate in this belief? **Compare/contrast** this aspect of America with that of another country, and explain reasons for any differences you perceive. You may need to **research** parts of this topic.

Pre-reading Activity   Write about a job that you or someone you know had to work at just to make money. Did you learn anything from it?

As You Read   Pick out the transitions used by the poet. Why are they important in the poem?

WHO BURNS FOR THE PERFECTION
OF PAPER
Martin Espada

Born in Brooklyn in 1957, **Martin Espada** *dropped out of the University of Maryland to work in a variety of positions: encyclopedia salesman, gas-station attendant, bouncer, and bindery worker in a printing plant. He went back to school to get degrees from the University of Wisconsin and North-eastern University, Boston. He is a lawyer, teacher of creative writing, and winner of a NEA fellowship. His books include* The Immigrant Iceboy's Bolero, Rebellion is the Circle of a Lover's Hands, *and* City of Coughing and Dead Radiators *(1993), from which this selection is taken.*

At sixteen, I worked after high school hours
at a printing plant
that manufactured legal pads:
Yellow paper
stacked seven feet high
and leaning
as I slipped cardboard
between the pages,
then brushed red glue
10 up and down the stack.
No gloves: fingertips required
for the perfection of paper,
smoothing the exact rectangle.
Sluggish by 9 PM, the hands
would slide along suddenly sharp paper,
and gather slits thinner than the crevices
of the skin, hidden.
Then the glue would sting,
hands oozing
20 till both palms burned
at the punchclock.

Ten years later, in law school,
I knew that every legal pad
was glued with the sting of hidden cuts,
that every open lawbook
was a pair of hands
upturned and burning.

Building Vocabulary

Define the words below, using *context clues* wherever possible and checking in a dictionary when necessary. Use them in sentences of your own.

sluggish (14)   crevices (16)
oozing (19)   punchclock (21)

Analyzing Content

1. **Paraphrase** the experience the poet is describing. What is lost in paraphrasing?
2. What has the poet learned through his job in the printing plant?
3. What is the significance of the title? Who is being referred to in it?

Analyzing Writing Techniques

1. Pick out the **metaphors** in this poem. What have they added to this selection?
2. What emotion does the writer wish to create in his readers? Which **images** in the poem help to bring about this emotion?

Group Activity

Have each member of your group pick out two words that they really liked in the poem. Make a **group list** of these words. Now, write a paragraph or a poem of your own into which you put as many of these words as you can.

Your Writing

1. Research a day in the life of a laborer in a printing plant, and write a paper in which you compare what Espada writes with what you have discovered. Do you think Espada has managed to capture the essence of the experience?
2. Find one or two other poets who write about physical labor in their poems, and write a paper in which you discuss the kinds of experiences they write about. What is their overall opinion of work? Do their ethnic or racial backgrounds influence their employment?

Pre-reading Activity   Do you feel women should be in the military? Why, or why not?

As You Read   Make a list of the **allusions** in this article. How many do you know? Look up some of the others after you have finished reading.

EQUALITY, YES—MILITARISM, NO
Annette Fuentes

Annette Fuentes, a freelance writer who lives in New York, is an assistant editor at Newsday. *She is also the chairperson of the Institute for Puerto Rican policy. This selection was first published in* Nation *in 1991.*

1   What had been unthinkable twenty years ago and unattainable ten years ago—the full integration of women into the voluntary service—is now on the horizon. On July 31 [1991], the Senate struck a blow for women's equality in the armed services when it voted to eliminate regulations that prohibited women in the Air Force and Navy from flying combat missions. The House had done the same in May. The forces fighting for women's equal opportunity seem to have scored a major, if mostly symbolic, victory at a time when women's rights are being sledgehammered by state legislatures, the courts and the Bush Administration. It's a victory, that is, if you consider elimination of combat exclusions an unadulterated feminist achievement.

2   In 1980, feminists of various stripes publicly wrestled with the question of women's relationship to the military. A case before the Supreme Court, *Rostker v. Goldberg,* filed by a men's veterans group, challenged the constitutionality of a male-only draft. *Rostker* was championed by the National Organization for Women. NOW and its president at the time, Eleanor Smeal, were criticized by many peace activists and antimilitarist feminists for their stance.

3   This time around, NOW is still advocating the equal opportunity position on women and the military, as are many other national women's legal and policy organizations. But the voices of feminists who consider combat inclusion a dubious advance have been muted. The sole debate has been between conservative types who think G.I. Jane will sabotage male bonding on the frontlines, and the equal rights advocates who argue that dropping all barriers to women in the military is not only fair, it contributes to military preparedness.

"The only thing exclusion protects is men's jobs," said Patricia Ireland, 　4
executive vice president of NOW. "It limits the services' ability to put the
best people in the jobs." When pressed, she acknowledged NOW's paci-
fist philosophy, but said that "women need to be in all the powerful institutions in society. As long as the military and Congress remain men's clubs,
women's perspective is excluded and public policy is worse for it."

The gulf war provided the main impetus to Congress's action. "Obvi- 　5
ously, as a result of Operation Desert Storm, attention has been focused
on the 1948 laws restricting women in the military," says Carolyn Becraft,
a former Army officer who works for Women's Research and Education
Institute. "The gulf war showed women in combat." Indeed, the 35,000
women deployed in the Persian Gulf were front and center in press coverage of that military action. Eleven women died in the war, five in combat. Two women were taken prisoner. Who could deny that women had
proved their mettle and deserved all the opportunities men get in the
armed forces?

Certainly not the U.S. public. A *Newsweek* poll taken during the war 　6
found that 63 percent of respondents approved of having women pilots,
53 percent said women should have combat assignments if they want them
and 50 percent believed any future draft should include women. The Pentagon has been testing the waters of public opinion regarding women in
combat situations since the 1983 invasion of Grenada. Press censorship
in that operation was so impenetrable that no images of the 170 women
soldiers sent to the island leaked out.

Panama was next, and the public got a closer look at 800 women who 　7
were getting a closer look at combat. Still, the military was sensitive to coverage of their participation. One wire story reported that two women drivers refused to ferry troops into Panama City during heavy fighting. But,
in an expert display of damage control, public affairs officers exonerated
the drivers in a statement that was attached to a release about two female
helicopter pilots who received medals of valor.

By contrast, the coverage of Desert Storm was a red, white and blue 　8
tribute to women soldiers. When a Scud missile destroyed a U.S. barracks
in Saudi Arabia, killing twenty-eight, including two women, it also seemed
to smash old definitions of frontline and combat zones. Predictions that
Americans couldn't tolerate women coming home in body bags were ex-
ploded, too. A majority of them apparently don't care about keeping
women out of harm's way anymore.

From the Pentagon's perspective, the use of women in the services is 　9
"a labor issue," says Linda De Pauw, a historian and founder of The Min-
erva Center on women and the military in Arlington, Virginia. "What's driving the extended use of women is military need, especially in the modern army. Military work has become increasingly technological."
Expanding the role of the growing number of female soldiers "fits in with
the idea of Workforce 2000 [the Hudson Institute's phrase for the work

force of the future], which is increasingly women and minority," she says. "Smart managers see they can't be bigots. It's counterproductive."

10   In fact, women of color make up 38 percent of all women (officers and enlisted) in the services; black women alone are 30 percent. In the Army, women of color are 55 percent of all enlisted women; black women are 47 percent. "The military has always provided equal opportunity. In that way, it is way ahead of the civilian sector," says Becraft. The retention of black women is very high, she says, because they have fewer opportunities in civilian life than black men.

11   Nonetheless, women of color aren't getting their fair share of the best jobs and highest ranks. Minority women are 41 percent of all enlisted women, yet only 19 percent of women officers. Statistics on the U.S. Army in Europe reveal that women of color occupy 50 percent of the lowest-ranking and lowest paid jobs in the military. In Germany, for example, they are 51 percent of all women soldiers and 3.5 percent of officers; three times as many white women are officers.

12   Rank is a primary factor in the discussions of combat restrictions. The women pilots who want access to combat missions are officers whose promotions and career paths are blocked without combat-related jobs. Just 324 women pilots in the Air Force and 248 in the Navy would immediately benefit from the legislative changes. The remaining statutory obstacles to women entering combat assignments are in the Navy and Marine Corps, which prohibit women from serving on ships on combat missions. In the Army, policy, not law, bars women from jobs considered to involve direct combat.

13   So the fight to end combat exclusions is driven from above. "It's absolutely true that officers are more supportive of repealing combat exclusions than enlisted," says Becraft. "Enlisted women are like blue-collar workers in their career progression. I don't think they want to be in the infantry." And who can blame them? A person might see the movie *Top Gun* and want to fly like Tom Cruise. But has anyone walked out of *Platoon* and signed up to be a grunt?

14   Although existing physical standards would exclude most women from ground combat roles should the Army change its policies, Phyllis Schlafly and other conservatives have harped on the image of women in muddy trenches to fire up the debate. The temptation to rebut their views and the choicest sexist statements emanating from old-timers at the Pentagon is certainly great. In June [1991] Gen. Robert Barrow told a Senate subcommittee addressing women and combat that "I may be old-fashioned, but I think the very nature of women disqualifies them from doing it. Women give life, sustain life, nurture life. They do not take it."

15   There was a time when feminists would make the very same argument and challenge the very existence of the military as well. But "women groups have been dealing with multicultural and multiracial organizing," says Sara Lee Hamilton, director of the Nationwide Women's Program of the American Friends Service Committee. "There's been less energy in the

movement left over to oppose militarism." Without a broader context into which to place the issue, some feminists have decided to go mano-a-mano with the boys, duking it out on their turf. "I see the issue of repealing combat exclusions as commensurate with improving military readiness," says Michele Beneke, a former air defense officer and legal intern for the American Civil Liberties Union who was liaison to the Gay and Lesbian Military Freedom Project. "I also see it as a citizenship issue. In American society, military service is a hallmark of citizenship. Women won't be full citizens until they can serve in any [every] capacity in the military." Proponents of this position say you've got to separate the nasty things the U.S. military actually does from its role as public employer. "You can be against the way the military is used and still say the structure should work with equal opportunity," says De Pauw. "The apparatus of the military is neutral. You can use the hierarchical organization for different things. The planet needs a lot of work. We could use armies to clean up toxic wastes."

Considering that the military is responsible for some of the worst toxic   16
waste sites, such an idea is ironic to Cynthia Enloe, Clark University professor of government and author of *Bananas, Beaches and Bases.* Enloe says, "What gets left out of the discussion is the very issue of militarism. The way the military is discussed makes it look like *General Hospital.* I'm dismayed that NOW hasn't articulated a position around militarism."

"If it took this long to get women into combat, how long will it take   17
to get everyone out?" asks theologian Mary Hunt, co-director of the Women's Alliance for Theology, Ethics and Ritual in Silver Spring, Maryland. "The issue is to be able to name those advances for women that aren't really feminist. Is the nomination of Judge Clarence Thomas really a civil rights achievement?" Hunt sees the issue of equal opportunity in the military as an example of what progressives face in the 1990s. "We're seeing cosmetic solutions, not substantive change. The advances are really retreats. And it requires the complicity of groups who seek to improve the lot of their members."

Advocates of women in the military frequently draw an analogy to   18
black history and civil rights struggles. Black men faced barriers to integration just as women do today, they say, and there is less racism in the services than in the civilian world. "African-Americans seek heroes. Even people who think we shouldn't have been in the Persian Gulf look at Colin Powell with awe," says Barbara Omolade, counselor at the Center for Worker Education at the City College in New York. "People have always said black people can't fight. So we join the Army to prove it. That same thrust has picked up around women. But blacks have not found true equality through military service. And having Powell at the top won't change foreign policy."

One pillar of the equal-opportunity argument is the concept of the   19
"new, improved Army": one that does good deeds, like delivering humanitarian aid to the Kurds. Forget that the U.S. Army helped make them refugees in the first place. It's the military of a new generation of men and

women developing "a new type of relationship . . . a nurturing relationship based upon respect, based on sharing the same hardships," in the words of Carol Barkalow, an Army captain and author of *In the Men's House.* Becraft says it's a less hierarchical military in which "young people have more similar value systems, are more willing to value difference—a multicultural work force."

20   This touchy-feely rhetoric implies that women soldiers will humanize a brutal male domain. Today's soldiers, like the Teenage Mutant Ninja Turtles of cartoon fame, will become warriors for peace. Of course, the idea of a downsized U.S. military as peacekeeping force goes hand-in-glove with the demise of the cold war's enormous standing Army. But if the Pentagon is selling the notion that its mission is changing, we don't have to buy it. "Do you call Grenada, Panama and the gulf war 'peacekeeping'?" asks Hunt.

21   Separating equal opportunity from military might is difficult for feminists with a global perspective. Can we be proud that a woman pilot might in the future strafe fleeing Iraqi women and children on a mop-up mission? Enloe is concerned that the only position on women, combat and the military being articulated is the equal-opportunity view. "The worrisome narrowness of the debate and the silence of U.S. antimilitarist feminists have a powerful effect [on] other countries." She says that, thanks to Cable News Network, U.S. women soldiers were a major story in NATO countries like Italy, Canada, Britain and Germany, where the issue of women and combat is a salient one. Italian women, who cannot join the military, will hold a conference in November [1991], says Enloe. "They're trying to figure out what Italian feminists should be thinking about militarism."

22   The current House-Senate negotiations on their bills to remove combat restrictions for women pilots offer another opportunity to examine the issue. Barriers to advancement for women who choose a military career should and probably will be dropped. Perhaps that will be the bone Congress tosses to women, instead of securing abortion rights and restoring welfare cuts.

23   But those whose vision of feminism extends beyond career trajectories to the search for wholeness inextricably tied to justice need to say there is another perspective on citizenship, valor and patriotism. A first-class female citizenship is founded on serving people, not destructive foreign policies. Let's not get so tangled up in yellow ribbons that we forget the connection between the battles women wage domestically to feed themselves and their families and a ravenous military machinery that swallows nations whole.

Building Vocabulary

Define the words below, using *context clues* wherever possible and checking in a dictionary when necessary. Use them in sentences of your own.

unattainable (1)   counterproductive (9)   respondents (6)
unadulterated (1)   integration (1)   repealing (15)
mettle (5)   dubious (3)

Journal Writing

Choose one or more of the three activities listed below, and make an entry in your journal. Focus on writing spontaneously rather than on structure and mechanics.

1. **Exploring:** Recall what you remember from other sources—your reading, your life experiences, movies and television, stories told to you by others—about the topic discussed by the writer. Choose one or two of these to write about. Which aspects of the topic did they bring up? What additional information did they provide? What emotions did they create in you?
2. **Taking Stock:** Which parts of the selection were most difficult for you to grasp? Which parts needed more explanation? Which parts required outside information to be understood? What kind of information was required (e.g., historical, culture-specific, technical, etc.)? Where might such information be found? Were there aspects of the writer's style you found particularly effective? Particularly difficult? Why?
3. **Responding:** Identify one or two of the writer's main concerns. What personal knowledge, if any, do you have of these issues? What is your opinion on these issues? Examine your response carefully to see what it teaches you about yourself.

Analyzing Content

1. What is the writer's opinion on the full integration of women into the military? What are some of her concerns?
2. How is the position of NOW different from the writer's?
3. What did the Gulf War demonstrate?
4. Describe the "new, improved army." What is the expected role of women soldiers in it?

Analyzing Writing Techniques

1. What technique does the writer use to make her point about the position of women of color in the services (paragraph 11)? Evaluate its effectiveness.
2. This essay provides several opposing viewpoints. Identify some of them. Why does the writer choose to bring these in, especially the ones she does not necessarily agree with?

Group Activity

Analyze the statement in paragraph 17, "The issue is to be able to name those advances for women that aren't really feminist." Do you agree that there are such "advances"? Have each group member come up with an example to support his or her answer.

Your Writing

1. The essay alludes to the fact that women's roles in the military have changed significantly during the last few decades. Write a research paper in which you explore this issue. What has changed? What remains the same? In your opinion, are the changes for the better?
2. In paragraph 13, the writer discusses the way in which movies might influence how a viewer feels about being in the military. Choose two movies that portray the services in very different ways, and write a paper in which you **analyze** what you learn about the military from each one.

Pre-reading Activity Think about a field that has changed during your lifetime. Note down how things used to be and how they are today.

As You Read Observe the writer's use of sense images. How do they strengthen her essay?

FISHY BUSINESS
Roz Batt

*Born in England in 1956, **Roz Batt** came to the United States in 1991 and later became a citizen. Her passions are photography, cooking, writing about food, and collecting English china. She is studying art at Foothill College.*

Never have I seen so much blood and guts. The concept of fish bleeding 1 as they are prepared to become food had never occurred to me until now, as I stand and make notes—inconspicuously, I hope—to one side of the Wah Fat Fish Market in San Francisco's Chinatown. Until now, I have done all my fish buying from supermarket chains, where I have been presented with fish that have been perfectly filleted, washed clean, and sanitarily wrapped in plastic. Here at Wah Fat, however, I am forced to come face to face with the real thing.

Around the edge of the market are huge water tanks filled with 2 grotesque-looking fish. I have not encountered such species before, let alone eaten them. The floor is slippery and covered with black mats. Miles of hose pipe lead from one tank to another. The walls, floor, and counter appear filthy, and the machinery is rusty. But the salty, sea smell of the market is of today's freshly caught fish, and above the humming of the tanks and regrigerators is the sound of someone's car stereo in the street, booming out the sounds of rap music, making us aware of lives being lived.

Although it is a sunny day outside, here in the market it is damp, cool, 3 and rather dark. The atmosphere feels comfortable somehow; the dim ceiling lights do not offend my eyes. Standing here, I suddenly realize how much I dislike the feeling of treading on the automatic door opener of a supermarket entrance. The large, metal-framed doors heave themselves open, and as I enter the impersonal surroundings, the mass of fluorescent light fixtures make me squint. It always takes me a moment to recover and adjust to these efficient but somehow hostile places.

In the center of the fish market is a huge, wooden preparation table; 4 above it hang all manner of deadly looking weapons. Standing behind the table are three men, each clothed in identical, blood-stained white overalls and black-rubber boots. One is wearing an uncharacteristic blue baseball cap—the influence of America in this bustling Asian enclave of the city. Although the men are not speaking to each other and have no expressions that I can discern on their faces, they are clearly working as a team. Each is performing his own laborious task. One slices off the fishes' fins, another scrapes off the scales, and the third slams the fish down onto the wooden board and chops off its head. They are all masters at using the cleaver, a terrifying instrument twice as long as their hands.

5   As I watch and wait for the men to speak to one another, I realize that they communicate through body language, working closely, side by side, in unison, almost as though they were in a silent, carefully choreographed dance. It feels as though these fishmongers have worked together for years, as though they are related. I wonder whether this is a family owned business.

6   Still, none of them has uttered a word. Their eyes are fixed on the job at hand. Then one looks up to scan the front of the market for possible customers. I am discovered. The older man in the baseball cap is coming toward me. His face looks hard and tired. How many hours has he been working today? My suspicion is since very early morning.

7   "You want something?" he asks.

8   "Not right at this moment, thank you," I reply, fingering my notepad awkwardly.

9   He walks away, clearly disappointed at a "no sale."

10   The market is now alive with all manner of customers—young and old, women and men—each determined to purchase the best catch of the day. Unlike in a supermarket, there is no question of picking a numbered ticket to be served in the order of arrival. No, here in the market we face more of a challenge. If you want a particular fish, you had better elbow your way to the front and speak up, or someone else will buy it first. Survival of the fittest.

11   Something in the atmosphere of the market has changed. Perhaps my presence has made the men self-conscious. They utter a few, brief words to each other, but I cannot hear what they are saying. The two younger men's eyes flash toward me. They resume their work, but at a slower, disjointed pace. Finally, the youngest of the trio places his cleaver carefully on the work table, and the others watch him intensely as he walks in my direction.

12   "Are you from Health, IRS, or what?" he asks me. His voice is timid, hesitant, the voice of the immigrant not yet at home in America and wondering what he has done wrong this time.

13   Quickly, I slip the pen and pad into my pocket and say, trying to put him at ease, "No, no, sorry, I'm writing a college assignment and I'm truly fascinated by your work."

14   There is relief on his face as he walks away. Embarrassed by my intrusion, I feel compelled to buy some fish.

15   Next to casting a line and catching the fish myself, or waiting for the early morning fishing trawlers to come to the dock to sell their products, purchasing my dinner at the fish market and watching it being made ready

seems to me the most authentic option. I choose a Rock Cod from one of the bubbling tanks. The fish is huge, with orange and brown speckles and vicious-looking fins. It is not particularly appealing to the eye, but I know from experience that it will taste delicious. Inspired by the smells wafting into the market from the numerous Chinatown restaurants close by, I begin to imagine steaming the fish with ginger, garlic, green onion, and soy sauce. Of course, it is possible to create wonderful meals from food that is bought from the supermarket, but having experienced the Wah Fat Fish Market, I feel it is not quite the same. Our supermarkets do not provide us with any connection between the food we buy and its live source. No intrigue. No uncomfortable feelings. No reality. And no sense of the hard work that has gone into its making.

My assignment complete, I leave the fish market with my dinner 16 tucked under my arm, feeling pleased that my purchase has cost me only three dollars. I have mixed feelings about my visit to the fish market—as do the fishmongers, who are still keeping an eye on me. I feel badly about how hard they are working to make a living, especially as I can see that the fish trade is not making them rich. However, they do have something money cannot buy: dedication and teamwork and pride in their expertise, in their ability to work efficiently and well with what supermarkets would regard as the most primitive of conditions and equipment.

In 20 years time, will we be able to find such personal service in food 17 stores? Will markets like the Wah Fat Fish Market still exist? Or will all food stores be pristine, sterile, and lacking any kind of human character? Will we even remember the presence of the "invisible" men and women who work so hard behind the scenes to bring us the "perfect" products, totally removed from the natural world, that today's consumers seem more and more to desire?

Structure and Strategy

1. What is the **thesis** of this essay? Is it implied or explicit? How is it related to the theme of Unit 6?
2. Where in this essay has the writer used **generalizations?** What effect do they have on the reader?
3. What rhetorical mode does the writer use in paragraphs 2–4? What is her purpose in using this mode? Where else does she use it?

Your Writing

1. Write an **observation** paper: View the workers and conditions in a workplace, and draw conclusions about work and our society.
2. What is Batt's point about the modern consumer? Do you agree? Write a paper about how the modern consumer's attitudes, needs, and desires are affecting the American workplace.

SYNTHESIS: QUESTIONS FOR CRITICAL THINKING AND WRITING

1. Several of these selections, particularly "Racism in Corporate America" and "Equality, Yes—Militarism, No," discuss the problems that women and minorities face in the work world of America. What is your view on this subject? Write a paper in which you **compare/contrast** your viewpoint with that of one or two of the authors in this section.

2. "Year of the Blue-Collar Guy" and "Who Burns for the Perfection of Paper" stress different aspects of manual labor. Write an essay in which you put together the two writers' ideas to weigh the pros and cons of such work and how it is viewed in the United States.

3. "Give Us Jobs, Not Admiration," "Earth Ambassador Aiding Indian Youth," and "Racism in Corporate America" illustrate that it sometimes is difficult to achieve career success when you do not fit the mold of the "good worker." What, in your opinion, is the image of the "good worker" that employers are seeking? Write an essay about this image and the problems it might cause.

4. The selections in this section depict many different attitudes toward work. Putting them together, what do you understand about the American ethic of work? How is work viewed? Why do people work? What are the satisfactions of work? The frustrations? Write an essay in which you put together your findings as well as your own opinions on the subject.

At Play

The influence that sports and important sports figures have on the American mind is immense—and not always for the best, as student Dan Frank argues in his essay "Violent Idols: Negative Effects of Professional Athletes on Children." For better or worse, however, sports have taken hold of the popular imagination and will not be letting go any time soon, so it is important to examine its various aspects and areas. The role of women in sports, for example, is analyzed in "Comes the Revolution," a *Time* article, and in "Why Men Fear Women's Teams," by Kate Rounds. The first essay looks at the enormous gains made by women's teams, and the second focuses on the problems women still experience and why they are often pushed into the background. "The Best Player of Her Time," by Curry Kirkpatrick, takes a different approach, showcasing the life and contributions of tennis player Martina Navratilova.

An inspiring sports figure can be an important influence, particularly for minority children who often encounter prejudice. This is the subject of poet Gary Soto's "Black Hair." And yet there are dangers in wanting to emulate one's sports hero—if for no other reason than the fact that very few ever make it to the top. This is why Arthur Ashe, the famous tennis player, urges African-American children to focus on the library rather than the playing field in "Send Your Children to the Libraries."

Sports can give a chance to minorities, but it can also label them, giving ethnic tags to their way of playing. We become aware of this in Jeff Greenfield's "The Black and White Truth about Basketball," in which he defines "black" and "white" styles of play. The definitions are given an ironic twist—unlike in many other areas of life, here the term *black* denotes superiority. The implications of this reach beyond the game and make us realize what several of the selections indicate: the world of sports, in many ways, mirrors the society that nurtures it.

Pre-reading Activity   Have you, or anyone you know, ever dreamed of being a professional athlete? What led to these dreams?

As You Read   Observe the writer's use of short paragraphs and the way he moves from point to point. How effective is this style?

SEND YOUR CHILDREN TO THE LIBRARIES
Arthur Ashe

Arthur Ashe (1943–1993) was the first African-American to attain world-wide prominence in men's tennis. He held some 33 titles in this field, including the topmost honors. He was also a social activist concerned with the plight of youth in inner cities, and he compiled a three-volume history of African-Americans in sports, A Hard Road to Glory. *The selection below was first published in the* New York Times *in 1977.*

Since my sophomore year at University of California, Los Angeles, I have   1
become convinced that we blacks spend too much time on the playing fields and too little time in the libraries.

Please don't think of this attitude as being pretentious just because I   2
am a black, single, professional athlete.

I don't have children, but I can make observations. I strongly believe   3
the black culture expends too much time, energy and effort raising, praising and teasing our black children as to the dubious glories of professional sports.

All children need models to emulate—parents, relatives or friends. But   4
when the child starts school, the influence of the parent is shared by teachers and classmates, by the lure of books, movies, ministers and newspapers, but most of all by television.

Which televised events have the greatest number of viewers? Sports—   5
the Olympics, Super Bowl, Masters, World Series, pro basketball playoffs, Forest Hills. ABC-TV even has sports on Monday night prime time from April to December.

So your child gets a massive dose of O. J. Simpson, Kareem Abdul-   6
Jabbar, Muhammad Ali, Reggie Jackson, Dr. J. and Lee Elder and other pro athletes. And it is only natural that your child will dream of being a pro athlete himself.

But consider these facts: For the major professional sports of hockey,   7
football, basketball, baseball, golf, tennis and boxing, there are roughly only 3,170 major league positions available (attributing 200 positions to golf, 200 to tennis and 100 to boxing). And the annual turnover is small.

8   We blacks are a subculture of about 28 million. Of the 13 1/2 million men, 5–6 million are under twenty years of age, so your son has less than one chance in a thousand of becoming a pro. Less than one in a thousand. Would you bet your son's future on something with odds of 999 to 1 against you? I wouldn't.

9   Unless a child is exceptionally gifted, you should know by the time he enters high school whether he has a future as an athlete. But what is more important is what happens if he doesn't graduate or doesn't land a college scholarship and doesn't have a viable alternative job career. Our high school dropout rate is several times the national average, which contributes to our unemployment rate of roughly twice the national average.

10   And how do you fight the figures in the newspapers every day? Ali has earned more than $30 million boxing, O. J. just signed for $2 1/2 million, Dr. J. for almost $3 million, Reggie Jackson for $2.8 million, Nate Archibald for $400,000 a year. All that money, recognition, attention, free cars, girls, jobs in the off-season—no wonder there is Pop Warner football, Little League baseball, National Junior League tennis, hockey practice at 5 A.M. and pickup basketball games in any center city at any hour.

11   There must be some way to assure that the 999 who try but don't make it to pro sports don't wind up on the street corners or in the unemployment lines. Unfortunately, our most widely recognized role models are athletes and entertainers—"runnin' " and "jumpin' " and "singin' " and "dancin'." While we are 60 percent of the National Basketball Association, we are less than 4 percent of the doctors and lawyers. While we are about 35 percent of major league baseball, we are less than 2 percent of the engineers. While we are about 40 percent of the National Football League, we are less than 11 percent of construction workers such as carpenters and bricklayers.

12   Our greatest heroes of the century have been athletes—Jack Johnson, Joe Louis and Muhammad Ali. Racial and economic discrimination forced us to channel our energies into athletics and entertainment. These were the ways out of the ghetto, the ways to that Cadillac, those alligator shoes, that cashmere sport coat.

13   Somehow, parents must instill a desire for learning alongside the desire to be Walt Frazier. Why not start by sending black professional athletes to high schools to explain the facts of life.

14   I have often addressed high school audiences and my message is always the same. For every hour you spend on the athletic field, spend two in the library. Even if you make it as a pro athlete, your career will be over by the time you are thirty-five. So you will need that diploma.

15   Have these pro athletes explain what happens if you break a leg, get a sore arm, have one bad year or don't make the cut for five or six tournaments. Explain to them the star system, wherein for every O. J. earning millions there are six or seven others making $15,000 or $20,000 or $30,000 a year.

But don't just have Walt Frazier or O. J. or Abdul-Jabbar address your   16
class. Invite a benchwarmer or a guy who didn't make it. Ask him if he
sleeps every night. Ask him whether he was graduated. Ask him what he
would do if he became disabled tomorrow. Ask him where his old high
school athletic buddies are.

We have been on the same roads—sports and entertainment—too   17
long. We need to pull over, fill up at the library and speed away to Congress and the Supreme Court, the unions and the business world. We need
more Barbara Jordans, Andrew Youngs, union cardholders, Nikki Gio-
vannis and Earl Graveses. Don't worry: We will still be able to sing and
dance and run and jump better than anybody else.

I'll never forget how proud my grandmother was when I graduated   18
from UCLA in 1966. Never mind the Davis Cup in 1968, 1969, and 1970.
Never mind the Wimbledon title, Forest Hills, etc. To this day, she still
doesn't know what those names mean.

What mattered to her was that of her more than thirty children and   19
grandchildren, I was the first to be graduated from college, and a famous
college at that. Somehow, that made up for all those floors she scrubbed
all those years.

Building Vocabulary

Define the words below, using *context clues* wherever possible and
checking in a dictionary when necessary. Use them in sentences of
your own.

pretentious (2)	instill (13)	exceptionally (9)
emulate (4)	expends (3)	benchwarmer (16)

Journal Writing

Choose one or more of the three activities listed below, and make an
entry in your journal. Focus on writing spontaneously rather than on
structure and mechanics.

1. **Exploring:** Recall what you remember from other sources—your
   reading, your life experiences, movies and television, stories told
   to you by others—about the topic discussed by the writer. Choose
   one or two of these to write about. Which aspects of the topic did
   they bring up? What additional information did they provide?
   What emotions did they create in you?
2. **Taking Stock:** Which parts of the selection were most difficult for
   you to grasp? Which parts needed more explanation? Which parts
   required outside information to be understood? What kind of information was required (e.g., historical, culture-specific, technical,

etc.)? Where might such information be found? Were there aspects of the writer's style you found particularly effective? Particularly difficult? Why?

3. **Responding:** Identify one or two of the writer's main concerns. What personal knowledge, if any, do you have of these issues? What is your opinion on these issues? Examine your response carefully to see what it teaches you about yourself.

Analyzing Content

1. Why do professional athletes have such a strong influence on young blacks?
2. Why, according to Ashe, is this negative?
3. How has he used statistics to strengthen his point?
4. What does he suggest as a tool to persuade young people to devote themselves more to education? Is this a good strategy? Explain why or why not.

Analyzing Writing Techniques

1. Where has the writer placed the **thesis** of the essay? Where else might it have been placed?
2. Analyze the conclusion. What is the writer trying to do? What is the technique he uses? Is this technique effective?

Group Activity

Have each member of your group list three names that come to their minds when they think "famous African-Americans." Analyze the group list. In what fields are these people? Do your findings support Ashe's ideas?

Your Writing

1. A related point Ashe makes is that entertainers are among the top role models today for children and young adults. Do you agree? Write an essay in which you analyze the kind of influence entertainers have on children and whether this is good or bad.
2. Write a letter to a young man or woman who is set on becoming a professional athlete. What advice would you give him/her? (You may use some of Ashe's points and examples, but be sure to bring in others of your own.)

Pre-reading Activity   Respond to the term *tomboy.* What images are associated with it in your mind? Does the term have a positive or a negative connotation for you?

As You Read   Note the writer's use of descriptive detail. In which paragraphs is it used? What effect is intended by it?

COMES THE REVOLUTION
Time

This piece was first published in Time *in 1978.*

Steve Sweeney paces the sideline, shoulders hunched against the elements. A steady downpour has turned an Atlanta soccer field into a grassy bog. A few yards away, his team of eight- and nine-year-olds, sporting regulation shirts and shorts, churns after the skittering ball. One minute, all is professional intensity as the players struggle to start a play. The next, there is childhood glee in splashing through a huge puddle that has formed in front of one goal. Sweeney squints at his charges and shouts, "Girls, you gotta pass! Come on, Heather!"   1

At eight, Kim Edwards is in the incubator of the national pastime—tee-ball. There are no pitchers in the pre–Little League league. The ball is placed on a waist-high, adjustable tee, and for five innings the kids whack away. Kim is one of the hottest tee-ball players in Dayton and a fanatical follower of the Cincinnati Reds. Her position is second base. She pulls a Reds cap down over her hair, punches her glove, drops her red-jacketed arms down to rest on red pants, and waits for the action. Kim has but a single ambition: to play for her beloved Reds. When a male onlooker points out that no woman has ever played big league baseball, Kim's face, a mass of strawberry freckles, is a study in defiant dismissal: "So?"   2

The raw wind of a late-spring chill bites through Philadelphia's Franklin Field, but it cannot dull the excitement of the moment. For the first time in the eighty-four year history of the Penn Relays, the world's largest and oldest meet of its kind, an afternoon of women's track and field competition is scheduled. The infield shimmers with color, a kaleidoscope of uniforms and warmup suits. One thousand college and high school athletes jog slowly back and forth, stretch and massage tight muscles, crouch in imaginary starting blocks, huddle with coaches for last-minute strategy sessions, or loll on the synthetic green turf, sipping cocoa and waiting. Susan White, a nineteen-year-old hurdler from the University of Maryland,   3 surveys the scene. There is a trace of awe in her voice: "When I was in high school, I never dreamed of competing in a national meet. People are finally accepting us as athletes."

4   Golfer Carol Mann is chatting with friends outside the clubhouse when a twelve-year-old girl walks up, politely clears her throat and asks for an autograph. Mann bends down—it's a long way from six-foot, three-inch Mann to fan—and talks softly as she writes. After several moments, the girl returns, wide-eyed, to waiting parents. Mann straightens and smiles. "Five years ago, little girls never walked up to tell me they wanted to be a professional golfer. Now it happens all the time. Things are changing, things are changing."

5   They are indeed. On athletic fields and playgrounds and in parks and gymnasiums across the country, a new player has joined the grand game that is sporting competition, and she's a girl. As the long summer begins, not only is she learning to hit a two-fisted backhand like Chris Evert's and turn a back flip like Olga Korbut's, she is also learning to jam a hitter with a fast ball. Season by season, whether aged six, sixty, or beyond, she is running, jumping, hitting, and throwing as U.S. women have never done before. She is trying everything from jogging to ice hockey, lacrosse and rugby, and in the process acquiring a new sense of self, and of self-confidence in her physical abilities and her potential. She is leading a revolution that is one of the most exciting and one of the most important in the history of sport. Says Joan Warrington, executive secretary of the Association for Intercollegiate Athletics for Women: "Women no longer feel that taking part in athletics is a privilege. They believe it is a right."

6   Spurred by the fitness craze, fired up by the feminist movement and buttressed by court rulings and legislative mandates, women have been moving from miniskirted cheerleading on the sidelines for the boys to playing, and playing hard, for themselves. Says Liz Murphy, coordinator of women's athletics at the University of Georgia: "The stigma is nearly erased. Sweating girls are becoming socially acceptable." . . .

7   If, as folklore and public have long insisted, sport is good for people, if it builds a better society by encouraging mental and physical vigor, courage and tenacity, then the revolution in women's sports holds a bright promise for the future. One city in which the future is now is Cedar Rapids, Iowa. In 1969, well before law, much less custom, required the city to make any reforms, Cedar Rapids opened its public school athletic program to girls and, equally important, to the less gifted boys traditionally squeezed out by win-oriented athletic systems. Says Tom Ecker, head of school athletics, "Our program exists to develop good kids, not to serve as a training ground for the universities and pros."

8   Some seven thousand students, nearly three thousand of them girls, compete on teams with a firm no-cut policy. Everyone gets a chance to play. Teams are fielded according to skill levels, and a struggle between junior varsity and C-squad basketball teams is as enthusiastically contested as a varsity clash. Cedar Rapids' schoolgirl athletes compete in nine sports,

guided by 144 coaches. Access to training equipment is equal too. The result has been unparalleled athletic success. In the past eight years, Cedar Rapids' boys and girls teams have finished among the state's top three sixty-eight times, winning thirty team championships in ten different sports.

Girls' athletics have become an accustomed part of the way of life in   9
Cedar Rapids. At a recent girls' track meet, runners, shotputters, hurdlers, high jumpers pitted themselves, one by one, in the age-old contests to run faster, leap higher, throw farther. For many, there were accomplishments they once would have thought impossible. A mile relay team fell into triumphant embrace when word came of qualification for the state finals. Team members shouted the joy of victory—"We did it!"—and then asked permission to break training: "Now can we go to the Dairy Queen, Coach?" Granted.

The mile run was won by seventeen-year-old Julie Nolan of Jefferson   10
High School. Sport is, and will remain, part of her life. "I've been running since the fifth or sixth grade. I want to run in college and then run in marathons." She admires Marathoner Miki Gorman, who ran her fastest when she was in her forties. "That's what I'd like to be doing," she says. Asked if she has been treated differently since she got involved in sports, this once-and-future athlete seemed perplexed: "I don't know, because I've always been an athlete."

Kelly Galliher, fifteen, has grown up in the Cedar Rapids system that   11
celebrates sport for all. The attitudes and resistance that have stunted women's athleticism elsewhere are foreign to Kelly, a sprinter. Does she know that sports are, in some quarters, still viewed as unseemly for young women? "That's ridiculous. Boys sweat, and we're going to sweat. We call it getting out and trying." She has no memories of disapproval from parents or peers. And she has never been called the terrible misnomer that long and unfairly condemned athletic girls. "Tomboy? That idea has gone out here." It's vanishing everywhere.

Building Vocabulary

Define the words below, using *context clues* wherever possible and checking in a dictionary when necessary. Use them in sentences of your own.

bog (1)	mandates (6)	buttressed (6)
incubator (2)	squints (1)	stigma (6)
spurred (6)	awe (3)	

Journal Writing

Choose one or more of the three activities listed below, and make an entry in your journal. Focus on writing spontaneously rather than on structure and mechanics.

1. **Exploring:** Recall what you remember from other sources—your reading, your life experiences, movies and television, stories told to you by others—about the topic discussed by the writer. Choose one or two of these to write about. Which aspects of the topic did they bring up? What additional information did they provide? What emotions did they create in you?

2. **Taking Stock:** Which parts of the selection were most difficult for you to grasp? Which parts needed more explanation? Which parts required outside information to be understood? What kind of information was required (e.g., historical, culture-specific, technical, etc.)? Where might such information be found? Were there aspects of the writer's style you found particularly effective? Particularly difficult? Why?

3. **Responding:** Identify one or two of the writer's main concerns. What personal knowledge, if any, do you have of these issues? What is your opinion on these issues? Examine your response carefully to see what it teaches you about yourself.

Analyzing Content

1. What is the "revolution" the article discusses? What does it **imply** about earlier practices?

2. Have any further changes occurred in this field since the article was written in 1978?

3. **Summarize** the main points about the Cedar Rapids program. What makes this program special?

4. **Analyze** the examples in the first four paragraphs. How is each different? What point is the writer making through each?

5. What is Liz Murphy referring to in paragraph 6 when she says, "The stigma is nearly erased"? Do you agree?

Analyzing Writing Techniques

1. In which paragraph does the **thesis** appear? Why has the writer placed it here? How does he lead up to it?

2. What do you notice about the backgrounds of the people quoted in this article? What do you think is the writer's intention in choosing these subjects?

Group Activity

Have each member of the group write a brief statement about what, if anything, sports has contributed to his/her life. Based on this, write a **collaborative** paragraph about the value of sports in our lives.

Your Writing

1. Expanding on your findings from the group activity and taking into account the points made in the *Time* article, write an essay about the importance of sports in our lives today. Examine both the pros and cons of the issue.

2. The Cedar Rapids athletic program's philosophy is that less gifted children have as much of a right to be included as the more talented athletes. It is opposed to "win-oriented" athletic programs. What is the policy, regarding this matter, at your educational institute? Research this topic, interviewing a few key people on campus, and then write a paper evaluating the athletic program.

Pre-reading Activity   Write a brief response to the title of this essay. What points do you think the selection will discuss?

As You Read   Identify the writer's position on the problems of women in team sports.

WHY MEN FEAR WOMEN'S TEAMS
Kate Rounds

Kate Rounds *is a freelance writer who often contributes to* Ms. *magazine, in which this essay first appeared in 1991.*

1   Picture this. You're flipping through the channels one night, and you land on a local network, let's say ABC. And there on the screen is a basketball game. The players are sinking three-pointers, slam-dunking, and doing the usual things basketball players do. They're high-fiving each other, patting one another on the butt, and then sauntering to the locker room to talk about long-term contracts.

2   Now imagine that the players aren't men. They're women, big sweaty ones, wearing uniforms and doing their version of what guys thrive on—bonding. So far, this scene is a fantasy and will remain so until women's professional team sports get corporate sponsors, television exposure, arenas, fan support, and a critical mass of well-trained players.

3   While not enough fans are willing to watch women play traditional team sports, they love to watch women slugging it out on roller-derby rinks and in mud-wrestling arenas. Currently popular is a bizarre television spectacle called *American Gladiators,* in which women stand on pastel pedestals, wearing Lycra tights and brandishing weapons that look like huge Q-Tips. The attraction obviously has something to do with the "uniforms."

4   The importance of what women athletes wear can't be underestimated. Beach volleyball, which is played in the sand by bikini-clad women, rates network coverage while traditional court volleyball can't marshal any of the forces that would make a women's pro league succeed.

5   It took a while, but women were able to break through sexist barriers in golf and tennis. Part of their success stemmed from the sports themselves—high-end individual sports that were born in the British Isles and flourished in country clubs across the U.S. The women wore skirts, makeup, and jewelry along with their wristbands and warm-up jackets. The corporate sponsors were hackers themselves, and the fans—even men—could identify with these women; a guy thought that if he hit the ball

enough times against the barn door, he too could play like Martina. And women's purses were equaling men's. In fact, number-one-ranked Steffi Graf's prize money for 1989 was $1,963,905 and number-one-ranked Stefan Edberg's was $1,661,491.

By contrast, women's professional team sports have failed spectacu- 6 larly. Since the mid-seventies, every professional league—softball, basketball, and volleyball—has gone belly-up. In 1981, after a four-year struggle, the Women's Basketball League (WBL), backed by sports promoter Bill Byrne, folded. The league was drawing fans in a number of cities, but the sponsors weren't there. TV wasn't there, and nobody seemed to miss the spectacle of a few good women fighting for a basketball.

Or a volleyball, for that matter. Despite the success of bikini volley- 7 ball, an organization called MLV (Major League Volleyball) bit the dust in March of 1989 after nearly three years of struggling for sponsorship, fan support, and television exposure. As with pro basketball, there was a man behind women's professional volleyball, real estate investor Robert (Bat) Batinovich. Batinovich admits that, unlike court volleyball, beach volleyball has a lot of "visual T&A mixed into it."

What court volleyball does have, according to former MLV executive 8 director Lindy Vivas, is strong women athletes. Vivas is assistant volleyball coach at San Jose State University. "The United States in general," she says, "has problems dealing with women athletes and strong, aggressive females. The perception is you have to be more aggressive in team sports than in golf and tennis, which aren't contact sports. Women athletes are looked at as masculine and get the stigma of being gay."

One former women's basketball promoter, who insists on remaining 9 anonymous, goes further. "You know what killed women's sports?" he says. "Lesbians. This cost us in women's basketball. But I know there are not as many lesbians now unless I'm really blinded. We discourage it, you know. We put it under wraps."

People in women's sports spend a lot of time dancing around the "L" 10 word, and the word "image" pops up in a way it never does in men's sports. Men can spit tobacco juice, smoke, and even scratch their testicles on national television and get away with it.

Bill Byrne, former WBL promoter, knows there isn't a whole lot women 11 can get away with while they're beating each other out for a basketball. "In the old league," he says, "my partner, Mike Connors, from *Mannix*—his wife said, 'Let's do makeup on these kids.' And I knew that the uniforms could be more attractive. We could tailor them so the women don't look like they're dragging a pair of boxer shorts down the floor."

The response from the athletes to this boy talk is not always outrage. 12 "Girls in women's basketball now are so pretty," says Nancy Lieberman-Cline. "They're image-conscious." The former Old Dominion star, who made headlines as Martina's trainer, played with the men's U.S. Basketball League, the Harlem Globe Trotters Tour (where she met husband Tim

Cline), and with the Dallas Diamonds of the old WBL. "Everyone used to have short hair," she says. "Winning and playing was everything. I wouldn't think of using a curling iron. Now there are beautiful girls out there playing basketball."

13   Lieberman-Cline says she doesn't mind making the concession. "It's all part of the process," she says. "You can't be defensive about everything."

14   Bill Byrne is so certain that women's professional basketball can work that he's organized a new league, the Women's Pro Basketball League, Inc. (WPBL), set to open its first season shortly. Byrne talks fast and tough, and thinks things have changed for the better since 1981 when the old league went under. "Exposure is the bottom word," he says. "If you get plenty of TV exposure, you'll create household names, and you'll fill arenas. It takes the tube. But I'll get the tube this time because the game of TV has changed. You have cable now. You have to televise home games to show people a product."

15   There's no doubt that many athletes in the women's sports establishment are leery of fast-talking guys who try to make a buck off women's pro sports, especially when the women themselves don't profit from those ventures. In the old league, finances were so shaky that some players claim they were never paid.

16   "We weren't getting the gate receipts," says Lieberman-Cline. "They'd expect 2,000, get only 400, and then they'd have to decide to pay the arena or pay the girls, and the girls were the last choice. There was a lot of mismanagement in the WBL, though the intent was good." She also has her doubts about the new league: "There are not enough things in place to make it happen, not enough owners, arenas, TV coverage, or players. It's going to take more than optimism to make it work."

17   Given the track record of women's professional team sports in this country, it's not surprising that the national pastime is faring no better. When Little League was opened to girls by court order in 1974, one might have thought that professional women's baseball could not be far behind. Baseball is a natural for women. It's not a contact sport, it doesn't require excessive size or strength—even little guys like Phil Rizzuto and Jose Lind can play it—and it's actually an individual sport masquerading as a team sport. Still, in recent years, no one's taken a serious stab at organizing a women's professional league.

18   In 1984, there was an attempt to field a women's minor-league team. Though the Sun Sox had the support of baseball great Hank Aaron, it was denied admission to the Class A Florida State League. The team was the brainchild of a former Atlanta Braves vice president of marketing, Bob Hope. "A lot of the general managers and owners of big-league clubs were mortified," Hope says, "and some players said they wouldn't compete against women. It was male ego or something."

19   Or something, says softball hall-of-famer Donna Lopiano. "When girls suffer harassment in Little League, that's not exactly opening up opportu-

nities for women," she says. "Girls don't have the access to coaching and weight training that boys have. Sports is a place where physiological advantages give men power, and they're afraid of losing it. Sports is the last great bastion of male chauvinism. In the last eight years, we've gone backward, not only on gender equity but on civil rights."

Women of color still face barriers that European American women   20 don't, particularly in the areas of coaching and refereeing. But being a woman athlete is sometimes a bond that transcends race. "We're all at a handicap," says Ruth Lawanson, an African American who played volleyball with MLV. "It doesn't matter whether you're Asian, Mexican, black or white."

Historically, baseball and softball diamonds have not been very hos-   21 pitable to black men and any women. Despite the fact that even men's softball is not a crowd pleaser, back in 1976, Billie Jean King and golfer Jane Blalock teamed up with ace amateur softball pitcher Joan Joyce to form the International Women's Professional Softball Association (IWPSA). Five years later, without sponsorship, money, or television, the league was history.

Billie Jean King has her own special attachment to the team concept.   22 As a girl, she wanted to be a baseball player, but her father gave her a tennis racket, knowing that there wasn't much of a future for a girl in baseball. The story is especially touching since Billie Jean's brother, Randy Moffitt, went on to become a pitcher with the San Francisco Giants. But even as a tennis player, Billie Jean clung to the team idea. She was the force behind World Team Tennis, which folded in 1978, and is currently the chief executive officer of TeamTennis, now entering its eleventh season with corporate sponsorship.

On the face of it, TeamTennis is a bizarre notion because it takes what   23 is a bred-in-the-bones individual sport and tries to squeeze it into a team concept. It has the further handicap of not really being necessary when strong women's and men's professional tours are already in place.

In the TeamTennis format, all players play doubles as well as singles.   24 Billie Jean loves doubles, she says, because she enjoys "sharing the victory." What also distinguishes TeamTennis from the women's and men's pro tours is fan interaction. Fans are encouraged to behave as if watching a baseball or basketball game rather than constantly being told to shut up and sit down as they are at pro tour events like the U.S. Open. The sense of team spirit among the players—the fact that they get to root for one another—is also attracting some big names. Both Martina Navratilova and Jimmy Connors have signed on to play TeamTennis during its tiny five-week season, which begins after Wimbledon and ends just before the U.S. Open.

But you have to go back almost 50 years to find a women's profes-   25 sional sports team that was somewhat successful—though the conditions for that success were rather unusual. During World War II, when half the population was otherwise engaged, women were making their mark in the formerly male strongholds of welding, riveting—and baseball. The All-American Girls Professional Baseball League (AAGPBL) fielded such teams as the Lassies, the Belles, and the Chicks on the assumption that it was better to have "girls" playing than to let the national pastime languish. The league lasted a whopping 12 years after its inception in 1943.

26   The success of this sandlot venture, plagued as it was by the simple-hearted sexism of the forties (the women went to charm school at night), must raise nagging doubts in the mind of the woman team player of the nineties. Can she triumph only in the absence of men?

27   It may be true that she can triumph only in the absence of competition from the fiercely popular men's pro leagues, which gobble up sponsorship. U.S. network television, and the hearts and minds of male fanatics. The lack of male competition outside the United States may be partly responsible for the success of women's professional team sports in Europe, Japan, South America, and Australasia. Lieberman-Cline acknowledges that Europe provides a more hospitable climate for women's pro basketball. "Over there, they don't have as many options," she says. "We have Broadway plays, movies, you name it. We're overindulged with options."

28   Bruce Levy is a 230-pound bespectacled accountant who escaped from the Arthur Andersen accounting firm 11 years ago to market women's basketball. "It's pretty simple," he says. "People overseas are more realistic and enlightened. Women's basketball is not viewed as a weak version of men's. If Americans could appreciate a less powerful, more scientific, team-oriented game, we'd be two-thirds of the way toward having a league succeed."

29   Levy, who represents many women playing pro basketball abroad, says 120 U.S. women are playing overseas and making up to $70,000 in a seven-month season. They include star players like Teresa Edwards, Katrina McClain, and Lynette Woodward. "A player like Teresa Weatherspoon, everybody recognizes her in Italy," he says. "No one in the U.S. knows her. If there were a pro league over here, I wouldn't be spending all day on the phone speaking bad Italian and making sure the women's beds are long enough. I'd just be negotiating contracts."

30   Levy claims that U.S. businesswomen aren't supporting women's team sports. "In Europe," he says, "the best-run and most publicized teams are run by women who own small businesses and put their money where their mouth is." Joy Burns, president of Sportswomen of Colorado, Inc., pleads no contest. "Businesswomen here are too conservative and don't stick their necks out," she says. MLV's Bat Batinovich, who says he's "disappointed" in U.S. businesswomen for not supporting women's team sports, figures an investor in MLV should have been willing to lose $200,000 a year for five years. Would Burns have done it? "If I'm making good financial investments, why should I?"

31   The prospects for women's professional team sports don't look bright. The reasons for the lack of financial support go beyond simple econom-

ics and enter the realm of deep-rooted sexual bias and homophobia. San Jose State's Lindy Vivas says men who feel intimidated by physically strong women have to put the women down. "There's always a guy in the crowd who challenges the women when he wouldn't think of going one-on-one with Magic Johnson or challenging Nolan Ryan to a pitching contest."

Softball's Donna Lopiano calls it little-boy stuff: "Men don't want to 32 have a collegial, even-steven relationship with women. It's like dealing with cavemen."

Building Vocabulary

Define the words below, using *context clues* wherever possible and checking in a dictionary when necessary. Use them in sentences of your own.

sauntering (1)	languish (25)	masquerading (17)
brandishing (3)	bizarre (3)	bastion (19)
stemmed (5)	marshal (4)	homophobia (31)
brainchild (18)		

Journal Writing

Choose one or more of the three activities listed below, and make an entry in your journal. Focus on writing spontaneously rather than on structure and mechanics.

1. **Exploring:** Recall what you remember from other sources—your reading, your life experiences, movies and television, stories told to you by others—about the topic discussed by the writer. Choose one or two of these to write about. Which aspects of the topic did they bring up? What additional information did they provide? What emotions did they create in you?
2. **Taking Stock:** Which parts of the selection were most difficult for you to grasp? Which parts needed more explanation? Which parts required outside information to be understood? What kind of information was required (e.g., historical, culture-specific, technical, etc.)? Where might such information be found? Were there aspects of the writer's style you found particularly effective? Particularly difficult? Why?
3. **Responding:** Identify one or two of the writer's main concerns. What personal knowledge, if any, do you have of these issues? What is your opinion on these issues? Examine your response carefully to see what it teaches you about yourself.

Analyzing Content

1. Why, according to the writer, do men fear women's teams?
2. By analyzing the evidence presented regarding which women's sports are successful and which are not, what **conclusions** can you draw?
3. Examine the role of television and corporate sponsorship in promoting women's team sports. What problems do you see?
4. Why is it easier for women athletes to succeed overseas?

Analyzing Writing Techniques

1. Where does the writer use the technique of **comparison/contrast?** Where does she bring in **illustration?** What other modes are used in the article?
2. This piece lacks a conventional conclusion. Write a final paragraph in which you summarize the article's main points.

Group Activity

Have each member of the group flip through TV channels one night, just as the writer suggests in the beginning of the essay, paying attention to the sports that are featured. Discuss your findings at the next class session. Based on your evidence, would you say the writer's evaluation of the problems faced by women's teams is accurate? Write a **group paragraph** on this topic.

Your Writing

1. The writer claims that homophobia is an important underlying reason why women's team sports are not adequately supported. Others seem to agree with her (see paragraphs 8 and 9). What is your opinion on this subject? Write an essay supporting your viewpoint with clear and specific examples.
2. **Compare/contrast** the situation of American women athletes in a particular sport with that of women athletes in a similar field in a different country. In what way is the American athlete better off? In what way is her situation worse?

Pre-reading Activity   Consider the title. Who would you consider a worthy recipient of this title? Why?

As You Read   Make a list of the adjectives that best describe Navratilova.

THE BEST PLAYER OF HER TIME
Curry Kirkpatrick

Curry Kirkpatrick is a freelance journalist who often writes for Newsweek, *in which this selection first appeared in 1994.*

She sprints onto the court, smiling and waving and whirling as she goes.   1
She arrives before the announcer can finish the intros, but long since the crowd has risen to its feet, clapped and shouted her along. After all those guilt-ridden years of rejection, suspicion, doubt and even fear—ours, not hers—it is good and proper and especially wonderful that here in Zurich and Filderstadt and Oakland and, for that matter, Tennis's Global Village, we have ultimately embraced her.

"I was born to be an American," Martina Navratilova once said. But   2
now, at the end, finally, her makeover from chubbette Euroqueen to Historical Eminence is complete. Navratilova has turned into far more than merely one of us. She is mentor, conscience, role model, our own World Icon. The best female athlete of all time, arguably. Grand-slam tennis champion, certainly. Above all, grande dame in humanity.

Navratilova, 38, has passed through a retirement year in which she came   3
this close to winning her 10th Wimbledon championship. She has not seemed so I-am-woman, hear-me-roar leonine as much as softer, vulnerable, even laid back. When she plays her last official engagement at the Virginia Slims Championships in New York next week—a tournament she has won, ho-hum, on seven occasions—first-time Martina gazers will invariably see her as warmer and more personable. And that's because she is.

Moreover, in the past year Navratilova has abandoned any pretense   4
to, as a friend says, "frilliness." This has resulted in yet another radical Martina makeover, this one in haberdashery: stark business suit, then jeans, in interviews with Barbara Walters and David Letterman; and for tournament play, floppy golf shirts and ugly black gym shorts.

But if this is about accentuating some lifestyle manifesto—*Hey, this is*   5
me. I don't care—Navratilova has got it all wrong. It's we who don't care anymore. Acceptance is history; her public shows up now with honor and

respect abounding. Rushing baseline to net with the same effort and enthusiasm as ever, she's been a revelation: old glad rags shining on a frol-
icking child at play.

6   And must not the genuinely happy crowd reaction be the best feeling
about the last tour? "I didn't think I'd care so much about how well I played
this year," Navratilova says. "But I can feel everybody wants me to win so
badly. I'm the home team everywhere." Remember, this is the foreign in-
vader who kept whipping up on America's sweetheart, Chris Evert. It was
the most ardent rivalry in all of sport; when Evert retired, Navratilova was
ahead 43-37.

7   It probably took Evert's friendship, then her own retirement, for the
public to come around to Martina. After all, it had taken a while for Chris,
who recently said that for a time Navratilova "wasn't nice to me," that han-
dlers "pumped her to hate me." How long could that have lasted? During
a break in their vicious on-court competition, Navratilova invited Evert to
Aspen and introduced her to the love of her life (now husband), Andy Mill.

8   In Martina's own remarkable life, Soviet tanks destroyed her homeland, her father committed suicide, her private affairs have been splashed
across a scrapbook from "Geraldo" hell. Probably no other public figure
has compiled so eclectic a roster of friends and companions—from best-
selling novelist to transsexual ophthalmologist to Texas beauty queen—the
variety of which may have led to the most memorable exchange in Wimbledon history:

9   **Reporter:** Are you still a lesbian?
10   **Martina:** Are you still the alternative?

11   Navratilova is a living textbook on dichotomy. She has always, as described by the essayist Frank Deford, "been the other; the odd one, alone:
left-hander in a right-handed universe, gay in a straight world; defector,
immigrant, the (last?) gallant volleyer among all those duplicate baseline
bytes . . . she was the European among Americans; she leaves as the American among Europeans—and the only grown-up left in the tennis crib."

12   **Parting shot:** It is hardly irony that in the year Navratilova leaves, her
14-year-old successors arrive: one *named* after her (Switzerland's Martina
Hingis), the other imitating her ferocious, attacking style (America's Venus
Williams). But Navratilova contributed a parting shot at their youthful
folly, as well: "Parents need to take better care of their kids. If the parent
allows her to get any toy, it's not the toy store's fault."

13   Navratilova wants her legacy to be her "passion." But last week another teenager named Marketa Kochta almost beat her in an early-round
match in Oakland. Kochta, Czech-born, said she came to the tournament
only because it was her last chance to play Martina. Later she whispered
to her opponent: "You are my hero."

14   And, surely, that should remain the grand old champion's most cherished legacy. Along with her courage and honesty and intellect, the divine

MN leaves behind her name, her game and her heroism against which all the future young women in tennis must measure themselves.

Building Vocabulary

Define the words below, using *context clues* wherever possible and checking in a dictionary when necessary. Use them in sentences of your own.

sprints (1)	ardent (6)	haberdashery (4)
grande dame (2)	mentor (2)	manifesto (5)
personable (3)	leonine (3)	eclectic (8)
accentuating (5)		

Journal Writing

Choose one or more of the three activities listed below, and make an entry in your journal. Focus on writing spontaneously rather than on structure and mechanics.

1. **Exploring:** Recall what you remember from other sources—your reading, your life experiences, movies and television, stories told to you by others—about the topic discussed by the writer. Choose one or two of these to write about. Which aspects of the topic did they bring up? What additional information did they provide? What emotions did they create in you?
2. **Taking Stock:** Which parts of the selection were most difficult for you to grasp? Which parts needed more explanation? Which parts required outside information to be understood? What kind of information was required (e.g., historical, culture-specific, technical, etc.)? Where might such information be found? Were there aspects of the writer's style you found particularly effective? Particularly difficult? Why?
3. **Responding:** Identify one or two of the writer's main concerns. What personal knowledge, if any, do you have of these issues? What is your opinion on these issues? Examine your response carefully to see what it teaches you about yourself.

Analyzing Content

1. What changes does the writer see in Navratilova during the last year? What reasons can you **infer** for these changes?
2. Describe the attitude of the public toward Navratilova today. What hints are we given that they were not always this way?
3. What do the details given about Navratilova's past indicate about her character?

4. Analyze Navratilova's legacy. Of all the things she leaves behind, which do you consider the most valuable?

Analyzing Writing Techniques

1. Each quotation by Navratilova has been chosen to illustrate a different side of her personality. Analyze the quotations, and indicate what they say about her.
2. What **metaphors** does the writer use to give a sense of Navratilova's character? Evaluate their effectiveness.

Group Activity

Have each member of the group find and **summarize** an article in praise of an athlete. Compare notes. For which qualities are these athletes praised? Do some qualities appear in more than one article?

Your Writing

1. Write a letter to an athlete you admire, explaining the reasons for your admiration and what, if anything, you have learned from his/her life.
2. The article touches on a trend that is growing in professional sports today: the inclusion of very young professional athletes. Write a paper in which you examine the pros and cons of this trend. What is gained and what lost, especially by the young players? Include specific examples.

Pre-reading Activity　Do you associate different sports with people of different races or nationalities? Why, or why not?

As You Read　Observe the way in which the writer presents reasons to support his opinions.

THE BLACK AND WHITE TRUTH ABOUT BASKETBALL
Jeff Greenfield

Jeff Greenfield is a native New Yorker, a writer, a speechwriter, and a television commentator. He holds degrees from the University of Wisconsin and Yale Law School. He has been published in most of the nation's major magazines and has written books on sports, the media, and politics. Some of his books are Where Have You Gone, Joe Di Maggio?, The World's Greatest Team: A Portrait of the Boston Celtics, Television: The First Fifty Years, *and* Playing to Win: An Insider's Guide to Politics. *The selection below was first published in* Esquire *in 1975 and then revised in 1981.*

The dominance of black athletes over professional basketball is beyond　1
dispute. Two thirds of the players are black, and the number would be greater were it not for the continuing practice of picking white bench warmers for the sake of balance. The Most Valuable Player award of the National Basketball Association has gone to blacks for eighteen of the last twenty-one years. In the 1979–80 season, eight of the top ten All-Stars were black. The NBA was the first pro sports league of any stature to hire a black coach (Bill Russell of the Celtics) and the first black general manager (Wayne Embry of the Bucks). What discrimination remains—lack of opportunity for lucrative benefits such as speaking engagements and product endorsements—has more to do with society than with basketball.

　　This dominance reflects a natural inheritance; basketball is a pastime　2
of the urban poor. The current generation of black athletes are heirs to a tradition half a century old: in a neighborhood without the money for bats, gloves, hockey sticks, tennis rackets, or shoulder pads, basketball is accessible. "Once it was the game of the Irish and Italian Catholics in Rockaway and the Jews on Fordham Road in the Bronx," writes David Wolf in his brilliant book, *Foul!* "It was recreation, status, and a way out." But now the ethnic names are changed; instead of Red Holzmans, Red Auerbachs, and McGuire brothers, there are Julius Ervings and Darryl Dawkins and

Kareem Abdul-Jabbars. And professional basketball is a sport with a national television contract and million-dollar salaries.

3   But the mark on basketball of today's players can be measured by more than money or visibility. It is a question of style. For there is a clear difference between "black" and "white" styles of play that is as clear as the difference between 155th Street at Eighth Avenue and Crystal City, Missouri. Most simply (remembering we are talking about culture, not chromosomes), "black" basketball is the use of superb athletic skill to adapt to the limits of space imposed by the game. "White" ball is the pulverization of that space by sheer intensity.

4   It takes a conscious effort to realize how constricted the space is on a basketball court. Place a regulation court (ninety-four by fifty feet) on a football field, and it will reach from the back of the end zone to the twenty-one-yard line; its width will cover less than a third of the field. On a baseball diamond, a basketball court will reach from home plate to just beyond first base. Compared to its principal indoor rival, ice hockey, basketball covers about one-fourth the playing area. And during the normal flow of the game, most of the action takes place on about the third of the court nearest the basket. It is in this dollhouse space that ten men, each of them half a foot taller than the average man, come together to battle each other.

5   There is, thus, no room; basketball is a struggle for the edge: the half step with which to cut around the defender for a lay-up, the half second of freedom with which to release a jump shot, the instant a head turns allowing a pass to a teammate breaking for the basket. It is an arena for the subtlest of skills: the head fake, the shoulder fake, the shift of body weight to the right and the sudden cut to the left. Deception is crucial to success; and to young men who have learned early and painfully that life is a battle for survival, basketball is one of the few games in which the weapon of deception is a legitimate rule and not the source of trouble.

6   If there is, then, the need to compete in a crowd, to battle for the edge, then the surest strategy is to develop the *unexpected;* to develop a shot that is simply and fundamentally different from the usual methods of putting the ball in the basket. Drive to the hoop, but go under it and come up the other side; hold the ball at waist level and shoot from there instead of bringing the ball up to eye level; leap into the air and fall away from the basket instead of toward it. All these tactics take maximum advantage of the crowding on a court; they also stamp uniqueness on young men who may feel it nowhere else.

7   "For many young men in the slums," David Wolf writes, "the school yard is the only place they can feel true pride in what they do, where they can move free of inhibitions and where they can, by being spectacular, rise for the moment against the drabness and anonymity of their lives. Thus, when a player develops extraordinary 'school yard' moves and shots . . . [they] become his measure as a man."

So the moves that begin as tactics for scoring soon become calling 8
cards. You don't just lay the ball in for an uncontested basket; you take the
ball in both hands, leap as high as you can, and slam the ball through the
hoop. When you jump in the air, fake a shot, bring the ball back to your
body, and throw up a shot, all without coming back down, you have
proven your worth in uncontestable fashion.

This liquid grace is an integral part of "black" ball, almost exclusively 9
the province of the playground player. Some white stars like Bob Cousy,
Billy Cunningham, Doug Collins, and Paul Westphal had it: the body control, the moves to the basket, the free-ranging mobility. They also had the
surface ease that is integral to the "black" style; an incorporation of the
ethic of mean streets—to "make it" is not just to have wealth, but to have
it without strain. Whatever the muscles and organs are doing, the face of
the "black" star almost never shows it. George Gervin of the San Antonio
Spurs can drive to the basket with two men on him, pull up, turn around,
and hit a basket without the least flicker of emotion. The Knicks' former
great Walt Frazier, flamboyant in dress, cars, and companions, displayed
nothing but a quickly raised fist after scoring a particularly important basket. (Interestingly, the black coaches in the NBA exhibit far less emotion
on the bench than their white counterparts; Al Attles and K. C. Jones are
statuelike compared with Jack Ramsey or Dick Motta.)

If there is a single trait that characterizes "black" ball it is leaping 10
agility. Bob Cousy, ex-Celtic great and former pro coach, says that "when
coaches get together, one is sure to say, 'I've got the one black kid in the
country who can't jump.' When coaches see a white boy who can jump
or who moves with extraordinary quickness, they say, 'He should have
been born black, he's that good.' "

Don Nelson, former Celtic and coach of the Milwaukee Bucks, recalls 11
that in 1970, Dave Cowens, then a relatively unknown Florida State graduate, prepared for his rookie season by playing in the Rucker League, an
outdoor Harlem competition that pits pros against playground stars and
college kids. So ferocious was Cowens' leaping power, Nelson says, that
"when the summer was over, everyone wanted to know who the white son
of a bitch was who could jump so high." That's another way to overcome
a crowd around the basket—just go over it.

Speed, mobility, quickness, acceleration, "the moves"—all of these are 12
catch-phrases that surround the "black" playground style of play. So does
the most racially tinged of attributes, "rhythm." Yet rhythm is what the black
stars themselves talk about; feeling the flow of the game, finding the tempo
of the dribble, the step, the shot. It is an instinctive quality, one that has
led to difficulty between systematic coaches and free-form players. "Cats
from the street have their own rhythm when they play," said college
dropout Bill Spivey, onetime New York high-school star. "It's not a matter
of somebody setting you up and you shooting. You *feel* the shot. When a
coach holds you back, you lose the feel and it isn't fun anymore."

13   Connie Hawkins, the legendary Brooklyn playground star, said of Laker coach Bill Sharman's methodical style of teaching, "He's systematic to the point where it begins to be a little too much. It's such an action-reaction type of game that when you have to do everything the same way, I think you lose something."

14   There is another kind of basketball that has grown up in America. It is not played on asphalt playgrounds with a crowd of kids competing for the court; it is played on macadam driveways by one boy with a ball and a backboard nailed over the garage; it is played in Midwestern gyms and on Southern dirt courts. It is a mechanical, precise development of skills (when Don Nelson was an Iowa farm boy his incentive to make his shots was that an errant rebound would land in the middle of chicken droppings), without frills, without flow, but with effectiveness. It is "white" basketball: jagged, sweaty, stumbling, intense. A "black" player overcomes an obstacle with finesse and body control; a "white" player reacts by outrunning or outpowering the obstacle.

15   By this definition, the Boston Celtics are a classically "white" team. The Celtics almost never use a player with dazzling moves; that would probably make Red Auerbach swallow his cigar. Instead, the Celtics wear you down with execution, with constant running, with the same play run again and again. The rebound triggers the fast break, with everyone racing downcourt; the ball goes to Larry Bird, who pulls up and takes the jump shot, or who fakes the shot and passes off to the man following, the "trailer," who has the momentum to go inside for a relatively easy shot.

16   Perhaps the most classically "white" position is that of the quick forward, one without great moves to the basket, without highly developed shots, without the height and mobility for rebounding effectiveness. What does he do? He runs. He runs from the opening jump to the last horn. He runs up and down the court, from base line to base line, back and forth under the basket, looking for the opening, for the pass, for the chance to take a quick step and the high-percentage shot. To watch San Antonio's Mark Olberding, a player without speed or moves, is to wonder what he is doing in the NBA—until you see him swing free and throw up a shot that, without demanding any apparent skill, somehow goes in the basket more frequently than the shots of any of his teammates. And to have watched Boston Celtic immortal John Havlicek is to have seen "white" ball at its best.

17   Havlicek stands in dramatic contrast to Julius Erving of the Philadelphia 76ers. Erving has the capacity to make legends come true; leaping from the foul line and slam-dunking the ball on his way down; going up for a lay-up, pulling the ball to his body and throwing under and up the other side of the rim, defying gravity and probability with moves and jumps. Havlicek looked like the living embodiment of his small-town Ohio background. He would bring the ball downcourt, weaving left, then right, looking for the path. He would swing the ball to a teammate, cut be-

hind a pick, take the pass and release the shot in a flicker of time. It looked plain, unvarnished. But there are not half a dozen players in the league who can see such possibilities for a free shot, then get that shot off as quickly and efficiently as Havlicek.

To former pro Jim McMillian, a black with "white" attributes, himself   18
a quick forward, "it's a matter of environment. Julius Erving grew up in a different environment from Havlicek—John came from a very small town in Ohio. There everything was done the easy way, the shortest distance between two points. It's nothing fancy, very few times will he go one-on-one; he hits the lay-up, hits the jump shot, makes the free throw, and after the game you look up and you say, 'How did he hurt us that much?' "

"White" ball, then, is the basketball of patience and method. "Black"   19
ball is the basketball of electric self-expression. One player has all the time in the world to perfect his skills, the other a need to prove himself. These are slippery categories, because a poor boy who is black can play "white" and a white boy of middle-class parents can play "black." Jamaal Wilkes and Paul Westphal are athletes who seem to defy these categories. And what makes basketball the most intriguing of sports is how these styles do not necessarily clash; how the punishing intensity of "white" players and the dazzling moves of the "blacks" can fit together, a fusion of cultures that seems more and more difficult in the world beyond the out-of-bounds line.

Building Vocabulary

Define the words below, using *context clues* wherever possible and checking in a dictionary when necessary. Use them in sentences of your own.

dominance (1)	agility (10)	inhibitions (7)
pulverization (3)	errant (14)	incorporation (9)
fundamentally (6)	lucrative (1)	tinged (12)
anonymity (7)	crucial (5)	finesse (14)

Journal Writing

Choose one or more of the three activities listed below, and make an entry in your journal. Focus on writing spontaneously rather than on structure and mechanics.

1. **Exploring:** Recall what you remember from other sources—your reading, your life experiences, movies and television, stories told to you by others—about the topic discussed by the writer. Choose one or two of these to write about. Which aspects of the topic did they bring up? What additional information did they provide? What emotions did they create in you?

2. **Taking Stock:** Which parts of the selection were most difficult for you to grasp? Which parts needed more explanation? Which parts required outside information to be understood? What kind of information was required (e.g., historical, culture-specific, technical, etc.)? Where might such information be found? Were there aspects of the writer's style you found particularly effective? Particularly difficult? Why?

3. **Responding:** Identify one or two of the writer's main concerns. What personal knowledge, if any, do you have of these issues? What is your opinion on these issues? Examine your response carefully to see what it teaches you about yourself.

Analyzing Content

1. What socioeconomic reason does the writer give for the dominance of blacks in basketball?
2. Why does the black player show no emotion during the game? Give examples from the text.
3. Define the term *rhythm*. Explain why the writer calls it a "racially tinged" attribute.
4. What reasons does the writer provide for calling the Celtics a classically "white" team?

Analyzing Writing Techniques

1. This is largely a **definition** essay. What is being defined? Where? What key words has the writer used to clarify the definition?
2. Pick out the sentence in which the writer **summarizes** the difference between "black" and "white" styles of play. Rewrite this sentence in your own words. What is the role of this sentence in the writer's argument?

Group Activity

Choose a sport that is familiar to members of the group. Discuss some of the famous figures who play this sport. What race/nationality are they? Do they have a particular style or styles? How far is this style a result of their racial background? Write a **collaborative** paragraph in which you **summarize** your discussion.

Your Writing

1. In this essay, one of the major points is that society and economics often affect the development of a sport and who plays it. Write

an essay in which you examine a *different* sport that you believe has been similarly affected.

2. Choose a sport *other* than basketball that you know well. Pick two of your favorite athletes in this sport, and **compare/contrast** their styles. Address the question of whether the ethnicity of the athletes influences their style of play.

Pre-reading Activity   Write about a public figure (in sports or otherwise) whom you idolized as a child.

As You Read   Observe the writer's use of language. What makes it special and different from the language of prose?

BLACK HAIR
Gary Soto

Born in 1952 in Fresno, California, **Gary Soto,** *once a migrant laborer in the San Joaquin Valley, is now a professor of Chicano Studies at the University of California at Berkeley and the author of several books of prose and poetry, including* The Elements of San Joaquin, Small Faces, Neighborhood Odes, *and* Local News. *The poem below is taken from* Black Hair *(1985).*

At eight I was brilliant with my body.
In July, that ring of heat
We all jumped through, I sat in the bleachers
Of Romain Playground, in the lengthening
Shade that rose from our dirty feet.
The game before us was more than baseball.
It was a figure—Hector Moreno
Quick and hard with turned muscles,
His crouch the one I assumed before an altar
10   Of worn baseball cards, in my room.

I came here because I was Mexican, a stick
Of brown light in love with those
Who could do it—the triple and hard slide,
The gloves eating balls into double plays.
What could I do with 50 pounds, my shyness,
My black torch of hair, about to go out?
Father was dead, his face no longer
Hanging over the table or our sleep,
And mother was the terror of mouths
20   Twisting hurt by butter knives.

In the bleachers I was brilliant with my body,
Waving players in and stomping my feet,
Growing sweaty in the presence of white shirts.
I chewed sunflower seeds. I drank water
And bit my arm through the late innings.

When Hector lined balls into deep
Center, in my mind I rounded the bases
With him, my face flared, my hair lifting
Beautifully, because we were coming home
To the arms of brown people.   30

Building Vocabulary

Define the words below, using *context clues* wherever possible and checking in a dictionary when necessary. Use them in sentences of your own.

bleachers (line 3)   torch (16)
lined (26)   flared (28)

Analyzing Content

1. Make a list of the baseball terms used in this poem and their meanings (looking up this information if necessary). What do they add or take away from the poem?
2. Explain line 16, "My black torch of hair, about to go out?"
3. Compare the narrator with Hector Moreno. Why does he identify with him?
4. What do you learn from this poem about the experience of being Mexican-American?

Analyzing Writing Techniques

1. Pick out a word or image that recurs in the poem, and analyze its significance. Is it symbolic in some way?
2. Analyze lines 17 through 20. Why has the writer inserted this information into a poem that seems to be about baseball?

Group Activity

Analyze the significance of the title. Why has the writer chosen this title? Have each member of the group come up with an alternate title.

Your Writing

1. Write a descriptive poem or essay about a sports activity you enjoyed (or hated) as a child. Try using **metaphoric** language to make part of your point clear to the reader.
2. As this poem illustrates, it often is crucial for minority groups to have heroes they can look up to. Choose a sports figure who is a hero for a particular minority, and write a paper analyzing the role that person has played in that community.

Pre-reading Activity   What are your feelings about the behavior of professional athletes today? Why?

As You Read   Note the writer's use of research sources and the ways in which he introduces them.

VIOLENT IDOLS: NEGATIVE EFFECTS OF PROFESSIONAL ATHLETES ON CHILDREN
Dan Frank

*Born in 1972, **Dan Frank** spent most of his growing-up years in the small mountain town of Running Springs, California. His favorite activities are hiking, climbing, fishing, and playing sports. He loves working with animals and is planning to become a veterinarian. He now lives in San Jose and attends Foothill College.*

1   In today's world of disintegrating families where the television set functions increasingly as a babysitter, sports have a major influence on how children view life. More than ever, young people look to the professional athlete for guidance. This is a problem, because although many athletes use their talents and celebrity power to help the less fortunate, many do not. Many athletes commit acts of crime and violence or take pride in displaying negative attitudes. Unfortunately, these are the ones that the media focuses on most often—O. J. Simpson is a case in point. As a result, children get the idea that violence and lawlessness is OK, and even admirable. After all, aren't their heroes turning to—and often getting away with—it?

2   The NBA is a good example of an organization with its share of problem athletes. It all begins with the coaches losing control of their players. A *Sports Illustrated* article by Phil Taylor quotes Dennis Rodman as saying, "I think I scare the NBA. They don't know what I'm going to do next." The article continues with Derrick Coleman of the Mets stating, "I miss practice, Chris misses practice, it's no big deal." (Taylor 18, 23). These quotes show a dangerous immaturity that is nonetheless attractive to kids. It gives them an excuse for the same kind of behavior, for showing lack of respect to teachers or parents, for back-talking a coach, for not caring, for developing an "attitude."

3   From here, it is only one step to the fights, which have become all too common in the NBA and often affect not only the players but the spectators as well. For instance, at a recent game between the New York Knicks

and the Chicago Bulls, a fight broke out between Bulls player Jo Jo English and Knicks player Dennis Harper. Almost immediately, both benches cleared, and the teams started exchanging blows. Soon, spectators joined in. The fight escalated to the point that a woman spectator had a $300 necklace ripped off and two little girls were almost smothered in the scuffle (McCullum, p. 75). What does a scene like this teach a young, impressionable observer? That physical violence is the accepted method of conflict resolution? That team loyalty means joining in a free-for-all, and never mind who gets hurt in the process?

Violence has even become part of the traditionally nonviolent sports   4
such as baseball. On April 13, 1994, Reggie Sanders of the Cincinnati Reds charged the mound in the eighth inning, because he thought that Montreal Expos pitcher Pedro Martinez was throwing too close to him. In a minute, both benches cleared, and players began exchanging blows. Another bench-clearing brawl occured on May 14, 1994, at Shea Stadium when Atlanta Braves pitcher John Smolts hit New York Mets player John Congelosi (McCullum 60).

Talking of peaceful sports, women's figure skating has always been   5
thought of as one of the most elegant events in sports history, sparking the imaginations of children all over the world and holding them rapt in beauty—until the Nancy Kerrigan incident in January 1994. After finishing a practice routine on the ice in Detroit during the U.S. nationals, Kerrigan, a top skater who hoped to go on to the Olympics, was clubbed viciously in the knee by an unknown male attacker. After he was later caught and questioned, the police suspected that Kerrigan's rival Tanya Harding— or at least her ex-husband—had hired him. Nonetheless, the Olympic Committee voted to allow Harding to proceed to the Olympics (where later, after not winning any medals, she would break down and confess to being an accessory in the Kerrigan attack). This sarcastic statement from *TV Guide* summed up the situation:

> When CBS paid $295 million to broadcast the Winter Olympic Games   6
> from Lillehammer, who would have thought it was buying the most riveting prime-time soap opera in recent history? The Women's event, 1994 style, features death threats, hit men, blackmail, divorce scandal and Grand Jury investigations. (Kellogg 8).

The incident leaves us with a bitter taste in our mouths, with our   7
childhood dreams of Olympic glory crumbling to ashes. We remember how we envisioned ourselves on the pedestal, holding up that gold medal for the honor of our country while the national anthem played in the background. It is all tainted by violence now.

The NFL, of course, is a prime hotbed of violence, the nature of foot-   8
ball being what it is. It is terrible the way more and more fights break out on the field—too many to even count. What is worse, however, is when

that violent behavior is carried to other parts of life—and every time, it seems, the cameras are there. When earlier this season the NFL was on hold because of the owners' lockout, a cameraman got hold of Chris Chellios of the Chicago Blackhawks and asked him how he felt. Chris answered, "Commissioner Gary Bettman must be crazy or stupid . . . messing up other people's lives. Someone just might take it the wrong way and decide to take it out on him." Of course, the media pounced on the remark. Headlines screamed, "Chris Chellios Threatens Commissioner Gary Bateman" (ESPN Sports Center News). This is what the youngsters will see and hear. How many children will come away from the incident feeling it is OK to threaten those we dislike? How many, perhaps, will follow it into action?

9   Another example: On April 6, 1994, quarterback Jim Everett was a guest on Jim Rome's show, *Talk 2.* Jim Rome is a well-known Los Angeles sportscaster with a reputation for taunting his guests, and he started off by referring to Jim as "Chris Everett" and questioning his toughness as a quarterback. After being called "Chris" several times, Jim warned his host not to do it again. When Jim Rome persisted, the 6-foot, 5-inch Everett stood up and shoved the table into Rome, smashing him to the floor. The entire scene was televised, including a panicked crew trying to break up the fight (Lapresti, column 1). Imagine the impact this might have on a young person watching his hero on this show. Imagine how he might act the next time he is provoked. And why not? The "big guys" do it, after all.

10   It is easy, it seems, to move from game-related violence into violence that destroys one's family life. In the Mets' off-season of 1986, Darryl Strawberry was ordered by the Los Angeles courts to stay away from his wife Lisa because of a beating that left her with a broken nose. The couple's problems continued as Strawberry began experimenting with alcohol and cocaine. On January 26, 1990, they got into a fight during which Strawberry pulled out a .25-caliber pistol and threatened Lisa with it. He was arrested and jailed briefly on suspicion of assault with a deadly weapon, but no charges were filed. After more abuse, Lisa finally divorced him in 1993. Less than 2 months later, Strawberry married Charisse Simon—3 months after he had been arrested on a battery charge for allegedly striking *her* (Verducci, pp. 18–35). Strawberry's is not an isolated case. In 1995, even as the O. J. Simpson trials for the alleged murder of his ex-wife dragged on, we remembered the case of boxing heavyweight champion Mike Tyson, convicted of raping Desiree Washington in March of 1992 (Corliss 60). Incidents like this, magnified by the media, can leave indelible impressions on children's mind. It is easy for them to rationalize that the violence is not as bad as it really is, and to condone it in their own life. Is there no connection between incidents like the ones above and the fact that domestic violence is escalating in our nation?

11   Perhaps the kind of behavior children have come to expect from their sports idols—and its dangerous influence on them—is best described by Jack McCallum in "Way Out of Control":

A friend of ours took his son to a baseball game last week and the kid   12
seemed really excited about going. Gee, Dad, the boy said, I hope we
see one today. . . . A homer? says the Dad. No, says the son, a brawl.
(McCallum, p. 60).

Works Cited

Corliss, Richard. "The Jock as Fallen Angel." *Time* 6 July 1994:
    60–62.
Kellogg, Mary Alice. "Sports Heroes in the News." *TV Guide* 12 Feb.
    1994
Lapresti, Mike, "Jim Everett." *San Jose Mercury News* 6 April 1994:
    D1.
McCullum, Jack. "Way Out of Control." *Sports Illustrated* 30 Jan.
    1995: 60–67.
Taylor, Phil. "Bad Actors." *Sports Illustrated* 30 Jan. 1995: 18–23.
Verducci, Tom. "The High Price of Hard Living." *Sports Illustrated*
    27 Feb. 1995: 18–35.

Structure and Strategy

1. How has the writer organized his major points? What **transition devices** (in addition to the traditional transition words) has he used?
2. What **rhetorical mode** does the writer use most effectively throughout the paper? Pick out one or two examples of this mode.
3. **Analyze** the conclusion. Do you think it is an effective end to the essay? Explain.

Your Writing

1. The field of athletics involves many people apart from the professional athlete. Who are some of these? Write a paper in which you examine *one* group of persons and the type of work they do. What kind of effect/influence do they have on the people around them?
2. Analyze the life of a famous athlete. What led to this person's success? What kind of influence did the athlete have on other people?

SYNTHESIS: QUESTIONS FOR CRITICAL THINKING AND WRITING

1. "Why Men Fear Women's Teams" and "Comes the Revolution" look at two aspects of women in sports. One essay argues that women have triumphed, and the other takes a more pessimistic view. Which essay do you agree with more closely? Write a paper in which you summarize the main points of the essay you agree with, supporting its thesis with additional points and examples of your own.

2. "Send Your Children to the Libraries" and "Violent Idols: Negative Effects of Professional Athletes on Children" examine some negative aspects of athletes' lives—not only when they fail but even when they succeed. According to you, what are some important hazards faced by athletes? Write a paper in which you **classify** these under various categories.

3. "The Black and White Truth about Basketball" discusses how race and ethnic identity can affect an athlete's style. Is this idea valid in other areas of life? Write a paper in which you discuss your opinion of this idea, using a field other than sports (e.g., music, dance, making business deals, etc.) to make your point.

4. The selections in this section, as well as some others in the book (e.g., "American Needs Its Nerds"), make the point that sports is given enormous importance (perhaps too much) in America. Do you agree? Write an essay in which you examine the role played by sports in American society today.

Language

The ability to use language is a unique gift that all humans share. Paradoxically, all humans do not share the same language, not even when they think that they do, and this leads to some interesting situations, humorous as well as painful, as several writers in this unit demonstrate.

In "His Talk, Her Talk," Joyce Maynard illustrates how men and women each have a different language of their own as well as different habits of conversation that flourish when they are among others of their own sex. In "Breaking the Hungry Teen Code," Ellen Goodman proves that what a parent might mean by "nothing to eat in the house" is totally different from what a teenager means. And in "Americanization is Tough on 'Macho'," Rose del Castillo Guilbault focuses on a single word to show how its connotations change totally depending on which side of the Mexican-American border you come from.

Language is power; thus, the lack of it can place us in positions of powerlessness. We see this in Amy Tan's "My Mother's English," in which an intelligent and able woman is often ignored or treated rudely because of her inability to express herself in standard English. Student Juan Chavez faces the flip side of this problem in "Do You Understand?" Living in America has made him lose his native language, Spanish, and this causes him to become the laughingstock of the village when he visits Mexico.

Chavez's painful experience shows that humans often wield the weapon of language to hurt others. Sometimes, it is not totally intentional, as James Willwerth shows us in "It Hurts Like Crazy," in which he examines the unthinking slurs about the mentally ill that exist in our everyday speech. At other times, however, it is willfully malicious, as Charles F. Berlitz documents in "The Etymology of the International Insult," a treatise that takes us across historical and geographical boundaries to show us—and hopefully sensitize us to—the use of negative racial epithets in many cultures and over many periods of time.

Pre-reading Activity Write about a situation in which you (or some-one you know) experienced communication difficulties because you did not know a language adequately.

As You Read Observe the kind of vocabulary the writer uses. Is there more than one level of diction in this essay?

MY MOTHER'S ENGLISH
Amy Tan

Amy Tan was born in Oakland, California, in 1952, soon after her parents immigrated to the United States from China. She won her first writing con-test at age 8. She has been a consultant to programs for disabled children and a freelance business writer. Her novels include The Joy Luck Club *and* The Kitchen God's Wife. *This selection is from a speech Tan delivered at the California Association of Teachers of English in 1990.*

As you know, I am a writer and by that definition I am someone who has always loved language. I think that is first and foremost with almost every writer I know. I'm fascinated by language in daily life. I spend a great deal of time thinking about the power of language—the way it can evoke an emotion, a visual image, a complex idea or a simple truth. As a writer, lan-guage is the tool of my trade and I use them all, all the Englishes I grew up with.

A few months back, I was made keenly aware of the Englishes I do use. I was giving a talk to a large group of people, the same talk I had given many times before and also with notes. And the nature of the talk was about my writing, my life, and my book *The Joy Luck Club*. The talk was going along well enough until I remembered one major difference that made the whole thing seem wrong. My mother was in the room, and it was perhaps the first time she had heard me give a lengthy speech, using a kind of Eng-lish I had never used with her. I was saying things like "the intersection of memory and imagination," and "there is an aspect of my fiction that re-lates to this and thus." A speech filled with carefully wrought grammati-cal sentences, burdened to me it seemed with nominalized forms, past per-fect tenses, conditional phrases, all the forms of standard English that I had learned in school and through books, a form of English I did not use at home or with my mother.

Shortly after that I was walking down the street with my mother and my husband and I became self-conscious of the English I was using, the

English that I do use with her. We were talking about the price of new and used furniture and I heard myself saying to her, "Not waste money that way." My husband was with me as well, and he didn't notice any switch in my English. And then I realized why: because over the twenty years that we've been together he's often used that English with me and I've used that with him. It is sort of the English that is our language of intimacy, the English that relates to family talk, the English that I grew up with.

4   I'd like to give you some idea what my family talk sounds like and I'll do that by quoting what my mother said during a recent conversation which I videotaped and then transcribed. During this conversation, my mother was talking about a political gangster who had the same last name as her family, Du, and how the gangster in his early years wanted to be adopted by her family which was by comparison very rich. Later the gangster became more rich, more powerful than my mother's family and one day showed up at my mother's wedding to pay his respects. And here's what she said about that, in part, "Du Yu Sung having business like food stand, like off the street kind; he's Du like Du Zong but not Tsung-ming Island people. The local people call him Du, from the river east side. He belong that side, local people. That man want to ask Du Zong father take him in become like own family. Du Zong father look down on him but don't take seriously until that man become big like, become a Mafia. Now important person, very hard inviting him. Chinese way: come only to show respect, don't stay for dinner. Respect for making big celebration; he shows up. Means gives lots of respect, Chinese custom. Chinese social life that way—if too important, won't have to stay too long. He come to my wedding; I didn't see it I heard it. I gone to boy's side. They have YMCA dinner; Chinese age I was nineteen."

5   You should know that my mother's expressive command of English belies how much she actually understands. She reads the *Forbes Report,* listens to *Wall Street Week,* converses daily with her stockbroker, reads all of Shirley MacLaine's books with ease, all kinds of things I can't begin to understand. Yet some of my friends tell me that they understand 50 percent of what my mother says. Some say maybe they understand maybe 80 percent. Some say they understand almost nothing at all. As a case in point, a television station recently interviewed my mother and I didn't see this program when it was first aired, but my mother did. She was telling me what happened. She said that everything she said, which was in English, was subtitled in English, as if she had been speaking in pure Chinese. She was understandably puzzled and upset. Recently a friend gave me that tape and I saw that same interview and I watched. And sure enough—subtitles— and I was puzzled because listening to that tape it seemed to me that my mother's English sounded perfectly clear and perfectly natural. Of course, I realize that my mother's English is what I grew up with. It is literally my mother tongue, not Chinese, not standard English, but my mother's English which I later found out is almost a direct translation of Chinese.

Her language as I hear it is vivid and direct, full of observation and   6
imagery. That was the language that helped shape the way that I saw
things, expressed things, made sense of the world. Lately I've been giving
more thought to the kind of English that my mother speaks. Like others I
have described it to people as broken or fractured English, but I wince
when I say that. It has always bothered me that I can think of no other way
to describe it than broken, as if it were damaged or needed to be fixed,
that it lacked a certain wholeness or soundness to it. I've heard other terms
used, "Limited English" for example. But they seem just as bad, as if everything is limited, including people's perceptions of the Limited English
speaker.

I know this for a fact, because when I was growing up my mother's   7
limited English limited my perception of her. I was ashamed of her English. I believed that her English reflected the quality of what she had to say.
That is, because she expressed it imperfectly, her thoughts were imperfect
as well. And I had plenty of empirical evidence to support me: The fact
that people in department stores, at banks, at supermarkets, at restaurants
did not take her as seriously, did not give her good service, pretended not
to understand her, or even acted as if they did not hear her.

My mother has long realized the limitations of her English as well.   8
When I was fifteen she used to have me call people on the phone to pretend I was she. In this guise, I was forced to ask for information or often-
times to complain and yell at people that had been rude to her. One time
it was a call to her stockbroker in New York. She had cashed out her small
portfolio and it just so happened that we were going to New York the next
week, our very first trip outside of California. I had to get on the phone
and say in my adolescent voice, which was not very convincing, "This is
Mrs. Tan." And my mother was in the back whispering loudly, "Why don't
he send me check already? Two weeks late. So mad he lie to me, losing
me money." Then I said in perfect English, "Yes, I'm getting rather concerned. You had agreed to send the check two weeks ago, but it hasn't arrived." And she began to talk more loudly, "What you want—I come to
New York, tell him front of his boss you cheating me?" And I was trying to
calm her down, making her be quiet, while telling this stockbroker, "I can't
tolerate any more excuses. If I don't receive the check immediately I'm
going to have to speak to your manager when I arrive in New York." And
sure enough the following week, there we were in front of this astonished
stockbroker. And there I was, red-faced and quiet, and my mother the real
Mrs. Tan was shouting at his boss in her impeccable broken English.

We used a similar routine a few months ago for a situation that was   9
actually far less humorous. My mother had gone to the hospital for an appointment to find out about a benign brain tumor a CAT scan had revealed
a month ago. And she had spoken very good English she said—her best
English, no mistakes. Still she said the hospital had not apologized when
they said they had lost the CAT scan and she had come for nothing. She

said that they did not seem to have any sympathy when she told them she was anxious to know the exact diagnosis since her husband and son had both died of brain tumors. She said they would not give her any more information until the next time; she would have to make another apppointment for that, so she said she would not leave until the doctor called her daughter. She wouldn't budge, and when the doctor finally called her daughter, me, who spoke in perfect English, lo-and-behold, we had assurances the CAT scan would be found, they promised a conference call on Monday, and apologies were given for any suffering my mother had gone through for a most regrettable mistake. By the way, apart from the distress of that episode, my mother is fine.

10   But it has continued to disturb me how much my mother's English still limits people's perceptions of her. I think my mother's English almost had an effect on limiting my possibilities as well. Sociologists and linguists will probably tell you that a person's developing language skills are more influenced by peers. But I do think the language spoken by the family, especially immigrant families, which are more insular, plays a large role in shaping the language of the child. . . . [While this may be true, I always wanted, however,] to capture what language ability tests can never reveal—her intent, her passion, her imagery, the rhythms of her speech, and the nature of her thoughts. Apart from what any critic had to say about my writing, I knew I had succeeded where it counted when my mother finished reading my first book and gave me her verdict. "So easy to read."

Building Vocabulary

Define the words below, using *context clues* wherever possible and checking in a dictionary when necessary. Use them in sentences of your own.

evoke (1)	budge (9)	fractured English (6)
transcribed (4)	conditional phrases (2)	portfolio (8)
vivid (6)	belies (5)	insular (10)
empirical (7)		

Journal Writing

Choose one or more of the three activities listed below, and make an entry in your journal. Focus on writing spontaneously rather than on structure and mechanics.

1. **Exploring:** Recall what you remember from other sources—your reading, your life experiences, movies and television, stories told to you by others—about the topic discussed by the writer. Choose one or two of these to write about. Which aspects of the topic did

they bring up? What additional information did they provide? What emotions did they create in you?

2. **Taking Stock:** Which parts of the selection were most difficult for you to grasp? Which parts needed more explanation? Which parts required outside information to be understood? What kind of information was required (e.g., historical, culture-specific, technical, etc.)? Where might such information be found? Were there aspects of the writer's style you found particularly effective? Particularly difficult? Why?

3. **Responding:** Identify one or two of the writer's main concerns. What personal knowledge, if any, do you have of these issues? What is your opinion on these issues? Examine your response carefully to see what it teaches you about yourself.

Analyzing Content

1. What are the two "Englishes" the writer speaks of? How are they different?

2. How did the writer feel about her mother because of her use of English? What did she learn later?

3. What point does paragraph 8 illustrate? Write a one-sentence **summary** of this paragraph.

4. What point does paragraph 9 illustrate? How does it relate to the previous paragraph?

Analyzing Writing Techniques

1. Examine the opening paragraphs. Why does the writer begin this way? Where does the **thesis** of this essay occur?

2. The writer tells us that her mother's English is "full of observation and imagery." Find examples of these qualities in the quotations we are given.

Group Activity

This essay was originally written as a speech. Pick out "speech-like" elements of the writing, and discuss how speeches differ from written passages. What limitations do speakers face that writers do not? What advantages do they have?

Your Writing

1. Tan claims that "the language spoken by . . . immigrant families, which are more insular, plays a large role in shaping the language

of the child." Do you agree? Write an essay examining the language used by first-generation immigrant children, gathering material from personal experience and observation or from your reading.
2. Write a letter to the writer expressing your understanding of the problems her mother faces and explaining what you see to be some reasons for these problems.

Pre-reading Activity Describe a situation in which you (or someone you know) had an insult term applied to you.

As You Read Think about why people choose to insult each other. The writer provides us with some reasons. Mark these. Can you come up with others?

THE ETYMOLOGY OF THE INTERNATIONAL INSULT
Charles F. Berlitz

Born in 1914, **Charles F. Berlitz** *is a linguist and the author of more than one hundred language-teaching books. This selection was originally published in* Penthouse *in 1970.*

"What is a kike?" Disraeli once asked a small group of fellow politicians. 1
Then, as his audience shifted nervously, Queen Victoria's great Jewish Prime Minister supplied the answer himself. "A kike," he observed, "is a Jewish gentleman who has just left the room."

The word kike is thought to have derived from the ending *-ki* or *-ky* 2
found in many names borne by the Jews of Eastern Europe. Or, as Leo Rosten suggests, it may come from *kikel,* Yiddish for a circle, the preferred mark for name signing by Jewish immigrants who could not write. This was used instead of an *X,* which resembles a cross. Kikel was not originally pejorative, but has become so through use.

Yid, another word for Jew, has a distinguished historic origin, coming 3
from the German *Jude* (through the Russian *zhid*). *Jude* itself derives from the tribe of Judah, a most honorable and ancient appellation. The vulgar and opprobrious word "Sheeny" for Jew is a real inversion, as it derives from *shaine* (Yiddish) or *schön* (German), meaning "beautiful." How could beautiful be an insult? The answer is that it all depends on the manner, tone or facial expression or sneer (as our own Vice President has trenchantly observed) with which something is said. The opprobrious Mexican word for an American—*gringo,* for example, is essentially simply a sound echo of a song the American troops used to sing when the Americans were invading Mexico—"Green Grow the Lilacs." Therefore the Mexicans began to call the Americans something equivalent to "los greengrows" which became Hispanized to *gringo.* But from this innocent beginning to the unfriendly emphasis with which many Mexicans say *gringo* today there is a world of difference—almost a call to arms, with unforget-

table memories of past real or fancied wrongs, including "lost" Texas and California.

4   The pejorative American word for Mexicans, Puerto Ricans, Cubans and other Spanish-speaking nationals is simply *spik,* excerpted from the useful expression "No esspick Englitch." Italians, whether in America or abroad, have been given other more picturesque appellations. *Wop,* an all-time pejorative favorite, is curiously not insulting at all by origin, as it means, in Neapolitan dialect, "handsome," "strong" or "good looking." Among the young Italian immigrants some of the stronger and more active—sometimes to the point of combat—were called *guappi,* from which the first syllable, "wop," attained an "immediate insult" status for all Italians.

5   "Guinea" comes from the days of the slave trade and is derived from the African word for West Africa. This "guinea" is the same word as the British unit of 21 shillings, somehow connected with African gold profits as well as New Guinea, which resembled Africa to its discoverers. Dark or swarthy Italians and sometimes Portuguese were called *Guineas* and this apparently spread to Italians of light complexion as well.

6   One of the epithets for Negroes has a curious and tragic historic origin, the memory of which is still haunting us. The word is *"coons."* It comes from *baracoes* (the *o* gives a nasal *n* sound in Portuguese), and refers to the slave pens or barracks *("baracoons")* in which the victims of the slave trade were kept while awaiting transshipment. Their descendants, in their present emphasizing of the term "black" over "Negro," may be in the process of upgrading the very word "black," so often used pejoratively, as in "blackhearted," "black day," "black arts," "black hand," etc. Even some African languages uses "black" in a negative sense. In Hausa "to have a black stomach" means to be angry or unhappy.

7   The sub-Sahara African peoples, incidentally, do not think that they are black (which they are not, anyway). They consider themselves a healthy and attractive "people color," while whites to them look rather unhealthy and somewhat frightening. In any case, the efforts of African Americans to dignify the word "black" may eventually represent a semantic as well as a socio-racial triumph.

8   A common type of national insult is that of referring to nationalities by their food habits. Thus "Frogs" for the French and "Krauts" for the Germans are easily understandable, reflecting on the French addiction to *cuisses de grenouilles* (literally "thighs of frogs") and that of the Germans for various kinds of cabbage, hot or cold. The French call the Italians *"les macaronis"* while the German insult word for Italians is *Katzenfresser* (Cat-eaters), an unjust accusation considering the hordes of cats among the Roman ruins fed by individual cat lovers—unless they are fattening them up? The insult word for an English person is "limey," referring to the limes distributed to seafaring Englishmen as an antiscurvy precaution in the days of sailing ships and long periods at sea.

9   At least one of these food descriptive appellations has attained a per-

manent status in English. The word "Eskimo" is not an Eskimo word at all but an Algonquin word unit meaning "eaters-of-flesh." The Eskimos naturally do not call themselves this in their own language but, with simple directness, use the word *Inuit*—"the men" or "the people."

Why is it an insult to call Chinese "Chinks"? Chink is most probably   10
a contraction of the first syllables of *Chung-Kuo-Ren*—"Middle Country Person." In Chinese there is no special word for China, as the Chinese, being racially somewhat snobbish themselves (although *not* effete, according to recent reports), have for thousands of years considered their land to be the center or middle of the world. The key character for China is therefore the word *chung* or "middle" which, added to *kuo*, becomes "middle country" or "middle kingdom"—the complete Chinese expression for "China" being *Chung Hwa Min Kuo* ("Middle Flowery People's Country"). No matter how inoffensive the origin of "Chink" is, however, it is no longer advisable for everyday or anyday use now.

Jap, an insulting diminutive that figured in the . . . [1968] national U.S.   11
election (though its use in the expression "fat Jap" was apparently meant to have an endearing quality by our Vice President) is a simple contraction of "Japan," which derives from the Chinese word for "sun." In fact the words "Jap" and "Nip" both mean the same thing. "Jap" comes from Chinese and "Nip" from Japanese in the following fashion: *Jihpen* means "sun origin" in Chinese, while *Ni-hon* (Nippon) gives a like meaning in Japanese, both indicating that Japan was where the sun rose. Europeans were first in contact with China, and so originally chose the Chinese name for Japan instead of the Japanese one.

The Chinese "insult" words for whites are based on the observations   12
that they are too white and therefore look like ghosts or devils, *fan kuei* (ocean ghosts), or that their features are too sharp instead of being pleasantly flat, and that they have enormous noses, hence *ta-bee-tsu* (greatnosed ones). Differences in facial physiognomy have been fully reciprocated by whites in referring to Asians as "Slants" or "Slopes."

Greeks in ancient times had an insult word for foreigners too, but one   13
based on the sound of their language. This word is still with us, though its original meaning has changed. The ancient Greeks divided the world into Greeks and "Barbarians"—the latter word coming from a description of the ridiculous language the stranger was speaking. To the Greeks it sounded like the "baa-baa" of a sheep—hence "Barbarians!"

The black peoples of South Africa are not today referred to as Negro   14
or Black but as Bantu—not in itself an insult but having somewhat the same effect when you are the lowest man on the totem pole. But the word means simply "the men," *ntu* signifying "man" and *ba* being the plural prefix. This may have come from an early encounter with explorers or missionaries when Central or South Africans on being asked by whites who they were may have replied simply "men"—with the implied though probably unspoken follow-up questions, "And who are you?"

This basic and ancient idea that one's group are the only people—at least   15 the only friendly or nondangerous ones—is found among many tribes throughout the world. The Navajo Indians call themselves *Dine*—"the people"—and qualify other tribes generally as "the enemy." Therefore an Indian tribe to the north would simply be called "the northern enemy," one to the east "the eastern enemy," etc., and that would be the *only* name used for them. These ancient customs, sanctified by time, of considering people who differ in color, customs, physical characteristics and habits—and by enlargement all strangers—as potential enemies is something mankind can no longer afford, even linguistically. Will man ever be able to rise above using insult as a weapon? It may not be possible to love your neighbor, but by understanding him one may be able eventually to tolerate him. Meanwhile, if you stop calling him names, he too may eventually learn to dislike *you* less.

Building Vocabulary

Define the words below, using *context clues* wherever possible and checking in a dictionary when necessary. Use them in sentences of your own.

etymology (title)   pejorative (2)   potential (15)
opprobious (3)   appelations (4)
physiognomy (12)

Journal Writing

Choose one or more of the three activities listed below, and make an entry in your journal. Focus on writing spontaneously rather than on structure and mechanics.
1. **Exploring:** Recall what you remember from other sources—your reading, your life experiences, movies and television, stories told to you by others—about the topic discussed by the writer. Choose one or two of these to write about. Which aspects of the topic did they bring up? What additional information did they provide? What emotions did they create in you?
2. **Taking Stock:** Which parts of the selection were most difficult for you to grasp? Which parts needed more explanation? Which parts required outside information to be understood? What kind of information was required (e.g., historical, culture-specific, technical, etc.)? Where might such information be found? Were there aspects of the writer's style you found particularly effective? Particularly difficult? Why?
3. **Responding:** Identify one or two of the writer's main concerns. What personal knowledge, if any, do you have of these issues? What is your opinion on these issues? Examine your response carefully to see what it teaches you about yourself.

Analyzing Content

1. The writer discusses many kinds of insults. What are some categories into which these insults may be divided?
2. A paradox that the writer points to is that many insults derive from terms that were originally positive ones. What transforms them into insults?
3. What do the terms *Inuit* and *Bantu* have in common? What worldview do they project? Which other peoples in the essay exhibit a similar worldview?
4. Pick out one example of a negative term that has been upgraded over time. How has this occurred?

Analyzing Writing Techniques

1. Analyze paragraph 1. What is its function?
2. Write a **thesis** paragraph for this essay. Where would you place such a paragraph?

Group Activity

Using the technique of **brainstorming,** come up with a list of other insult terms. Have each group member choose one such term and research its sources, then do a group presentation for the entire class.

Your Writing

1. This selection was written in 1970. How many of the terms mentioned in it are still being used? What new terms have come into use? (You may consult the group activity for ideas.) Write an essay, using Berlitz as a model, in which you analyze some of the popular insult terms of today.
2. What point is Berlitz making in the final paragraph? Do you agree or disagree? Write an essay exploring this idea, bringing in examples of your own.

Pre-reading Activity   Write about an experience in which you were confused by a word or expression because it was being used differently from the way you were accustomed to using it. (An example may be a **slang** expression, **jargon,** or a word from another language.)

As You Read   Note the writer's use of comparison/contrast techniques and anecdotes to make her point.

AMERICANIZATION IS TOUGH ON "MACHO"
Rose del Castillo Guilbault

Rose del Castillo Guilbault was born in Ciudad Obregon, Mexico, and currently lives in the San Francisco Bay Area. She is director of public affairs for a San Francisco TV station and a syndicated writer for the Pacific News Service. This selection, first published in 1989, is taken from This World, *the weekly magazine of the* San Francisco Chronicle.

1   What is *macho?* That depends which side of the border you come from.

2   Although it's not unusual for words and expressions to lose their subtlety in translation, the negative connotations of *macho* in this country are troublesome to Hispanics.

3   Take the newspaper descriptions of alleged mass murderer Ramon Salcido. That an insensitive, insanely jealous, hard-drinking, violent Latin male is referred to as *macho* makes Hispanics cringe.

4   *"Es muy macho,"* the women in my family nod approvingly, describing a man they respect. But in the United States, when women say, "He's so macho," it's with disdain.

5   The Hispanic *macho* is manly, responsible, hardworking, a man in charge, a patriarch. A man who expresses strength through silence. What the Yiddish language would call a *mensch.*

6   The American *macho* is a chauvinist, a brute, uncouth, selfish, loud, abrasive, capable of inflicting pain, and sexually promiscuous.

7   Quintessential *macho* models in this country are Sylvester Stallone, Arnold Schwarzenegger and Charles Bronson. In their movies, they exude toughness, independence, masculinity. But a closer look reveals their machismo is really violence masquerading as courage, sullenness disguised as silence and irresponsibility camouflaged as independence.

8   If the Hispanic ideal of *macho* were translated to American screen roles, they might be Jimmy Stewart, Sean Connery and Laurence Olivier.

In Spanish, *macho* ennobles Latin males. In English it devalues them. 9
This pattern seems consistent with the conflicts ethnic minority males experience in this country. Typically the cultural traits other societies value don't translate as desirable characteristics in America.

I watched my own father struggle with these cultural ambiguities. He 10
worked on a farm for twenty years. He laid down miles of irrigation pipe, carefully plowed long, neat rows in fields, hacked away at recalcitrant weeds and drove tractors through whirlpools of dust. He stoically worked twenty-hour days during harvest season, accepting the long hours as part of agricultural work. When the boss complained or upbraided him for minor mistakes, he kept quiet, even when it was obvious the boss had erred.

He handled the most menial tasks with pride. At home he was a good 11
provider, helped out my mother's family in Mexico without complaint, and was indulgent with me. Arguments between my mother and him generally had to do with money, or with his stubborn reluctance to share his troubles. He tried to work them out in his own silence. He didn't want to trouble my mother—a course that backfired, because the imagined is always worse than the reality.

Americans regarded my father as decidedly un-*macho.* His character 12
was interpreted as nonassertive, his loyalty non-ambition, and his quietness, ignorance. I once overheard the boss's son blame him for plowing crooked rows in a field. My father merely smiled at the lie, knowing the boy had done it, but didn't refute it, confident his good work was well known. But the boss instead ridiculed him for being "stupid" and letting a kid get away with a lie. Seeing my embarrassment, my father dismissed the incident, saying "They're the dumb ones. Imagine, me fighting with a kid."

I tried not to look at him with American eyes because sometimes the 13
reflection hurt.

Listening to my aunts' clucks of approval, my vision focused on the 14
qualities America overlooked. "He's such a hard worker. So serious, so responsible." My aunts would secretly compliment my mother. The unspoken comparison was that he was not like some of their husbands, who drank and womanized. My uncles represented the darker side of *macho.*

In a patriarchal society, few challenge their roles. If men drink, it's be- 15
cause it's the manly thing to do. If they gamble, it's because it's how men relax. And if they fool around, well, it's because a man simply can't hold back so much man! My aunts didn't exactly meekly sit back, but they put up with these transgressions because Mexican society dictated this was their lot in life.

In the United States, I believe it was the feminist movement of the early 16
'70s that changed *macho*'s meaning. Perhaps my generation of Latin women was in part responsible. I recall Chicanas complaining about the

chauvinistic nature of Latin men and the notion they wanted their women barefoot, pregnant and in the kitchen. The generalization that Latin men embodied chauvinistic traits led to this interesting twist of semantics. Suddenly a word that represented something positive in one culture became a negative prototype in another.

17   The problem with the use of *macho* today is that it's become an accepted stereotype of the Latin male. And like all stereotypes, it distorts truth.

18   The impact of language in our society is undeniable. And the misuse of *macho* hints at a deeper cultural misunderstanding that extends beyond mere word definitions.

Building Vocabulary

Define the words below, using *context clues* wherever possible and checking in a dictionary when necessary. Use them in sentences of your own.

subtlety (paragraph 2)	upbraided (10)	masquerading (7)
alleged (3)	transgressions (15)	stoically (10)
patriarch (5)	connotations (2)	menial (11)
quintessential (7)	cringe (3)	semantics (16)
recalcitrant (10)	promiscuous (6)	

Journal Writing

Choose one or more of the three activities listed below, and make an entry in your journal. Focus on writing spontaneously rather than on structure and mechanics.

1. **Exploring:** Recall what you remember from other sources—your reading, your life experiences, movies and television, stories told to you by others—about the topic discussed by the writer. Choose one or two of these to write about. Which aspects of the topic did they bring up? What additional information did they provide? What emotions did they create in you?
2. **Taking Stock:** Which parts of the selection were most difficult for you to grasp? Which parts needed more explanation? Which parts required outside information to be understood? What kind of information was required (e.g., historical, culture-specific, technical, etc.)? Where might such information be found? Were there aspects of the writer's style you found particularly effective? Particularly difficult? Why?
3. **Responding:** Identify one or two of the writer's main concerns. What personal knowledge, if any, do you have of these issues? What is your opinion on these issues? Examine your response carefully to see what it teaches you about yourself.

change the oil filter and vacuum the upholstery to avoid. There is a way women talk with other women, and, I gather, a way that men talk when in the company of other men. They are not at all the same.

I think I know my husband very well, but I have no idea what goes on when he and his male friends get together. Neither can he picture what can keep a woman friend and me occupied for three hours over a single pot of coffee.

The other day, after a long day of work, my husband, Steve, and his friend Dave stopped at a bar for a few beers. When he got home, I asked what they had talked about. "Oh, the usual." Like what? "Firewood. Central America. Trucks. The Celtics. Religion. You know."

No, not really. I had only recently met with my friend Ann and her friend Sally at a coffee shop nearby, and what we talked about was the workshop Sally would be holding that weekend concerning women's attitudes toward their bodies, Ann's 11-year-old daughter's upcoming slumber party, how hard it is to buy jeans, and the recent dissolution of a friend's five-year marriage. Asked to capsulize our afternoon's discussion, in a form similar to my husband's outline of his night out, I would say we talked about life, love, happiness and heartbreak. Larry Bird's name never came up.

I don't want to reinforce old stereotypes of bubble-headed women (Lucy and Ethel), clinking their coffee cups over talk of clothes and diets while the men remove themselves to lean on mantels, puff on cigars and muse about world politics, machines and philosophy. A group of women talking, it seems to me, is likely to concern itself with matters just as pressing as those broached by my husband and his friends. It might be said, in fact, that we're really talking about the same eternal conflicts. Our styles are just different.

When Steve tells a story, the point is, as a rule, the ending, and getting there by the most direct route. It may be a good story, told with beautiful precision, but he tells it the way he eats a banana: in three efficient chews, while I cut mine up and savor it. He can (although this is rare) spend 20 minutes on the telephone with one of his brothers, tantalizing me with occasional exclamations of amazement or shock, and then after hanging up, reduce the whole conversation for me to a one-sentence summary. I, on the other hand, may take three quarters of an hour describing some figure from my past while he waits—with thinly veiled impatience—for the point to emerge. Did this fellow just get elected to the House of Representatives? Did he die and leave me his fortune?

In fairness to Steve, I must say that, for him, not talking about something doesn't necessarily mean not dealing with it. And he does listen to what I have to say. He likes a good story, too. It's just that, given a choice, he'd rather hear about quantum mechanics or the history of the Ford Mustang. Better yet, he'd rather play ball.

Building Vocabulary

Define the words below, using *context clues* wherever possible and checking in a dictionary when necessary. Use them in sentences of your own.

innate (1)	tantalizing (9)	dissolution (7)
contamination (1)	anatomy (1)	broached (8)
segregate (3)	redistributed (3)	quantum (10)
bubble-headed (8)		

Journal Writing

Choose one or more of the three activities listed below, and make an entry in your journal. Focus on writing spontaneously rather than on structure and mechanics.

1. **Exploring:** Recall what you remember from other sources—your reading, your life experiences, movies and television, stories told to you by others—about the topic discussed by the writer. Choose one or two of these to write about. Which aspects of the topic did they bring up? What additional information did they provide? What emotions did they create in you?
2. **Taking Stock:** Which parts of the selection were most difficult for you to grasp? Which parts needed more explanation? Which parts required outside information to be understood? What kind of information was required (e.g., historical, culture-specific, technical, etc.)? Where might such information be found? Were there aspects of the writer's style you found particularly effective? Particularly difficult? Why?
3. **Responding:** Identify one or two of the writer's main concerns. What personal knowledge, if any, do you have of these issues? What is your opinion on these issues? Examine your response carefully to see what it teaches you about yourself.

Analyzing Content

1. Examine the topics generally discussed by men and those generally discussed by women, according to this essay. What differences do you perceive?
2. What differences does the author find in the styles of conversation between men and women? What **analogy** has she used to bring out this difference?
3. Examine the first sentence of paragraph 10, "In fairness to Steve. . . ." What does it **imply** about one of the roles of conversation?

4. Who do you think is the intended audience of this piece? What clues are we given as to this audience?

Analyzing Writing Techniques

1. What is the purpose of paragraph 1? What is its relationship to the **thesis**?
2. What **rhetorical mode** does the writer employ to clarify her thesis? Pick out an example of this in the essay.

Group Activity

View a short portion of a movie or video that focuses on a conversation between people of the same sex. (Or, alternately, discuss a similar conversation scene from a movie you have all seen recently.) What do you notice about this conversation? Does it support what Maynard claims?

Your Writing

1. How far do you agree with Maynard's thesis about the differences between "his talk" and "her talk"? Write an essay supported by examples from your observation and at least *one* research source.
2. In the first paragraph, the writer refers to "nonsexist childrearing." What is your opinion on such a method? Is it important? Is it valuable? Is such a method possible in today's society? Write an essay in which you address these and other related questions and come to a clear conclusion of your own.

Pre-reading Activity   Describe a common expression that you often hear teenagers use. In what context do they use this term? What is its meaning or connotations?

As You Read   Observe the style and level(s) of diction. What do they tell you about the intended audience of this selection?

BREAKING THE HUNGRY TEEN CODE
Ellen Goodman

Born in Boston in 1941, **Ellen Goodman** *holds a degree from Radcliffe College and has worked as a reporter for* Newsweek. *Her writing has been published in* McCall's, Harper's Bazaar, *and* Family Circle. *She is a columnist for the* Boston Globe, *in which this piece first appeared in 1986. Her column, "At Large," is syndicated and appears in nearly 400 newspapers across the country. Her books, in which her columns have been collected, include* Turning Points, At Large, *and* Keeping in Touch.

1   As a parent who works with words for a living, I have prided myself over many years for a certain skill in breaking the codes of childspeak. I began by interpreting babytalk, moved to more sophisticated challenges like "chill out" and graduated with "wicked good."

2   One phrase, however, always stumped me. I was unable to crack the meaning of the common cry echoing through most middle-class American households: "There's Nothing to Eat in This House!"

3   This exclamation becomes a constant refrain during the summer months when children who have been released from the schoolhouse door grow attached to the refrigerator door. It is during the summer when the average taxpayer realizes the true cost-effectiveness of school: It keeps kids out of the kitchen for roughly seven hours a day. A feat no parent is able to match.

4   At first, like so many others, I assumed that "NETH!" (as in "Nothing to Eat in This House") was a straightforward description of reality. If there was NETH, it was because the children had eaten it all. After all, an empty larder is something you come to expect when you live through the locust phase of adolescence.

5   I have one friend with three teenage sons who swears that she doesn't even have to unload her groceries anymore. Her children feed directly from the bags, rather like ponies. I have other friends who only buy ingredients for supper on the way home so that supper doesn't turn into lunch.

Over the years, I have considered color-coding food with red, yellow   6
and green stickers. Green for eat. Yellow for eat only if you are starving.
Red for "touch this and you die."

However, I discovered that these same locusts can stand in front of a   7
relatively full refrigerator while bleating the same pathetic choruses of
"NETH! NETH!" By carefully observing my research subjects, I discovered
that the demand of "NETH!" has little to do with the supply.

What then does the average underage eater mean when he or she   8
bleats "NETH! NETH!" You will be glad to know that I have finally broken the code for the "nothing" in NETH and offer herewith my translation.

NETH includes: 9

1. Any food that must be cooked, especially in a pan or by convectional
    heat. This covers boiling, frying or baking. Toasting is acceptable under
    dire conditions.
2. Any food that is in a frozen state with the single exception of ice cream.
    A frozen pizza may be considered "something to eat" only if there is a
    microwave oven on hand.
3. Any food that must be assembled before eaten. This means tuna that is
    still in a can. It may also mean a banana that has to be peeled, but only
    in extreme cases. Peanut butter and jelly are exempt from this rule as
    long as they are on the same shelf beside the bread.
4. Leftovers. Particularly if they must be re-heated. (See 1.)
5. Plain yogurt or anything else that might have been left as a nutrition
    trap.
6. Food that must be put on a plate, or cut with a knife and fork, as op-
    posed to ripped with teeth while watching videos.
7. Anything that is not stored precisely at eye level. This includes:
8. Any item on a high cupboard shelf, unless it is a box of cookies
    and:
9. Any edible in the back of the refrigerator, especially on the middle
    shelf.

While divining the nine meanings of "NETH!" I should also tell you   10
that I developed an anthropological theory about the eating patterns of
young Americans. For the most part, I am convinced, Americans below
the age of 20 have arrested their development at the food-gathering stage.

They are intrinsically nomadic. Traveling in packs, they engage in   11
nothing more sophisticated than hand-to-mouth dining. They are, in effect, strip eaters who devour the ripest food from one home, and move on
to another.

Someday, I am sure they will learn about the use of fire, not to men-   12
tion forks. Someday, they will be cured of the shelf-blindness, the inability to imagine anything hidden behind a large milk carton. But for now,
they can only graze. All the rest is NETH-ing.

Building Vocabulary

Define the words below, using *context clues* wherever possible and checking in a dictionary when necessary. Use them in sentences of your own.

childspeak (1)	intrinsically (11)	convectional (9)
locust (4)	larder (4)	divining (10)
bleating (7)	pathetic (7)	nomadic (11)
exempt (9)		

Journal Writing

Choose one or more of the three activities listed below, and make an entry in your journal. Focus on writing spontaneously rather than on structure and mechanics.

1. **Exploring:** Recall what you remember from other sources—your reading, your life experiences, movies and television, stories told to you by others—about the topic discussed by the writer. Choose one or two of these to write about. Which aspects of the topic did they bring up? What additional information did they provide? What emotions did they create in you?
2. **Taking Stock:** Which parts of the selection were most difficult for you to grasp? Which parts needed more explanation? Which parts required outside information to be understood? What kind of information was required (e.g., historical, culture-specific, technical, etc.)? Where might such information be found? Were there aspects of the writer's style you found particularly effective? Particularly difficult? Why?
3. **Responding:** Identify one or two of the writer's main concerns. What personal knowledge, if any, do you have of these issues? What is your opinion on these issues? Examine your response carefully to see what it teaches you about yourself.

Analyzing Content

1. Describe the different stages of the writer's ability to interpret "childspeak." What is her ultimate achievement?
2. What problem do paragraphs 5 and 6 describe? What insight do they give us into the behavior patterns of teenagers?
3. Analyze the list of "NETH" items. What activities do teenagers seem unable to perform?
4. Examine the conclusion of this essay. Which paragraphs form the conclusion? How do they relate to the **thesis?**

Analyzing Writing Techniques

1. The term *childspeak* is an **allusion** to a well-known novel. Which one? (You might need to research this item). What **connotations** are created by this allusion?
2. **Tone** is a central element in the reader's understanding of this piece. What is the tone? Choose one paragraph in which the tone is clearly expressed, and analyze how it works.

Group Activity

Going back to the pre-reading activity, examine the expressions that you wrote about. Did any group members choose the same expressions? Discuss what these expressions tell us about the lifestyles and attitudes of teenagers.

Your Writing

1. An important premise underlying this essay is that parents and children speak a different "language" and, therefore, often find it difficult to communicate with each other. Do you agree? Write a paper illustrating with examples the difference (or similarity) in parent/child languages.
2. In the voice of a teenager, write a letter addressed to a parent concerned with the problem of NETH. Indicate ways in which this problem might be solved. You may choose either a serious *or* a humorous tone for this assignment.

Pre-reading Activity   What does this title bring to your mind? Write down your ideas, then check the essay to see how close you were to the writer's topic.

As You Read   Continue considering the title. How does it relate to the **thesis?** Is it well chosen? Which elements should a good title possess?

IT HURTS LIKE CRAZY
James Willwerth

James Willwerth *is a columnist for* Time, *in which this piece originally appeared in 1993.*

1   DC comics Superman editor Mike Carlin, hoping to boost newsstand sales, declares that "an escapee from a cosmic lunatic asylum" named Doomsday will murder the Man of Steel. The state of Pennsylvania touts itself as a place for "multiple personalities" to suggest it has much to offer tourists. A character on "Roseanne" argues that only "murderers, psychos and schizos" can beat a lie-detector test. On election eve, Ross Perot tells a cheering crowd, "We're all crazy again now! We got buses lined up outside to take you back to the insane asylum."

2   At a time of growing sensitivity to racist and sexist language, no such caution governs the use of the vocabulary of mental illness, whether as a metaphor, a plot device or a put-down. "There is hardly a moment when we turn on television or read newspapers that we don't see violent stereotypes or hear bad jokes at the expense of the mentally ill," says Nora Weinerth, cofounder of the National Stigma Clearinghouse, which organizes protests against prejudicial images of mental illness in the media. "When children are told that a superhero will be killed by someone who is mentally ill, it stigmatizes us." Backed by research showing that mental illness is biological in origin—like cancer or heart disease—patients and advocates are gearing up a national antidefamation campaign.

3   With the help of the New York State Alliance for the Mentally Ill, Weinerth and New York City activist Jean Arnold set up the clearinghouse operation in January 1990. Its efforts reflect more than concerns over hurt feelings or political correctness. A stream of negative images, advocates argue, makes it harder for recovering patients to find work, obtain housing or participate fully in society. "We're not language police," concludes Arnold. "We don't expect the word *crazy* to disappear. But we're hoping

for the day when these stereotypes are as unacceptable as racist and sexist remarks."

The stigma borne by present-day patients "is harder to live with than   4
the illness itself," laments Joanne Verbannic, a Michigan grandmother employed at the Ford Motor Credit Co., who at age 25 had paranoid schizophrenia diagnosed. "Every time I read about a 'paranoid killer' or hear on TV that the weather will be 'schizophrenic,' I feel like someone has put a knife in me."

Experts who work with the mentally ill are especially concerned about   5
the misinformation spread by the jokes and casual use of medical terms. When *Time* uses the word *schizophrenic* to describe internal conflict within the Republican Party, the metaphor perpetuates a misunderstanding, as does a *New York Times* article describing the hyena's laughlike calls as "psychotic in pitch." Schizophrenia, a brain disorder whose symptoms can include hearing voices, has nothing to do with multiple or "split" personalities. Psychotic refers to a period of severe, treatable and often terrifying disorientation.

The label *psychotic killer,* a favorite of headline writers and Hollywood   6
producers, reinforces an inaccurate link between mental illness and violence. According to recent studies, slightly more than 11 percent of the mentally ill are prone to violence, roughly the same percentage as in the general population. In reality, most mentally ill patients are withdrawn, frightened and passive. For 25 years, researchers at the University of Pennsylvania's Annenberg School for Communication tracked television portrayals of the mentally ill in prime time: more than 72 percent of the characters were portrayed as violent.

Activists have directed much of their fire at Madison Avenue. In late   7
1991, the communications giant GTE ran an ad featuring a man who was "temporarily insane" because he heard strange voices on his non-GTE system. The New York State Lottery game Crazy 8s last year had an ad showing a "typical" customer bragging that he was "crazy, nuts. I'm out of control." Ads have run recently for "psycho" sunglasses and "Skitzocolor" T shirts.

Some of the protests have been successful. Former First Lady Rosalynn   8
Carter, a leading mental-health advocate, persuaded one North Carolina company to pull ads featuring cans of peanuts in straitjackets promoting a product line called Certifiably Nuts. One of her annual mental-health-policy symposiums at Emory University's Carter Center was devoted entirely to stigma issues. "We are all concerned about stigma," she says. "It holds back progress in the whole field."

Deere & Co. listened to protests and pulled catalog ads for a "schiz-   9
ophrenic" power mower, putting in its place a public service ad that read, "The most shocking thing about mental illness is how little people understand about it." Wordstar took "loony bin," "bobby hatch" and "funny farm" out of its thesaurus list of synonyms for "institution."

10   But such victories are sporadic at best. Last spring a Manhattan and New Jersey discount clothier named Daffy's ran an ad showing a strait-jacket with the caption, "If you're paying over $100 for a dress shirt, may we suggest a jacket to go with it?" Protesters picketed a store, wrote letters and petitioned the New York City Commission on Human Rights. A Daffy's spokesperson insisted that the ad was humorous and called the protest unfair.

11   The stigma is even being passed on to the next generation. DC Comics insists that Superman's killer was never meant to be portrayed as mentally ill, but another of its comics features a character named Shade. "Greetings from the mental states of America," said one of its early promotion circulars, "where every citizen has the right to remain deranged!"

Building Vocabulary

Define the words below, using *context clues* wherever possible and checking in a dictionary when necessary. Use them in sentences of your own.

schizo (1)	perpetuates (5)	misinformation (5)
clearinghouse (2)	put-down (2)	sporadic (10)
antidefamation (2)	stigmatizes (2)	

Journal Writing

Choose one or more of the three activities listed below, and make an entry in your journal. Focus on writing spontaneously rather than on structure and mechanics.

1. **Exploring:** Recall what you remember from other sources—your reading, your life experiences, movies and television, stories told to you by others—about the topic discussed by the writer. Choose one or two of these to write about. Which aspects of the topic did they bring up? What additional information did they provide? What emotions did they create in you?
2. **Taking Stock:** Which parts of the selection were most difficult for you to grasp? Which parts needed more explanation? Which parts required outside information to be understood? What kind of information was required (e.g., historical, culture-specific, technical, etc.)? Where might such information be found? Were there aspects of the writer's style you found particularly effective? Particularly difficult? Why?
3. **Responding:** Identify one or two of the writer's main concerns. What personal knowledge, if any, do you have of these issues? What is your opinion on these issues? Examine your response carefully to see what it teaches you about yourself.

Analyzing Content

1. Why are jokes using the terms of mental illness a problem?
2. What is the goal of the National Stigma Clearinghouse? Why?
3. What connection does the popular media make between mental illness and violence? Use the statistics provided in the essay to evaluate the accuracy of this connection.
4. Describe some successful protests against stereotyping the mentally ill. What led to their success? Why are these victories called "sporadic"?

Analyzing Writing Techniques

1. Note the use of quotation marks in the essay. What are the various ways in which they are used?
2. What is the main point of this essay? Write it out in your own words. Which example seems to best illustrate this point?

Group Activity

Have each member of the group listen carefully to conversations for a whole day, listening for terms related to mental illness. Discuss how many terms each person heard, what the context of the usage was, and whether it "stigmatized" the mentally ill.

Your Writing

1. Write a paper in which you study the images of the mentally ill portrayed by TV or the movies in recent years. Are they largely accurate, or do they, as this writer claims, perpetuate harmful stereotypes? Support your opinion with examples.
2. Think of other groups that are "stigmatized" by the unthinking use of language (e.g., the handicapped, gays and lesbians, etc.). Using this essay as a model, choose *one* such group, and write a paper in which you illustrate the problem they face.

Pre-reading activity   Write about a misunderstanding that you experienced because of unclear language or someone's inability to express his or her feelings.

As You Read   Note the writer's use of **chronology** as an organizational tool.

DO YOU UNDERSTAND?
Juan Chavez

Born in 1974, **Juan Chavez** *is a first-generation Mexican-American who grew up on the rough streets of East Palo Alto, California. As a youth, he was a member of various gangs. "My best friends," he says, "were hustlers and drug dealers." At 16, he was kidnapped, taken to Los Angeles, and held for ransom for 15 days before police could rescue him. This incident changed his views on life. Today, he helps his father with family businesses, running a nightclub in the United States and working on their cattle ranch in Mexico in the summer. Juan is a student at Foothill College.*

1   With each new year, I feel a sense of distance growing between my parents and myself. The older we become, the less we seem to know each other. It's not because I don't see them or spend time with them—I'm in contact with them everyday. It's not because of our different points of view—we have many similar values. Our problem arises because of one simple reason: their limited comprehension of the English language and my equally limited understanding of Spanish.

2   As a child, the first words I said were in Spanish, because my parents spoke only this language. My English was limited to the few expressions I learned from watching cartoons, words like *Superman, spinach* (from Popeye), *Jeepers,* and, of course, *Scooby Dooby Doo.* This was not a problem, for at this time in my life none of the people I needed and loved knew any English.

3   During these childhood years, when my English vocabulary was at its lowest level—the same level as my parents'—my father and mother and I were the closest to each other. I could describe to them exactly how I felt, sad or happy or angry. I could do this clearly and fluently, without stammering or worrying about pronounciation. I could hold a conversation without having to wrack my brain for the right word, and I could fully understand what they said to me. Our bond went beyond that of blood. It

was the bond of a common language, with its sounds, its nuances, and its music.

With the start of school, this bond began to fray. Running home from school each day, I would be so happy, so proud of myself, because I'd learned another new English word. In those days, I learned fast. It was because of the way the school was set up. It was a school in the "white" part of town. The poor, the Mexicans, my family—we lived on the other side. For some reason, however, a few of us Mexican kids attended the anglo school. We learned a lot of things at that school. We knew what prejudice meant, and what being a minority was, long before we knew the words. And we learned English. A lot of English. You see, in this school, anyone caught speaking Spanish was punished. First, the teacher would scold him, then he would be made to do a menial task—clean the blackboard, clap the dusty erasers, or pick up the garbage in the schoolyard while the other kids watched. It didn't take us long to learn that Spanish was regarded as something bad, something not allowed, something to be avoided if we wanted to succeed in the world of school.

In this way, through the years, English became my primary language. The only place where I spoke Spanish was in our house, where, ironically, English was not allowed. My father and mother believed that speaking English in a Mexican home was a betrayal of Mexican pride. So I spoke Spanish—at dinner, or as I came into the house and my mother asked where I had been. I spoke it every day, but my knowledge of Spanish never expanded—perhaps because I had already internalized the attitude of the anglo world, that it was of no value. As a result, the Spanish I spoke as a child was the same Spanish I used as a young man—basic.

I remember watching an American action movie on TV one day with my father. As the scene changed from people shooting at each other to people shouting at each other, my father asked me to translate what the actors were saying. I tried, but it was difficult. I was stuttering, pausing in the middle of sentences, because I couldn't find the right words. Soon, it became impossible. I was annoyed that I was missing out on the movies as I tried to tell my father what was going on. I was also a little ashamed, and that made me more annoyed. So I made up a story, something simple that was easy to say in Spanish. When I was done, I remember my father gave me an odd look, a sad look. For years, I believed that it was because he had known somehow that I was lying to him, but now, I wonder if it was the sadness of a Mexican father who couldn't understand what his Mexican-American son was trying to say.

I was 16 when I finally realized what I had unknowingly lost while I had focused so hard on improving my English. In that year, my father sent me to his hometown in Mexico. There, my uncle Ramiro, who hadn't seen me in 10 years, welcomed me warmly. That evening, all my relatives from nearby towns came to his house to meet me. As they asked questions, I replied. As I replied, they laughed. It took me only a short while to real-

ize that they weren't responding to my wit. It was my words—mispro-
nounced, wrongly used, sometimes meaningless. Baby words. All through
my 2-week stay, I was the joke of the town. Everywhere I went, all I had
to do was open my mouth and laughter would follow. It grew so bad that
finally I stopped talking completely.

8   When I got home, I described to my parents what had happened, what
a terrible, humiliating situation it had been. They took me in their loving
arms. Then they, too, laughed.

9   Recently, my grandmother, my mother's mother, passed away. It was
a sudden thing. I had been very attached to her as a child, and the news
of her death left me in shock. For 2 months, I held the anger and sadness
inside my heart. Then finally, one day, I went to my mother. I desperately
needed someone to talk to. Someone to whom I could tell how hurt I was,
how my grandmother's death was like a dull knife slowly twisting in my
heart. I wanted to tell her how much I had wanted to see my grandmother
before she died, to hold her in my arms so tightly that we would hear our
hearts saying goodbye to each other. All this I wanted to tell my mother.
Surely she, of all people, would understand.

10   I talked and talked, but I couldn't find those damn words. Not the right
ones. As I talked, I looked into my mother's eyes. The expression in them
was the same as that in my father's eyes the day I lied to him about the TV
show. The same confused, disappointed stare. It was then that I realized
she couldn't understand me. Sure, she knew that I was hurt—but the
depths of my feeling, or how I thought about my grandmother, about
death—she couldn't comprehend that. A deeper sorrow pressed down on
my soul at that moment. Had my parents *ever* really understood anything
I tried to say?

11   Many people tell me I'm fortunate to have two languages. My English-
speaking friends envy that I can travel throughout Mexico and make myself understood at hotels and bars and bus stations and stores. My Mexican friends believe that my knowledge of English gives me more job
opportunities in America, and prestige as well. That's what they say, but I
know better. Caught between two languages, neither of which feels like
my own, I watch helplessly as my parents recede further and further into
the distance.

Structure and Strategy

1. What is the **tone** of this essay? How is it different from "Violent
   Idols," the student essay in Unit 7?
2. How does the writer achieve this tone? Pick out some examples of
   this from the text.
3. Make a list of other kinds of tones the writer could have used. Select one of these, and rewrite the first paragraph to bring out this
   tone.

4. Analyze the devices used by the writer to support the main point. What makes them effective? What other kinds of proof might he have used?

Your Writing

1. Write a process paper about how one can best communicate with one's parents or children. What steps should one take in the early years? Does the process need to change as the children grow? What pitfalls should one watch out for?
2. Chavez writes about the way in which the educational system deprived him of his mother tongue. Is this still a problem in schools today? Research this subject, and write a paper on the current educational philosophy regarding non-English languages in the area where you go to school.

SYNTHESIS: QUESTIONS FOR CRITICAL THINKING AND WRITING

1. "My Mother's English," "Breaking the Hungry Teen Code," and "Do You Understand?" deal with the communication gaps that often open up between parents and children. Write an essay in which you examine the reasons for such a communication gap.
2. "My Mother's English" points to the many difficulties immigrants face because they are not completely fluent in their use of English. But immigrants are not alone in having problems with language. Point to another group in America that has difficulties because of the kind of language they use, and write an essay in which you analyze their situation.
3. "His Talk, Her Talk," points to some differences between men's conversation and women's. Are these distinctions valid in other cultures? Write an essay about another culture you are familiar with, discussing how men and women communicate with people of the same sex.
4. "Do You Understand?" points to the way in which communication between parents and children diminishes as a result of the child acquiring English language skills. However, this problem seems not to have occurred in "My Mother's English." Examine both essays, then write a paper in which you analyze what can be done in the home and in society to prevent the erosion of such communication.

Identity

Who am I? This question has intrigued humankind from the beginnings of our existence. The answer may be attempted from many levels—personal, psychological, professional, spiritual—and will vary accordingly. This unit, which deals mainly with cultural identity, indicates that the answer becomes increasingly complex in a diverse society such as America.

Is it even worthwhile to attempt to define identity—one's own, and especially that of another group? Jack G. Shaheen points to the harm this might create if done without care in "The Media's Image of Arabs," in which he shows us the painful stereotypes he and his family have often had to endure. In "The Handicap of Definition," William Raspberry declares that the negative connotations created by the word *black* have caused African-American children to feel limited in tragic ways. And in "Freedom from Choice," Brian A. Courtney, who comes from a mixed heritage, wishes to be free of the pressure to define himself as one race or the other—and thus be forced always to deny part of himself.

Identity, which often sets us apart from other groups, can have very different kinds of influences depending on who we are and how comfortable we feel with our "otherness." As Margaret A. Gibson illustrates in "Cultural Barriers and the Press to Americanize," an essay about Punjabi teenagers in an American school, holding on to one's identity can be a very difficult and stressful task for young adults whose home lives are so different from those of their classmates. In "A Taste of Greece," student Bill Vourthis is more at ease with who he is, perhaps because he has found a community and a suitable venue to express his Greek identity and to share it with non-Greeks.

In today's America, however, the demarkations between ethnic identities are increasingly blurred. Richard Rodriguez demonstrates in "Does America Still Exist?" that the many races coming together—peacefully enough, most of the time—on our city streets are constantly learning from and influencing each other. And in "Child of the Americas," Aurora Levins Morales celebrates the different ancestries that have contributed to her identity, joining and coalescing and transforming themselves through her until she has become a true American.

Pre-reading Activity   Consider the title. How can definition be a handicap?

As You Read   Observe the way in which the writer repeats certain terms to build continuity and reinforce ideas throughout the essay.

THE HANDICAP OF DEFINITION
William Raspberry

*Born in 1935 in Okolona, Mississippi, African-American writer **William Raspberry** is a syndicated columnist for the* Washington Post. *He has taught at Howard University, been on the Pulitzer Prize board, and received the Liberty Bell Award from the Federal Bar Association for "outstanding community service." This selection, an excerpt from a longer piece titled "Instilling Positive Images," was first published in the* Washington Post *in 1982.*

I know all about bad schools, mean politicians, economic deprivation and racism. Still, it occurs to me that one of the heaviest burdens black Americans—and black children in particular—have to bear is the handicap of definition: the question of what it means to be black.   1

Let me explain quickly what I mean. If a basketball fan says that the Boston Celtics' Larry Bird plays "black," the fan intends it—and Bird probably accepts it—as a compliment. Tell pop singer Tom Jones he moves "black" and he might grin in appreciation. Say to Teena Marie or The Average White Band that they sound "black" and they'll thank you.   2

But name one pursuit, aside from athletics, entertainment or sexual performance in which a white practitioner will feel complimented to be told he does it "black." Tell a white broadcaster he talks "black," and he'll sign up for diction lessons. Tell a white reporter he writes "black" and he'll take a writing course. Tell a white lawyer he reasons "black" and he might sue you for slander.   3

What we have here is a tragically limited definition of blackness, and it isn't only white people who buy it.   4

Think of all the ways black children can put one another down with charges of "whiteness." For many of these children, hard study and hard work are "white." Trying to please a teacher might be criticized as acting "white." Speaking correct English is "white." Scrimping today in the interest of tomorrow's goals is "white." Educational toys and games are "white."   5

6 An incredible array of habits and attitudes that are conducive to success in business, in academia, in the non-entertainment professions are likely to be thought of as somehow "white." Even economic success, unless it involves such "black" undertakings as numbers banking, is defined as "white."

7 And the results are devastating. I wouldn't deny that blacks often are better entertainers and athletes. My point is the harm that comes from too narrow a definition of what is black.

8 One reason black youngsters tend to do better at basketball, for instance, is that they assume they can learn to do it well, and so they practice constantly to prove themselves right.

9 Wouldn't it be wonderful if we could infect black children with the notion that excellence in math is "black" rather than white, or possibly Chinese? Wouldn't it be of enormous value if we could create the myth that morality, strong families, determination, courage and love of learning are traits brought by slaves from Mother Africa and therefore quintessentially black?

10 There is no doubt in my mind that most black youngsters could develop their mathematical reasoning, their elocution and their attitudes the way they develop their jump shots and their dance steps: by the combination of sustained, enthusiastic practice and the unquestioned belief that they can do it.

11 In one sense, what I am talking about is the importance of developing positive ethnic traditions. Maybe Jews have an innate talent for communication; maybe the Chinese are born with a gift for mathematical reasoning; maybe blacks are naturally blessed with athletic grace. I doubt it. What is at work, I suspect, is assumption, inculcated early in their lives, that this is a thing our people do well.

12 Unfortunately, many of the things about which blacks make this assumption are things that do not contribute to their career success—except for that handful of the truly gifted who can make it as entertainers and athletes. And many of the things we concede to whites are the things that are essential to economic security.

13 So it is with a number of assumptions black youngsters make about what it is to be a "man": physical aggressiveness, sexual prowess, the refusal to submit to authority. The prisons are full of people who, by this perverted definition, are unmistakably men.

14 But the real problem is not so much that the things defined as "black" are negative. The problem is that the definition is much too narrow.

15 Somehow, we have to make our children understand that they are intelligent, competent people, capable of doing whatever they put their minds to and making it in the American mainstream, not just in a black subculture.

16 What we seem to be doing, instead, is raising up yet another generation of young blacks who will be failures—by definition.

Building Vocabulary

Define the words below, using *context clues* wherever possible and checking in a dictionary when necessary. Use them in sentences of your own.

deprivation (1)	inculcated (11)	innate (11)
academia (6)	scrimping (5)	concede (12)
quintessentially (9)	devastating (7)	

Journal Writing

Choose one or more of the three activities listed below, and make an entry in your journal. Focus on writing spontaneously rather than on structure and mechanics.

1. **Exploring:** Recall what you remember from other sources—your reading, your life experiences, movies and television, stories told to you by others—about the topic discussed by the writer. Choose one or two of these to write about. Which aspects of the topic did they bring up? What additional information did they provide? What emotions did they create in you?
2. **Taking Stock:** Which parts of the selection were most difficult for you to grasp? Which parts needed more explanation? Which parts required outside information to be understood? What kind of information was required (e.g., historical, culture-specific, technical, etc.)? Where might such information be found? Were there aspects of the writer's style you found particularly effective? Particularly difficult? Why?
3. **Responding:** Identify one or two of the writer's main concerns. What personal knowledge, if any, do you have of these issues? What is your opinion on these issues? Examine your response carefully to see what it teaches you about yourself.

Analyzing Content

1. What is the first sentence in the essay doing? How does it relate to the second sentence? Judge the effectiveness of this beginning.
2. What are paragraphs 2 and 3 doing? What **rhetorical mode** is employed in these paragraphs? How are they related to paragraph 4?
3. **List** the problems the writer believes are inherent in the implications of what it means to be "black."
4. What point is he trying to persuade the readers of? Where is it most clearly stated?

Analyzing Writing Techniques

1. Analyze the structure of paragraph 4. Is it effective? Explain why or why not. How does it differ from a conventional paragraph?
2. Because he uses short paragraphs, as is common when writing for newspapers, Raspberry often organizes his points into **blocks** of paragraphs (e.g., paragraphs 5–7). Find another such block, and analyze its focus.

Group Activity

Discuss the idea of the "positive ethnic tradition" (paragraph 11). Is there such a thing? Can it be developed? How is it different from stereotyping? Find some examples of activities we believe certain groups of people do well.

Your Writing

1. In paragraph 15, the writer mentions a "black subculture." Think about the idea of a subculture. What does it mean? What are some other subcultures in America today? Write a paper choosing any *one* subculture and exploring its characteristics and its role in the larger societal structure.
2. What reasons does the writer give for the fact that many blacks are unable to achieve financial success in America? Do you agree with his reasons? Write a paper in which you examine the problem of black poverty and offer some reasons of your own for this situation.

Pre-reading Activity   Write about a situation in which your family values conflicted with those of the outside world.

As You Read   Observe the writer's use of interviews. How do they strengthen her writing?

CULTURAL BARRIERS AND THE PRESS
TO AMERICANIZE
Margaret A. Gibson

Margaret A. Gibson *is the author of* Accommodation without Assimilation: Sikh Immigrants in an American High School *(1988), from which this excerpt is taken.*

All Punjabi students were faced with conflicting sets of expectations regarding appropriate behavior, one set applicable to their Punjabi world and the other to the world of school. At home, for example, Punjabi young people learned to defer to their elders and to remain respectfully quiet in their presence. When Punjabis first entered American schools, whether as small children or teenagers, they were reluctant to speak in class except to respond with factual information to a teacher's direct question. Punjabi students were especially uncomfortable with the American technique of "brainstorming," one elementary teacher observed, and fell silent when expected to express their own ideas. High school teachers made similar observations. " 'I don't know,' is their answer almost before the question is asked," one English teacher responded, when asked if Punjabi students participated in class discussions. It was rare, said another, for Punjabi girls "to be outgoing enough to initiate conversation in class." Part of the difficulty stemmed from the coeducational nature of American high schools.   1

In Punjab villages teenage boys and girls traditionally avoid conversation with one another and even eye contact. In Indian schools, girls are not faced with the necessity of mixing with boys or speaking up in their presence. Classroom interaction is structured differently and, in most cases, secondary schooling is segregated by sex. At Valleyside High the Punjabi girls, including those born in America, participated only with great reluctance in coeducational activities, especially those that appeared competitive, such as physical education classes. They did not wish to draw attention to themselves in the presence of the opposite sex.   2

Just talking to boys could pose difficulty, particularly for the newer ar-   3 rivals: "A family that has just come over gets really upset if they see their [teenage] daughter talking to some guy," one student explained. Even for the American-educated students informal conversation between the sexes did not always come easily: "When I came here [to the high school] from eighth grade and saw girls talking to guys I thought, 'Oh my God, what are you doing?' I had never thought of myself doing that. And if a guy came I'd go the other way." Most Punjabi girls did talk to boys at school, we discovered, but not in front of their parents. One student explained in an interview.

4   **Interviewer:** Does it bother your parents if you just speak to fellow students who are guys?

5   **Girl:** A lot of guys . . . come by [my house] and say "Hi, how are you?" I tell them not to stop [by] . . . because my mom and dad would get mad. They say, "Okay, we understand." I talk to guys here at school, and if my parents were to find out they would probably kick me out of school.

6   **Interviewer:** Just for chatting with them?

7   **Girl:** They are afraid . . . the guy might start liking me.

8   **Interviewer:** How do they feel about your making friends with American girls?

9   **Girl:** They don't say anything about that, just as long as I stay away from boys and going out on dates.

10 **Interviewer:** So you can mix with all kinds of girls?

11 **Girl:** Yes . . . I enjoy talking to everybody. I even like to talk to boys. I've always been shy, but I enjoy talking to them. . . . If you don't talk to people they might say, "She thinks she's too good." I don't consider myself too good to talk to anybody. I think everybody is equal.

12 **Interviewer:** It must be awfully hard on the girls when they know their parents would really get upset.

13 **Girl:** Just about every girl here [at the high school] talks to everybody. If their parents were to be with them, they would have to face the other way. It's like in India. You hardly can look at anybody at all.

14 Punjabi students had learned to behave one way at home, another at school, but even in school the separation between the sexes remained. In sharp contrast to Valleysider social patterns, Punjabi boys and girls were never seen walking or sitting together. In group meetings, such as a get-together of the Asian Club, girls and boys sat separately. Most girls also refrained from speaking up in these sorts of gatherings, not, they said, because they felt incompetent to do so, but because it was their way of showing respect for the opposite sex.

15   Coeducational schooling posed the most obvious difficulties for Punjabis, but the constant attention given to preparing young people to go off on their own and to make decisions in accordance with individual rather

than family wishes provided equal cause for tension. The entire high school curriculum carried an implicit emphasis on teaching students that they had both the responsibility and the right to make decisions independent of their elders' views. So strong was the individualist orientation that it had become formalized in a social studies course titled "On Your Own." This course or one similar to it was required for graduation.

In this class students learned how to rent an apartment, get married, 16 plan the family budget, and even arrange a funeral—all on their own. Punjabi students were distinctly uncomfortable with this class, which from start to finish presumed white, middle-class values. Lessons dealing with marriage and family life, always taught from a Western point of view, were embarrassing to Punjabi adolescents, as were units dealing with contraception, abortion, and divorce, particularly in the coeducational setting of the American classroom. Outside of class Punjabi girls were teased by Punjabi boys for having to pair off with members of the opposite sex for some of their assignments, in accordance with the teacher's instructions. In spite of their discomfort with this and many other class assignments, however, the girls reported that "whatever the teacher says, we have to do."

Even some Valleysider parents expressed concern about the heavy em- 17 phasis by school personnel on independent decision making for young people. The high school, they felt, was undercutting parental authority, teaching students, for example, not to believe something just because "your parents believe it." Some objected to the message that at age eighteen the child, then legally an adult, could "do as he pleases, at school, at home, or any place else, and the parents don't have anything to say about it." Those Valleysiders who wished the schools would do more to support parental authority were also those who reinforced the legitimacy of school authority. In this respect, some Valleysider parents sounded very much like their Punjabi counterparts.

Most Punjabi students in time learned to juggle the different demands 18 and expectations of home and school. There were occasions, however, when Punjabi girls resisted complying with class requirements, even at the risk of losing credit. Physical education raised the most difficult problems. Two years of physical education were mandatory for high school graduation. Students received full credit if they attended class regularly, changed into gym clothes (short shorts and shirt), and made a reasonable effort to do what was asked of them. Although requirements seemed straightforward to Valleyside teachers, for many of the Punjabi girls in the senior sample they were simply beyond the pale. "Our children cannot change for sports," said one Punjabi parent; "this is against our culture." Almost no Punjabi parents wanted their daughters to expose their legs in the presence of boys or men. Some girls wore street clothes to class until they realized they would fail. Then they changed to sweat pants, no matter the temperature. . . .

19   Quite a few Punjabi parents were opposed to all sports for adolescent girls, especially if they were expected to run around in the presence of boys or men. In Punjab villages, only little girls played outside. An older girl, one man pointed out, would be seen "walking with her head low." Right or wrong, he concluded, Punjabi parents wanted the same from their daughters in Valleyside. . . .

20   In spite of all the pressures and counterpressures, Punjabi students made every effort to meet the demands of the formal curriculum, only rarely refusing to comply with a teacher's demands or school regulations, and then only in matters perceived to affect family and community honor. This was true even though Punjabi students often found the values of the classroom incompatible with those advocated by their parents. The easy give and take between the sexes and between students and teachers, the emphasis on individual decision making and on asserting one's own ideas, and the underlying assumption that majority-group norms should prevail were examples of home-school discontinuities with which all Punjabi students had to contend and with which, in fact, they were successfully contending, by working out a multicultural modus vivendi.

21   Punjabis did not view compliance with school rules or doing what one must to succeed academically as symbols of majority-group conformity, and they rewarded those who excelled in school. Diligence in matters academic and the acceptance of school authority were not equated, in the Punjabi view, with "acting white" or "like the Americans." Furthermore, although Punjabi teenagers condemned peers who acted "like whites," they enjoyed American burgers, wore designer jeans, and, if they could possibly manage it, zoomed down a highway standing on the seat in an open Trans Am.

Building Vocabulary

Define the words below, using *context clues* wherever possible and checking in a dictionary when necessary. Use them in sentences of your own.

defer (1)	counterpressures (20)	legitimacy (17)
stemmed (1)	initiate (1)	discontinuities (20)
incompetent (14)	segregated (2)	

Journal Writing

Choose one or more of the three activities listed below, and make an entry in your journal. Focus on writing spontaneously rather than on structure and mechanics.

1. **Exploring:** Recall what you remember from other sources—your reading, your life experiences, movies and television, stories told to you by others—about the topic discussed by the writer. Choose one or two of these to write about. Which aspects of the topic did they bring up? What additional information did they provide? What emotions did they create in you?

2. **Taking Stock:** Which parts of the selection were most difficult for you to grasp? Which parts needed more explanation? Which parts required outside information to be understood? What kind of information was required (e.g., historical, culture-specific, technical, etc.)? Where might such information be found? Were there aspects of the writer's style you found particularly effective? Particularly difficult? Why?

3. **Responding:** Identify one or two of the writer's main concerns. What personal knowledge, if any, do you have of these issues? What is your opinion on these issues? Examine your response carefully to see what it teaches you about yourself.

Analyzing Content

1. What is the basic conflict facing Punjabi students in the American high school?

2. Describe the classroom behavior of Punjabi students. Why is this a problem in an American school?

3. Which courses present the greatest difficulties for the Punjabi girls? Why?

4. How do the Punjabi students deal with the conflicts they face? According to the writer, are they successful?

Analyzing Writing Techniques

1. Explain the term *modus vivendi.* From where does it come? Is it a good writing technique to use expressions such as these in an English essay?

2. What do the ellipses (. . .) in the excerpt stand for? Why does the writer need to use ellipses? What are some pros and cons of using them?

Group Activity

Using the technique of **brainstorming,** come up with a list of the values held by Punjabi parents according to this excerpt. Discuss each value. How many of them are common values held by mainstream American parents?

Your Writing

1. This essay gives you a glimpse into the life of a teenage Punjabi/Indian girl. Using research if necessary, write a paper in which you **compare/contrast** such a person's life with an American teenager's. Based on your findings, what conclusions can you draw about cultural values?

2. Some of the problems faced by the Punjabi students seem to result from the way in which classes are set up at Valleyside High. Write a letter to the school board in which you suggest some changes that could be made relatively easily and would help these conflict-torn students.

Pre-reading Activity Write a response to the title, searching your memory for what you remember of media portrayals of Arabs.

As You Read Observe the way in which the writer has blended personal examples with objective, observed detail.

THE MEDIA'S IMAGE OF ARABS
Jack G. Shaheen

Born in Pittsburg in 1935, **Jack G. Shaheen** *is a first-generation Lebanese-American. He holds degrees from Carnegie Tech, Penn State, and the University of Missouri. He teaches mass communication at Southern Illinois University and is a freelance reporter. His books include* The TV Arab *and* The Hollywood Arab. *This selection was first published in* Newsweek *in 1988.*

America's bogyman is the Arab. Until the nightly news brought us TV pictures of Palestinian boys being punched and beaten, almost all portraits of Arabs seen in America were dangerously threatening. Arabs were either billionaires or bombers—rarely victims. They were hardly ever seen as ordinary people practicing law, driving taxis, singing lullabies or healing the sick. Though TV news may portray them more sympathetically now, the absence of positive media images nurtures suspicion and stereotype. As an Arab-American, I have found that ugly caricatures have had an enduring impact on my family. 1

I was sheltered from prejudicial portraits at first. My parents came from Lebanon in the 1920s; they met and married in America. Our home in the steel city of Clairton, Pa., was a center for ethnic sharing—black, white, Jew and gentile. There was only one major source of media images then, at the State movie theater where I was lucky enough to get a part-time job as an usher. But in the late 1940s, Westerns and war movies were popular, not Middle Eastern dramas. Memories of World War II were fresh, and the screen heavies were the Japanese and the Germans. True to the cliché of the times, the only good Indian was a dead Indian. But when I mimicked or mocked the bad guys, my mother cautioned me. She explained that stereotypes blur our vision and corrupt the imagination. "Have compassion for all people, Jackie," she said. "This way, you'll learn to experience the joy of accepting people as they are, and not as they appear in films. Stereotypes hurt." 2

Mother was right. I can remember the Saturday afternoon when my son, Michael, who was seven, and my daughter, Michele, six, suddenly called out: "Daddy, Daddy, they've got some bad Arabs on TV." They were 3 watching that great American morality play, TV wrestling. Akbar the Great, who liked to hear the cracking of bones, and Abdullah the Butcher, a dirty fighter who liked to inflict pain, were pinning their foes with "camel locks." From that day on, I knew I had to try to neutralize the media caricatures.

4   It hasn't been easy. With my children, I have watched animated heroes Heckle and Jeckle pull the rug from under "Ali Boo-Boo, the Desert Rat," and Laverne and Shirley stop "Sheik Ha-Mean-le" from conquering "the U.S. and the world." I have read comic books like the "Fantastic Four" and "G.I. Combat" whose characters have sketched Arabs as "lowlifes" and "human hyenas." Negative stereotypes were everywhere. A dictionary informed my youngsters that an Arab is a "vagabond, drifter, hobo and vagrant." Whatever happened, my wife wondered, to Aladdin's good genie?

5   To a child, the world is simple: good versus evil. But my children and others with Arab roots grew up without ever having seen a humane Arab on the silver screen, someone to pattern their lives after. Is it easier for a camel to go through the eye of a needle than for a screen Arab to appear as a genuine human being?

6   Hollywood producers must have an instant Ali Baba kit that contains scimitars, veils, sunglasses and such Arab clothing as *chadors* and *kufiyahs*. In the mythical "Ay-rabland," oil wells, tents, mosques, goats and shepherds prevail. Between the sand dunes, the camera focuses on a mock-up of a palace from "Arabian Nights"—or a military air base. Recent movies suggest that Americans are at war with Arabs, forgetting the fact that out of twenty-one Arab nations, America is friendly with nineteen of them. And in "Wanted Dead or Alive," a movie that starred Gene Simmons, the leader of the rock group Kiss, the war comes home when an Arab terrorist comes to the United States dressed as a rabbi and, among other things, conspires with Arab-Americans to poison the people of Los Angeles. The movie was released last year.

7   The Arab remains American culture's favorite whipping boy. In his memoirs, Terrel Bell, Ronald Reagan's first secretary of education, writes about an "apparent bias among mid-level, right-wing staffers at the White House" who dismissed Arabs as "sand niggers." Sadly, the racial slurs continue. At a recent teacher's conference, I met a woman from Sioux Falls, S.D., who told me about the persistence of discrimination. She was in the process of adopting a baby when an agency staffer warned her that the infant had a problem. When she asked whether the child was mentally ill, or physically handicapped, there was silence. Finally, the worker said: "The baby is Jordanian."

8   To me, the Arab demon of today is much like the Jewish demon of yesterday. We deplore the false portrait of Jews as a swarthy menace. Yet a similar portrait has been accepted and transferred to another group of Semites—the Arabs. Print and broadcast journalists have started to challenge this stereotype. They are now revealing more humane images of Palestin-

ian Arabs, a people who traditionally suffered from the myth that Palestinian equals terrorist. Others could follow that lead and retire the stereotypical Arab to a media Valhalla.

It would be a step in the right direction if movie and TV producers de- 9 veloped characters modeled after real-life Arab-Americans. We could then see a White House correspondent like Helen Thomas, whose father came from Lebanon, in "The Golden Girls," a heart surgeon patterned after Dr. Michael DeBakey on "St. Elsewhere," or a Syrian-American playing tournament chess like Yasser Seirawan, the Seattle grandmaster.

Politicians, too, should speak out against the cardboard caricatures. 10 They should refer to Arabs as friends, not just as moderates. And religious leaders could state that Islam like Christianity and Judaism maintains that all mankind is one family in the care of God. When all imagemakers rightfully begin to treat Arabs and all other minorities with respect and dignity, we may begin to unlearn our prejudices.

Building Vocabulary

Define the words below, using *context clues* wherever possible and checking in a dictionary when necessary. Use them in sentences of your own.

bogeyman (1)	whipping boy (7)	vagrant (4)
caricatures (1)	nurtures (1)	swarthy (8)
neutralize (3)	gentile (2)	

Journal Writing

Choose one or more of the three activities listed below, and make an entry in your journal. Focus on writing spontaneously rather than on structure and mechanics.

1. **Exploring:** Recall what you remember from other sources—your reading, your life experiences, movies and television, stories told to you by others—about the topic discussed by the writer. Choose one or two of these to write about. Which aspects of the topic did they bring up? What additional information did they provide? What emotions did they create in you?

2. **Taking Stock:** Which parts of the selection were most difficult for you to grasp? Which parts needed more explanation? Which parts required outside information to be understood? What kind of information was required (e.g., historical, culture-specific, technical, etc.)? Where might such information be found? Were there aspects of the writer's style you found particularly effective? Particularly difficult? Why?

3. **Responding:** Identify one or two of the writer's main concerns. What personal knowledge, if any, do you have of these issues? What is your opinion on these issues? Examine your response carefully to see what it teaches you about yourself.

Analyzing Content

1. Why is the writer concerned about the absence of positive media depictions of Arabs?
2. Select three negative media images presented by the writer in this essay, and list them in order of magnitude.
3. What relationship between America and the Arab nations do recent movies suggest? What is the truth?
4. Explain the writer's proposed solution. Is it an effective one? Explain why or why not.

Analyzing Writing Techniques

1. In paragraph 3, what is the role of the first sentence, "Mother was right"? Where else has the writer used this device?
2. What is the writer doing in the second paragraph? Why is this important to his argument?

Group Activity

Do some library research on the Gulf War. What media images of Arabs were prevalent at that time in America? Discuss how this might have affected both Arab-Americans and non-Arab-Americans.

Your Writing

1. Throughout the essay, the writer refers to other groups that have been stereotyped by the media. Choose *one* such group, and write an essay about the kind of stereotyping you have observed.
2. Imagine that you are about to produce a TV show. What kinds of characters would you include in your show to generate some positive media images for minorities? Write a paper in which you describe a few of your main characters and what you hope to achieve through them.

Pre-reading Activity   If someone asked you, "Where are you from?" how would you respond? Examine your answer to see how you identify yourself.

As You Read   Observe the writer's use of generalization. **Underline** some of the general statements that seem particularly accurate to you.

DOES AMERICA STILL EXIST?
Richard Rodriguez

*Born in 1944 in San Francisco, **Richard Rodriguez** holds degrees from Stanford and Columbia Universities. His best-known work is* Hunger of Memory: the Education of Richard Rodriguez. *He is a freelance writer and lecturer who often debates the merits of bilingual education. This selection first appeared in* Harper's *in 1984.*

For the children of immigrant parents the knowledge comes easier. America exists everywhere in the city—on billboards, frankly in the smell of French fries and popcorn. It exists in the pace: traffic lights, the assertions of neon, the mysterious bong-bong-bong through the atriums of department stores. America exists as the voice of the crowd, a menacing sound— the high nasal accent of American English. 1

When I was a boy in Sacramento (California, the fifties), people would ask me, "Where you from?" I was born in this country, but I knew the question meant to decipher my darkness, my looks. 2

My mother once instructed me to say, "I am an American of Mexican descent." By the time I was nine or ten, I wanted to say, but dared not reply, "I am an American." 3

Immigrants come to America and, against hostility or mere loneliness, they recreate a homeland in the parlor, tacking up postcards or calendars of some impossible blue—lake or sea or sky. Children of immigrant parents are supposed to perch on a hyphen between two countries. Relatives assume the achievement as much as anyone. Relatives are, in any case, surprised when the child begins losing old ways. One day at the family picnic the boy wanders away from their spiced food and faceless stories to watch other boys play baseball in the distance. 4

There is sorrow in the American memory, guilty sorrow for having left something behind—Portugal, China, Norway. The American story is the story of immigrant children and of their children—children no longer able to speak to grandparents. The memory of exile becomes inarticulate as it 5

still true today? Write an essay on the subject, supporting your opinion with current examples.

2. In paragraph 15, Rodriguez claims that assimilation is "reciprocal." Do you agree? Write an essay in which you examine the ways that the American identity has (or has not) been influenced by immigrants.

will continue to
other.

Job applicati
individuals to ch
marked BLACK be
ever, I could just
these forms, I thii
whoever sees the
cepting a big x by
not truly represer
added the categc
heard that a few s

One of the g
pose them to boi
the end society m
CIAL will not magi
people to stop ju
we really are—bi

Building Voca

Define the word
checking in a di
your own.

biracial (3)
derogatory (8)
shun (8)

Journal Writin

Choose one or n
entry in your jou
structure and m

1. **Exploring:** R
   reading, your
   to you by oth
   one or two of
   they bring u|
   What emotioi
2. **Taking Stock**
   you to grasp?
   required outs

Pre-reading Activity   Using the device of **clustering,** write your responses to the term *biracial.*

As You Read   Observe how the writer moves from the problem to a
discussion of its solution.

FREEDOM FROM CHOICE
Brian A. Courtney

Brian A. Courtney *studies journalism at the University of Tennessee. This
piece first appeared in the "My Turn" column of* Newsweek *in 1995.*

As my friend Denise and I trudged across the University of Tennessee   1
campus to our 9:05 A.M. class, we delivered countless head nods, "Heys"
and "How ya' doin's" to other African-Americans we passed along the way.
We spoke to people we knew as well as people we didn't know because
it's an unwritten rule that black people speak to one another when they
pass. But when I stopped to greet and hug one of my female friends, who
happens to be white, Denise seemed a little bothered. We continued our
walk to class, and Denise expressed concern that I might be coming down
with a "fever." "I don't feel sick," I told her. As it turns out, she was referring to "jungle fever," the condition where a black man or woman is at-
tracted to someone of the opposite race.

This encounter has not been an uncommon experience for me. That's   2
why the first 21 years of my life have felt like a never-ending tug of war.
And quite honestly, I'm not looking forward to being dragged through the
mud for the rest of my life. My white friends want me to act one way—
white. My African-American friends want me to act another—black. Pleas-
ing them both is nearly impossible and leaves little room to be just me.

The politically correct term for someone with my racial background   3
is "biracial" or "multiracial." My mother is fair-skinned with blond hair and
blue eyes. My father is dark-complexioned with prominent African-
American features and a head of woolly hair. When you combine the ge-
netic makeup of the two, you get me—golden-brown skin, semi-coarse hair
and a whole mess of freckles.

Someone once told me I was lucky to be biracial because I have the   4
best of both worlds. In some ways this is true. I have a huge family that's
filled with diversity and is as colorful as a box of Crayolas. My family is
more open to whomever I choose to date, whether that person is black,
white, biracial, Asian or whatever. But looking at the big picture, American society makes being biracial feel less like a blessing than a curse.

5   O
to labe
egorie
pro-lif
Ameri
lem fc
rest of
tify wi
who v

6   G
Tenn.,
minor
of my
Over
black
only *h*
dressii
and m
identit

7   M
Ameri
campi
have t
white
me I d
a pair
kind c
admit
let it r
said ir

8   O
sweep
peopl(
These
materi
herita;
same |
for sor

9   I (
lems i
knowl
like m
white
whate

formation was required (e.g., historical, culture-specific, technical, etc.)? Where might such information be found? Were there aspects of the writer's style you found particularly effective? Particularly difficult? Why?

3. **Responding:** Identify one or two of the writer's main concerns. What personal knowledge, if any, do you have of these issues? What is your opinion on these issues? Examine your response carefully to see what it teaches you about yourself.

Analyzing Content

1. Why is the writer's friend upset with him in the first paragraph? What values are implied in her reaction?
2. How is the writer lucky to be biracial?
3. How is being biracial a difficult experience for him?
4. What, according to the writer, is the underlying problem regarding biracial children? What solution does he propose? How will it improve the situation?

Analyzing Writing Techniques

1. **List** the transition terms used by the writer to connect different parts of his argument. What would be lost from the essay if they were removed?
2. **List** the metaphors used by the writer. Why does he use them? How do they aid his argument or enhance his style?

Group Activity

Have each member of the group interview people of different ethnic origins, including biracial people, asking them what advantages and disadvantages they think biracial individuals face. Compile your findings into a **collaborative** paragraph.

Your Writing

1. Do you agree with the writer that our need to label everything into categories is negative, or do you feel that labeling is important and necessary? Is it OK to label certain things but not others? Write a paper in which you support your opinion with specific examples.
2. Write a letter to the writer explaining how you feel about the issue of biracial identity. Propose a different solution that you feel will improve the situation.

Pre-reading Activity   Briefly trace your ancestry. Where did your parents come from? Do you belong to more than one race? Which language(s) do you speak?

As You Read   Observe the use of words from other languages in the poem. Think about what the poem gains from this kind of diction.

CHILD OF THE AMERICAS
Aurora Levins Morales

Born in Puerto Rico in 1954, **Aurora Levins Morales** *came to the United States in 1967. She is the daughter of a Puerto Rican mother and a Jewish father and a writer of short stories, essays, and poetry. This selection was written in 1986.*

I am a child of the Americas,
a light-skinned mestiza of the Caribbean,
a child of many diaspora, born into this
    continent at a crossroads.

I am a U.S. Puerto Rican Jew,
a product of the ghettos of New York I have
    never known.
An immigrant and the daughter and
    granddaughter of immigrants.
I speak English with passion: it's the tongue
    of my consciousness,
a flashing knife blade of crystal, my tool, my
    craft.

I am Caribeña,[1] island grown. Spanish is in
    my flesh,
ripples from my tongue, lodges in my hips: 10
the language of garlic and mangoes,
the singing in my poetry, the flying gestures
    of my hands.

----

[1]Caribbean woman

I am of Latinoamerica, rooted in the history
   of my continent:
I speak from that body.

I am not african. Africa is in me, but I
   cannot return.
I am not taína.[2] Taíno is in me, but there is
   no way back.
I am not european. Europe lives in me, but I
   have no home there.

I am new. History made me. My first
   language was spanglish.[3]
I was born at the crossroads
20 and I am whole.

Building Vocabulary

Define the words below, using *context clues* wherever possible and
checking in a dictionary when necessary. Use them in sentences of
your own.

mestiza (line 2)   lodges (10)   craft (9)
ghettos (6)   diaspora (3)   spanglish (18)

Analyzing Content

1. Examine the writer's different heritages. In what way is she the
   product of New York ghettos if she has never been to one?
2. What role does English play in her life?
3. What role does Spanish play? How do we know the writer feels
   differently about this language compared with English?
4. Explain the meaning of the fourth stanza.

Analyzing Writing Techniques

1. **Analyze** the structure of the poem. What is the subject of each
   stanza?
2. **Pick out** the metaphor used by the writer in the first stanza. How
   is it changed or developed when repeated in the final stanza?

----

[2]*Taínos* were the Indians indigenous to Puerto Rico
[3]Mixture of Spanish and English languages

Group Activity

Do a "Roots" project in which you trace the ancestry of a public figure the group chooses, noting the influence of this person's racial heritage on him or her.

Your Writing

1. In the first stanza, the writer states that she is a child of many diaspora. Write a paper on *one* diaspora that has been an important influence on American culture and society, giving specific details.
2. Do you think the multiracial, multicultural identity is a particular American one, or do people in other countries share this aspect of society? Write a paper in which you elaborate on your opinions with examples drawn from different nations.

Pre-reading Activity   Complete the sentence "I am a(n). . . ." How did you define/identify yourself? Write a paragraph elaborating on that idea.

As You Read   Observe the different categories the writer has given us in the essay as ways to experience and understand the Greek identity.

A TASTE OF GREECE
Bill Vourthis

Born in 1976 in Redwood City, California, **Bill Vourthis** *is a first-generation Greek-American. His recent travels to Greece have sparked a growing interest in his roots. He wishes to dedicate this essay to his family and to other Greek college students. Bill is a student at Foothill College.*

1   Every year during the Labor Day weekend, Greeks from all over the Bay Area—San Jose, Oakland, San Mateo, and San Francisco—flock to the Church of the Holy Cross in Redwood City. They are coming to attend the Greek Festival, to experience once more what it is that makes them Greek: the foods and wines, the dances and music, the crafts and the religious history they brought with them years ago when they came to this country.

2   The festival lasts only 3 days, but it takes the organizers a long time to prepare. The preparation is an experience in itself and allows the local Greek community to bond and pass down traditions and values. It begins with the women. Old and young, they meet at the church to discuss what to cook and to portion out duties. Many nights are then spent chopping, simmering, baking, stuffing—and talking. Not only are culinary secrets passed down from generation to generation, but also the stories. The old women reminisce about their mothers and grandmothers, how each had her special way of making a dish turn out just right. They remember weddings and baptisms in the villages where women used to gather and gossip, just as they are doing now. The talking, the cooking, the secrets shared—it all creates a special bond among the women, a reinforcement of the traditional cultural roles. It becomes an initiation for the young into maturity, into Greek womanhood.

3   Meanwhile, the men, too, are busy, for they also have an important role to play in making the festival successful. Not surprisingly, their job is to build the booths. No one is too unskilled to be included. The older men teach the younger ones how to set up the entire area so that it re-

sembles an ancient Greek town: first the *agora* or marketplace, which used to be the center of commercial life; then the theater, with tiers of semicircular benches rising around it, where the performances will be held. Patiently, they hammer and saw and instruct until plywood is transformed into painted pillars that give each booth the feel of an ancient temple.

Food is at the heart of the festival, just as it is at the heart of every cul- 4 ture. Perhaps that is why when the festival opens, the food booths are the ones people rush to first, to taste the delicacies no longer found every day in their homes: fried kalamari served with a squeeze of lemon, rice pilafi, golden honey-dipped loukomades, tiropita stuffed with cheese, dolmades made from grape leaves, and whole roasted lamb. The most popular booths are the ones selling gyros and Greek salads, the two items that possibly best embody Greek culture. The gyro is the perfect balanced meal. To make it, one first toasts the rolled out gyro bread until it is golden. Meanwhile, the meat, marinated in spices, has been sizzling in a pan. At the right moment, it is laid on top of the bread and topped off with garden-fresh tomatoes, green and yellow onions, and crisp chives, but the secret of the gyro lies in the last ingredient, without which the sandwich lies naked: the white tangy garlic sauce that is poured over everything. Now the bread is ready to be rolled up and devoured!

The Greek salad that accompanies the gyro is a work of art. It consists 5 of plump red tomatoes, sliced red onions, green peppers, crunchy cucumbers, kalamata olives, crumbled feta cheese, and anchovies—all tossed in olive oil that gleams like the sun. The amount of pride people take in serving the best, most authentic, most *Greek* ingredients is seen in the fact that the olive oil is sent to the festival each year direct from the motherland, from people who grow and process it themselves.

Another item sent directly to the festival from Greece is the wine, dis- 6 tilled and aged to perfection. What makes this wine the best there is, as any Greek will tell you, is retsina, the sap from a special tree that is added during distillation. As one sips this dry, heady drink, surely the landscapes of Greece flash through one's mind.

Once the inner being is satisfied, people gravitate toward the lively 7 music. The bouzooki is playing its clear, bright notes, accompanied by a violin and flute and maybe drums. The tempo is upbeat, because this is a time of celebration, and the young men, who have been practising all summer, are showing off their skill. The lead dancer explains the meaning of the dances to the audience. First is a dance that men used to perform before going off to battle the Turks. It is a dance that requires stamina and discipline; the dancers keep their backs straight while doing a squat walk. This dance honors those who have died for the independence of Greece. A popular dance performed by the women is the suicide dance, and there is history behind this one, too. It commemorates women who chose to jump from a cliff to their deaths rather than be enslaved by the Turks. Dance groups from several cities come to perform at this festival. The stage throbs with a fierce sense of competition as well as cultural pride, and the enthusiastic cheers from the audience show how closely they share these emotions.

8   To another side is a display of Greek art, many of the booths manned by the artists themselves. There is a great variety—paintings, jewelry, vases. A popular subject of the paintings is the Greek landscape, made more picturesque through nostalgia. The jewelry comes in many forms—wreaths and diadems for the head, and tiny animal and bird shapes strung into necklaces and earrings. The most prominent piece of jewelry is the Cross; the most popular statues are the forms of Greek gods. It is an interesting blend of the pagan and the Christian. The art items may not be masterpieces but are eagerly purchased, because they are all created by Greeks—and they are beautiful.

9   Religion is the most important part of this festival and, for the people who create the festival, of Greek life. It is to show dedication to Jesus that the festival is held at a church and not a convention center or park. A strong sense of religious ritual permeates the festival. Before the performances begins, for example, the priest leads the audience in prayer. When the food booths open, before anyone begins to eat, there is another prayer. Many people come to the festival mainly to view the display of archaic religious items brought together from many different places for the devout to admire. The ancient Bibles, communion cups, orthodox icons, crosses, and censors give one a sense of going back in time. A tour of the church is a popular part of the festival, and people who have been inside sometimes exchange amazed whispers about how they felt a sudden warmth flooding them as they stepped up to the cool altar.

10   What does it mean to be Greek? It means to share in the spirit of the artists and philosophers, the playwrights and poets from the Golden Age, which was possibly the greatest formative influence on the development of European civilization. It means to feel lucky that such a richness is part of who you are. It means to carry on those traditions and ideas, to cook and share the foods and drinks loved by the ancients, to dance the dances, to sing the old songs, to enjoy and wear the jewelry, and to carry home the traditional artifacts that have decorated Greek houses for centuries. It means to bond, old and young, from far and near, through work and storytelling and prayer in the special way the Greek festival makes possible.

Structure and Strategy

1. Examine the title of the essay. Is it effective in giving the reader an idea of the subject? Where in the essay is it reinforced?
2. What is the major **rhetorical mode** used in this essay, and what is its purpose? Analyze a paragraph in which this rhetorical mode comes across clearly, and evaluate its effectiveness on the reader.

3. The writer makes a general statement that food is at the heart of every culture. How does he develop this idea? What kind of transition sentence(s) does he use in that paragraph?
4. Analyze the organization of the essay. Why do certain points come earlier and others later? What would be lost if the paragraphs are moved around?

Your Writing

1. Although this paper is written in the **third person,** it is based on firsthand observation. Attend a cultural event in your community that you feel enhances people's sense of who they are, and write an essay describing it and explaining its value. (You may choose to write it in **first person** or **third person.**)
2. Imagine that you are on a planning committee for a cultural festival to enhance your community's sense of pride and identity. Which kinds of activities, booths, events, and such would you focus on? Why? Write a paper explaining your thinking process, supporting your ideas with specific, practicable examples.

The preceding units have given us many different ideas and experiences that relate to the roles we play in a multicultural society. This unit focuses on possibly the most important aspect of living with others who are unlike us: how do we deal with their "differentness"? How do we deal with situations in which our own differentness causes others to react negatively to us? Are there some behaviors or values we can learn that will help us to coexist more peacefully in a world that promises to be more and more cross-cultural?

In "For My Indian Daughter," Lewis P. Johnson shares the ignorance and prejudice toward Native-Americans that he has faced for many years. He also shows how they have spurred him to discover himself, however, and have given him the strength to teach his young daughter how to live in a country that will not always be accepting of her. In "Fire, Hope and Charity," Jeanne Marie Laskas points to forgiveness and generosity as the virtues that help to heal a crime of sweeping violence against the Amish and to ally them more solidly with their neighbors. And in "The Culture of Cuisine," which analyzes the cosmopolitan eating habits of America, John Naisbitt and Patricia Aburdene illustrate how enjoyable and enriching the process of acceptance can become once we are willing to begin.

Perhaps a good starting point is to recognize the contributions made by those we characterize as "other" instead of holding them responsible for all our social ills. This is Chang-Lin Tien's belief in "America's Scapegoats." Perhaps from there it is easier to reach the point at which we appreciate each group for what it has to offer, as demonstrated by the lovable central character in José Burciaga's "My Ecumenical Father." But the central ingredient to help remedy relationships in a diverse world seems best described by Langston Hughes in "I, Too, Sing America," the poem that inspired the title of this book. It is a confidence that manages to steer clear of anger, that makes the best of one's situation, and that believes strongly in one's one inner worth and the ultimate possibility of friendship—even across the barriers of a history of hate.

Pre-reading Activity   What does "I am the darker brother" (from stanza 2) mean to you? Write a line that begins similarly, "I am—," and complete it in a way that illustrates how society (or part of it) looks at your race.

As You Read   Observe how the poem is structured: stanzas, line breaks, presence or absence of rhyme, and use of repetition.

I, TOO, SING AMERICA
Langston Hughes

Langston Hughes (1902–1967) is a major African-American poet of the Harlem Renaissance of the 1920s. Responsible for bringing the rhythm of the blues and the urban black dialect into American poetry, he is the author of 16 books of poetry, two novels, three collections of stories, 20 dramatic pieces, eight children's books, and two volumes of autobiography. This selection illustrates his dictum that "poetry should be direct, comprehensible and the epitome of sincerity."

I, too, sing America.

I am the darker brother.
They send me to eat in the kitchen
When company comes,
But I laugh,
And eat well,
And grow strong.

Tomorrow,
I'll be at the table
When company comes.   10
Nobody'll dare
Say to me,
"Eat in the kitchen,"
Then.

Besides,
They'll see how beautiful I am
And be ashamed—

I, too, am America.

Analyzing Content

1. Who is the "I" or **narrator** of the poem?
2. Pick out and explain the **metaphor** created and reinforced by the author throughout the poem.
3. What historical/social condition(s) does the metaphor portray?
4. Pick out the turning point of the poem. What change occurs in the author's attitude? What is his hope?

Analyzing Writing Techniques

1. **List** the transition terms used by the writer in this poem. How are they different from those used in prose?
2. **Examine** the first and last lines of the poem, and comment on their difference. What is the writer trying to convey through them?

Group Activity

Go through an anthology of Langston Hughes' works, and pick out another poem that illustrates the social condition of being black in America in the 1920s and 1930s. Discuss as a group the message that Hughes is trying to convey and the images he uses to do it.

Your Writing

1. Write a poem or prose piece that illuminates your experience, or that of someone you know, of being treated in a particular way (either negative or positive) because of your race. What did you learn from the incident?
2. The statement "Besides, they'll see how beautiful I am" reminds one of the "Black is beautiful" movement that became popular in the United States during the 1960s. Write a paper analyzing this movement and its effect on black identity and culture.

Pre-reading Activity   Think of a situation in which you (or some-one you know) stood out in a group. How did the group react to this? How did you feel?

As You Read   Observe the movement from paragraph 1 to paragraph 2. What is the effect on the reader? Look for other places in the essay where the writer effects the same kind of movement.

FOR MY INDIAN DAUGHTER
Lewis P. Johnson

Born in 1935, **Lewis P. Johnson** *is a full-blooded Potawatomi Ottawa Indian who also goes by the name Lewis Sawaquat. He works for the U.S. Department of Agriculture and lives near Lake Leelanau in Michigan. This selection, his first published piece, originally appeared in* Newsweek *in 1983.*

My little girl is singing herself to sleep upstairs, her voice mingling with   1
the sounds of the birds outside in the old maple trees. She is two and I am
nearly 50, and I am very taken with her. She came along late in my life,
unexpected and unbidden, a startling gift.

Today at the beach my chubby-legged, brown-skinned daughter ran   2
laughing into the water as fast as she could. My wife and I laughed watching her, until we heard behind us a low guttural curse and then an unpleasant voice raised in an imitation war whoop.

I turned to see a fat man in a bathing suit, white and soft as a grub, as   3
he covered his mouth and prepared to make the Indian war cry again. He
was middle-aged, younger than I, and had three little children lined up
next to him, grinning foolishly. My wife suggested we leave the beach, and
I agreed.

I knew the man was not unusual in his feelings against Indians. His   4
beach behavior might have been socially unacceptable to more civilized
whites, but his basic view of Indians is expressed daily in our small town,
frequently on the editorial pages of the county newspaper, as white people speak out against Indian fishing rights and land rights, saying in essence,
"Those Indians are taking our fish, our land." It doesn't matter to them that
we were here first, that the U.S. Supreme Court has ruled in our favor. It
matters to them that we have something they want, and they hate us for
it. Backlash is the common explanation of the attacks on Indians, the
bumper stickers that say, "Spear an Indian, Save a Fish," but I know better. The hatred of Indians goes back to the beginning when white people

came to this country. For me it goes back to my childhood in Harbor Springs, Mich.

5   **Theft:** Harbor Springs is now a summer resort for the very affluent, but a hundred years ago it was the Indian village of my Ottawa ancestors. My grandmother, Anna Showanessy, and other Indians like her, had their land there taken by treaty, by fraud, by violence, by theft. They remembered how whites had burned down the village at Burt Lake in 1900 and pushed the Indians out. These were the stories in my family.

6   When I was a boy my mother told me to walk down the alleys in Harbor Springs and not to wear my orange football sweater out of the house. This way I would not stand out, not be noticed, and not be a target.

7   I wore my orange sweater anyway and deliberately avoided the alleys. I was the biggest person I knew and wasn't really afraid. But I met my come-uppance when I enlisted in the U.S. Army. One night all the men in my barracks gathered together and, gang-fashion, pulled me into the shower and scrubbed me down with rough brushes used for floors, saying, "We won't have any dirty Indians in our outfit." It is a point of irony that I was cleaner than any of them. Later in Korea I learned how to kill, how to bully, how to hate Koreans. I came out of the war tougher than ever and, strangely, white.

8   I went to college, got married, lived in La Porte, Ind., worked as a sur-veyor and raised three boys. I headed Boy Scout groups, never thinking it odd when the Scouts did imitation Indian dances, imitation Indian lore.

9   One day when I was 35 or thereabouts I heard about an Indian pow-wow. My father used to attend them and so with great curiosity and a strange joy at discovering a part of my heritage, I decided the thing to do to get ready for this big event was to have my friend make me a spear in his forge. The steel was fine and blue and irridescent. The feathers on the shaft were bright and proud.

10   In a dusty state fairground in southern indiana, I found white people dressed as Indians. I learned they were "hobbyists," that is, it was their hobby and leisure pastime to masquerade as Indians on weekends. I felt ridiculous with my spear, and I left.

11   It was years before I could tell anyone of the embarrassment of this weekend and see any humor in it. But in a way it was that weekend, for all its silliness, that was my awakening. I realized I didn't know who I was. I didn't have an Indian name. I didn't speak the Indian language. I didn't know the Indian customs. Dimly I remembered the Ottawa word for dog, but it was a baby word, *kahgee,* not the full word, *muhkahgee,* which I was later to learn. Even more hazily I remembered a naming ceremony (my own). I remembered legs dancing around me, dust. Where had that been? Who had I been? "Suwaukquat," my mother told me when I asked, "where the tree begins to grow."

12   That was 1968, and I was not the only Indian in the country who was feeling the need to remember who he or she was. There were others. They

had powwows, real ones, and eventually I found them. Together we re-searched our past, a search that for me culminated in the Longest Walk, a march on Washington in 1978. Maybe because I now know what it means to be Indian, it surprises me that others don't. Of course there aren't very many of us left. The chances of an average person knowing an average Indian in an average lifetime are pretty slim.

Circle: Still, I was amused one day when my small, four-year-old [13] neighbor looked at me as I was hoeing in my garden and said, "You aren't a real Indian, are you?" Scotty is little, talkative, likable. Finally I said, "I'm a real Indian." He looked at me for a moment and then said, squinting into the sun, "Then where's your horse and feathers?" The child was simply a smaller, whiter version of my own ignorant self years before. We'd both seen too much TV, that's all. He was not to be blamed. And so, in a way, the moronic man on the beach today is blameless. We come full circle to realize other people are like ourselves, as discomfiting as that may be sometimes.

As I sit in my old chair on my porch, in a light that is fading so the [14] leaves are barely distinguishable against the sky, I can picture my girl asleep upstairs. I would like to prepare her for what's to come, take her each step of the way saying, there's a place to avoid, here's what I know about this, but much of what's before her she must go through alone. She must pass through pain and joy and solitude and community to discover her own inner self that is unlike any other and come through that passage to the place where she sees all people are one, and in so seeing may live her life in a brighter future.

Building Vocabulary

Define the words below, using *context clues* wherever possible and checking in a dictionary when necessary. Use them in sentences of your own.

unbidden (1)	masquerade (10)	iridescent (9)
fraud (5)	backlash (4)	moronic (13)
powwow (9)	comeuppance (7)	

Journal Writing

Choose one or more of the three activities listed below, and make an entry in your journal. Focus on writing spontaneously rather than on structure and mechanics.

1. **Exploring:** Recall what you remember from other sources—your reading, your life experiences, movies and television, stories told to you by others—about the topic discussed by the writer. Choose one or two of these to write about. Which aspects of the topic did

they bring up? What additional information did they provide? What emotions did they create in you?

2. **Taking Stock:** Which parts of the selection were most difficult for you to grasp? Which parts needed more explanation? Which parts required outside information to be understood? What kind of information was required (e.g., historical, culture-specific, technical, etc.)? Where might such information be found? Were there aspects of the writer's style you found particularly effective? Particularly difficult? Why?

3. **Responding:** Identify one or two of the writer's main concerns. What personal knowledge, if any, do you have of these issues? What is your opinion on these issues? Examine your response carefully to see what it teaches you about yourself.

Analyzing Content

1. Explain the term *backlash* in the context of this piece. Why does the writer follow the term with the statement "I know better"?
2. What does the writer learn in the U.S. Army? Why does he end paragraph 7 by describing himself as "white?"
3. Describe what the writer discovers at his first powwow. In what way is this an "awakening" for him?
4. Infer what the writer means by his statement in paragraph 12 that "I now know what it means to be Indian."

Analyzing Writing Techniques

1. **Examine** the title. What does it tell us about the purpose of the piece? Where in the piece itself is this idea reinforced?
2. **Analyze** the placement of the examples chosen by the writer. What progression do they show in terms of how he feels about the ignorance and prejudice of non-Indians?

Group Activity

Examine the subheadings of the essay, "Theft" and "Circle." What points are they emphasizing? Come up with some new subheadings for the essay that point to other important concerns. (You may use phrases as well as single-word headings and break up the sections differently.)

Your Writing

1. Write a paper in which you examine another group that has suffered from "backlash" recently. Set out the original problem, the

advances made, and the new problems faced, using research where necessary.

2. One problem the writer faces early in his life is that he is no longer in touch with his Indian culture. This is also true for many other Native-Americans. Write a paper in which you explore the causes that have led to such a situation.

Pre-reading Activity   What is your favorite food? To which ethnic cuisine does it belong? How did you become fond of it?

As You Read   Observe the way in which the writers use the actual names of brands, restaurants, places, etc. What does this technique add to their argument?

THE CULTURE OF CUISINE
John Naisbitt and Patricia Aburdene

John Naisbitt and Patricia Aburdene are "futurists," consultants who work with leaders in government, business, and science to predict the new directions American society is taking. Their books include Megatrends *and* Megatrends 2000, *from which this selection is excerpted.*

1   West Los Angeles is the home of Gurume, a Japanese-run restaurant whose speciality—Gurume chicken—is Oriental chopped chicken and green beans in an Italian marinara sauce, served over spaghetti, with Japanese cabbage salad, Texas toast, and Louisiana Tabasco sauce. It is a symbol of what is happening to world lifestyle and cuisine.

2   We are tasting one another's cuisines with great gusto. Americans are exporting seafood delicacies to Japan, Tex-Mex is all the rage in Paris, and the United States is importing sushi bars as if they were Toyotas.

3   "Three years ago the world had never tasted soft-shells [crabs] and now we export to twenty-two countries," said Terrence Conway, owner of the John T. Handy Company, a Chesapeake Bay firm that in 1986 exported 270,000 pounds of crabs, mainly to Japan. (In 1988 the company was bought by a Japanese firm.)

4   Tex-Mex cuisine is prepared kosher in Israel, where former Houstonian Barry Ritman's Chili's restaurant comes complete with a Lone Star beer sign, armadillo art, and cactus garden.

5   "There just wasn't anyplace here to buy the tacos, chili, or chips I ate back in Texas," says Ritman, who satisfied his Southwest cravings while introducing Israelis to tacos, tortillas, and margaritas.

6   In 1985 San Antonio-based Papa Maya, one of a handful of Tex-Mex restaurants in Paris, received the city's Best Foreign Food award. Since then Tex-Mex has become Paris's hot new exotic cuisine. Chic young Parisians now fill the house at La Perla, Café Pacifico, and the Studio.

7   There were 19,364 Oriental restaurants in the United States in 1988, according to RE-COUNT, a service of the Restaurant Consulting Group,

Inc., in Evanston, Illinois. Oriental restaurant growth outpaces all other restaurant categories, having increased 10 percent just in 1987 and 1988 while restaurants grew 4 percent overall, says RE-COUNT.

In 1975 there were only about 300 sushi bars in the United States; by 1980 there were more than 1,500, reports *Palate Pleasers,* the first Japanese food magazine for Americans printed in the United States. Today there are thousands.   8

"At least five to ten new sushi bars open in New York City and Los Angeles every month," according to Susan Hirano of *Palate Pleasers.* And the sushi craze has broken out of the big city.   9

You can order sushi in American beef country: Des Moines, Iowa; Wichita, Kansas; and Omaha, Nebraska. The Japanese Steak House, in Grand Rapids, Michigan, boasts a floating sushi bar. The Kroger supermarket in Buckhead, Georgia, sells sushi. More adventurous Georgians order the octopus and eel.   10

If Americans are crazy about sushi, the Japanese have shown they have an all-American sweet tooth. Tokyo is overflowing with the latest American confectioneries: Häagen-Dazs, Famous Amos, Mrs. Field's, and David's Cookies stores. Even lesser-known outlets like Steve's and Hobson's ice-cream shops are open in Tokyo.   11

In the United States ethnic food is one of the hottest segments in the restaurant business. Eating out in Middle America used to mean steak and potatoes. Now it is Mexican, Chinese, Korean, Afghan, and Ethiopian. Between 1982 and 1986 overall restaurant traffic in the United States increased 10 percent, but Asian restaurants saw business grow 54 percent, Mexican restaurants 43 percent, and Italian restaurants 26 percent. In a one-block area of the Adams Morgan neighborhood of Washington, D.C., you can eat Ethiopian, Jamaican, Italian, Mexican, French, Salvadorean, Japanese, Chinese, Caribbean, Indian, or American.   12

Building Vocabulary

Define the words below, using *context clues* wherever possible and checking in a dictionary when necessary. Use them in sentences of your own.

kosher (4)   cravings (5)   confectioneries (11)
chic (6)   outpaces (7)
sweet tooth (11)

Journal Writing

Choose one or more of the three activities listed below, and make an entry in your journal. Focus on writing spontaneously rather than on structure and mechanics.

1. **Exploring:** Recall what you remember from other sources—your reading, your life experiences, movies and television, stories told to you by others—about the topic discussed by the writer. Choose one or two of these to write about. Which aspects of the topic did they bring up? What additional information did they provide? What emotions did they create in you?

2. **Taking Stock:** Which parts of the selection were most difficult for you to grasp? Which parts needed more explanation? Which parts required outside information to be understood? What kind of information was required (e.g., historical, culture-specific, technical, etc.)? Where might such information be found? Were there aspects of the writer's style you found particularly effective? Particularly difficult? Why?

3. **Responding:** Identify one or two of the writer's main concerns. What personal knowledge, if any, do you have of these issues? What is your opinion on these issues? Examine your response carefully to see what it teaches you about yourself.

Analyzing Content

1. Why do the writers call Gurume in Los Angeles "a symbol of what is happening to world lifestyle?" Pick out another example of this trend.

2. How have American eating habits changed in other parts of the United States? Which example did you find most surprising? Why?

3. How has American food affected the rest of the world? Give examples.

4. The writers make a particular mention of sushi. Describe this dish, and explain why the writers choose this food item rather than some other foreign dish (e.g., pizza) to make their point.

Analyzing Writing Techniques

1. What use do the writers make of statistics? Explain how they do or do not aid the argument.

2. Analyze the introduction. Is it effective? Explain why or why not. What other kinds of introductions might be used?

Group Activity

Because this is an excerpt, it does not have a separate conclusion. Discuss what a good conclusion should achieve, then have each person in the group write a conclusion paragraph. Compare the conclusions.

Your Writing

1. Do you agree with the writer that American eating habits are changing? Do you think this is a positive trend, or is something being lost as a result? Write a paper exploring this issue, providing examples to support your viewpoint.

2. Imagine that you are planning to open a new restaurant in your neighborhood. What kind of restaurant would you choose? Why? Write a proposal describing the restaurant, the food, the prices and ambiance, and the kinds of customers you would target. Present an argument as to why you think this kind of restaurant would succeed.

Pre-reading Activity   Who do you think the title refers to? Explain.

As You Read   Think about the way the writer presents opposing aspects of America to lead to his final point. Is this an effective technique? Why, or why not?

AMERICA'S SCAPEGOATS
Chang-Lin Tien

Chang-Lin Tien *is Chancellor of the University of California at Berkeley and A. Martin Berlin Professor of Mechanical Engineering. This selection was first published in* Newsweek *in 1994.*

1   My life has been far more satisfying than I dreamed possible when I arrived in the United States, 38 years ago. I am privileged to head a world-class institution, the University of California, Berkeley. My former Ph.D. students are professors at major universities. My engineering research has contributed to America's space technology, nuclear-reactor, safety and energy technology.

2   Yet no matter the scope of my accomplishments, when many Americans see my face and hear my Chinese accent, they think of me as an immigrant, first and foremost. In the eyes of many, that has come to mean a drain on public services, a competitor for jobs and a threat to a cohesive society.

3   I have watched the campaign to discourage immigration with growing concern. Whether we preside over universities or work the fields, immigrants are becoming the scapegoats for America's ills. I don't object to controlling the volume of immigration. Today, with unprecedented shifts in the global population, no nation can afford to throw its borders wide open. But we are in danger of forgetting that America was built by immigrants, and that our immigrant heritage is the wellspring of our nation's strength and vitality.

4   Even as a university chancellor, I am no stranger to the sharp sting of anti-immigrant hostility. Perhaps the most dramatic incident took place when I represented Berkeley a few years ago at a football rally after the Citrus Bowl. As I walked to the stage, a few people in the audience chanted, "Buy American, Buy American." This was profoundly disturbing. I am American and proud of it.

5   Just looking like an immigrant can make you the target of heckling. Any of us of Asian, Latin American and Middle Eastern heritage knows

this. Several friends and family members have been subjected to taunts of "Go back to your own country." It's difficult for them to respond; like Bruce Springsteen, they were born in the U.S.A. This anti-immigrant mood is not new. Throughout our history, whenever the economy suffered, immigrants became easy targets. But today, it is not only the immigrants who suffer. Ultimately, all Americans stand to lose, native and foreign born alike.

Now our nation faces the formidable challenge of forging a unified   6
society from highly diverse constituencies. The population is undergoing a rapid transformation, and by the middle of the 21st century, the major- ity of Americans will trace their roots to latin America, Africa, Asia, the Middle East and the Pacific Islands.

Evolving into a cohesive society based on respect and understanding   7
is far from automatic. Throughout human history, racial and ethnic ten- sions have divided and destroyed peoples and countries. The ethnic strife that ripped apart Brooklyn's Crown Heights and South-Central Los Ange- les is a sobering reminder of the challenge posed by rapid diversification.

Yet if there is a nation that promises to be a model for how to make   8
diversity work, it is the United States. This is the nation with the strongest and deepest democratic roots. This is a nation with a living Constitution that guarantees rights to all its citizens. This is a nation that has taken pride not in its homogeneity, but in its immigrant heritage.

It was America's promise that drew me here in 1956. Even as a pen-   9
niless graduate student from China, I believed I could make a contribu- tion in this land of opportunity. Indeed, I am deeply grateful to America for offering opportunities difficult to find anywhere else in the world.

Today, however, in the headlong rush to restrict immigration, we are   10
jeopardizing this promise. Hundreds of state and federal measures have been introduced to curb legal and illegal immigration. The backers of these proposals often rely on inflammatory anti-immigrant rhetoric to rivet the attention of Americans, ignite their rage and move them to action.

In the hoopla, the debate is now moving away from the legitimate   11
question of how much immigration America can sustain. Instead, we're blaming immigrants for many of our most urgent problems and trying to convince ourselves that we'll solve them by simply restricting immigration.

Effective immigration policy must be grounded in reason, not emo-   12
tion. Racial and cultural hostilities fanned by the present anti-immigration frenzy must cool down. Then I am confident, we can make immigration work for America, just as it has from the time of our nation's infancy.

After all, in my 38 years here, I have seen this nation make amazing   13
progress. When I came here to study in the South, I encountered Jim Crow segregation. Whites rode in the front of buses and blacks in the back. This racial system did not apply to Asian-Americans and left us in an ugly limbo. It troubled me and left a lifelong impression. The rest of the coun- try was not free from racial discrimination. When I joined the Berkeley fac-

ulty, in 1959, my wife and I could not live in certain Bay Area neighborhoods.

14   In less than four decades I have seen the enactment of civil-rights legislation that has created opportunities for all Americans. I have seen universities open doors to students who reflect our diverse society. I have seen women and men of all backgrounds become leaders in government, business, science, arts and education. Now I look forward to seeing the promise of America fulfilled. We can turn our national motto of *e pluribus unum,* or "one out of many," into more than an expression in a dead language. What it will take is the same kind of unwavering commitment that forged one nation from highly diverse colonies more than two centuries ago.

15   Immigrants are not the cause of America's major problems. It's time America stopped putting all the blame on immigrants and started facing up to the difficult reality of a world in transition. Let's seize the opportunity to transform America into a model of diversity for the future.

Building Vocabulary

Define the words below, using *context clues* wherever possible and checking in a dictionary when necessary. Use them in sentences of your own.

cohesive (2)	hoopla (11)	jeopardizing (10)
wellspring (3)	preside (3)	limbo (13)
constituencies (6)	heckling (5)	

Journal Writing

Choose one or more of the three activities listed below, and make an entry in your journal. Focus on writing spontaneously rather than on structure and mechanics.

1. **Exploring:** Recall what you remember from other sources—your reading, your life experiences, movies and television, stories told to you by others—about the topic discussed by the writer. Choose one or two of these to write about. Which aspects of the topic did they bring up? What additional information did they provide? What emotions did they create in you?

2. **Taking Stock:** Which parts of the selection were most difficult for you to grasp? Which parts needed more explanation? Which parts required outside information to be understood? What kind of information was required (e.g., historical, culture-specific, technical, etc.)? Where might such information be found? Were there aspects of the writer's style you found particularly effective? Particularly difficult? Why?

3. **Responding:** Identify one or two of the writer's main concerns. What personal knowledge, if any, do you have of these issues? What is your opinion on these issues? Examine your response carefully to see what it teaches you about yourself.

Analyzing Content

1. List the writer's accomplishments. In spite of them, what disadvantage does he often face?
2. What ironic fact do anti-immigrant crowds not realize when they tell people who look "foreign" to go home?
3. Why does the writer believe that the United States promises to be a country in which diversity can work?
4. Summarize the writer's attitude toward immigration.

Analyzing Writing Techniques

1. **List** the personal examples the writer uses to make his point. In what way are they effective?
2. **Explain** the following allusions: Citrus Bowl, South-Central Los Angeles, Jim Crow, *e pluribus unum*. How do they relate to the writer's main thrust?

Group Activity

Trace the roots of the word *scapegoat*. Where did it come from? How did it rise? How has the meaning changed in modern times? Now discuss whether or not the metaphor of the scapegoat is effectively used by the writer in this essay.

Your Writing

1. The writer asserts strongly that immigrants are not the cause of America's major problems. Do you agree or disagree? Write a paper in which you choose a major social problem, and explore how immigrants have or have not affected this problem
2. In paragraph 10, the writer refers to state and federal measures to curb immigration. Choose one such measure, and evaluate its effects on the immigrant as well as the larger society

Pre-reading Activity   Write about a disaster, natural or man-made, that you have some knowledge of. How did people—those who observed it as well as those who experienced it—respond to it?

As You Read   Observe how the writer brings alive the character of Sam Z. What techniques does she use?

FIRE, HOPE AND CHARITY
Jeanne Marie Laskas

Jeanne Marie Laskas *is a freelancer who often writes for* Life, *in which this first piece appeared in 1992.*

1   Late on the night of March 14, someone came down Coffee Run Road and lit Sam Z. Yoder's 90-year-old barn on fire. This was in the Kishacoquillas Valley, known as Big Valley, a narrow strip of farmland in central Pennsylvania. Sam Z.—everyone here uses middle initials because there are only three or four last names in Big Valley—is an Amish bishop, 68 years old. The events of that night probably won't ever leave him. His granddaughter woke up first, hearing something crackling. The whole family came charging out. Sam Z. went for the horses. The horses ran into the fire, as horses will do, confused and terrified. Then they turned around and ran right over Sam Z., trampling him. His cows were howling. He struggled to his feet. He had to get to his cows. But his barn was a fireball, and soon it was spitting hot cinders onto the roof of his house.

2   Meantime, another Amish barn down on Back Mountain Road was torched, and another, and another, and another on Church Lane. It seemed the whole valley was lighting up. Trucks from 24 different fire companies charged into the chaos. Non-Amish neighbors came roaring through the valley in their pickups, alerting farmers to protect their barns. Eventually Sam Z. found himself standing there all beat up, holding a garden hose. He was squirting his house, protecting it from the flames engulfing his barn, listening to the echoes of those cows. When the sun came up on Sunday morning, the fires had destroyed six Amish barns. The corpses of 139 cows and 38 horses lay among the debris. All through the valley the air was thick with a horrible stench.

3   "And we just don't know why it was done," says Sam Z., standing in the mud where his barn used to be, his hat drooping, his beard reaching clear down to his chest. His is the question that echoes loudest through the valley. The FBI is on the case; special agents in wing tips and blue suits have come out to Sam Z.'s farm with their questions. They go home with

few clues and terribly muddy shoes. Sam Z. doesn't have much insight to offer about the culprits. He occupies himself with larger thoughts, which seem to come over him without warning.

"When they did this, it hurt everybody," Sam Z. says, speaking with all the authority of a holy man.   4

All of the Amish?   5

"No, I mean it hurt everybody," he says.   6

All of the people in Big Valley?   7

"No, I mean, when they did this, it hurt everybody all over the world," he says. "I feel this. I do feel this."   8

News of the Big Valley barn fires indeed went around the world— partly, perhaps, because the Amish, who moved to this valley in 1791, are always a curiosity and a fascination. These are peace-loving people determined to live a life of simplicity, sheltering themselves from the outside world—no cars, no electricity, no telephones—so as to better focus on the spiritual world. Their lifestyle is a display of innocence, of what the world could be like if life weren't so frantic and hurried. To see these people fall prey to seemingly random acts of violence is to see a brutal victimization, like watching a child get smacked in the face. It demands notice, which explains the donations coming in, and attention from the FBI, CNN, the *Today* show and, even Geraldo Rivera. The barn fires of the Kishacoquillas Valley lit something in a lot of people.   9

Watching an Amish barn-raising is a sight to behold, a gift for the soul. At dawn on March 31 the men start arriving at Sam Z.'s. Just two weeks have passed since the night of the fires, and already Sam M.'s barn on Back Mountain Road is up and so is Sam I.'s over at Plum Bottom. Sam Z. is awed by the turnout. "We feel we're not worth it," he says. It's help from the outside world that has him feeling especially humble.   10

The Amish divide the world into two. You are either Amish or you are "English." You are either on the inside or the outside. The Amish strive to keep their world from becoming too infected by ours, so they keep away from us. But for this brief moment following the fires, the two worlds have met and the outside is getting a rare peek at the inside.   11

Sam Z. is still trying to contain in his mind all the money that has come in from places as far away as Hawaii and Germany. The Kishacoquillas Valley National Bank says the Big Valley Barn Fire Relief Fund has grown to $600,000, all of it English money, and contributions are still coming in every day. Sam Z. is thinking of all the livestock and feed that have been donated, all the backhoes and bulldozers that came in and did the cleanup, all the cakes and pies, the great mounds of Kentucky Fried Chicken, the bags upon bags of paper plates and dishwashing detergent donated by the workers of the local Jamesway discount department store. It is hard for Sam Z. to receive all this charity. Ordinarily, the Amish do not accept help from outsiders. They refuse social security checks, and they don't take out insurance policies. To the Amish, worldly things take your mind off what's   12 real: the spiritual world, God's world. And so the Amish have rules to assure that they will not become attached to society.

13   The 1,500 Amish people living in Big Valley are divided into three sects, each identified by the colors of their horse-drawn buggies: yellow, black or white. Those with yellow tops are the least conservative sect; next come the black toppers; and finally, the most conservative, the white toppers. White toppers do not paint their houses or barns. They do not have indoor plumbing. Black and yellow toppers allow paint and plumbing, and they socialize with one another. White toppers are left pretty much alone down in their end of the valley.

14   The point behind all the rules is to avoid pride—in yourself, in how you think, in how you look. You must look like everyone else: Men get the same bowl haircuts, do not grow mustaches and are allowed beards only when they come of age. No zippers are allowed on clothes. White toppers are not allowed to show buttons on their jackets—they must use hooks and eyes. Women use straight pins to fasten their clothes. Their hair must not be cut, and heads must be covered. The idea is to avoid becoming stylish or drawing attention to yourself.

15   Amish behavior is nearly as circumscribed as Amish fashion. Children stop school after the eighth grade. Men do men things and women do women things. You will not see a woman sawing logs at a barn-raising. She will be inside cooking. In the Amish world, human imagination, innovation, intellect and, above all, individuality are intentionally squashed. Outsiders can't help but wonder why anyone would want to live like that.

16   Already, by eight A.M. on barn-raising day, three walls of Sam Z.'s barn are up. Even Sam Z. thinks that's pretty fast. The cutting of the wood and figuring of the plan have all been done in advance. The wood is green, cut just a week ago up on Jack's Mountain and sawed into lumber at the Plum Bottom mill. The posts and beams have been connected to form the skeletons of walls and the whole thing has been laid out just so on the ground, ready for the barn-raising to happen. When enough people show up, the walls are hoisted, then fitted into the floor in mortice joints. Wooden pegs driven deep will keep it all in place. A school bus arrives with even more workers, so they are sent down to help put up Esle Hostetler's barn near Milroy. Sam Z. has more than 200 men here. They are all gathered in clumps, and while each group has a purpose, it seems no one clump, or individual, is in charge. A community instinct has taken over.

17   Interestingly, of the six burned barns, all but one belonged to the most conservative Amish, the white toppers. Three belonged to bishops. These facts have a lot of people surmising that whoever did the terrible deed had a purpose in mind. You don't hear many Amish people worrying about who the arsonist was. It is not their way to focus on evil. Still, there are a lot of theories. Almost all the theories come from the English. Perhaps the arsonist was a shunned Amish person, someone who had left the church. Worse, maybe it was someone who is still Amish. But no one wants to entertain

the thought that an Amish person could act out so violently, so these theories get whispered, then are dropped.

"I may be wrong, but I think it was some young fellas out on a spree," says Ruth Peachey, who helps her husband, Ivan, run the local branch of the Mennonite Disaster Service. 18

"I've heard that these barns were burned in order to test the Amish to see if they won't become indignant and arrogant and vengeful," says Lee Kanagy, a Mennonite minister. "It could be. I don't know." 19

"I think it was more a matter of who was in the firebug urge," says Clair DeLong, a former county farm extension agent. 20

"I think it was some kind of a cult, and this was their initiation," says a farmer. 21

"I think the police know who it is, and they won't tell us," says a local dairyman. "We keep giving them our evidence, and then they never tell us what happened with it." 22

"You just can't sit down over a cup of coffee and tell everyone how your day went in your investigation," says FBI agent Jack Shea. 23

Just as there is no consensus on the culprits, there is no unanimity on the punishment that should be meted out if an arsonist is caught. "Death penalty," says Blair Auman, an English dairy farmer who would offer this punishment only after a period of torture. "Make him dig them dead burnt animals out with his bare hands. Then let him eat what he dug out." The Amish way, on the other hand, is to forgive, forget and build. They do not press charges. They do not testify in court. An Amish farmer from Back Mountain Road thinks the arsonist should be invited out to watch one of the barn-raisings, then invited inside for a nice Amish dinner—maybe mashed potatoes and roasted chicken, with moon pies for dessert. "That really puts a dig into you," says Auman. "To have these people turn around and invite you in and share food with you, that really cheapens your act, I think." 24

By noon the superstructure of Sam Z.'s barn is up. Most of the siding is up, and the roof is going on. There has been only one injury. Eli Byler had a hammer come falling down on his head. He was taken to the hospital, and now he is back showing the four stitches he got. "And two shots, one in each arm," he is saying to a group of onlookers. Sam Z. is handing him a self-addressed stamped envelope to put the bill in when he gets it. Amish health insurance is a lot like Amish barn insurance. Just wait a bit and somebody will come around and take care of it. 25

By 2:45 children are running down Coffee Run Road with their empty lunch boxes. Home from school, they see that in the spot where there was just wind blowing this morning a barn now stands. Jacob Y. Hostetler is in there sweeping out the sawdust. The children enter timidly and eventually skip in circles, testing the sureness of the new floor. Sam Z. is inside, too, looking up, saying, "Big barn." He seems overwhelmed, unable to say much else. And everybody comments on the pungent smell of the green 26 wood. Pretty soon the first sparrow arrives. It soars among the rafters, checking the place out, as if to wonder, "Where did this barn come from?" It came from God, Sam Z. says, refusing to rejoice in the strength and ingenuity of mankind, refusing to show pride in his new barn. Pride is sinful. Be humble, but be careful. Don't become proud of your humility.

27   People from the outside world wonder how the Amish can live such secluded rule-bound lives. But such doubters have never seen an Amish barn-raising. You watch all those men dressed alike in their dark clothes and straw hats, all crawling so nimbly over the fresh wood standing against the sky, and you can't help but notice what they look like. They look like ants. It isn't such a bad image. One ant can't do much, but a million ants working together can perform miracles. An Amish barn-raising is a belief system in action: Sacrifice individuality—forget about your self, your clothes, your hair, your creative longings—in favor of the common good.

28   A visitor from New York City walks up to Sam Z. She has been shaking her head all day in disbelief, watching this barn emerge. "If my house in Brooklyn burned down," she says, "I don't think my neighbors would come around to rebuild it." Sam Z. ponders that piece of information, then says, "We would."

Building Vocabulary

Define the words below, using *context clues* wherever possible and checking in a dictionary when necessary. Use them in sentences of your own.

cinders (1)	arsonist (17)	circumscribed (15)
wing tips (3)	unanimity (24)	hoisted (16)
victimization (9)	stench (2)	consensus (24)
innovation (15)	prey (9)	superstructure (25)

Journal Writing

Choose one or more of the three activities listed below, and make an entry in your journal. Focus on writing spontaneously rather than on structure and mechanics.

1. **Exploring:** Recall what you remember from other sources—your reading, your life experiences, movies and television, stories told to you by others—about the topic discussed by the writer. Choose one or two of these to write about. Which aspects of the topic did they bring up? What additional information did they provide? What emotions did they create in you?

2. **Taking Stock:** Which parts of the selection were most difficult for you to grasp? Which parts needed more explanation? Which parts required outside information to be understood? What kind of in-

formation was required (e.g., historical, culture-specific, technical, etc.)? Where might such information be found? Were there aspects of the writer's style you found particularly effective? Particularly difficult? Why?

3. **Responding:** Identify one or two of the writer's main concerns. What personal knowledge, if any, do you have of these issues? What is your opinion on these issues? Examine your response carefully to see what it teaches you about yourself.

Analyzing Content

1. Describe briefly the catastrophe that occurs. How do the Amish react to this disaster?
2. Explain what the reaction of the Amish tells us about their values.
3. According to the writer, what do outsiders find most difficult to accept about the Amish way of life?
4. Why, in spite of the Amish's careful separateness, did the outside world respond so generously to their trouble?

Analyzing Writing Techniques

1. **Analyze** paragraph 12. What is its purpose? Which sentence in the paragraph seems most important? Could it be placed more effectively elsewhere in the paragraph?
2. **Pick out** the **metaphor** used by the writer toward the end of this piece. Is it an effective one? Why, or why not?

Group Activity

In the last few years, there have been several films, both educational and popular, produced about the lifestyle of the Amish. Have group members choose and view *one* of these, and then discuss and write a **collaborative** paragraph about one major difference between the Amish and other Americans.

Your Writing

1. Based on this essay as well as your observance and experience, write a paper in which you **compare/contrast** the sense of community among the Amish with the attitude toward neighbors in another specific setting (e.g., your neighborhood, New York, a rural setting in the Midwest, etc.). What conclusions can you draw from the evidence you have examined?
2. Write an essay in which you weigh the pros and cons of Amish life. Use information from other sources to support your ultimate opinion.

Pre-reading Activity   Think about the title. What one word would *you* use to describe a family member you are close to? Write a title, like Burciaga's, that captures a central aspect of this person's character.

As You Read   Observe the writer's use of humor to make a point.

MY ECUMENICAL FATHER
José Burciaga

José Burciaga *was raised in the West Texas border town of El Paso. He is a Chicano cultural activist and muralist and the founder of the comedy group* Culture Clash. *His book of poems,* Undocumented Love, *won the 1981 Before Columbus American Book Award. His other books include* Spilling the Beans *and* Drink Cultura, *from which this selection is taken.*

1   ¡Feliz Navidad! Merry Christmas! Happy Hanukkah! As a child, my season's greetings were tricultural—Mexicano, Anglo and Jewish.

2   Our devoutly Catholic parents raised three sons and three daughters in the basement of a Jewish synagogue, Congregation B'nai Zion in El Paso, Texas. José Cruz Burciaga was the custodian and *shabbat goy*. A shabbat goy is Yiddish for a Gentile who, on the Sabbath, performs certain tasks forbidden to Jews under orthodox law.

3   Every year around Christmas time, my father would take the menorah out and polish it. The eight-branched candleholder symbolizes Hanukkah, the commemoration of the first recorded war of liberation in that part of the world.

4   In 164 B.C., the Jewish nation rebelled against Antiochus IV Epiphanes, who had attempted to introduce pagan idols into the temples. When the temple was reconquered by the Jews, there was only one day's supply of oil for the Eternal Light in the temple. By a miracle, the oil lasted eight days.

5   My father was not only in charge of the menorah but for 40 years he also made sure the Eternal Light remained lit.

6   As children we were made aware of the differences and joys of Hanukkah, Christmas and Navidad. We were taught to respect each celebration, even if they conflicted. For example, the Christmas carols taught in school. We learned the song about the twelve days of Christmas, though I never understood what the hell a partridge was doing in a pear tree in the middle of December.

7   We also learned a German song about a boy named Tom and a bomb—*O Tannenbaum.* We even learned a song in the obscure language

of Latin, called "Adeste Fideles," which reminded me of, *Ahh! d'este fideo,* a Mexican pasta soup. Though 75% of our class was Mexican-American, we never sang a Christmas song *en Español.* Spanish was forbidden.

So, our mother—a former teacher—taught us "Silent Night" in Spanish: *Noche de paz, noche de amor.* It was so much more poetic and inspirational.   8

While the rest of El Paso celebrated Christmas, Congregation B'Nai Zion celebrated Hanukkah. We picked up Yiddish and learned a Hebrew prayer of thanksgiving. My brothers and I would help my father hang the Hanukkah decorations.   9

At night, after the services, the whole family would rush across the border to Juarez and celebrate the *posadas,* which takes place for nine days before Christmas. They are a communal re-enactment of Joseph and Mary's search for shelter, just before Jesus was born.   10

To the posadas we took candles and candy left over from the Hanukkah celebrations. The next day we'd be back at St. Patrick's School singing, "I'm dreaming of a white Christmas."   11

One day I stopped dreaming of the white Christmases depicted on greeting cards. An old immigrant from Israel taught me Jesus was born in desert country just like that of the West Texas town of El Paso.   12

On Christmas Eve, my father would dress like Santa Claus and deliver gifts to his children, nephews, godchildren and the little kids in orphanages. The next day, minus his disguise, he would take us to Juárez, where we delivered gifts to the poor in the streets.   13

My father never forgot his childhood poverty and forever sought to help the less fortunate. He taught us to measure wealth not in money but in terms of love, spirit, charity and culture.   14

We were taught to respect the Jewish faith and culture. On the Day of Atonement, when the whole congregation fasted, my mother did not cook, lest the food odors distract. The respect was mutual. No one ever complained about the large picture of Jesus in our living room.   15

Through my father, leftover food from B'nai B'rith luncheons, Bar Mitzvahs and Bat Mitzvahs, found its way to Catholic or Baptist churches or orphanages. Floral arrangements in the temple that surrounded a Jewish wedding *hutpah* canopy many times found a second home at the altar of St. Patrick's Cathedral or San Juan Convent School. Surplus furniture, including old temple pews found their way to a missionary Baptist Church in *El Segundo Barrio.*   16

It was not uncommon to come home from school at lunch time and find an uncle priest, an aunt nun and a Baptist minister visiting our home at the same time that the Rabbi would knock on our door. It was just as natural to find the president of B'nai Zion eating beans and tortillas in our kitchen.   17

My father literally risked his life for the Jewish faith. Twice he was assaulted by burglars who broke in at night. Once he was stabbed in the   18 hand. Another time he stayed up all night guarding the sacred Torahs after anti-semites threatened the congregation. He never philosophized about his ecumenism, he just lived it.

19   Cruz, as most called him, was a man of great humor, a hot temper and a passion for dance. He lived the Mexican Revolution and rode the rails during the Depression. One of his proudest moments came when he became a U.S. citizen.

20   September 23, 1985, sixteen months after my mother passed away, my father followed. Like his life, his death was also ecumenical. The funeral was held at Our Lady of Peace, where a priest said the mass in English. My cousins played mandolin and sang in Spanish. The president of B'nai Zion Congregation said a prayer in Hebrew. Members of the congregation sat with Catholics and Baptists.

21   Observing Jewish custom, the cortege passed by the synagogue one last time. Fittingly, father was laid to rest on the Sabbath. At the cemetery, in a very Mexican tradition, my brothers, sisters and I each kissed a handful of dirt and threw it on the casket.

22   I once had the opportunity to describe father's life to the late, great Jewish American writer Bernard Malamud. His only comment was, "Only in America!"

Building Vocabulary

Define the words below, using *context clues* wherever possible and checking in a dictionary when necessary. Use them in sentences of your own.

tricultural (1)	mandolin (20)	communal (10)
Yiddish (2)	synagogue (2)	anti-semites (18)
inspirational (8)	commemoration (3)	cortege (21)
surplus (16)		

Journal Writing

Choose one or more of the three activities listed below, and make an entry in your journal. Focus on writing spontaneously rather than on structure and mechanics.

1. **Exploring:** Recall what you remember from other sources—your reading, your life experiences, movies and television, stories told to you by others—about the topic discussed by the writer. Choose one or two of these to write about. Which aspects of the topic did they bring up? What additional information did they provide? What emotions did they create in you?
2. **Taking Stock:** Which parts of the selection were most difficult for you to grasp? Which parts needed more explanation? Which parts

required outside information to be understood? What kind of information was required (e.g., historical, culture-specific, technical, etc.)? Where might such information be found? Were there aspects of the writer's style you found particularly effective? Particularly difficult? Why?

3. **Responding:** Identify one or two of the writer's main concerns. What personal knowledge, if any, do you have of these issues? What is your opinion on these issues? Examine your response carefully to see what it teaches you about yourself.

Analyzing Content

1. Give examples of the Anglo influence on the writer's childhood.
2. How did the Jewish community respond to the writer's father? Why?
3. Do a brief character analysis of the father. What important values did he impart to his children?
4. Explain the meaning of the comment in the last paragraph.

Analyzing Writing Techniques

1. **Analyze** paragraph 12. What role does it play in the writer's overall argument?
2. The writer makes several allusions to the Jewish religion and culture or symbolic items relating to them. Find these, and explain each reference. What do such details add to the essay?

Group Activity

Look up and discuss the roots of the word *ecumenical*. Why does the writer use this term to describe his father? Is the term well chosen? Have each member of the group write a paragraph about whether he or she knows an ecumenical person. Discuss these paragraphs, then choose the best one to read to the class.

Your Writing

1. Think about the final comment of the essay, "Only in America!" Now write an essay about another aspect of society/lifestyle that you consider to be uniquely American, explaining why you think it is so.
2. What is the writer's attitude about the necessity of being "ecumenical" in American society today? What is your attitude? Write an essay in which you explore this issue, giving clear reasons for your viewpoint.

Pre-reading Activity   Have you, or someone you know, lived in two places with very different lifestyles? List the major differences between those two places.

As You Read   Note the comparison/contrast mode used by the writer. Think about a different comparison/contrast structure she could have used.

IT'S A LONG WAY FROM JERUSALEM TO SAN FRANCISCO
Noga Eshban Laderman

Noga Eshban Laderman *was born in France in 1962 but grew up in Jerusalem. At the age of 22, she came to the United States, where she worked as a make-up artist in Hollywood for 8 years and then returned to school. She is now pursuing a degree in cinema at San Francisco State University and plans to become a documentary film producer. She wrote this essay while at Foothill College.*

1   "Don't forget the car sale we have to go to on Saturday," my husband told me as he left for work early Thursday morning. Still half-asleep in bed, I nodded in agreement, but after he left, I couldn't go back to sleep. His words kept echoing in my head. They took me back to Israel, to the peaceful and meaningful Saturdays I enjoyed growing up in Israel. Yearning for the Shabbat in my home town, I thought back on the life I had led in Israel, the important role my family and friends played, the communal lifestyle I experienced, and the values I believed in. Inevitably, I found myself comparing life in Israel to my life today in the United States.

2   During the weekdays, Jerusalem—like any other big city—is a busy and noisy place. Traffic is heavy most hours of the day, and the little stores are always crowded with hot-tempered people. The coffee houses are packed with locals and tourists, and it seems that the streets need to be stretched to give everyone breathing space. The busiest time of the week is Friday morning, when we, religious and secular Jews both, prepare for the coming Shabbat, our day of rest. Our preparations include cleaning house and doing last-minute shopping before the shops close. The religious Jews must also cook all the Shabbat meals, for they are not allowed to do any type of work that will interfere with their rest and prayer day.

3   It never ceased to amaze me how, just like magic, the energy of the city changed as Friday afternoon arrived. At 4 PM, most of the stores closed down, the traffic stopped, and the streets were empty of people. By sun-

set, Jerusalem had transformed into a quiet, peaceful city. As the Shabbat began, I could hear from my house the songs and prayers from the many synagogues. The rhythm of the prayers floating over the quiet streets would put me into a mood of inexplicable peace and relaxation.

Friday evening in Jerusalem, with its spiritual ambiance, is the special time when families gather for the Shabbat dinner. A strong sense of community fills the air as we hurry home to be with our loved ones. I can still smell the aromas from my mother's kitchen as I write these lines. My mother spoiled us by cooking our favorite dishes for Shabbat: chicken with curry and almonds, simmered on a low flame for hours until it became soft enough to melt in our mouths; bell peppers stuffed with spiced ground beef and rice; a variety of spicy colorful Moroccan salads; and an assortment of honey-based sweets. During dinner, we discussed everything. From daily issues such as buying a new showerhead to solving the world's latest problems to sharing our intimate feelings, nothing was considered inappropriate. I especially loved listening to my parents' stories about their childhoods. I could picture my mother as a little girl with curly black hair, helping my grandmother bake the "Halla" bread for their Shabbat dinner in Morocco many years ago. These gatherings and the sense of continuity they provided helped me to feel protected and loved. I knew my family's love was unquestionable and that I could always trust and rely on them.

My family were not the only ones I could rely on when I lived in Jerusalem. Lifelong friendships are an important element of the culture of Israel, and several such friends played an important part in my life. These friends became an extended part of my family, and like an extended family, they felt free to come over to our house at any time. My mother's best friend from high school and her children are part of my earliest memories. I treated them just as I treated my own parents and siblings. We spent our vacations and celebrated the Jewish holidays together. We shared our disappointments and successes. They were always there for me, just like my family, when I lost a boyfriend or failed an exam. When something exciting happened to one of us—a baby being born, or a longed-for promotion at work—we would all join in the celebration. These friends gave me a strong sense of community, a set of clear expectations as to what friendship means, and ultimately, helped me to develop my sense of self during my adolescent years.

This was my background when I arrived in the United States during my early twenties. Not surprisingly, I would have to go through some major changes and adjust my expectations of society before I grew used to living in America.

My initial months here were immensely exciting. The beauty of San Francisco, my first American city, captured my heart. Its many hills and candy-colored Victorian buildings gave me a sense that I was in a wonderland, gorgeous but slightly unreal. I spent a lot of time touring the different neighborhoods of the city, enjoying the diversity of the crowds.

Weekends were particularly hectic. To acclimatize myself to this new society, I found myself going to endless barbecues, dances, and tailgate parties before baseball and football games. My holiday season, like that of most Americans, was filled with vacation trips or, if I stayed in town, visits to the malls to catch the many sales. Busy having fun, I did not think about the special meaning of the Shabbat day and did not realize, until years later, what I lost as its calmness and traditional family activities passed out of my life.

8   Soon after my arrival in the United States, I also realized that I needed to change my expectations regarding friendships. I was lonely and miserable without the friends of my childhood, with whom I was used to sharing my meals, my thoughts, and my daily life. I desperately wanted to form meaningful connections in this new country, people who would again be like an extended family, people I could depend on, but I soon learned a valuable lesson about the cultural differences between my old and my new environments.

9   My first hopeful encounter was with an American woman at the table next to mine in a cafe. I was reading a newspaper when she asked if she could look at a section. We started talking, and it seemed like we had many interests in common. She was very friendly and animated, and when it was time to leave, she said that we "must do lunch" and exchanged phone numbers with me. I was so excited about this possible friendship that I called my parents in Israel to let them know about this experience, but when I phoned my new friend a few days later, she said she was going to be very busy for a couple of weeks but that we should meet soon after. I called her up again a few weeks later, and again after a couple of months, but our lunch meeting never took place. She was always "too busy." It took me awhile to realize that she had used "let's do lunch" only as a conversational phrase and had no intention of actually meeting me. Similarly, I was confused during my first few months when people would ask "How are you doing today?" In the beginning, I would be grateful for all this interest—from virtual strangers—and would begin telling them how I was new to the city and feeling homesick. I stopped when I finally realized that no one was listening to my answers. Once again, I had mistaken polite conversation and friendliness for a desire to form friendships. It would take me 10 years to establish a deep friendship in America. During these years, I would learn how rare and precious such friendships—which I took as a matter of course in Israel—are. I would learn to feel fortunate whenever they did happen.

10   Moving from a culture that focused on the community to one that focused on the individual was a difficult transition for me. Painful as it was, I learned many valuable things in the process. I learned to live alone and be independent. I learned to be company for myself. I learned to gain strength and self-esteem from within myself and my relationship with my husband, and no longer to depend on constant support from a large group

of family and friends. In many ways, living in America has been a very liberating experience, and I feel particularly proud that I have adjusted so well to a society so different from that of my childhood.

There are other changes in myself, though, that I am not as happy with. 11 I have developed a sense of "space" and often speak of the need for it as vital to my life, whereas in Israel, I was never bothered by the lack of it. I enjoy the anonymity of my American life, the freedom to act without a whole group of people commenting on my actions, but I do not enjoy that when someone knocks on my door without calling me first—a common situation in Israel—I often feel upset.

When one moves away from home to a different culture, changes are 12 bound to occur. As one adjusts to new surroundings, one loses some things and gains others. In my case, I am keenly aware of both. America has given me much—freedom and the power to make my own decisions, and a strong sense of my individuality—yet I am reluctant, sometimes, to change my thinking to fit more fully into this culture. For with every step I take into America, I know I am moving further from Jerusalem.

Structure and Strategy

1. In this essay, the writer uses **comparison/contrast** to make many of her points. Find an example of this rhetorical mode *(a)* within a paragraph and *(b)* within a larger section.
2. **Outline** the overall structure of the essay. How else may comparison/contrast essays be structured?
3. This essay could also be written as a **pro/con** paper that examines the advantages and disadvantages of the societies the writer is looking at. How would you structure such a paper using the same points the writer is making?

Your Writing

1. In her conclusion, Laderman makes the point that learning to adjust to "difference" has both positive and negative aspects. Do you agree? Write about an experience in which you, or someone you know, had to adjust to a new situation. (Your topic need not be limited to a cultural situation.) What did you, or the person you are writing about, gain or lose because of this experience?
2. Laderman's essay points to the fact that different cultures value different qualities. She points to individualism as a quality held in high regard in America. What are other qualities are valued in this society? Write a paper in which you discuss two or three such qualities and how they influence daily living in this country.

SYNTHESIS: QUESTIONS FOR CRITICAL THINKING AND WRITING

1. Examine "The Culture of Cuisine" and "My Ecumenical Father," and analyze the attitude of the people mentioned in each of these pieces. What allows them to deal with diversity in a positive way? Compare and contrast where necessary.

2. "Fire, Hope and Charity" and "I, Too, Sing America" are both pieces in which a negative experience of being different is turned into a positive one. Write a paper in which you analyze each experience, focusing on the transformation and the reasons for it.

3. "America's Scapegoats" discusses how people who are different may have much to contribute to the society in which they live. Look through the book to find one or two other authors with similar ideas. Do you agree or disagree with them? Summarize their points, and either support or refute them.

4. All of the writers in this section have presented different ways in which they deal with or have dealt with difference. What have you learned from them about dealing successfully with the predicament of being different? Write a paper in which you bring together the ideas of the writers in this section as well as your own experiences and observation.

Glossary

Allusion Brief reference to a person, place, and so on in another literary work or to an historical event, usually for the purpose of comparision or clarification.

Analogy Comparison of something, point by point, with something similar.

Audience Intended readership of a literary work.

Cliché An expression so worn out that it conveys little meaning.

Connotation The associations created by a word. Its flavor.

Context Background, beyond the actual text, that helps readers understand a piece.

Diction The type of language chosen for a piece. Can be formal or informal.

Epigraph Brief quotation from a person or a literary work at the beginning of a piece.

Focus Angle of vision from which a narrative is presented and the characters are viewed.

Image, imagery Description, visualization, or representation of something, often through comparision with something else that is more familiar. Examples include *simile* and *metaphor.*

Mood Atmosphere of a work, often suggested by images and vocabulary.

Narrator Person who "tells" or presents a story, poem, essay, etc. Sometimes, this is a character in the story; sometimes, it is the voice of the author.

Paradox Apparent contradiction that may hint at a complex truth.

Paraphrasing Putting an idea into one's own words.

Personification   The giving of human characteristics to non-human objects.
Plagiarism   Using someone else's words or ideas without giving proper credit.
Plot   The action of a piece (i.e., what occurs and why).
Point of view   See *Focus.*

Setting   Location and context within which the action of a literary piece takes place.
Speaker   See *Narrator.*
Sprintwriting   Writing informally and quickly for a limited period without stopping to edit.
Symbol   Something standing for, or suggesting, something else that is more complex or greater than itself (e.g., a flag or a cross).

Theme   Idea or concept of central importance to a literary work.
Thesis   The main idea of an essay.
Tone   Attitude of a speaker or writer toward a subject.
Transition   Link between ideas or sections in an essay.

Credits

Allen, Paula Gunn. "Womanwork" by Paula Gunn Allen, 1982. Reprinted by permission of the author and Shadow Country of the University of California.   145

Alvarez, Julia. "Hold the Mayonnaise" by Julia Alvarez. Copyright © 1992 by Julia Alvarez. First published in *The New York Times Magazine*, January 12, 1992. Reprinted by permission of Susan Bergholz Literary Services, New York. All rights reserved.   55

Ashe, Arthur. "Send Your Children to the Libraries" by Arthur Ashe, *The New York Times*, February 6, 1977. Copyright © 1977 by of The New York Times Co. Reprinted by permission.   229

Barrett, Katherine. "Old Before Her Time" by Katherine Barrett, *Ladies Home Journal*, 1983. Copyright © 1983, Meredith Corporation. All rights reserved. Used with the permission of Ladies' Home Journal® magazine.   40

Berlitz, Charles F. "The Etymology of the International Insult" by Charles F. Berlitz, *Penthouse*, 1970. Reprinted by permission of Penthouse, © 1970, General Media Communications, Inc.   271

Bernikow, Louise. "Never Too Old: 'The Art of Getting Better' " by Louise Bernikow. Courtesy *Mademoiselle*. Copyright © 1983 by the Conde Nast Publications, Inc. Reprinted by permission.   34

Bigler, Eric. "Give Us Jobs, Not Admiration" by Eric Bigler, *Newsweek*, 1987. Reprinted by permission of the author.   201

Brandt, Anthony. "Children of Divorce" by Anthony Brandt which appeared in *Parenting,* 1981. Reprinted by permission of the author.   20

Burciaga, Jose Antonio. Reprinted from *Drink Cultura: Chicanismo* by Jose Antonio Burchiaga, 1993. Published by Joshua Odell Editions, Santa Barbara, California.   354

Chira, Susan. "The Good Mother: Searching for an Ideal" by Susan Chira, *The New York Times*,

Index

A

B

C